DATE DUE

NOV 2 9 1993	
APR 2 9 1996	
MAR 2 1 1999	
APR 1 4 2004	
MAR 2 4 2006	
APR 3 0 2009	

BRODART, INC.   Cat. No. 23-221

THE BOOK OF COSTUME

Annotated Edition

THE COUNTESS OF WILTON.

THE BOOK OF COSTUME:

or Annals of Fashion (1846)
by
A Lady of Rank

Annotated Edition

Containing a biography of the Countess of Wilton
plus additional notes on Needlework in Costume & The Field of Cloth of Gold

WRITTEN BY:
The Countess of Wilton
R.L. Shep

TRANSLATIONS & EDITING BY:
Pieter Bach

R.L. Shep
Lopez Island

Annotated and Enlarged Edition, which also contains an
unabridged reproduction of the original of 1846
Printed in the United States of America
ISBN 0-914046-04-7
LC# 86-90527

Library of Congress Cataloging-in-Publication Data

Wilton, Mary Margaret Stanley Egerton, Countess of,
    1801-1858.
    The book of costume, or, Annals of fashion.

    "Written by the Countess of Wilton."
    Originally published: London : H. Colburn, 1846.
    Includes index.
    1. Costume--History. I. Shep, R. L., 1933-   .
II. Title. III. Title: Book of costume. IV. Title:
Annals of fashion.
GT510.W6 1987   391'.009   86-90527
ISBN 0-914046-04-7

Published by:

R. L. SHEP
Box 668
Mendocino, CA 95460

CONTENTS

Page numbers in brackets [ ] indicate material added to the original

PREFACE

Reprinting **THE BOOK OF COSTUME** has been a long-term goal, and the book has been hidden away in a trunk for years, waiting for the right time to do it. Little did we know how much work would be involved when we finally got it out and started to look at it critically.

The Countess of Wilton is probably the first woman ever to have written a book of this kind, certainly one this complete. She had a classical education of the type that few people can boast of these days, and she was writing for her peers. Luckily, she usually manages to define the costume terms she mentions as she goes, but she presumes a lot when it comes to other references.

It soon became evident that we would have to put in a good table of contents, identify the illustrations, and index the work. It also became clear that we would have to do something about identifying the people she mentions: Swinburn, Lady Millar, Coxe, Lady Wortley Montague, et al. And so a whole new world opened up, the world of 18th and early 19th century travellers and their accounts of distant lands, their peoples, and their clothing. It also opened up the world of Ranjit Singh (The Lion of the Punjab), Khyber Ali, and people like Thomas Moore who, having been no farther east than Paris, wrote all about the East, and later managed to destroy Byron's memoirs!

We have also added three appendices: the first contains translations of all the French passages in the book, of which there are many; the second is an excerpt from **The Art of Needle-Work, from the Earliest Ages**, which was edited by the Countess of Wilton – the section is from "Needlework in Costume" and our purpose in including it is to give further insight into her views of fashion and the people who were needed to keep the industry going; the third is an excerpt from the same book, part of the section entitled "The Field of the Cloth of Gold", giving additional descriptions of this great event, which is briefly discussed in **The Book of Costume**.

In annotating this work we have, however, done nothing about the original Introduction, with the exception of translating some French words. In this introduction, Lady Wilton looks at some of the elements of costume (jewellery, beards, lace, silk, etc.), rather than looking at countries and historical periods. It is an interesting overview.

The scope of **The Book of Costume** is very broad for its day, taking in many parts of Asia and the Middle East. It does not, however, contain any information on the Americas, Australia, Africa, or Indonesia. It barely touches on Japan (Admiral Perry did not open that country to foreigners until 1853). It also does not record ancient Egyptian costume, as that country was not to become popular in England until the Suez Canal was opened in 1869.

It is interesting that Lady Wilton was very much aware of the United States, even though it probably was a political sore point in her childhood. In the excerpt from "Needlework in Costume" which we have included as Appendix B, she mentions the Yankee Tie, which she claims is the only true innovation of the day. She is also very much aware of the cotton trade, naturally so for one living just outside Manchester, and refers to "the 'New World', the magnificent and imperial empress (that is to be) of the whole earth".

One of the greatest complications we ran into in our research was the spelling of names. The printer set the work from her handwritten pages and many of the people she mentions do not seem to exist until variant spellings of their names are tried. We have shown in our notes the spellings as given and then what we finally found in our research, along with their dates when possible and what they wrote or did, etc.

It is well known, by the way, that Mary Margaret Egerton, the second Countess of Wilton, is the author of this book. What is not so well known is that the original illustrations were done by G. B. Standfust, a member of the Royal Academy and quite famous in his day. It should be noted that, no matter what the subject matter, the illustrations have a very definite Victorian flavor to them. The actual engravings were done by William James Linton, 1812-1897, who started engraving for the "London Illustrated News" in 1842 and was considered the best engraver of his day. He moved to the United States in 1867 and set up a printing press in New Haven, Connecticut.

And what of the Countess of Wilton? Who was she? That became the most intriguing question of all. To answer it better, we made a trip to England to visit the house where she lived and to do research at some of the libraries where she must have done her own research in the 1840's. We learned firsthand just how difficult it is to find out anything about a woman. The subject has to be approached obliquely – by looking up her husband, her father, her sons, and other men in her life. The pieces all came together as one bit of information led to the next. What we found was a thoroughly interesting woman who deserves to be known in her own right. The results of this research will be found in a short biography of the Countess of Wilton begining on page [9].

The illustration we have used for the frontispiece is one of those lucky finds made by asking questions, following up leads, and going to the right shop on the right day. The original painting, by Sir Thomas Lawrence, is presumably lost, as none of the catalogues or other sources we consulted contained any information on it.

———————

I would like to thank Pieter Bach, without whose advice, assistance, and encouragement this project would have bogged down long ago.

I would like to give special thanks to the members of The Costume Society of England for their encouragement and help.

I would also like to thank the following people and libraries:

J. J. Bagley, University of Liverpool (ret.), and author;
Charles Brown, Research Consultant, London;
The Earl of Derby and his staff at Knowsley Hall;
Suzanne Diamond, Professor of French (ret.);
Dale Gluckman, Assistant Curator, Textiles and Costume, Los Angeles County Museum of Art;
Irene Joshi, Librarian, University of Washington, and fashion authority;
Robert Kaufmann, Librarian, Costume Institute, Metropolitan Museum of Art;
Sandra Schugren, Librarian, Lopez Memorial Library;
Allie Smaalders, Librarian, Amsterdam Public Library and University of Southern California (ret.);
James Snowden, Librarian, Nottingham Public Library, and author;
Alan Suddon, Librarian, Metropolitan Toronto Library;
Diana Winterbotham, Local Studies Librarian, Lancashire County Library;
and
British Library, Reading Room;
British Library, Map Library;
British Library, Science Reference Library;
Camden Borough Libraries;
Guildhall Library, City of London;
Lopez Memorial Library;
Manchester Central Library;
Manchester Art Galleries and the staff at Heaton Hall;
Scottish National Library.

R. L. Shep

THE COUNTESS OF WILTON
A Biography

Although she was an author and was in the mainstream of the artistic and social life of her day, nothing really has been written about the Countess of Wilton. There are no records left at Heaton Hall, which was her home; and virtually no records of her at Knowsley Hall, where she was born and grew up. Peerages seem to feel that women are only worth noting in terms of their husbands; in fact, many do not even record the birth of female children. What that means is that any biography written about her, 130 years after her death, can only be sketchy at best, relying in large part on circumstantial evidence.

Any enquiry into the life of Mary Margarent Stanley Egerton, 2nd Countess of Wilton, must begin with her mother, Elizabeth Farran. Elizabeth Farran came from Liverpool; her father was (at various times) an apothecary, a surgeon, and an actor. Her mother was the daughter of a pub owner/brewer. Miss Farran became a leading actress in the late 1700's, appearing in Bath, Liverpool, and finally, in 1777, in London, where she made her debut as Lady Hardcastle in **She Stoops to Conquer.**

It was sometime during this period that she met Edward Smith-Stanley, the 12th Earl of Derby. He was married but, according to Cockayne's **Peerage**, was estranged from his wife, having caught her in an affair with the Duke of Dorset. He refused to divorce her, thereby preventing her from marrying the duke; and Elizabeth Farran, it is said, refused to become his mistress. However, they were constant companions, chaperoned by her mother. Lord Derby was an avid horse racer (the "Derby" is named for him) and he was so taken with Miss Farran that he often named his race horses after her roles on the London stage. A few weeks after his wife's death in 1797, he married Elizabeth Farran and she, then at the height of her career, playing Lady Teazle in **The School for Scandal**, bade farewell to the London stage. She became the Countess of Derby, wife of one of the wealthiest and most powerful men in England.

It is worth noting that Elizabeth Farran's portrait was painted in 1790 by Sir Thomas Lawrence. This portrait hung at Heaton Hall after the death of Lord Derby and was featured in a retrospective exhibit of Lawrence's paintings in 1890. It was purchased by Pierpont Morgan and went to the Metropolitan Museum of Art in New York, where it now hangs. It is quite distinctive because of the large muff Miss Farran holds at her side which almost drags on the floor. It appears in Millia Davenport's **Book of Costume** as illustration #2222.

The marriage was apparently very successful, and Mary Margaret was born 22 March 1801, the last of their three children. Elizabeth Farran died in 1829, and Lord Derby in 1834. The title passed to his eldest son, who was from the first marriage.

There is little record of Mary Margaret's childhood. Mr. Bagley says in his **The Earls of Derby** that Knowsley Hall became the home of a large family of lively children, which included the Earl's grandchildren from his first family and numerous cousins. The quality of her education can be assumed from the depth of knowledge and ease with foreign languages which she exhibits in **The Book of Costume**. Knowsley Hall is quite near Liverpool, in Lancashire, but at that time it was peaceful and remote from the ever increasing industrial city squalor, and it was here that they spent most of their time. They did, of course, have a house in London as well, where they would stay. One must remember that travel was still by coach and horses; one didn't just run up to London for the day. Lord Derby was in the middle of both the political and horse racing worlds and he was host at Knowsley to most of the important figures of the day, including the Prince of Wales. It was certainly a heady atmosphere for a child growing up. These years saw the defeat of Napoleon, the abolition of slavery in England, the mental decline of George III, the Regency, the accession of George IV and his problems with Queen Caroline (over which he and Lord Derby had a falling out), and the increasing momentum of the Industrial Revolution.

It is about this time that Thomas Grosvenor comes into the picture. He was the second son of the Marquess of Westminster and, as such, had little prospect of succeeding to the title. But his mother was the only child of the Earl of Wilton, so when his maternal grandfather died in 1814, he succeeded to that title, being only 15 at the time. On the 27th of November 1821, he was allowed by Royal licence to take the name and arms of Egerton (the family name of the Earls of Wilton). On the 29th, he married Mary Margaret Stanley, who then became the second Countess of Wilton. They were wealthy and the family seat was at Heaton Hall, just outside Manchester and close enough to Knowsley that the two estates might even have had a common border at some point. And so two of the great landowning families of Lancashire were joined by marriage.

The young Wiltons have been described as being unattractive. Lady Elizabeth Grosvenor, their sister-in-law, said that they took no pains to make themselves agreeable in public, and that Lady Wilton "has as much sensitivity as a deal board, by which those that live with her may also be a deal bored". As far as I can tell, Lady Elizabeth Grosvenor did not have much to recommend her except social position, money, and an acid tongue. I am sure that none of these people ever let Lady Wilton forget that she was the daughter of an actress; it is, in fact, mentioned in everything that I read about her. I am equally certain that to the Grosvenors, who were then and are now probably the richest family in England, Lord Wilton was very much second best, having given up the family name. It is at least partially due to these social slights, I believe, that Lady Wilton set out to prove herself to the world.

This 'boring' woman ran one of the most interesting houses in all of England, kept a chef reputed to be the best in the country (Monsieur Rotival), and entertained some of the most interesting and more raffish people of the Regency and early Victorian period. They entertained, amongst others, the young Disraeli, the Duke of Wellington, Fanny Kemble, Sir Francis Grant, William Huskisson, and Count d'Orsay. Disraeli, of course, became one of the most famous Prime Ministers of the Victorian Age. Huskisson was also a famous statesman of his day and was known for having saved the Bank of England from disaster in the panic of 1826. Sir Francis Grant was president of the Royal Academy of Art at that time.

Arthur Wellesley, the Duke of Wellington, who defeated Napoleon at Waterloo and was another major statesman of the day, wrote 599 letters to Lady Wilton, many of which can be found in **Wellington and his Friends: Letters of the first Duke of Wellington.** These letters are interesting in terms of the politics of the day, as Wellington was more than candid about many subjects, including the young Queen Victoria and her temper, his own slights at court, whether or not the Queen would marry Prince Albert, the Precedency Bill about which Queen Victoria was angry as it did not give Prince Albert precedence over other members of the British Royal Family, etc. Unfortunately, the letters have been edited to exclude most references to Lady Wilton herself, except for references to of her trip to Portugal in 1839 and other travels abroad in 1846. This at least gives us the sense that she had some knowledge of the Continent. Also at one point there is mention that Lady Wilton felt she would do well in politics herself because of her intense interest in the subject, although this was not possible for a woman in those days. It is known that Wellington usually destroyed the correspondence he received, but somehow 233 of Lady Wilton's replies have survived among the private family papers of the Dukes of Wellington. It is unfortunate for us that none of them is reproduced in **Wellington and his Friends.** Early in his career, and before being granted his title, Arthur Wellesley had served in India for several years, during the time that his brother was Governor-General; his memories may well have stimulated the interest in India which Lady Wilton exhibits in **The Book of Costume.**

Alfred, Count d'Orsay is another fascinating figure of the day. He was the son of one of Napoleon's generals and came to England in 1821. He met Marguerite, the Countess of Blessington, who persuaded him to marry her daughter. The marriage was not successful, as it was the Countess herself who was the object of his desire, and upon the death of her husband the fact of their relationship became fairly open knowledge. They maintained a well attended salon in London. The Count was a dandy, and set the taste in both fashion and literary matters in English society, while remaining very controversial. In some ways, he reminds one of an early Oscar Wilde. It is also interesting that the man in top hat and monocle that **The New Yorker** uses on its masthead and on its last February cover each year is a caricature of d'Orsay and his dandyism. There are paintings by him and a self-portrait bust in the National Portrait Gallery in London. It is said that he finally fled to Paris in 1849 to escape his debts.

Fanny Kemble was a famous actress of the time. She talks of visits, with her mother, to Heaton Hall in her **Record of Childhood.** In that book, she says that Lady Wilton was "strikingly handsome in person, and extremely attractive in her manners. She was tall and graceful, the upper part of her face, eyes, brow, and forehead were radiant and sweet, and, though the rest of her features were not regularly beautiful, her countenance was noble, and her smile had a peculiar charm of expression, at once winning and mischievous." This hardly agrees with the opinion of Lady Elizabeth

Grosvenor. Even more enlightening is Margaret Armstrong's **Fanny Kemble: A Passionate Victorian**, in which there is a good deal of information about the Wiltons and life at Heaton Hall, the dinners and all the famous and well placed people who dined there. She describes one dinner at which there were a Hungarian Count and Countess; Alexander Baring, Baron Ashburton, who negotiated the boundary between Maine and Canada; Lord Francis, Earl of Ellesmere, who was the Secretary for War; and numerous other fashionable people of the day. Fanny Kemble used to stay at Heaton Hall when performing at the Theatre Royal, Manchester, and would come down to dinner fully made up as Lady Macbeth, Portia, or whatever role she was playing that night, and then be driven to the theatre in time for the performance. She speaks well of Lady Wilton, who would lend her a riding habit and let her ride her favorite horse. As she says, "no one could be kinder than Lady Wilton; she was Lord Derby's daughter but her mother had been an actress, the celebrated Miss Farren (sic) . . ."

It was about this time that the first railway came into being. This was the Liverpool-Manchester railway; the land for it was obtained through an enabling bill, which was voted against by both Lord Derby and Lord Wilton. However, the bill finally passed and they gave in to it. The area was undoubtedly chosen because Manchester was and is one of the biggest manufacturing centers of England as the center of the cotton textile industry, and Liverpool is its port. Mr. Bagley says that Lady Wilton organized a party for one of the pre-opening runs in November of 1829, and that the train was reported to have travelled 5 miles in 15 minutes (all of 20 miles an hour!). Fanny Kemble described the official opening of the railway in September of 1830, when she took the run along with Lord and Lady Wilton, the Duke of Wellington, and several others. She was staying at Heaton Hall at the time. This occasion was called 'The Iron Duke meets the Iron Horse', i.e., the Duke of Wellington met Stephenson's steam locomotive. At one point, the train stopped for water and apparently Huskisson alighted to shake hands with the Duke of Wellington, who was leaning out of his carriage, when another engine ran Huskisson down and crushed his leg. Lord Wilton tied off the artery and rushed him to a doctor, but to no avail: Huskisson died as a result of his injury.

Lord Wilton was a sportsman, politician, and musician. There is a small, beautiful organ in Heaton Hall on which he composed a number of hymns, which were played at the church in Prestwich, of which he was the patron. These hymns remain in the Anglican hymnal. Fanny Kemble says that he encouraged his peasantry to keep up their ancient customs such as pageants and morris dancing. He was also Lord Steward of the Household in 1835, Colonel of the "Queen's Own" Light Infantry regiment of the London Militia in 1840, and Envoy Extraordinary and Minister Plenipotentiary with the Garter, sent by Queen Victoria to the King of Saxony at Dresden in 1842 (being made a Knight of the Crown of Rue of Saxony at the same time). One gathers from this that the Wiltons, like most of the notables of the day, spent a great deal of time in London. His critics say he was artificial and proud and that on the journey to Dresden he would try on the Order of the Garter to see how it looked on him.

Lord and Lady Wilton are described in the **New Sporting Gazette** magazine of September 1838 as follows:

"Whilst on his switch-tail'd bay, with wand'ring eye
Attenuated W----n canters by;
His character how difficult to know,
A compound of psalm tunes and Tallo-ho!
A forward rider half inclin'd to preach,
Tho' not dispos'd to **practise** as to **teach**,
An amorous lover, with the **saintly twist**,
And now a **sportsman**, now an **organist**.

"W----n's pale Countess of her lineage proud,
Urges her phaeton thro' the admiring crowd;
Diana's self could scarcely match the team,
That fairy body, and those steeds of cream!"

But not all of her life consisted of parties and social events. Lady Wilton bore her first son in 1825; he died in less than a year. She had a second son in 1831 and he died in less than two months. She had two more sons, one in 1833 (who succeeded to the title in 1882) and another in 1839 (who succeeded to the title in 1885, as his brother died without issue). But one has to look in Burke's **Peerage and Baronetage** to find that she also had three daughters. It must have been hard on Lady Wilton to have seven children, especially in those days. In 1829, when her mother died, she took on the added burden of running her father's household at Knowsley until his death in 1834.

Lady Wilton was also known for her works of charity and became a well loved local figure in the area of Heaton Park and Prestwich. She had an intense interest in botany and it was for her that the Orangery was added to Heaton Hall. And of course, more to the point, she edited Mrs. Stone's **Art of Needlework** in 1840, and wrote **The Book of Costume** in 1846 (which went into a second printing in 1847). **The Book of Costume** was an ambitious work which involved her in a great deal of research. One of its great strengths is the fact that she quotes from firsthand accounts, not only for period costume but also for the folk costume of various countries. She is probably the first woman to have attempted a work of this scope and, in the tradition of her day, did not allow her name to be used in connection with it (Jane Austen's novels, for example, did not bear her name until printings made after her death).

The picture that emerges from all this is of a woman who raised a large family, was devoted to her father (especially in his later years), was intensely interested in the poor, in politics, in progress, in botany, in textiles and costume, as well as acting as hostess to some of the more interesting people of her times. It is hardly a sketch of a boring woman who did not know how to handle herself in public and in society.

Lady Wilton died unexpectedly on 16 December 1858, aged 57, at Egerton Lodge near Melton Mowbray, between London and Nottingham. We checked the record office in London and there was no record of a will. We did, however, find two accounts of her death in the London "Times", one being a reprint of an article from the Manchester "Guardian", and another article in the London "Times" devoted to her funeral. There were ten private carriages, closed; two mutes (hired professional mourning attendants) bearing the arms of the family; two mutes bearing plumes; a horseman bearing her coronet on a crimson cushion; the hearse, drawn by six black horses; nine mourning coaches, each drawn by four horses. And then there follows a list of the people in the coaches. In tribute, they said that many of the poor walked from Manchester (some five miles away) to be present as the funeral cortege passed. "It is not because she occupied a high station, but because her virtues would have distinguished her as a noble woman in any station that the death of the Countess of Wilton is so universally bewailed. The many public and private duties that devolved upon her were fully and lovingly performed. She was ever ready with a kind word, and with more practical evidences of sympathy, to gladden the hearts of all round her who needed help. And it will be a joy, although full of sadness, to those whose grief is a sanctity that we may not lightly mention, to look upon the records which her Ladyship has left of the kindly, the almost motherly, concern she felt for her poorer neighbours." Thus she was remembered both for her compassion and for her charity. She should also be remembered for her interest in the arts, and especially for her interest in costume, fashion, and the needle arts.

Heaton Hall was rebuilt in 1772 by James Wyatt, to a plan which destroyed all traces of the original house of 1684. The Wyatt designs were exhibited at the Royal Academy and had a great deal of influence on other residences built both in England and on the Continent. The Orangery was built by Lewis Wyatt circa 1823. The Park landscaping was formal before 1770, but then between 1770 and about 1807 it was laid out by William Emes, a follower of Lancelot "Capability" Brown. It was further worked on after that by John Webb, a pupil of Emes. The style, based on "Capability" Brown's ideas, was one of making everything look like a painting of a country landscape. Both Heaton Hall and the Park were sold to the City of Manchester in 1902 for £230,000. There followed 'two disastrous sales in 1902 and 1906' during which all the furnishings were sold off, including books, furniture, paintings and effects. The grounds were converted to a golf course, and parts of the house used for locker rooms, mass catering, and storage. The Manchester City Art Galleries are now responsible for Heaton Hall; it is being restored and they are trying to refurnish it with pieces true to the period. So far, it remains pretty bare. The grounds are still partially a golf course, partially a park, and partially a zoo.

The Countess of Wilton was painted seated in an arm chair by Sir Thomas Lawrence (see frontispiece), and again by him in a bust-length. There was also a portrait of her by A. E. Chalon (also a member of the Royal Academy) which is a half-length, a copy of which can be seen at Heaton Hall. Another portrait of her, a watercolor by Chalon, is shown in **Wellington and his Friends**, but is not listed in any other source. There is no record of either of the Lawrence portraits having survived but, luckily, engravings were taken of them.

Sources:

Armstrong, Margaret. **Fanny Kemble: A Passionate Victorian**, Macmillan, 1938;

Bagley, J. J. **The Earls of Derby 1485-1985**, Sidgwick & Jackson, 1985;

Burke's **Peerage & Baronetage**;

Cockayne's **Peerage**;

Debrett's **Illustrated Peerage**;

Kemble, Frances Anne. **Record of a Childhood**, 1898;

Lomax, James. **The First & Second Earls of Wilton and Heaton House**, 1983;

The London **Times**, December, 1858;

Manchester City Art Galleries. **Heaton Hall**, 1984;

Wellington, the 7th Duke (ed.). **Wellington and his Friends: Letters of the first Duke of Wellington**, 1965.

Heaton House.

THE SEAT OF THE RIGHT HONORABLE THE EARL OF WILTON,
PATRON OF THE CHURCH IN PRESTWICH.

THE

BOOK OF COSTUME:

OR,

ANNALS OF FASHION,

FROM THE EARLIEST PERIOD TO THE PRESENT TIME.

By A LADY OF RANK.

ILLUSTRATED

With numerous Engravings on Wood,

BY THE MOST EMINENT ARTISTS.

LONDON:

HENRY COLBURN, PUBLISHER,

13 GREAT MARLBOROUGH STREET.

1846.

LONDON:
GEORGE BARCLAY, CASTLE STREET, LEICESTER SQUARE.

ADVERTISEMENT.

THE Book of Costume! Though the philosopher
and the politician may, perhaps, at the first glance,
be disposed to regard with some degree of disdain
the subject of which the writer has ventured to treat
in this volume, yet a little reflection will be sufficient
to convince them that, after all, it is not so frivolous
as they may have imagined.

Costume, comprehending all that relates to Dress
and Fashion, furnishing a standard of civilization, in-
volving the interests of the arts and of commerce, is, in
fact, an important element in the prosperity of States.
The study of its changes, their causes, and their
consequences, cannot, therefore, be unworthy the attention of the scholar or the statesman — of the man
of business, or the man of pleasure; while there are
few readers of the gentler sex to whom it can fail
to prove a theme of exciting interest.

To exhibit the various phases of Costume during the succession of ages, whether induced by climate or locality, by political revolutions, or the capricious decrees of Fashion, among the various nations of the world, in their progress from barbarism to the highest refinement of civilized life, is the aim of the work here submitted to the public.

It will easily be perceived that it has required a wide range of reading to collect the scattered traits necessary for composing this picture, historical and graphic, of the costumes of both sexes, from the earliest times to the present day. Though preferring little claim to the merits of extensive erudition or deep antiquarian research, still the writer presumes to hope that it will be found a useful and pleasing record of all that is most desirable to be known on the subject of dress: a subject of universal interest to the human family, and which must continue to excite attention while our race endures.

CONTENTS,

AND

ILLUSTRATIONS

FROM DESIGNS BY EMINENT ARTISTS.

COSTUME IN GERMANY.

COSTUME IN POLAND.

COSTUME IN RUSSIA.

COSTUME IN TURKEY, WALLACHIA, &c.

COSTUME IN GREECE.

COSTUME IN ALBANIA.

COSTUME IN INDIA.

COSTUME IN THE MOGUL EMPIRE.

COSTUME IN THE BIRMAN EMPIRE.

COSTUME IN PERSIA.

COSTUME IN BOKHARA, CIRCASSIA, AND CASHMERE.

COSTUME IN AFFGHANISTAN.

COSTUME IN CHINA.

COSTUME IN PALESTINE AND SYRIA.

COSTUME IN ARABIA.

THE

BOOK OF COSTUME.

Dress, considered merely as a covering for the body, and as a means of promoting warmth, needs no explanation. In the early ages, it was simple as the manners of the people who invented it. Leaves, feathers, and skins, formed the clothing of our first parents. As civilization gradually spread over the world, and as the invention and genius of man found means to change a raw hide into leather, the wool of sheep into cloth, the web of a worm into silk, flax and cotton into linen ; to extract from herbs, flowers, woods, minerals, and insects, dyes and colours that vie with the rainbow in richness and variety; mankind gave way to the caprices of vanity; they quitted the simple garments of their forefathers, and gradually gave themselves up to an almost incredible degree of luxury and extravagance in the adornment of their persons.

So extensively, and so rapidly, did this passion for dress and finery of every kind, spread over the world, that edicts, laws, and ordinances, have been passed, from time to time, by many nations, to arrest the growing evil; an evil created by that desire for personal distinction which dwells, more or less, in every human breast, whether male or female, and which marks the untaught savage of the Sandwich Isles, as well as the enlightened and well-educated inhabitant of Britain.

It may appear incredible, to those who have not dived into the mysteries of dress and fashion, to learn that revolutions have been caused at different times, and among different nations, from the determined resistance opposed to the various laws and decrees which have been directed against the too great love of dress and ornament; and so powerfully has this passion exhibited itself in the human mind, that blood has actually been shed to support it.

In the history of China, we find that even that meek, quiet people were roused to fury, when their Tartar conquerors ordered their luxuriant tresses to be cut off; and so strenuously did they oppose the arbitrary decree, that, in more than one instance, the unfortunate Chinese preferred losing their heads to parting with their beloved ringlets. We are also told that the Tartars waged a long and bloody war with the Persians, and declared them to be infidels, because they would not clip their whiskers after the fashion of the former.

Even so late as the eighteenth century, a very serious *émeute* took place in Madrid, on an attempt being made to banish the *capa* and *sombrero;* and, marvellous as it may seem, the obstinate resistance opposed to those who wished to change the fashion of these cherished articles of dress, caused the disgrace and flight of the prime minister.

In our own country many laws and edicts have been made at different times to check, not only extravagance in dress itself, as regards the richness and splendour of its materials, and the ornaments that decorate it, but also to correct and regulate the shape of various parts of the apparel of both men and women. Several of our early kings waged war against the ridiculous and enormous length of *piked* shoes, and by enacting a law, restraining their points to a certain standard, hoped to correct the evil. But Fashion was not to be so ruled by the will of a monarch: angry at her wishes being disobeyed, she immediately put it into the heads of her followers to invent a mode equally absurd; the *crakowes* and *poulaines* disappeared, but were soon replaced by shoes of so extravagant a width, that another law was, ere long, found necessary to circumscribe their breadth.

Queen Elizabeth, though herself so devoted a follower of fashion, and so passionately fond of dress, still made many laws respecting the attire of her subjects. She commanded the lower orders to wear on the Sabbath-day a cap of a peculiar shape; and, perhaps to restrain the love of foreign fashions which had long been so prevalent in England, she enacted that this

émeute: riot
capa and sombrero: cape & hat
crakowes and poulaines: types of shoe known only by those names, having long, narrow pointed toes

head-dress should be made of wool, knit, thicked, and dressed in Britain. She also made a decree to limit the size of the ruffs and swords worn by her courtiers, to the standard she considered fitting for subjects to assume; and, fearful that so arbitrary a law might be in some way or other evaded by the votaries of fashion, she appointed officers, whose sole duty it was to break every man's sword exceeding the limited length, and clip all the ruffs whose size infringed upon her regal ordinance.

Although these arbitrary laws caused some slight troubles at first, among gallants who could not brook the shortening of their cherished weapons, still no serious consequences ensued, and on the whole the English have ever borne the attacks made upon their dress with becoming *sang froid*.

Elizabeth, too, busied herself in arranging the costume usually worn in the inns of court, and particularized the shapes and colours of the garments, and the embroideries she considered befitting so grave an assembly.

Under Elizabeth's successor, a serious debate took place in Parliament, concerning the enormous size of verdingales; and some years afterwards laws were passed to put a stop to patching and painting.

The Turks, despotic in every thing, will not allow the Grecian ladies the poor privilege of wearing petticoats of the length that fashion in their country has declared to be proper and fitting; they have officers whose duty it is to nibble off as much of the jupe as ventures to extend beyond the length fixed by their barbarous masters.

The Turks also have laws by which none but their

sang froid: composure

own august persons are allowed to wear yellow slippers; and, while their haughty brows were encircled with turbans of the finest and brightest-coloured muslins, with silks of the richest dyes, or with shawls of the gayest tints and most delicate texture, their Grecian subjects were condemned to wear dark cotton caps, as a mark of their servitude; the Armenians, too, they oblige to appear in ridiculous-looking, balloon-shaped cappas; and the crouching Jews look doubly miserable when forced to bend to the Turkish law, which only permits their heads to be covered with brimless caps, much resembling inverted flowerpots.

These despots have, however, themselves been, within the last few years, constrained to bend to the decree of Sultan Mamhoud, who ordered that a red cloth fez, or military cap, should be worn by the followers of the faithful, instead of the lofty calpac, or ample turban. This law was, however, received with the most determined and indignant remonstrance and opposition, and so obnoxious to the Turkish feelings was this new-fashioned head-dress, that the discontented party set fire to the houses of those who were favourable to the change; and, though the Sultan's wishes passed into a law, his subjects are still highly disgusted with their forced adoption of any coiffure in the place of the turban so long worn by their forefathers.

Besides the many decrees made by our monarchs concerning dress, a particular costume was arranged by Charles the Second and his council, for the nobility to appear in, and one in which great extravagance of gold, silver, lace, and jewels, was not necessary;

for during this reign, in England, the immense sums lavished upon dress and ornaments were almost incalculable.

Gustavus of Sweden also invented, or at least ordered, a court habiliment, in which all who wished to be admitted to his presence, both men and women, were obliged to appear, and Buonaparte followed his example, to the no small disgust of his officers, and to the despair and anger of *les belles Françaises*. Even during the Revolution, when blood, murder, and misery, were spread over devoted France, — when the prisons echoed with the groans of the unfortunate victims of political despotism, — when the scaffolds were crowded with the dead and the dying, — dress was not forgotten, and stormy were the debates on this important subject held in the National Convention!

In various countries of Europe sumptuary laws have at different times been enacted, to restrain extravagance in apparel. In Switzerland, Italy, and Germany, the legislature frequently found it necessary to interfere, and for this reason, probably, the national costume still remains in full force among the peasantry, who hitherto have resisted the approach of Fashion, and her handmaids, Caprice and Vanity.

While on this subject we must not omit to mention the peculiar privileges relating to dress, belonging to the family of Andrea Doria. When, owing to the luxury and profusion which characterized the Genoese of his day, the senate found it absolutely necessary to check the growing evil, and forbade the wearing of jewels and brocade, the patriot admiral, doubtless to shew his country's sense of the services he had

les belles Françaises: the French beauties (or) beautiful Frenchwomen

rendered to it, was allowed to expend what sums he pleased upon the adornment of his person; and this privilege was afterwards extended to his family.

Woman is defined by an ancient writer to be, an "animal that delights in finery;" and it is to be feared the annals of dress in every land, the most savage as well as the most civilized, will but prove the truth of the assertion. Certain it is that the peacock, in all its pride, does not glitter in more various and gaudy trappings than does a modern woman of fashion.

But while thus speaking of woman's love of finery, which appears from the most ancient writers to have belonged to her since the world began, we must not omit to mention that man also was, and in most countries still is, as much devoted to this passion as the fair sex. Though in these days, at least in most civilized nations, it is considered effeminate for men to adorn their persons with trinkets and embroidered garments, still those who peruse the "Book of Costume" will find that, however extravagant women have been in these respects, men have equalled, if not surpassed, them in profusion and magnificence. Among savage nations, to this day, the warriors deck their persons with all the finery they can procure, with feathers, shells, beads, and paint; while their wives are often obliged to content themselves with their blanket covering, and but few ornaments.

In Exodus we read of the "jewels of silver, and jewels of gold," borrowed by the Israelites from the Egyptians. In Isaiah, also, we find a long account of the varieties of female apparel in the time of the Prophet.

Having thus pointed out to our readers the antiquity of the Toilette, we will speak of Fashion, who, "sole arbitress of dress," with the caprice for which she is so celebrated, has enacted, that what is the proper standard for attire in one country, and at one time, shall be equally the contrary in other climes, and at other periods.

Of all nations, the two that pay the most devoted attention to the decrees of Fashion, in the size, shape, and colour of every trifle relating to the Toilette, are the English and the French; and it seems a reflection worthy the consideration of the philosopher, why these two (we may truly say the most enlightened nations of the world) should, of all others, be the most determined and devoted followers of this feather and flower-decked goddess.

COSMETICS.

Among the numerous inventions for the improvement of beauty, painting the neck and arms with white, the cheeks with red, the eyelids with black, and the fingers with rose colour, is, perhaps, the most ancient. Almost every nation of the world, men as well as women, whatever complexion Nature may have bestowed upon them, have, at one time or another, followed this baneful fashion. In the second Book of Kings, we read, "Jezebel painted her face, and tired her head;" and in the East the custom remains in full force to this day. The Turkish and Arabian women especially devote much time to colouring their eyelids and the tips of their fingers; but, in England, rouge and enamel powders are alone employed for beautifying the complexion, and rendering it clear and transparent.

One of the dangers of this practice is illustrated by an amusing anecdote. A lady who piqued herself on the beauty, freshness, and pure white and red of her complexion, went to attend a chemical lecture. She had not been there long, when suddenly her face was observed by all present to become perfectly blue. Unconscious of the change, or of the attention directed to her ghastly features, she smilingly continued talking to her acquaintance, and, if she remarked the wondering eyes turned towards her, doubtless attributed their gaze to the fairness of which she was so vain. At length one of her companions ventured to whisper in her ear the strange and alarming alteration that had taken place, and which, on her making a precipitate retreat, was attributed by the lecturer to its true cause;—the cosmetic she had used being affected by some salt, or acid, employed in his experiments, had caused the marvellous transfiguration.

The danger to health from this practice is very great; and illnesses of serious kinds are said to be consequent on the use of enamelling. Cosmetics, too, and washes employed to render the skin soft and smooth, are equally deleterious; and the approach of wrinkles and age is in reality hastened by their frequent use. The Jewish women carried this practice to a most intemperate excess; and some years since, in France, even the young and beautiful, whose charms required no adventitious aid or ornament, were still, by the arbitrary laws of fashion, obliged to follow the reigning mode, till, as Lady W. Montague expresses it, "they looked monstrously unnatural in their paints."

The Arabic and Persian writers frequently mention painting and cosmetics, and speak of the line of antimony which, in those countries, it is usual to draw between the eyelids, to give additional lustre to the eyes. Even in the days of Ezekiel, this practice was very common: "Thou didst wash thyself, painted thine eyes, and deckest thyself with ornaments," says the prophet; and so it continues to this day. The Eastern ladies are much celebrated for their knowledge in compounding and inventing cosmetics and washes; and after them the Calmuck Tartars and Grecian women are most versed in this art. But these nations, not content with white and red paints, use also black, yellow, and saffron-coloured lotions.

Cosmetics, it is said, were unknown in England till the reign of Elizabeth, when they were brought from Italy, and were soon extensively adopted by the higher ranks.

Another extraordinary fashion, also derived from Arabia, is that of wearing upon the face patches of black silk, cut into every grotesque shape. Among Eastern nations, where a black mole is considered a great beauty, and descanted upon by their poets with rapture and admiration, it is not surprising that those beauties to whom Nature has denied this fancied charm should endeavour to imitate it by means of art; but, in England, there was no such excuse for this custom, which was in full force throughout the reign of Queen Anne, but gradually declined under her successor.

Among the Greeks, even now, a small patch of gold leaf is often worn by a bride.

While speaking on this subject, we must mention the savage custom so prevalent among the wild, uncivilized nations of America, Africa, and the South Sea Islands, of tattooing, which, in those countries, is considered a necessary addition to beauty. How so extraordinary a custom first originated, it is impossible to discover; but, when we consider the pain endured by the votaries of beauty, we cannot help remembering the old French saying, "Il faut souffrir pour être belle." The operation of tattooing is sometimes performed with an instrument full of small teeth, which, having been dipped into a mixture of black paint and oil, is stuck into the skin, and leaves an indelible stain. At other times, figures are burnt in with gunpowder, leaving long scars and deep cuts, which often traverse the forehead, cheeks, chin, and various parts of the body. Some of these devices frequently denote the rank of the person upon whom they have been inflicted.

A strange fashion prevails among the upper classes of the Chinese, of contracting the feet till they become of a small size, but quite deformed. The moment a female child comes into the world, the little unfortunate's toes are turned under the foot, and bandaged tightly. Of course, the pain endured by the poor infant must be very great, for these ligatures are renewed daily until the feet stop growing. At length they are released, and the Chinese beauty waddles about, proud of an embellishment which by every other nation is looked upon as a deformity.

THE COIFFURE.

Among the numerous caprices of Fashion, she has, at various times and in different countries, changed the natural covering of the human head, the hair, till it is impossible to enumerate her vagaries. Though

"Il faut souffrir pour être belle": One must suffer to be beautiful

the gift of Nature, and the greatest ornament of youth, this capricious goddess tortures the tresses, that would if left alone wave with graceful elegance, into every variety of shape. Sometimes she bids the ruthless scissors clip the luxuriant ringlets close to the head; straightway her commands are obeyed; and nothing is seen but crops. Then, tired of heads like those of charity children, she orders the hair to be allowed to grow, and hang in long braids down the back. Again she changes her mind, and, stiffened with pomatum and powder, the hair is drawn over a cushion, and held firm by the aid of pins and combs, till the wearers look several inches taller than they really are.

The ancient Gauls were proud of long hair, and, when conquered by Julius Cæsar, he made them cut it off, as a mark of servitude. In France, it was long considered the peculiar privilege of royalty to have flowing tresses; and to cut off the hair of a prince, under the first race of kings, was to declare him excluded from the succession to the throne, and to debase him to the rank of a subject. Indeed, of so much consequence was this considered among the French, that their historians have taken the trouble to record the length of the hair of many of their early monarchs.

After Christianity spread over the world, the clergy vehemently opposed the hair being worn long; and there is a canon still extant, dated the year 1096, which declares that they who wear it so shall be excluded from the church while living, and not prayed for when dead.

The longest hair we hear of in any country is that of a tribe of North American Indians; and this is the more remarkable, as the men only possess this wonderful length of tresses, the women of the same tribe having, in comparison, short hair.

The peruke, or, at all events, false hair, was much used by the ancients. It is supposed that the perukes then worn were made of painted hair, glued together. An account is given of that worn by the Emperor Commodus; it is described as having been powdered with gold, and previously oiled and perfumed, to cause the gold to adhere to it. In the British Museum, may be seen a peruke found in the Temple of Isis, at Thebes, the curling and arranging of which would puzzle many a modern coiffeur. It is of a large size, and each ringlet is arranged with the greatest nicety: apparently, the Theban perruquiers possessed a secret unknown to modern *artistes* in *wigology*,—that of preserving the curl in the hair; for although thousands of years have, perhaps, passed away since this peruke was first made, it preserves its pristine shape, form, and hue.

In France, the reign of perukes lasted for a very long time: it began at the commencement of the seventeenth century, and the fashion soon spread throughout all Europe. As may easily be imagined, young people at first resisted the sacrifice of their natural hair, to be replaced by a cumbersome wig. But, ere long, Fashion's will overcame their scruples, and all ages adopted the reigning mode. The clergy even could not resist the wig mania, and many learned and grave divines preached against " vanity in dress," forgetting the example they themselves were setting to their parishioners. At length, however, this practice was considered scandalous and improper, and it was prohibited among the clergy.

When the hair was once more allowed to grow, and decorate the head, instead of the immense curled, oiled, pomatumed wig, it was made to resemble a peruke as much as possible. After that came the *pig-tails*, or *queues*, which have only disappeared within the last few years.

The various coiffures worn by women will be found in the countries and reigns to which they belong. We will only add here that woman's hair has ever been left to adorn its fair possessor, without calling down either the animadversion of the preacher, or the censure of the critic.

THE BEARD.

Beards have ever held a high rank in the estimation of all nations, and, by many, this venerable appendage to the chin has been regarded with almost superstitious reverence. Among the Tartars, many of their religious ceremonies consist in the proper management of the beard. The Greek and Romish churches have long been bitter enemies on this subject; the former enforce the wearing long beards, while the latter have made edicts which enjoin shaving.

The Chinese, to whom Nature has allowed but a very scanty crop of hair upon the face, regard the long beards of other nations with envy and admiration, and devote much time and attention to the care and cultivation of the few straggling hairs they can coax to grow upon their chins. The Russians formerly wore enormous beards; but their czar Peter ordered them all to be shaved off. His injunction, however, met with so much opposition, that he found it necessary to appoint officers to cut off the beards of his refractory subjects by violence, since they would not part with them quietly. Perhaps this despotic ruler was of the same opinion respecting them as Alexander, who ordered all the Macedonians to be shaved, lest the length of their beards should afford a handle to their enemies!

The Eastern nations are remarkable for the length of their beards. Formerly, the kings of Persia, and even some of the earlier monarchs of France, wore them plaited, and woven with gold thread. To the present day, in Persia, a barber is a man of great importance, as he must not only be well versed in the intricacies of his art, but also be very trustworthy, particularly he to whose care is entrusted the beard of the king—the pride of the nation.

In India, there is a nation who devote their beards and whiskers to the goddess of destruction, and who look upon the preservation of life even as of slight importance, when compared with the loss of one hair from their beards.

At one time, beards and unshaven chins were, by different nations, looked upon as signs of grief and mourning,—as they are by the Jews of the present day. When the Roman people adopted shaving, they wore beards to mark any great sorrow. The Greeks, on the contrary, if in any deep affliction, shaved off the beard. Among the ancient Egyptians, the priests alone appeared with smooth chins. All slaves, in the time of the Romans, had long beards and flowing tresses; and, when made freemen, they shaved, and covered their heads. The abolition of the beard among the Greeks took place, it is said, about the time of Alexander; among the Romans, about the year 300. The ancient Germans are said to have shaved the beard; also the ancient Goths, Franks, and Britons. The Danes and Saxons wore beards till the introduction of Christianity.

Though the anathemas of preachers, and the censures of learned divines, have succeeded in banishing this venerable appendage throughout most parts of Europe, still the bushy whisker and fierce curling moustache are highly prized by the *petit maîtres* of our days. A curious fact relating to the latter must not be omitted, as it proves the estimation in which moustaches were once held. It is mentioned, in the introduction to the "Lusiad," that John de Castro, the noble governor of Goa (which place he held for his master, the Portuguese king), being in want of a large loan from the citizens, to enable him to fit out a military expedition, was in great distress for a good security to offer in return for the required money. At first, he thought of pledging the bones of his gallant son, Don Fernando; but, on opening the grave, it was found necessary to relinquish this intention. He therefore offered the next most precious object he possessed in the world, namely, one of his moustaches. This act of generous and devoted patriotism was fully appreciated by the inhabitants of Goa, who, emulating the liberality of their governor, received the precious security with every mark of respect, and, presenting to Don Juan more than the sum demanded, also returned him his inestimable pledge.

King Robert of France gloried in a beard of so luxuriant a growth, that it is difficult to say which was most venerated, his renown as a warrior, or the

petit maîtres: dandies, coxcombs

appendage that ornamented his chin. A Sultan formerly only allowed his beard to grow from the time of his ascending the throne. Among the Mahommedans, it is considered a sin to cut the beard off when once it has been allowed to grow, as they say " the angels dwell in them."

Many nations dye their beards; the Persians, particularly, never think they can be of a sufficiently intense and shining black without the aid of art; and though the operation is very troublesome, they never fail to undergo it about once every fortnight. While the process is performing, the beard assumes various different shades and tints; first orange, then green, and, lastly, black; but sometimes an unlucky application of one dye before the former has properly saturated the beard, to the no small disgust of the Persian *petit maitre*, leaves his chin of a fiery red, a purple, a blue, or a particoloured tint. Mr. Morier, speaking of the Persian's affection for a beard, says, in his work on that country, " It is inconceivable how careful they are of this ornament: all the young men sigh for it, and grease their chins to hasten the growth of the hairs; because, until they have there a respectable covering, they are not supposed fit to enjoy any place of trust."

The beards of Cardinal Pole and Sir Thomas More have long been celebrated; but, with all the care and attention bestowed upon them, few modern beards can equal those of the patriarchs.

INVENTIONS AND MANUFACTURES CONNECTED WITH DRESS.

We must now proceed to dress itself, and to those innumerable manufactures and inventions which mankind has created for the adornment of the person. Silks, satins, velvets, brocades, linens, cottons, muslins, gauzes, laces, assume, under the nimble fingers of Fashion's handmaids, every variety of shape, form, and hue.

JEWELLERY.

The love of jewels and ornaments has been prevalent among all nations, from the earliest ages. The savages deck their limbs and bodies with shells and bones, and admire these rude ornaments as much as does the fair European, when delightedly gazing at the brilliant treasures contained in her velvet-lined *écrin*, whose golden clasps encircle the gifts of all lands. This passion is frequently mentioned in the Scriptures, and the most ancient authors speak of ear-rings, nose and lip-rings, necklaces, chains, bracelets, anklets, and every other variety of ornament. Their shape, size, and the materials of which they are composed, are changeable as the thoughts of the fickle goddess who superintends their structure; while every land is searched for gems of the brightest hue, and even the ocean is forced to give up her treasures, to satisfy this universal love of splendour and magnificence.

" It is a curious fact," remarks a modern traveller in Egypt, " that the love of ornament, prevalent as it is throughout the world, appears to be carried to the

écrin: jewel box

greatest excess by the most civilized and the most uncivilized nations,—the inhabitants of the deserts of
Nubia, and the *élégantes* of England and France."
The former pride themselves upon their beads, shells,
and berries; while the latter glitter in diamonds from
Golconda, sapphires and rubies from Peru, onyxes
from Arabia, turquoises from Persia, emeralds from
South America, garnets and amethysts from the East,
topazes from Ethiopia, changeable opals from Egypt,
and last, though not least, among this galaxy of glittering gems, pearls from the recesses of the deep blue
ocean, in the Persian Gulf and Gulf of Mexico.

EAR-RINGS.

Ear-rings, or, as they were formerly called, pendants, are worn by all nations. In Europe men have,
for the most part, abandoned this fashion, though
in some lands they still wear rings in their ears;
but in almost all the numerous countries and tribes
of Africa, Asia, and America, both sexes wear them.
In the East Indies they are made the size of saucers,
and are generally of gold and valuable jewels. In
order to admit this immense ear-ring, an incision
is made through the ear, and a filament, formed of
cocoa-nut leaves tightly rolled together, is thrust into
the opening. This filament is constantly enlarged,
till it has stretched the orifice to two inches in diameter. The perfection required being then attained,
the wound is allowed to heal, and the ear laden with
every kind of ornament.

The ear of a European lady would be looked upon
with contempt by these Eastern fashionables of both

sexes, for men as well as women wear the ear loaded with coins, jewels, flowers, or any thing they can procure; but among some of the Indian tribes, the *noblesse* alone are allowed the high privilege of having an orifice through the ear more than three inches in diameter, while the lower orders are restricted to that size. In the Sandwich Islands, the inhabitants enlarge the incision to such an extent, that the ear is dragged down to the waist. The Indians, Africans, and savages of America, also wear nose and lip-rings.

ARMLETS.

The armilla, or bracelet, is of very high antiquity. It is mentioned in Genesis, chap. xxiv. verse 22:— "And it came to pass as the camels had done drinking, that the man took a golden ear-ring of half a shekel weight, and two bracelets for her hands of ten shekels weight of gold."

This was formerly the most universal of all ornaments, and was worn either upon the wrist or upon the arm. Sometimes bracelets were very massive: Livy speaks of those worn by the Sabine women, as being of great weight, and the Roman matrons are said to have had them frequently of from six to ten pounds in weight.

Armillæ, we are informed by all the Greek and Roman historians of ancient times, were formerly regarded with great veneration, and were frequently presented as the reward of valour; these, however, were exclusively formed of silver, those of gold being reserved for Roman citizens. Ælian tells us the Persian kings rewarded ambassadors from all nations with armillæ, and in the book of Exodus they are included among the gifts for the tabernacle.

It is supposed that bracelets were formerly used as a badge of power in Eastern countries. M. d'Herbelot states, that when the Caliph Cayem Bemrillah granted the investiture of some dominions which had been possessed by his predecessors, it was performed by the Caliph sending with the firman a crown, a chain, and bracelets. Even at the present day in Persia, these latter ornaments are only allowed to be worn by the king and his sons. At various times, both in England and Ireland, armillæ have been dug out of the chalk-cliffs or out of the bogs, and one was found on the wrist of a skeleton, in the East Riding of Yorkshire. Among the ruins of Herculaneum was found a golden Venus, with golden bracelets and anklets on the arms and legs.

RINGS.

The annulus, or ring, is also a very ancient ornament. Pliny tells us that the inventor of it is not known, but it was used by the Babylonians, Chaldeans, Persians, and Greeks, though Pliny thinks the latter were unacquainted with it at the time of the Trojan war, as Homer does not mention it. In the Scriptures the signet-ring is frequently named, and Quintus Curtius tells us that Alexander wore one. Pliny gives us much information respecting the ancient use of rings, which were not, as at present, mere ornaments, worn for the adornment of the fingers. Among the Romans, before they were set with stones, it was the custom to wear them on whichever hand or fingers the wearer pleased ; but when the stones were added to

them, it would have been considered the excess of
foppery to have the right hand adorned with one.
The Greeks wore them exclusively on the fourth finger
of the left hand, and gave as a reason for this custom,
that this finger communicated by a small nerve with
the heart. The Gauls and Britons, Pliny informs us,
wore them on the middle finger. He also adds, that
the ancients had three different kinds of rings, in gold,
in silver, and in iron, each of which served to distinguish different conditions or qualities.

NECKLACES.

Necklaces, or torques, as they were formerly called,
were as much worn by the ancients as bracelets. The
brooch also is mentioned by almost all old writers; it
was used to fasten the cloak on one shoulder, or to
confine its folds on the breast.

Chains were a favourite ornament among the ancients. The Gauls are represented to have worn
them in battle, to distinguish the commanders from
their subordinates. Homer and Virgil frequently
mention them; also belts or girdles of gold and embroidery.

FRENCH FASHIONS IN ENGLAND.

Colbert declared that the surest means of paving the
way for universal monarchy was to render the French
language and French fashions prevalent throughout
Europe. In establishing the supremacy of *la mode
Parisienne*, he has certainly fully succeeded, though,
happily, his great and deep-laid plan has been over-

thrown. The devotion shewn by the English to every French mode that appears is, indeed, extraordinary. Even when the two nations were filled with feelings of jealousy towards each other, when war shewed the sentiments of hatred that actuated them, England still greedily seized upon every variation in *la mode Parisienne*, and, detesting the inventors, nevertheless slavishly followed their decrees. Evelyn, in his essay called the " Mode," alludes to this mania. " I have frequently wondered," he says, " that a nation so well conceited of themselves as I take our countrymen to be, should so generally submit to the mode of another, of whom they speak with so little kindnesse. That the *Monsieurs* have universally gotten the ascendant over every other part of Europe, is imputable to their late conquests; but that only their greatest vanity should domineer over this kingdome, speaks us strangely tame. For myself, though I love the French well (and have many reasons for it), yet I would be glad to pay my respects in any thing rather than my *clothes*, because I conceive it so great a diminution to our native country, and to the discretion of it."

In another place, speaking of the mutability of fashion, he says, " But, be it thus excusable in the French to alter and impose the mode on others, for the reasons deduced, 'tis no less a weakness and a shame in the rest of the world, who have no dependancy on them, to admit them, at least to that degree of levity, as to turn into all their shapes without discrimination; so as when the freak takes our *Monsieurs* to appear like so many farces or Jack-puddings on the stage, all the world should alter shape, and play the pantomimes with them.   Methinks a French taylor, with his ell in his hand, looks like the enchantress Circe over the companions of Ulysses, and changes them into as many forms."

Those who peruse these pages will be surprised to see for how many years French fashions have prevailed in England ; and to such an extent is this mania carried, that English manufactures cross the Channel to be rendered fit for Englishmen and women to wear, by receiving their shape and form from the fingers and needles of French *tailleurs* and *modistes*.

THE MANUFACTURE OF SILK, &c.

However baneful a passion for dress may become, when allowed, under certain circumstances, to degenerate into extravagance and profusion, it is still wonderful to contemplate the support that thousands derive from the capricious laws of fashion.   Spinning, dyeing, weaving, give employment to multitudes of people, and the very mutability of the mode is greatly to their benefit.

The manufacture of silk was, it is said, discovered in the island of Cos, and as it now forms so principal a part of a lady's attire, it may not be uninteresting to mention, that its first invention is attributed to Pamphylia, the daughter of Platis.   Her name is recorded by ancient authors, as being the first person who made the silk-worms' labours subservient to the adornment of beauty ; and well does she deserve the gratitude of past and present ages.   The looms of Persia, China, and Italy, are the most celebrated for the manufacture

tailleurs & modistes: dressmakers and milliners

of silks, velvets, satins, and brocades; and within the last few years, slight and beautifully coloured threads of glass have been interwoven with them, forming a new and much-admired production.

Linen is a most useful and necessary addition to the clothing of mankind. Its origin is so ancient that it is unknown, but, in the time of Herodotus, it was an article of export from Egypt, whence the Greeks and Romans procured it. The mummies are frequently found wrapped in it, which is a sufficient proof of its antiquity.

Cotton is also another manufacture that was known in the early ages. Its invention is attributed to the Persians, and Pliny mentions its use among the Egyptians; but though in ancient delineations brought from the latter country, flax is frequently seen, there is no indication of the cotton-plant.

Cloth, which was a manufacture known to the Egyptians, Romans, and Greeks, was brought from Rome into Britain, and the conquerors instructed their new subjects in the art of fabricating it, and established a manufactory at Winchester. It fell into decay, however, under the Danes and Saxons, but revived when Alfred came to the throne, and ever since that time it has gradually improved, till at last the woollen trade has become a principal source of the wealth and riches of England.

MANUFACTURE OF LACE.

The antiquity of lace, that favourite addition to a lady's toilette, is not supposed to be nearly so great as the fabrics we have already mentioned. In Beckman's

" History of Inventions," we read the following account: " It seems very difficult, if not impossible, to determine the antiquity of lace. I remember no passage in the Greek or Roman authors that seems to allude to it; for those who ascribe works of this kind to the Romans, found their opinions on the expression, ' art of the Phrygians,' which consisted only of needle-work. Lace worked by the needle may be found among old church furniture. We read in various authors, that the art of making lace was brought from Italy, particularly from Genoa and Venice, to Germany and France; but this only seems to allude to the oldest kind, or that worked by the needle. I am firmly of opinion that lace worked by the needle is much older than that made by knitting. I will venture to assert that knitting lace is a German invention, first known about the middle of the sixteenth century. The inventress was a Saxon lady named Barbara, wife of Christopher Uttman."

In a French work, entitled " La Vie de Colbert," we read of the first introduction of the lace manufacture into France, but *point* is the only kind mentioned. The Count de Marsan, says the author, brought from Brussels to Paris his former nurse, named Du Mont, and her four daughters, and procured for her the exclusive right to establish and carry on the lace manufacture in that capital. In a little time Du Mont and her daughters collected two hundred women, some of whom were of good families, and they soon produced such excellent work, that it was, ere long, pronounced very little, if at all, inferior to that imported from foreign countries. The laces now the most prized and sought after are Brussels point, Mechlin, Valenciennes, Lisle, Chantilly, and blonde.

EMBROIDERY.

Embroidery is a very ancient invention, and was much admired and practised among the early nations. It is supposed that the Phrygians first discovered this art, and employed coloured silks, and gold thread or wire, for ornamenting their dresses. In the Bible we find that the high-priest's robe had on the bottom of the skirt figures of pomegranates, wrought with blue, scarlet, and purple. The ephod, also, was embroidered in blue, purple, scarlet, and gold; the girdle of needle-work, too, we are informed by Josephus, was embroidered with flowers in colours. Homer and Virgil frequently mention this art; thus, in the "Odyssey," we read : —

> " Close by the stream a royal dress they lay,
>   A vest, and robe with rich embroidery gay."

And Virgil also says : —

> " A noble present to my son she brought,
>   A robe, with flowers on golden tissue wrought."

The "Æneid," too, speaks of "robes of tissue, stiff with golden wire." We may, therefore, suppose this to be the same as the gold mentioned in Exodus, which was " beat into thin plates, and cut into wires, to work it in the blue, and in the purple, and in the scarlet, and in the fine linen, with cunning work."

" Threads of the dearest and most malleable metal, gold," says Beckman, " seem to have been early employed for ornamenting different articles of dress.

People, however, soon began to weave or knit dresses of gold thread, without the addition of any other materials. The weaving of gold threads with cloth is ascribed by Pliny to King Attalus. In the third century gold was interwoven with linen, and that linen was embroidered in gold thread. It was not till a much later period that silver was formed into threads, and interwoven with cloth. It has been fully proved that silver threads were so interwoven in the time of the last Greek emperors."

In the time of Moses, embroidery appears to have been performed by men; for, in Exodus, we read that Aholiah was a cunning workman, and an "embroiderer in blue, and in purple, and in scarlet, and fine linen."

Homer and Virgil frequently mention this art, which appears, from their poems, to have been brought to perfection, and constantly practised, by the Tyrian and Phrygian ladies, who not only embroidered vests, tunics, and girdles, but also pictures and carpets. Thus we read:—

> " Fair thrones within from space to space were raised,
> Where various carpets with embroidery blazed,
> The work of matrons."

And again:—

> " The queen her hours bestowed
> In curious works; the whirling spindle glowed
> With crimson threads; while busy damsels cull
> The snowy fleece, or twist the purple wool."

The women in many of the Greek Islands were also renowned for their great proficiency in embroidery. The Anglo-Saxons, too, practised it with great success;

and Edward the Elder is mentioned in history as having "had his daughters taught to exercise the needle and the distaff."

WEAVING AND DYEING.

Weaving is another art in which the ladies of the "olden time" also excelled, and it appears that they frequently employed themselves in making garments for their lords. Thus we find in the "Æneid:"—

"The queen, on nearer view, the guest surveyed,
Robed in the garments her own hands had made."

And of Andromache we read:—

"Far in the close recesses of the dome,
Pensive she plies the melancholy loom;
A growing work employed her secret hours,
Confusedly gay with intermingled flowers."

The ancients were much celebrated for their knowledge of various beautiful dyes, some of which are unknown to modern ages. Tyre was renowned for the invention of the purple dye, which was formerly the symbol of regal and sacerdotal dignity. Homer has stamped its value and antiquity, by representing his heroes in purple robes; and habits of the same precious colour were given by the Israelites to Gideon. Pliny describes this colouring matter, and says that it was extracted from two kinds of shell-fish, and was contained in a small bag in their throats; each fish only yielding one drop. As may be imagined, it was very expensive, from the immense quantities required to dye one piece of cloth; but that the colour was very durable, may be believed from the testimony of Plutarch, who, in his life of Alexander, says, that the Greeks found in the treasury of the kings of Persia a large quantity of purple cloth, which was as beautiful as when first made, though it was one hundred and ninety years old.

Among the Greeks, dyeing appears to have been little practised or known ; but the Romans bestowed much pains and expense upon this art, and, in the public games, the different parties were known by the colours of their garments.   Virgil alludes to this celebrated dye in the " Æneid," when he says : —

> " Each leader shining in his Tyrian vest."

HEAD-DRESSES.

Perhaps the most ancient head-dress that we find mentioned in history is the tiara.   Strabo informs us that it was in the form of a tower.   But it appears, by the remarks of many other authors, to have had various shapes.   Among the Persians, the king alone was permitted to wear it erect and straight, the priests and lords of the country being obliged to bend it down in front.   Xenophon tells us that it was frequently encompassed with the diadem, and often had a half moon embroidered on it.   The tiara is seen carved upon ancient medals, and Servius calls it a Phrygian cap. The kings and heroes of Homer and Virgil wore this head-dress : —

> " This royal robe and this tiara wore
>   Old Priam."

THE VEIL.

The veil, that ancient and graceful covering for the head, which has been, and still is, worn by almost every nation of the world, is generally, in Europe, composed of lace or gauze. This "transparent shade" is the most beautiful part of the costume of a bride, and, in the words of the poets, "adds another charm to the loveliness it seems to hide." Homer frequently mentions the veil, as a part of the attire of the Grecian and Trojan ladies. Of Helen, he says : —

> "O'er her fair face a snowy veil she threw,
>   And, softly sighing, from the loom withdrew."

In the "Odyssey," too, we find that, in those days, queens and ladies of rank wove them for themselves. Among Eastern nations, to the present day, the veil is very different from what it is with us. It is formed of large sheets of different materials, which, falling over the head, hang down to the feet, and, being held in folds in front, thus envelope the whole person. Ladies of distinction have them of silk, women of inferior grade of linen or cotton. Ruth's veil, mentioned in the Scriptures, was most probably of the latter material. The Turkish women make them of horse-hair; so that they are transparent from within, but opaque without.

THE CAUL.

A caul is a very ancient head-dress; it is mentioned in the Bible, and by most old writers; it was usually made of net-work, of gold, or silk, and enclosed all the hair. Some were set with jewels, and were very heavy and of great value. In the time of Virgil, cauls were much worn:—

> " Her head with ringlets of her hair is crowned,
> And in a golden caul the curls are bound."

And also in Homer:—

> " Her hair's fair ornaments, the braids that bound,
> The net that held them, and the wreath that crowned."

THE PIN.

Among the rich and beautiful accessories to a lady's toilette, we must not omit to mention one which, however insignificant in itself, adds greatly to the proper arrangement of the dress,—I mean that useful little implement, the *pin*. Before it was known in its present form, its place was supplied by pins of pointed wood or thorns, which materials, though rude and uncivilised, were in common use among our ancestors. The modern pin is said to owe its birth to Germany; and some of my readers will, perhaps, be surprised to hear that eighteen, some even say twenty-five, workmen assist in its formation.

PERFUMES.

Perfumes must not be forgotten in this little treatise on dress. They are of very ancient origin, and the Hebrews and Eastern nations, it is said, constantly used them, before the Greeks and Romans were acquainted with their value. Moses, in Exodus, gives an account of an anointing oil and a perfume, the former composed of myrrh, cinnamon, sweet calamus, cassia, and olive oil; the latter of sweet spices and frankincense, both of which were to be used in the tabernacle. All kinds of fragrant and powerful perfumes were used by the ancients for embalming, and they are mentioned in various parts of the Old Testament, as being known to, and used by, the Hebrews. They were afterwards much esteemed by the Greeks and Romans, who imported the most precious from Syria and India. Perfumes were used in their sacrifices to the gods, and also at their feasts, to give an agreeable scent to their garments and apartments. We often read, too, in the old poets, that

" Fragrant oils the stiffened limbs anoint."

In the camp of Darius, Alexander found, among the other treasures of which he became master, quantities of rich perfumes and precious ointments.

The love of odours of all kinds soon spread over the world, and Pliny laments their being allowed even in the Roman camp, where the eagles, standards, and ensigns, were perfumed, " as if to reward them for conquering the world." Nero is said to have expended on the funeral pile of his wife more incense than the scented groves of Arabia could produce in a whole year.

The fair ladies of our own day perfume their garments and apartments with the odours which are extracted from flowers and herbs, more frequently than with the scented and odoriferous drugs formerly used. The attar of roses, the sweetest, the most precious of

all perfumes comes from the East, and the fête held in
its honour in those countries is thus beautifully described by Moore:—

> " But never yet, by night or day,
>   In dew of spring or summer ray,
>   Did the sweet valley look so gay
>   As now it shines, all love and light,
>   Visions by day and feasts by night!
>   A happier smile illumes each brow,
>   With quicker spread each heart uncloses,
>   And all is ecstasy—for now
>   The valley holds its feast of roses!"

THE FAN.

Fans, which in some countries may almost be considered as a part of the costume, so necessary do they
appear to the fashionables of both sexes, must not be
forgotten.   The use of them was first introduced
amongst us from the East, where the hot climate
renders them almost indispensable.   In the Greek
church, a fan is put into the hands of the deacons, in
the ceremony of their ordination, in allusion to a part
of their office in that church, which is to keep the flies
off the priests during the celebration of the sacrament.

In Japan, where neither men nor women wear
hats, except as a protection against rain, a fan is to
be seen in the hand or the girdle of every inhabitant.   Soldiers and priests even are never without
them.   In that country, they serve a great many different purposes.   Visitors receive the dainties offered
them, upon their fans; the beggar, imploring charity,
holds out his fan for the alms his prayers may obtain.
According to Siebold, the fan here serves the dandy

in lieu of a whalebone switch; the pedagogue, instead of a ferule, for the offending school-boy's knuckles; and a fan, presented upon a peculiar kind of salver to the high-born criminal, is said to be the form of announcing his death-doom, his head being struck off at the same moment as he stretches it towards the fan.

In the book of "Table Talk" we read: "In the south of Italy, men still continue to use the fan, and, in hot weather, one may often see a captain of dragoons moustached, and 'bearded like the pard,' fanning himself with all the graces and dexterity of a young coquette."

In England, fans were almost unknown till the reign of Queen Elizabeth. Under Charles the Second they were much used; but, during the reign of Queen Anne, they became almost a part of the lady's costume; at ball or supper, in the morning promenade or the evening's drive, one hand still held a fan of feathers, of silk, or of painted paper.

ARTIFICIAL FLOWERS.

Artificial flowers, those beautiful imitations of the "stars of the earth," are now brought to such perfection, that they almost rival the blossoms they are intended to imitate. Paris, the emporium of all the gems of the toilette, as usual, surpasses all other cities, in her delicate and faithful imitations of the flowers, buds, and blossoms, that bloom in every quarter of the globe; and, not content with copying each varying tint, each delicate fibre, the fair *floriste* adds to their beauty and charm, by giving to each a drop of the perfume peculiar to it. Near Genoa, there is a con-

floriste: maker of artificial flowers

vent where the holy sisters devote their leisure hours to this elegant employment, and their skill is celebrated throughout all Europe.

In England, artificial flowers were unknown till the reign of Edward the Third.

MOURNING COSTUME.

The outward signs of woe and sorrow have always, in almost all nations, been demonstrated by some peculiarity in the colour or shape of the attire; but different countries have adopted different modes of expressing their grief.

The Roman women, on these melancholy occasions, laid aside their gold, purple, and embroidered dresses. Under the republic, they wore black robes, but, under the emperors, these were changed to white; they also covered their heads.

The men of Rome, after they had adopted the custom of shaving the beard, allowed it to grow long when in mourning, as a sign of their affliction. They also clothed themselves in black, a custom supposed to have been derived from the ancient Egyptians; and sometimes they wore garments made of the skins of beasts.

In Greece, where the beard was always retained, it was considered a sign of sorrow to shave it off; so opposite are the customs of various nations, in every thing relating to the adornment of the person. Often, too, they cut off the hair, and laid it on the corpse. We read in Homer,—

> " They shaved their heads, and covered with their hair
> The body."

Both men and women wore black garments, and laid aside all their ornaments, and the latter often tore or shaved off their hair, and they always muffled up and concealed their faces.

The Chinese, Siamese, and Japanese, wear white mourning, for their superstitions teach them to believe that the dead become beneficent genii. The Turks wear blue, or violet; the Ethiopians, grey; the Peruvians, mouse colour; the Spaniards formerly wore white serge. Herrera observes, that the last time it was used was in 1498, at the death of Prince John.

The Jews formerly neither shaved nor saluted any one during mourning; they never wore black; their outward token of mourning was to retain upon their persons the garments they had on when their friend or relative died.

In Italy, the women used to wear white mourning, and the men brown; in Syria and Armenia we see them in blue, and in Egypt in yellow robes, or such as are of the colour of dead leaves. In the Barbary States old soiled garments testify grief, and they are frequently passed through water, to give them that appearance. In Lycia and Argos, white was the mourning colour; at Delos, shaving the hair was the only sign of affliction.

In France, the mourning habit was formerly white, and continued so till the reign of Charles the Eighth. Leopold, Emperor of Germany, who died so late as the year 1705, when in deep affliction, followed the custom of the Jews, and let his beard grow.

In England, as early as the fifteenth century, the immense expense incurred in mourning habiliments caused an edict to be framed to limit the richness and size of the garments allowed to the nobility, as well as to those of the lower orders.

The following explanation has been given of the cause of the adoption of different colours for the symbol of mourning :—

White is the emblem of purity; celestial blue indicates the space where the soul ranges after death; yellow (or dead leaf) exhibits death as the end of hope, and man falling like the leaf in autumn; grey is the colour of the earth, our common mother; black, the colour of mourning now general throughout Europe, indicates eternal night. " Black," says Rabelais, " is the sign of mourning, because it is the colour of darkness, which is melancholy, and the opposite to white, which is the colour of light, of joy, and of happiness."

THE TOILETTE IN ENGLAND.

CHAPTER I.

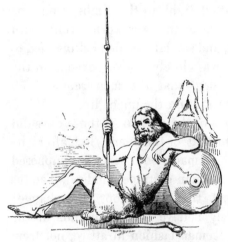

Ancient Briton

NCIENT authors disagree in the accounts they give of the dress of the first inhabitants of Britain. Some assert that, previously to the first descent of the Romans, the people wore no clothing at all; other writers, however (and, probably, with more truth), state, that they clothed themselves with the skins of wild animals; and as their mode of life required activity and freedom of limb, loose skins over their bodies, fastened, probably, with a thorn, would give them the needful warmth, without in any degree restraining the liberty of action so necessary to the hardy mountaineer.

Julius Cæsar gives us reason to think that the mantles he observed in use, were made by fastening the ends of hair into some sort of coarse cloth ; but it is impossible at the present time to say in what manner this was done.

Another dress mentioned by ancient writers, indicates a progress towards civilization. The year in which it was worn is not given, but it may be considered the second era in the history of the toilette of the rude and warlike Britons. It consisted of a sort of trousers, which fitted tight to the limbs, from the waist to the ankles ; over this was worn a tunic with long sleeves, a cloak, and sandals, made of skins, tied to the feet. The head was closely shaven, except on the crown, and Cæsar adds, that the men removed all their beard excepting that on the upper lip.

Probably the dress of the women of those days did not differ much from that of the men ; but after the second descent of the Romans, both sexes are supposed to have followed the Roman costume ; indeed, Tacitus expressly asserts that they did adopt this change; though we may safely believe that thousands of the natives spurned the Roman fashion in attire, not from any dislike of its form or shape, but from the detestation they bore towards their conquerors.

The beautiful and intrepid Queen Boadicea is the first British female whose dress is recorded. Dio mentions, that when she led her army to the field of battle, she wore " a various-coloured tunic, flowing in long loose folds, and over it a mantle, while her long hair floated over her neck and shoulders." This war-

Julius Cæsar: 100 B.C.–44 B.C.; invaded Britain 55 B.C.
Tacitus: historian, circa 55 A.D.–117 A.D.
Queen Boadicea: Queen of Norfolk and Sussex; died 62 A.D.

like queen, therefore, notwithstanding her abhorrence of the Romans, could not resist the graceful elegance of their costume, so different from the rude clumsiness of the dress of her wild subjects ; and, though fighting valiantly against the invaders of her country, she succumbed to the laws which Fashion had issued!—a forcible example of the unlimited sway exercised by the flower-crowned goddess over the female mind.

It may not be uninteresting here to describe the Roman costume, at the period when it was adopted by the British. The *toga*, or gown without sleeves, was usually of a pure white, and being gracefully thrown around the shoulders, descended nearly to the ground behind, and was occasionally used as a covering for the head. A purple border was a mark of dignity. The generality of people wore the tunic, without the toga ; it was the in-door dress, and completely covered the body. At first, the sleeves of the tunic only reached to the elbow; soon, however, they extended to the wrist, and at last increased in length till they touched the ankles. The feet were covered with sandals. As improvements in dress became more common, the *stola* (resembling a chemise) was worn by the women. It was always white, had long sleeves, and frequently a narrow border of gold round the bottom. Over it was thrown the mantle, or cloak, and sandals encircled the feet of the wearer. The Roman ladies were very fond of ornaments, and wore rings, bracelets, armlets, and torques, or necklaces.

With the Saxon invasion came war and desolation, and the elegancies of life were necessarily neglected. The invaders clothed themselves in a rude and fantastic manner. It is not unlikely that the Britons

Saxon invasion: 6th century A.D.

may have adopted some of their costume. From the Saxon females, we are told, came the invention of dividing, curling, and turning the hair over the back of the head. Ancient writers also add, that their garments were long and flowing.

The Romans for many years looked upon a shirt as belonging to women only; but at length they also adopted it, and the Saxon military men did not disdain to wear it richly embroidered.

Gradually, additions and improvements in costume were made. Over the linen shirt was worn a linen or woollen tunic, which reached to the knees; it had long sleeves, and was put on like a shirt. Frequently the border and collar were ornamented, and a girdle usually confined it at the waist. Long drawers, or trousers, covered the lower limbs, and leathern stockings, or buskins, were also used. Often bands of cloth or woollen were wrapped round the legs: over these stockings were worn, and the shoes were generally black, tied by a leathern thong.

The Anglo-Saxons appear to have admired bright colours, and red or blue hose were generally worn. Silk, when imported about the eighth century, was at first too costly a material to be much used, but afterwards it became a favourite article of dress. Weaving and embroidery were well known to the English females, even at that early period. William of Malmesbury says also, that "gold chains and bracelets were favourite ornaments of both sexes."

The women wore long tunics, or gowns, and a mantle. The sleeves were confined at the wrists by bracelets or borders of embroidery, and the cloak often formed a graceful festoon in front. A veil of linen or

William of Malmesbury: circa 1090-1143: wrote "Acts of the Kings of the English" (original in Latin, "Gesta Regum Anglorum") in 1125, a history covering the 5th-12th centuries

silk always encircled the head. Matthew Paris thus describes the costume of the Anglo-Saxons: "The dress of the gentlemen was a loose cloak, which reached down to the ankles, and over that a long robe, fastened over both shoulders, on the middle of the breast, by a clasp or buckle. These cloaks and robes were frequently lined with rich furs, and bordered with gold and embroidery. The soldiers and common people wore close coats, only reaching to the knee, and short cloaks, hanging over the left shoulder, and buckled on the right. These had sometimes an edging of gold. They wore caps that came to a point in front, which were probably made of the skins of beasts. The women wore a long loose robe, reaching to the ground. On their heads hung a veil, which, falling down before, was gathered up at the corners, and folded round their necks and over their bosoms. The robe was usually ornamented with a broad border, coloured and embroidered. Slippers were worn by men and women of fashion, and the men had a crossed bandage in lieu of a stocking. The hair of the men was worn long and flowing, and the beard was permitted to grow on the upper lip."

The Anglo-Saxon ladies seldom, if ever, went with their heads bare; sometimes the veil, or *head-rail*, was replaced by a golden head-band, or it was worn over the veil. Half circles of gold, necklaces, bracelets, ear-rings, and crosses, were the numerous ornaments worn at that period by the women. It is supposed that mufflers (a sort of bag with a thumb) were also sometimes used.

Great uncertainty exists respecting the true character of a garment much used by the Anglo-Saxon

Matthew Paris: 1200-1259; wrote a history of England (in Latin) from William the Conqueror to the reign of Henry III (whose reign extended to 1272)

ladies, called a *kirtle*. Some writers suppose it to have meant the petticoat; others, that it was an under robe. But, though frequently mentioned by old authors, nothing can be correctly determined respecting it.

Little appears to be known concerning the costume in Britain under the Danes; but we are told that the latter "were effeminately gay in their dress, combed their hair once a day, bathed once a week, and often changed their attire."

An ancient and celebrated piece of tapestry, kept in the Church of Bayeux, contains some curious representations of the dress of the Northmen. This immense *tableau* of the conquest of England has survived the ravages of time, and is still in a wonderful state of preservation. It measures two hundred and twelve feet in length, but only eighteen inches in breadth, and is engraved in Montfaucon's "Monarchie Française." Till of late years, Matilda, the consort of William the Conqueror, was supposed to have been the embroideress of this beautiful memorial of her husband's conquests; now, however, doubts on this subject have been raised, and it is said to have been worked in later ages.

We confess our disposition to believe that, notwithstanding the testimony of learned antiquaries, Matilda was the inventress of this ancient tapestry; and, even now, we can fancy the royal lady surrounded by the fair dames of her court, each armed with a needle, gaily recording the triumphs of the Norman Conqueror. How many fair fingers must have assisted in this curious work! how many bright eyes must have smiled at the curious emblems and devices it contains!

King Edward is represented, in this work, habited in a long robe, emblazoned round the bottom; it is

Danes: the Danes invaded in successive waves in the 8th–10th centuries
Bayeux Tapestry: depicts the Norman Conquest of England (1066); 234 ft. by $19\frac{1}{2}$ in.
Montfaucon, Bernard de: 1655–1741
Matilda: crowned 1068; died 1083
William the Conqueror: 1027–1087
King Edward: circa 1002–1066

fastened at the neck and waist by a band, and the sleeves are long and nearly tight. He has shoes on his feet, and a bushy beard and moustaches. Montfaucon, in his description of the tapestry, supposes Edward, who is seated on his throne, to be in the act of desiring Harold to go and inform William of Normandy that he has appointed him his successor to the British crown. The beard and moustaches of the monarch are very luxuriant, and seem to intimate that his majesty did not like his subjects to imitate the Norman fashions. William of Malmesbury accuses the Britons, at this time, "of transforming themselves into Normans and Frenchmen, employing their strange speech and manners, and also the very fantastic costume of their nation,—that of wearing short tunics, or clipping their hair, and shaving the beard."

King Harold

Harold and his attendants are very differently habited from the monarch. Each wears on his head a kind of bonnet, and though the beard is close shaven, and no hair is seen underneath the head-dress, the moustaches are allowed to remain. They wear tunics reaching to the knees, and small cloaks, that much resemble the Greek *chlamydes*, are fixed on the right shoulder with a brooch. Their feet are covered with clumsy-looking shoes. The riding-dress is the same, with the addition of spurs.

Harold: Harold II, 1066
William of Malmesbury: see p. 42

After William the Conqueror came to the throne, the Norman dress was very generally adopted; but the curious fashion of shaving the back of the head was a mode that the Anglo-Saxons appear never to have followed; and we are told by William of Poitou, "that when William returned to Normandy, accompanied by several of his new subjects, the courtiers of the regent were much astonished at the beauty of the long-haired English, and their rich embroidered habits."

William the Conqueror: reigned 1066–1087
William of Poitou: unknown; Poitou is also known as Aquitaine and lies along the West Coast of France, in the area of Bordeaux; it passed back and forth between France and England as a result of wars and marriage settlements

Chapter 2 – England, 12th to early 14th Century

CHAPTER II.

THE ladies' dress continued much the same as we have described in the preceding chapter, till the reign of Henry the First, when the sleeves and veils were worn so immensely long, that they were tied up in bows and festoons, and *la grande mode* then appears to have been, to have the skirts of the gowns also of so ridiculous a length, that they lay trailing upon the ground. Laced bodies were also sometimes seen, and tight sleeves with pendant cuffs, like those mentioned in the reign of Louis the Seventh of France. A second, or upper tunic, much shorter than the under robe, was also the fashion; and, perhaps, it may be considered as the

Lady in the Reign of Henry I

Henry the First: 1100–1135
Louis the Seventh: 1120–1180

surcoat generally worn by the Normans. The hair was often wrapped in silk or riband, and allowed to hang down the back; and mufflers were in common use. The dresses were very splendid, with embroidery and gold borders.

The gentlemen's habiliments, during the above reigns, varied much more than those of the fair sex; and the writers of the time charge the reign of William Rufus with many abuses and extravagances in dress. Every article relating to the toilette was composed of the richest materials. The finest cloths, linen, and silks, adorned with gold and embroidery, and lined with costly furs, formed the costume of the higher classes. The tunic, formerly reaching to the knees, was now considerably lengthened, and the sleeves hung down nearly to the feet, while the inner garment swept the ground.

William of Malmesbury mentions a mantle presented to Henry by the Bishop of Lincoln, which cost 100*l.*, and describes it as being made of the finest cloth, lined with black sables. The same writer greatly censures the long hair, loose flowing robes, ridiculously pointed shoes, and effeminate appearance, of the men of that period.

It is said that a laughable incident occurred when Henry was in Normandy. A preacher so eloquently declaimed against the sin and wickedness of wearing long hair, that the monarch and his attendants actually wept. Delighted with the impression his eloquence had made upon the king and his subjects, the prelate determined to follow up his advantage, and not lose the golden opportunity; he therefore took from the folds of his sleeve a large pair of shears, and cropped the whole congregation!

William Rufus: 1087–1100
William of Malmesbury: see p. 42
Henry: Henry I, 1100–1135
"A preacher": Bishop Serlo

Perhaps to this act may be attributed the fashion of wearing wigs; for, in Stephen's reign, we first find them mentioned; and it is not unlikely but the profusion of flowing locks, left as a mark of the preacher's eloquence upon the floor of the church, may have furnished some cunning *coiffeur* with the idea of restoring them to the heads of their former possessors, in another form. Certain it is that but few months had elapsed before long hair again graced the heads of the courtiers, and Serlo and his sermon were forgotten.

This story reminds us of a similar anecdote related of Thomas Conecte, who preached so eloquently against the high head-dresses of the ladies, that, moved by his words, his fair listeners pulled off the obnoxious coiffures, and consigned them to the flames.

The length of the beard soon afterwards became an object of animadversion with the clergy, and also the extraordinary shape of the fashionable boots and shoes. The latter are represented as having had points like a scorpion's tail, and were named *pigaciæ*. Sometimes they were stuffed, so as to allow them to be twisted like a ram's horn. The boots, called *ocreæ rostratæ*, were of an equally ridiculous form. Both these extravagant fashions were inveighed against by the monks, though without success.

In the reign of Henry the Second, *court manteaux*, and jagged or fringed garments, appear to have been introduced, and the absurdities and extravagances of dress became every day greater. One fashion succeeded another in rapid succession, and the inventive genius of man and woman seemed exerted only to disco-

Stephen: 1135–1154
coîffeur: hairdresser
Serlo: see p. 48

Thomas Conecte: preached moral reform; burned at the stake in Rome, 1433
Henry the Second: 1154–1189
court manteaux: short cloaks

ver new methods of adorning the human frame. In too many of these ridiculous modes, taste was wholly disregarded or forgotten; caprice, or a love of singularity and variety, was frequently the author of many an extravagant costume, which, being invented, perhaps, by some person of rank, was, however frightful, followed by others in a lower grade of society, till gradually the mode became extended throughout the country.

So has it ever been, from year to year, up to the present period. Fashions the most ridiculous and *outré* have always found admirers, or, at least, followers; provided a dress is supposed to be fashionable, it matters little to the willing slaves of the fickle goddess whether it be becoming or not. Thus, the peaked shoes are said to have been invented by a gentleman who had a deformed foot; and, in later years, the *ruff* is attributed to a lady who first wore it to conceal a wen. Probably, could we trace the birth of many other fashions, we should find they arose from similar causes.

State garments, in this reign, were profusely ornamented; and gloves were worn by the men, some of them embroidered, and with jewelled backs; and even in the sacerdotal habits, splendour was carried to such an extent, that Lord Lyttleton declares the accounts of the magnificence of Beckett to be "incredible."

Alarmed at the extent to which pomp and luxury of attire were brought, the legislature interfered, and framed several severe laws and edicts on this momentous subject. It would afford no little amusement, at the present day, to listen to deep debates on the width

outré: outrageous
Lord Lyttleton: wrote a history of Henry II in 1767
Beckett: Thomas à Becket, 1118-1170; Archbishop of Canterbury; canonized 1173

of a tunic, the point of a shoe, or the length of a beard; to see the learning and rank of the country consulting gravely together about wigs and peaked boots, and solemn divines launching anathemas from the pulpit against absurdities in costume.

Matthew Paris says, that King Henry, when interred at Fontevraud, "was arrayed in the royal vestments, having a golden crown on the head, and gloves on the hands; boots, wrought with gold, on the feet, and spurs."

In an inventory of the dress of King John, hose are mentioned, and sandals of purple cloth, fretted with gold. The pantaloons, or *chausses*, were worn; also a pointed cap, or a capuchon. In the same reign, the *petit-maîtres* are accused of curling their hair with irons, and binding it up with ribands.

The Normans, some writers affirm, were remarkable for choosing the gaudiest colours for their garments, yellow alone excepted, which was ordered to be worn by the Jews, as a mark of infamy. Their shirts are represented as having been made of fine linen; their doublets fitted tight to their bodies, and the nobles wore them reaching to the ankles: frequently, too, an embroidered girdle, adorned with jewels, encircled the waist. But it was upon the *court manteaux* that the greatest magnificence was displayed. One that belonged to Richard the First is described as having been "nearly covered with half moons and shining orbs of solid silver, to imitate the heavenly bodies."

About the beginning of the thirteenth century, the ladies found their long narrow cuffs, hanging to the

Matthew Paris: see p. 43
King Henry: Henry II, died 1189
King John: 1199–1216
petit maîtres: dandies
court manteaux: short cloaks
Richard the First: Richard the Lionhearted, 1189–1199

ground, very uncomfortable; they therefore adopted tight sleeves. Pelisses, trimmed with fur, and loose surcoats, were also worn, as well as *wimples*, an article of attire worn round the neck under the veil. Embroidered boots and shoes formed, also, part of their wardrobe.

Lady in the Reign of Henry III

In a work like the present, it is impossible to give all the numerous varieties in the costume of those early days. We shall, therefore, only mention the appearance of any great novelty in the annals of fashion, and dilate more largely upon those dresses, the shape, form, and materials of which are recorded in later times by the painter, the poet, and the sculptor.

Matthew Paris says, that in the thirteenth century, he was more disgusted than pleased with the foppery of the times. He also adds, that the nobility who attended the marriage of the daughter of Henry the Third with the King of Scotland were attired in habits of silk called *cointises*. Velvet is also mentioned as a new material just imported. Another garment, called an *over-all*, being a cloak with sleeves and a hood, was now worn. The shoes were embroidered in chequers; the hood had fringed edges; and round hats and caps came into fashion. Moreover, the sportsmen of those days, when preparing for

Henry the Third: 1216–1272
daughter of Henry III: Margaret, who married Alexander III of Scotland in 1251
cointises: not defined in any of our sources; Boucher says "habit" meant garments
    in general; in French, the word has associations of sharpness, or smartness

the chase, enveloped their heads in a white coif tied under the chin!

Under the chivalric and excellent King Edward the First, few, if any, ridiculous modes appeared; the *noblesse* had a long tunic and mantle, and sometimes an upper tunic, called a *cyclas*, and a surcoat of rich stuff lined with fur. The hose were worked in gold, and the hair and beard were carefully curled. We hear, too, of purple robes, fine linen vestments, and mantles woven with gold.

The ladies' costume, during the reigns of Henry and Edward, was very splendid. The veils and wimples were richly embroidered, and worked in gold; the surcoat and mantle were worn of the richest materials; and the hair was turned up under a gold caul.

Towards the year 1300, the ladies' dress fell under the animadversion of the malevolent writers of that day. The robe is represented as having had tight sleeves and a train, over which was worn a surcoat and mantle, with cords and tassels. "The ladies," says a poet of the thirteenth century, "were like peacocks and magpies; for the pies bear feathers of various colours, which Nature gives them; so the ladies love strange habits, and a variety of ornaments. The pies have long tails, that trail in the mud; so the ladies make their tails a thousand times longer than those of peacocks and pies."

The pictures of the ladies of that time certainly present us with no very elegant specimens of their fashions. Their gowns or tunics are so immensely long, that the fair dames are obliged to hold them

King Edward the First: 1272–1307
Henry & Edward: Henry III and Edward I

up, to enable them to move; whilst a sweeping train trails after them; and over the head and round the neck is a variety of, or substitute for, the wimple, which is termed a *gorget*. It enclosed the cheeks and chin, and fell upon the bosom, giving the wearer very much the appearance of suffering from sore throat or toothache.

Lady in the Reign of Edward II

When this head-dress was not worn, a caul of net-work, called a *crespine*, often replaced it, and for many years it continued to be a favourite coiffure.

The writers of this time speak of tight lacing, and of ladies with small waists.

In the next reign, an apron is first met with, tied behind with a riband. The sleeves of the robe, and the petticoat, are trimmed with a border of embroidery; rich bracelets are also frequently seen; but, notwithstanding all the splendour of the costume, the gorget still envelopes the neck.

The gentlemen in the reign of Edward the Second first adopted the party-coloured habits so much admired in after-years; but neither the cause nor inventor of these curious habiliments is recorded. The garments now became much shorter, and the hood, instead of concealing the head like a cowl, was frequently twisted into a smart coiffure, not unlike a turban. Beards were now worn, and long hair.

Edward the Second: 1307–1327

Chapter 3 – England, 14th Century

THE TOILETTE IN ENGLAND.

CHAPTER III.

THE long and glorious reign of Edward the Third presents us with many novelties in fashion. Many modes were brought from foreign lands. "The Englishmen," says the Monk of Glastonbury, "haunted so much unto the folly of strangers, that every year they changed them in diverse shapes and disguisings of clothing, now long, now large, now wide, now strait, and every-day clothingges new and destitute and devest from all honesty of old arraye or good usage ; and another time to short clothes, and so strait-waisted, with full sleeves, and *tapetes* of surcoats, and hodes, over-long and large, all so nagged and knib on every side, and all so shattered, and also buttoned, that I with truth shall say, they seem more like to tormentors or devils in their clothing, and also in their shoging (shoeing) and other array, than they seem to be like men."

Edward the Third: 1327–1377
Monk of Glastonbury: Douglas, who wrote "The Chronicles of England" in 1480
tapetes: possibly brocaded fabric
nagged, knib, shattered: no definitions of these terms could be found in relation
  to costume

Though Edward himself is represented as having been, in his own person, an enemy to dress and extravagance, his *noblesse* did not follow his example. The long garments entirely disappeared, and a vest that fitted quite tight to the body, down to the middle of the thigh, replaced it. This new invention was made of the richest materials, covered with embroidery, and buttoned down the front, whilst a girdle confined it over the hips. Like the similar garment worn by the ladies some years afterwards, it was called a *côte-hardie*. But the most fantastical parts of this dress were the sleeves; they reached as far as the elbows (having others underneath), and from the bottom of them hung long white cuffs, exactly similar to those worn by the ladies from their wrists. This ridiculous mode must have had a curious effect when worn by men on horseback, and as they gallopped along, the cuffs must have resembled streamers fluttering in the breeze. A cloak, of an unusually great length, generally covered this fantastic attire; it had a row of buttons on the right shoulder, and the edges were frequently indented or stamped, so as to imitate leaves of flowers.

In an inventory of this reign, we read of a jupon of blue tartan, powdered with blue garters, decorated with buckles, and pendants of silver gilt; also a doublet of linen, having round the skirts and sleeves a border of long green cloth, embroidered with clouds and vine-stalks in gold.

Again the parliament found it necessary to interfere, and to make new laws respecting dress. The nobility, as usual, were permitted to amuse themselves with all the varieties of fashions, and to wear the

noblesse: nobility

richest habiliments; but persons under the rank of knights were forbidden the use of silks and embroidery, or ornaments of gold and silver, or jewellery. Rings, buckles, ouches, girdles, and ribands, were expressly forbidden them, and if they infringed the statute, they were to forfeit the ornament or dress so worn.

The beard at this period was usually long, and pointed; Edward's is quite patriarchal. The hair, also, was flowing on the shoulders, and a popular saying then was,—

> " Long beirds hertiless,
> Peynted hoods witless,
> Gay cotes graceless,
> Maketh England thriftless."

In an illumination on a grant made by this king, about 1350, to Thomas de Brotherton, we find that his majesty wore a beard and whiskers, but the latter has neither; his hair, too, is short, his body enclosed in armour, with a doublet-sleeve to the wrist, and a surcoat of his arms, without a collar, but having a handsome trimming. The king's shoes are long and pointed, without heels, and have a square opening over the instep.

Drawings made about this time, give us representations of men wearing caps made the shape of the head, surrounded by a border, which is either embroidered splendidly, or profusely ornamented with jewels. Some are clad in long gowns, open before, with sleeves reaching to the wrists.

Edward the Third is described as wearing a mantle or cloak of velvet, embroidered in gold, ornamented with precious stones, and lined with ermine; this cloak was fastened with a velvet band, covered with jewels. The robe was a rich gold and coloured brocade, or a manufacture much resembling it. It reached from the neck, which was then always uncovered, down to the ankles; the hose were of scarlet silk, and the shoes profusely embroidered with precious stones.

The dress of ladies of "high degree" was no less splendid; velvet shirts, trimmed with rich furs, and jackets fitting tight to the shape, embroidered in gold and silks, with a mantle of gold and silver cloth, sometimes studded with jewels, formed their usual costume.

Lady in the Reign of Edward III

A surcoat was a garment greatly in fashion at this time. It was worn by men, and fitted close to the body down to the hips, when it became very full, the bottom being usually covered with embroidery; the sleeves were large and hanging, and a flowing mantle, descending from the shoulders, and reaching nearly to the ground, was generally thrown over it.

The sleeves of the ladies' gowns were also long and hanging; sometimes they reached nearly to the ground, but others were always worn under them; the upper sleeve was only pinned to the dress, and was therefore easily detached from it.

These being the days of chivalry and tournaments, when lances were shivered for the love of the fair ladies whose bright eyes glanced round the lists, when rewards were given to the conqueror, and many a love-token was presented by jewelled fingers to the true and faithful knight, we may readily suppose that even, as Cressida exclaims, "There, Diomed, keep this sleeve," this part of a lady's attire might be given as a pledge " to wear on the helm," as well as a glove or scarf. It is supposed, however, by some old authors, to have meant an ornamental cuff.

One remarkable peculiarity in the dress of the men at this time was the manner of wearing the capuchon, or hood. It had a long tail that hung down the back in a point, and was buttoned close up to the chin. Other gallants twisted it up in a fantastic form, and carelessly poised it on the top of the head, and sometimes even placed a beaver hat over it. These capuchons were for many years the fashion in France, and as long ages have elapsed since they were worn, we may be allowed to surmise that these hoods, added to their shaven faces and short hair, must have made them appear very like a nation of monks; indeed, some chroniclers affirm that it was the fear of this *sobriquet* that induced Francis the First to set the fashion of velvet caps in his kingdom.

Gentleman in the Reign of Edward III

The admiration for gaudy colours was very great at this period. Frequently, if the doublet were of scarlet velvet, the mantle would be blue, with white

Cressida: from Shakespeare's play "Troilus & Cressida"
Diomed: Diomede/Diomedes; one of the principal Greek warriors of the Trojan War; this
   reference is to Shakespearean costume, not Greek dress
sobriquet: epithet or nickname

linings, the hose also blue, and the shoes of scarlet, trimmed with gold. The caps now in fashion were of a curious shape, with a broad lap, like a fan, on one side, usually of velvet to match the mantle, and lined with the same. Some, however, were of a round form, ornamented with jewels.

Fig. 1.

Shoe of Edward III

Although pointed shoes were much worn at the beginning of this reign, their shape changed towards the end; some, too, were curiously ornamented in patterns in embroidery. *Fig.* 1 is the drawing of a shoe represented on the monument of Edward the Third, in Westminster Abbey; and *Fig.* 2 is from the effigy of his son, in the Minster, at York.

Fig. 2.

Shoe of Prince William

In a print of the king, we find him drawn with a hat, which may, perhaps, be looked upon as the commencement of the fashion; for, at that time, caps were mostly worn by all classes: they were of every shape.

Now, too, we first find a feather gracing the cap of the gallants of the fourteenth century. It was usually stuck straight up in front of the cap; for, as yet, they had not arrived at the careless grace and elegance of the plume which, two centuries afterwards, was known by the title of the "panache à la Henri Quatre."

son of Edward the Third: Prince William of Hatfield, his second son; the only royal
   tomb in York Minster, dates from the 14th century
panache à la Henri Quatre: hat plume in Henri IV style (1399–1413), generally white

Chapter 4 – England, 14th and 15th Centuries

THE TOILETTE IN ENGLAND.

CHAPTER IV.

FASHION now assumed a most important place in the annals of England, and many new modes were, in the reign of Richard the Second, brought from Italy, Bohemia, Poland, Spain, France, and Germany. Indeed, but little seemed left to English taste and invention, for foreign countries supplied numerous novelties in dress, which our countrymen and countrywomen did not fail to follow and adopt, with their usual eagerness when any thing relating to that important subject, *la toilette*, is concerned.

To begin with the costume of the ladies, they were extremely partial to party-coloured robes, and wore *sous jupes*, or kirtles, of rich satin, or brocade, flowered with gold and silver. Richard the Second's first queen, Anne, introduced Bohemian fashions among her new subjects, and certainly was herself a most celebrated leader of fashion.

From Bohemia came, perhaps, the vest, or *côte-*

Richard the Second: 1377–1399
Anne: Anne of Bohemia, 1366–1394

hardie, a most curious garment. It somewhat resembled a waistcoat, for it was made quite tight to the shape as far as the hips, and was frequently trimmed with a broad border of fur all round, and with buttons down the front. Across the bosom it was cut quite square, and it had sleeves fitting tight to the wrist. Sometimes, in imitation, probably, of the French, an *escarcelle*, or modern reticule, was suspended from the border, and hung down in front. There was also a sleeveless or sideless robe worn at this period, which is frequently confounded with the *côte-hardie*, under which was worn a petticoat, or kirtle, of a different material from the robe, with a tight body and sleeves, the latter adorned with buttons. Some fair dames adopted the mode of wearing stomachers of jewels; and the whole dress, robe, kirtle, and mantle, were very often emblazoned with the arms of the family of the lady, and that of her husband. Sometimes, too, curious mottoes, or quaint devices, were worked on the borders.

Towards the end of this reign, the trains of the gowns became so ridiculously long, that a clergyman published a tract against them.

The head-dresses were various, and not remarkable for beauty or elegance. The gentlemen having adopted one that was peculiarly ugly, the ladies probably thought it but seemly that they should do likewise; they therefore wore one called a *caput*, which was stiff, formal, and inelegant. It was fitted quite close to the crown of the head, and had a broad border across the forehead, arched out and escaloped. Sometimes, to improve its beauty, two lappets were appended, and hung as low as the waist. Other coiffures resembled basins laid on the top of the head, and formed of gold net-work ; while some, again, had points like a bishop's mitre ; but all were low and small. The hair was parted on the forehead, and drawn back in short curls or plaits behind the ears.

The *gorget*, or *chevesail*, was worn, but was sometimes replaced by a broad band round the neck, and the ornamented girdle, instead of spanning the waist, was allowed to fall over the hips. The shoes were usually pointed ; but those of the ladies never approached to the extravagance of shape so much reprobated in the attire of the men.

During this reign, so eventful in new fashions, Queen Anne is said to have introduced, besides " the new guise of Beme " (Bohemia), the custom of riding on side-saddles. Camden asserts this ; and the old poet Gower certainly speaks of ladies who " everich one ride on side." But female equestrians are seen on seals of much earlier date riding in this fashion, and it is therefore probable that Anne of Bohemia only introduced some improvement in the saddle, or the science of equitation.*

The extravagant profusion displayed in gentlemen's habiliments now increased to a great degree ; from King Richard himself down to the lowest of his subjects, every thought seemed centred in dress, and, occupied as they were with new fashions and fopperies, we cannot better describe them than by copying the words of a work called " Eulogium," written, it is supposed,

---

* An example may be seen in the second number of the " Journal of the British Archæological Association," p. 145, being an engraving from a seal of Joanna de Stuteville, appended to a document dated 1227.

Camden: probably William Camden, 1551-1623, author of many histories
Gower: John Gower, circa 1330-1408; Chaucer called him "Moral Gower"
Eulogium: anonymous work of the period, mentioned also in G. W. Rhead's "Chats on
  Costume"

at this period : " The commons were besotted in excess of apparel, in wide surcoats reaching to their loins ;

Man in the Reign of Richard II

some in a garment reaching to their heels, close before, and strutting out on the sides ; so that on the back they make men seem women, and this they call by a ridiculous name, *gowne*. Their hoods are little, tied under the chin, and buttoned like the women's, but set with gold, silver, and precious stones. Their *liripipes*, or tippets, pass round the neck, and, hanging down before, reach to the heels, all jagged. They have another *weed* of silk, which they call *paltock*. Their hose are of two colours, or pied with more, which they tie to their *paltocks*, with white lachets, called *herlots*, without any breeches. Their girdles are of gold and silver, and some of them worth twenty marks. Their shoes and *pattens* are snouted and piked, more than a finger long, crooking upwards, which they call *crakowes*, resembling devil's claws, and fastened to the knees with chains of gold and silver."

" Alas !" exclaims another writer of that day, " may not a man see, as in our days, the sinful costly array of clothing ; and, namely, in too much superfluity of clothing, such that maketh it so dear, to the harm of the people ; not only the cost of embroidery, the disguising, indenting, or barring, ounding, paling, winding, or bending, and semblable waste of cloth in vanity, but there is also the costly furring in their gowns; so much pouncing of chisel to make holes, so much dagging of shears, with the superfluity in length of the aforesaid gowns, trailing in the mire, on horse and also on foot, as well of man as of woman."

The testimony of two writers at the end of the fourteenth century, has fully established the extravagance and splendour of the costume of that time; and it is not to be wondered at that it continued, and even increased rapidly: for Richard himself was fond of the most varied and costly apparel, and, says Holinshed, "he had one cote, which he caused to be made for him, of gold and stone, valued at thirty thousand marks."

Dr. Grey remarks, that "Richard's expense in regard to dress was very extraordinary." In a picture of the king, painted in 1377, he is represented in a robe adorned with white harts and broom pods, alluding to his mother's arms and his own name of *Plantagenista*.

The gentlemen, like the ladies, besides emblazoning their robes, and wearing them embroidered with precious stones, had letters, mottoes, and various devices worked upon them, and the mantles were frequently "jagged" and "indented." Jackets, cassocks, and party-coloured garments, were also the mode. Sometimes the robe was exactly divided into two colours, or the hose were different, the one leg being clothed in red, the other in blue. The tight sleeves also vanished, and large wide ones supplied their place. "They were called," says the Monk of Evesham, "the devil's receptacles, for stolen goods were easily concealed in them. Some fell to the feet, others swept

Holinshed: Ralphael Holinshed, wrote "Chronicles of England, Scotland & Ireland", 1577; died 1580
Dr. Grey: Dr. Thomas Grey, 1716-1771; historian
Monk of Evesham: "The Revelation of the Monk of Evesham or Vissio Monachi de Eynsham", 1483

the ground, and were full of slashes :" and we are told these wonderful inventions gloried in the euphonous title of *Pokys*.

At this time, the hair was worn long and curled, the beard large, and the moustaches very thick and drooping. Hats, hoods, and caps were worn. One of the latter was particularly frightful; it rose in an immense cone, and part of the material of which it was composed fell down the back, forming the segment of a circle, the edges retiring towards the temples. This cap, when, as was frequently the case, it was ornamented with grotesque figures of men, women, and animals, and worn with armour, must have had a very ridiculous effect; but the magic name of Fashion overcame all objections that Taste brought forward, and this ugly coiffure was long admired by all.

Double vests were now introduced. The upper one was without a collar, and open down the sides, with large sleeves, and an embossed girdle; and the under garment, or doublet, had very tight sleeves.

Many of the London citizens, at this period, wore their hair short and curled. Their caps were of two kinds; one was tied under the chin; the other had a peak in front, and was turned up at the sides. They also had doublets with sleeves, short coats, with enormous sleeves, collars, and flaps, surcoats, hoods, and scarlet gowns.

Soon afterwards, other caps, round and high, banished those just described. It is said, that among the lower classes, cloth stockings, breeches, and a doublet buttoned in front, were worn. " The vanity of the common people in their dress was so great," says Knighton, " that it was impossible to distinguish the rich from the poor, the high from the low, the clergy from the laity, by their appearance."

Richard, alarmed at the extent to which extravagance in dress was now carried, made various sumptuary laws, but very little attention was paid to them. The *crakowes* were supposed to be of Polish invention ; they were as ridiculous as the *choppines*, which, some years later, were imported from Italy.*

In the succeeding reign, the *côte-hardie* was universally worn by all classes. The gowns had long trains, and the sleeves, which were generally tight, had very small *ruffles* at the wrist. The girdle rested negligently on one hip, and fell down loosely on the other side, having a jewel or golden ornament appended to it. From the latter hung a *châtelaine*, or *cordelière*, curiously wrought in gold and precious stones.

Besides this habit, a long mantle was generally worn, and the ornaments then the mode were rich and beautiful. They consisted of a necklace, composed of four rows of precious stones, and a cross on the bosom ; the mantle was confined at the neck with brooches or golden trinkets ; and the girdle often hung to the feet, and was terminated with tassels. This costume was altogether a very graceful and elegant one, and, if we except the head-dress, few of the succeeding fashions can be compared with it.

The coiffure to which we allude was not very

---

* Chaucer's description of the Canterbury pilgrims may be referred to for information respecting the dress of nearly all ranks at the end of the fourteenth century, from the knight to the poor ploughman.

Knighton: Henry Knighton, chronicler and historian, died circa 1396
Chaucer: 1340-1400

much unlike the pediment of a portico, with two square horns standing out side-ways from the forehead. It was composed of a variety of mate-rials, generally of silk or fine linen, interwoven in a curious manner with bands of riband and gold and silver cord; from it was suspended behind, a dra-

Lady's Head-Dress in the
Reign of Henry IV

pery or veil, edged with embroidery. The hair was seldom seen underneath this mighty fabric. Some ladies, however, preferred a crescent-shaped coiffure, with long lappets; some a heart-shaped head-dress; and others shewed their taste by merely confining the hair in a net-work covering, over which was placed a long veil.

A French writer of this period severely censures the female costume. He declaims with much elo-quence against the quantities of fur employed for trim-ming the *tails* of the gowns, the hoods and the sleeves, and laments that the love of useless and extravagant fashions has become so prevalent among the lower classes.

It is stated by authors of the time, that some ladies, not content with the shapes that Nature had bestowed upon them, stuffed their petticoats at the hips, till they resembled the far-famed and much-reviled hoop of later years.

An illumination painted during this reign, repre-sents the gentlemen habited in close gowns, with arm-holes opposite the elbows; a tight vest underneath, and the dress confined by a girdle, which supports the sword.

The hair was now worn short and curled, and old people let the beard and whiskers grow. Broad-brimmed hats are sometimes seen. The doublets were often striped, or party-coloured, and had large sleeves. The tunics were long, and embroidered, and large copes frequently covered the back and shoulders; the inner tunic, and a splendidly-embroidered mantle, were adorned with cords, tassels, and jewelled bands. Long tunics, then called *houppelandes*, were a new fashion, imported, it is suggested by Mr. Planché, from Spain.

Henry revived most of the laws of his predecessors for restricting dress within reasonable limits; but the orders of a king, backed though they were by his ministers, were of no avail, and Fashion ruled with undisputed power over every rank and class in Britain. Gowns and mantles were allowed to be worn short by persons of and above the rank of a lord; all other gentlemen were obliged to wear them as low as the knees, or pay a fine of twenty shillings, which in many cases was most willingly forfeited to his majesty.

Shortly afterwards, robes cut and slashed, and or-namented with devices and flowers, were prohibited, and the unlucky tailor who should venture to make the said habiliments was to be imprisoned. Cloth of velvet and gold, and several of the rich furs, were also restricted to the use of the nobility, and various other laws on the same subject were enacted.

The gentlemen's costume in the reigns of the two succeeding Henrys, greatly resembled that of the time we have just recorded. Short gowns and long ones, tunics that swept the ground, or that reached only to the knees, immense sleeves, and hoods, formed the general features of dress. Buskins also became the

Mr. Planché: James Robinson Planché, 1796–1880, noted author of books on English cos-
    tume
Henry: Henry IV, 1399–1413
two succeeding Henrys: Henry V, 1413–1422; Henry VI, 1422–1461 and 1470–1471

fashion, and we now for the first time hear of short *cotes*. The hair was worn short, and beards nearly disappeared,

The ladies' dress altered very little, except that the *côte-hardie* assumed rather more the shape of a spencer or jacket than of a waistcoat, and that the girdle, instead of slipping over the hips, encircled the waist, and gave a much more graceful appearance to the costume.

The reign of Henry the Fifth is noted in the annals of fashion for the introduction into England of that celebrated monstrosity, the horned head-

Lady's Head-Dress in the
Reign of Henry V

dress, so much admired by the ladies, and so much disliked and found fault with by writers and preachers of the fifteenth century. It was compared to a horned snail, to a gibbet, and to many other equally frightful objects. But the abuse levelled at their favourite coiffure only made the fair wearers more determined to persevere in continuing it, and the *élégantes* of England and France nobly resisted every effort to deprive their heads of so admired an ornament.

There were, however, some other coiffures worn, by those whose courage sank beneath the determined opposition the horned head-dress met with. As in the former reign, golden net-work round the head was sometimes seen, and a peaked coiffure, with a veil falling behind.

Towards the close of this reign, the sleeves of

Henry the Fifth: 1413–1422

gowns became immensely long and wide, so that the ends often fell to the ground, and served as a muff to conceal the delicate hands; for as yet gloves were only worn by men.

When the *côte-hardie* disappeared, ladies must have wondered at the metamorphosis in their shapes, occasioned by its banishment; for certainly it was any thing but an elegant garment, and probably its departure first suggested the wearing stays, which appeared towards the end of the fifteenth century.

Chapter 5 – England, 15th and 16th Centuries

THE TOILETTE IN ENGLAND.

CHAPTER V.

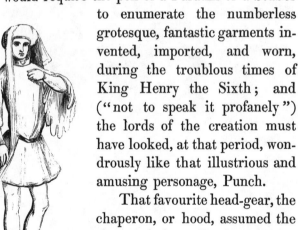

Gentleman in the Reign of Henry VI

It would require the pen of a Paradin or a Stubbs to enumerate the numberless grotesque, fantastic garments invented, imported, and worn, during the troublous times of King Henry the Sixth; and ("not to speak it profanely") the lords of the creation must have looked, at that period, wondrously like that illustrious and amusing personage, Punch.

That favourite head-gear, the chaperon, or hood, assumed the shape of the roll of a turban, with a point standing up from the middle, like a handle. Over this was sometimes thrown a long piece of linen, which hung to the ground, or was carried

Paradin: Guillaume Paradin, wrote "Mémoire de l'Histoire de Lyon" in 1573
Stubbs: Phillip Stubbs, ca. 1555-1610, wrote "Anatomy of Abuses" (in dress) in 1583
King Henry the Sixth: 1422-1461 and 1470-1471
Punch: perhaps a double reference to both the Punch of Punch and Judy plays and the then new and radical magazine "Punch", which had been founded in 1841

over the arm. Frequently by this streamer, called " the Tippet," the hood was allowed to hang negligently on the back of the wearer.

Chausses, made very tight, continued in fashion, and they were still seen of two colours. The *bottines* of the former reign grew longer in the leg, and the points shot out to a most amazing length, ending with a point like a needle. How the gallants of that time contrived to walk in them, must remain a mystery. Although they did not turn upwards, like the *crakowes* formerly mentioned, yet they were quite as ridiculous. Paradin, speaking of these *poulaines*, says : " When men became tired of these pointed shoes, they adopted others in their stead, denominated *duck-bills*, having a bill or beak before, of four or five fingers in length."

The cloaks and mantles were frequently covered with the most grotesque embroidery, in every variety of pattern. There were often circular arm-holes, trimmed with fur, and a small cape, cut round, and lying flat, permitting the throat to appear. The jacket, or doublet, allowed an under-vest or waistcoat to be seen, the tight sleeves of which peeped out from underneath the wide ones of the upper garment. Sometimes the doublet reached to the knees; but the mode of wearing it short was gradually becoming the fashion, and banishing the long gowns and tunics.

The horned coiffure still engrossed the admiration of the ladies, but several alterations were gradually made in it. Instead of standing out sideways to an immense width, it was raised upwards in the shape of a fork, with long lappets hanging down on either side. Other head-dresses were not unlike *tocques*. But in every coiffure the hair was carefully concealed; and

chausses: stockings
bottines: boots or shoes

though queens, on the day of their coronation, usually allowed their luxuriant tresses to hang down in all their native richness, their fair subjects appeared to think such a mode by no means an ornamental one.

One coiffure of this period was shaped like a heart, with a semicircular opening at the lower part, for the admission of the head, round which was a border, generally ornamented with jewels. Another of these

Ladies' Coiffures in the Reign of Henry VI

curious structures was very high and pointed, and the veil, or fall of linen, spread itself over the two forks, and fell down behind. But in no picture do we find the veil drawn over the face, or apparently used for any thing but an ornament.

The queen of Charles the Sixth of France is accused of having introduced these curious coiffures into that country, from her native land, Bavaria, and, like all other foreign modes, they quickly crossed the Channel, and appeared in England.

The waists of the gowns throughout this reign were remarkable for their excessive shortness, so different from the hour-glass form given by the now despised

The queen of Charles the Sixth of France: Isabelle of Bavaria, 1371–1435, married Charles and came to France in 1385; see note p. 201

côte-hardie. Some robes, with capes or collars of fur, also appeared; and stomachers of various colours, terminating in a point, varied the sameness of the costume.

A picture of the poet Chaucer, mentioned in Granger's "Biographical History of England," has the following lines written under it, and the date 1436. They are characteristic of the dress of that day, though not complimentary to the bard, who, however, is said to have been the handsomest man of his time:—

> " His stature was not very tall,
> Lean he was, his legs were small,
> Hosed within a stock of red,
> A buttoned bonnet on his head."

The caps, or, as they were then called, bonnets, were made of fine cloth, silk, and velvet, and were perfectly dazzling with jewellery. Another picture represents a lady in the costume of the year 1454. Around her head she wears a broad embroidered bandeau, from which, on the right side, is suspended, in a festoon, a large string of pearls. The graceful folds of a flowing veil cover the rest of the head, and form a coiffure infinitely preferable to the horned towers we before described. The garment is a long loose vest, plaited in front; it has a richly embroidered collar, and the sleeves are tight down to the wrist, and trimmed with buttons.

The reign of Edward the Fourth may be termed the era of short garments. The gowns and tunics disappeared, except in state and official costumes; and the *petit maîtres* of England appeared in jackets (which they called *pourpoints*) of a most unseemly

Chaucer: lived 1340-1400; 1436 therefore cannot be a correct date
Granger: James Granger, 1723-1776, wrote "Biographical History of England from
    Egbert the Great to the Revolution" in 1769
Edward the Fourth: 1461-1470 and 1471-1483
petit maîtres: dandies

brevity, and padded out to a wonderful extent.   The
sleeves were frequently very short, and puffed at the

Man in the Reign of Edward IV

shoulders, and beneath them extended to the wrist the long sleeves
of their shirts.   The collar of the
pourpoint lay flat, and underneath
it hung a rich gold chain.   The
chausses were quite tight to the
feet, and usually terminated by
poulaines.   To finish the costume
of these *élégants* of the fifteenth
century, their hair was dressed so
as to fall over their eyes, and their
heads gloried in caps rivalling in
height the steeple coiffure of the
ladies.   The rank of the wearer
was then known by the length of
the far-famed *poulaines*.   "The
men," says Paradin, "wore them
with a point before, half a foot long; the richer and
more eminent personages wore them a foot; and
princes, two feet long."

With a view to check such absurd modes, the king
ordered that no one under the rank of a lord should
wear shoes more than ten inches long, or short jackets,
padded or wadded; and all tailors and cobblers making
the like were to pay a fine, and to be *cursed* by the
clergy.   Other sumptuary laws relating to rich furs,
to cloth of gold, and various manufactures, were also
made.

The ladies' coiffures again occupy much attention
during this reign.   They were often tall and pointed,
like steeples; or, to use the words of Paradin, "they

Paradin: Guillaume Paradin, fl. 1573; see p. 72

resembled asses' ears." Here are drawings of two of the most curious : —

Ladies' Coiffures in the
Reign of Edward IV

Gowns with bodices laced in front now became the fashion. Strutt imagines they were stays, from their being called *corse*. Trains were banished, and the ladies' gowns were trimmed with rich fur; they had also sumptuous girdles, with clasps, and long gold chains encircled their necks.

In a print of Richard the Third, contained in Walpole's life of that monarch, we find him represented with long, curling hair, but neither beard, whiskers, nor moustaches. His *pourpoint* appears to be embroidered with the royal arms across the breast; his pantaloons, or *chausses*, are quite tight, reach to the feet, and are without ornament; his large shoes are barred across; his sleeves tight, with rosettes at the elbows; and a sort of puffed handkerchief, not unlike a ruff, encircles his neck; his cloak has a train that sweeps along the ground, and is lined with ermine.

Richard the Third: 1483–1485
Walpole: Horace Walpole, 1717–1797

On his head he wears a crown. His queen has long hair, hanging to her waist, and parted over the forehead; her robe is splendid; her furred mantle (embroidered with the arms of England, and of her own family) is closed at the throat with a magnificent brooch, so that but little of the under garment is visible.

Walpole gives a curious memorandum of the dress of the unfortunate Edward the Fifth, which was ordered for him to wear at his uncle's coronation. The account is preserved in the royal wardrobe roll, and is as follows:—" A short gowne, made of two yards and three quarters of crymsy cloth of gold; lyned with two yards $\frac{3}{4}$ of blue velvet; a long gowne made of vi. yards $\bar{5}$ of crimsy cloth of gold, lyned with six yards of green damask; a short gowne, made of two yards $\frac{3}{4}$ of purpell velvet, lyned with two yards $\frac{3}{4}$ of green damask; a doublett, and a stomacher of two yards of blue satin, and a bonet of purpell velvet." The mandate from Richard the Third to his wardrobe-keeper, dated from York, also contains a list of splendid dresses of this period.

The shape of the shoes worn at this time is curious. The dress of Henry the Seventh at his coronation, in 1485, consisted of a shirt of fine lawn, a vest of crimson silk, with an opening in the front; crimson sarcenet *chausses*, laced with ribands to the coat, which was lined with ermine, decorated with bows of gold and riband, and trimmed with minever. The mantle was of crimson satin, laced with silk, and adorned with tassels. To this magnificent dress was added a crimson rose made of satin.

Walpole: Horace Walpole, 1717-1797
Edward the Fifth: April–June, 1483
Richard the Third: 1483-1485
Henry the Seventh: 1485-1509

The female coiffure of this day, as will be seen by the picture annexed, had greatly changed; it was three-cornered on the face, and in form not unlike a church porch; it fell over the shoulders behind, and had long lappets reaching to the waist.

Lady in the Reign of Henry VII

But there were many other head-dresses introduced during this reign. The hair usually fell in all its luxuriance down the back, unfettered by comb or fillet, and very beautiful were the long fair ringlets of many of the dames and maidens of Britain. Some of the coiffures are not unlike ornamented turbans; others resemble the capuchon worn by the men; and others, again, are round and pointed, but not high. So various and so strange were many of these head-dresses, that we may almost imagine Fashion was at this time amusing her own fancies at the expense of her votaries, and forcing her followers to render themselves ridiculous, and even ugly, to shew her power over them.

The waists of the robes were now made so as to pinch in the figure; they were cut square over the bosom, or reached to the throat, and were confined by a girdle, or belt, with a splendid ornament in front, terminated with a *cordelière* and tassel. The petticoats, or kirtles, were full, but without trains, and usually had a coloured border round the bottom. The sleeves were as various as the coiffures; sometimes they were very full, and held in at the wrist by a narrow band, or the fulness confined into two or three large puffs down the arm; some, however, were left quite loose, and hanging, not unlike those worn a few years since in England, and they were not unfrequently trimmed with a border to match the bottom of the robe.

Elizabeth, queen of Henry the Seventh, wore a splendid dress the day before her coronation. It is described in Cotton's manuscript, and consisted "of a mantle of white cloth of gold damask, furred with ermines, fastened on her breast with a large lace curiously wrought with gold and silk, with rich knoppes of gold at the end tasselled." On the day of her nuptials, the same queen wore, according to Leland, her long fair hair hanging down her back, with "a calle of pipes over it."

"At the close of the fifteenth century," says Strutt, "the dress of the English was exceedingly fantastical and absurd." How often may not this phrase be repeated when diving into the annals of the toilette of both men and women!

To begin with the head, the hair was parted back from the forehead, and fell in long-flowing ringlets upon the shoulders, which made the warriors of that day look very effeminate, particularly as the face was divested of beard, whiskers, and moustaches; which latter appendages to the upper lip were never seen but on the faces of the aged.

As a covering to the curling locks, velvet caps were worn, with such towers of plumes of different colours standing upright from the head, or negligently drooping over one side, that they appeared at a distance like a forest of pine-trees waving beneath a

Elizabeth, queen of Henry the Seventh: daughter of Edward IV by his second wife, Elizabeth Wydville, who was a granddaughter of Henry IV; the marriage took place in 1486
Cotton: Sir Robert Bruce Cotton, 1571-1631, antiquarian and collector of ancient manuscripts; his collection is now in the British Museum
Leland: John Leland, circa 1503-1552; antiquarian
Strutt: Joseph Strutt, 1749-1802; wrote "Dresses & Habits of the English People" in 1796-9

summer breeze. Those gallants who did not approve of these splendid head-dresses wore broad felt or fur hats ; and the hood, so favourite a covering for the head ever since the reign of Edward the Third, now nearly disappeared.

Slashed garments were very much worn ; the sleeves, particularly, were covered with puffings and ornaments. The shirts, too, were embroidered in silk, and had full long sleeves of fine linen, which were seen below the upper sleeve of the doublet. In this reign, an old author says, gentlemen wore "*petty cottes, doublettes, long cottes, stomachers, hozen, socks, shoen.*"

The fashion of wearing broad shoes, which commenced in the preceding reign, was now very prevalent ; their appearance was most ridiculous, the more so from their contrast to the late peaked ones ; and they must have been very uncomfortable to the wearer. It is asserted that they were first brought into England from Holland.

The upper part of the *chausses*, or hosen, was now beginning to be formed of a different material and colour from the lower part, and was frequently puffed with satin, like the doublet, and gaily embroidered.

On the day of his coronation, Henry the Eighth's dress was splendid in the extreme. His coat was literally embossed with gold ; the *placardo* covered with every kind of precious stone ; the *bawdrech* on his neck with *balesses*, and the mantle of crimson velvet was lined with ermine. His queen wore a long gown of embroidered white satin, and her hair, like that of Queen Anne, hung down her back.

A great many authors appear to have written upon

Edward the Third: 1327-1377
Henry the Eighth: crowned 1509
placardo: garment worn beneath the coat or gown
bawdrech: baldric, a necklace
balesses: ballas rubies, a type of rose-pink spinel
His queen: Catharine of Aragon

dress during this reign, for even the clergy had caught the fashionable infection, though some chroniclers assert that they did not attempt to wear silk and embroidery till Cardinal Wolsey set them the example. Authors of that, and indeed later periods, wrote much and strongly against the prevalence of confounding the different degrees of society, by allowing all ranks to wear the same dress ; much also was preached, written, and said, against " pride of hair," as an ancient author termed the profusion of hair worn at this time, and the extravagant manner in which it was " *plaited, braided, bowed,* and *combed.*"

Henry the Eighth is represented in an old picture,

Henry VIII

at the time of his interview with Francis the First, when both monarchs displayed every kind of magnificence and extravagance, as habited in a garment composed of cloth of gold, over a jacket of rose-coloured velvet. His collar was composed of rubies and pearls, set in alternate rows, and on his breast hung a rich jewel of St. George, suspended by a riband. His boots were of yellow leather, and his hat of black velvet, with a white feather turning over the brim, and beneath it a broad band of rubies, emeralds, and diamonds, mixed with pearls. His pages were splendidly attired in crimson, with the union Rose embroidered on the back of the doublet, between a

Cardinal Wolsey: circa 1457–1530
Frances the First: King of France, 1515–1547; they met at the Field of the Cloth of
    Gold, 1520; see Appendix C

dragon and a greyhound. Their breeches and sleeves also were slashed, and curiously puffed out with fine cambric, and they had white stockings and shoes.

The exact time when ruffs were first worn is not known. It is said they were invented by a Spanish lady, to hide a wen upon her neck ; it is, however, certain that they were much in fashion in the reign of Henry the Eighth, and flourished greatly through this and several succeeding reigns.

The doublet was now worn with slashes and cuts, and the waistband, reaching just below the arm-pits, had eight kinds of skirts appended to it.

In a picture by Holbein of the lovely but unfortunate Anne Boleyn, we see the dress she wore on the day she became Queen of England. It is much the same as the one we have described as worn by Elizabeth. Stowe gives the following account of another, in which she appeared about that time : " Then," says he, " proceeded forth the queene, in a *circote* and robe of purple velvet, furred with ermine, in her hayre coife and circlet. After her followed ladies, being lords' wives, which had circotes of scarlet, with narrow sleeves, the breast all lettice, with barres of pouders, according to their degrees ; and over that they had mantles of scarlet, furred, and every mantle had lettice about the necke,

Anne Boleyn

Holbein: Hans Holbein, circa 1497-1543; appointed court painter to Henry VIII in 1536
Anne Boleyn: her coronation took place 1 June 1533
Stowe: John Stowe, 1525-1605; chronicler and antiquarian, began his career as a tailor
Elizabeth: probably a reference to Elizabeth I

like a neckerchiefe, likewise poudered, so that by their pouderings their degrees might be knowne. Then followed ladies, being knights' wives, in gownes of scarlet, with narrow sleeves, without traines, only edged with lettice."

The hair is gracefully arranged in Holbein's picture. It is drawn back from the forehead in small curls; a broad plait hangs from the top of the head, over one ear; and the crown, placed far back, is held in its place by an ornamented caul and wreath of gold.

In another portrait, Anne is represented with her hair braided over her forehead, and hanging down over her shoulders; on her head is a cap, adorned with precious stones, and a tassel falling behind. Her train is not long, and her sleeves are large, wide, open down the outside, and ornamented with three bows of riband. But this cannot be strictly considered the English costume of this reign; for, Anne having passed many years in France, it is likely that she might adopt the fashions of that nation—amongst others, that of wearing lappets.

During the reign of a monarch who delighted so much in splendour and display of every kind, in masques, tournaments, and jousts, and who, we are told, even on ordinary occasions, wore a collar of *ballas rubies* pendant from his neck, diamonds inserted in his bonnet, and rings clustering round his fingers, it is to be supposed that his courtiers vied with each other in splendour and magnificence of apparel. The grave churchmen, too, had an example of extravagance and display set before them, which they were not slow to follow, for nothing could surpass the richness of the

Holbein: see note p. 83
ballas rubies: rose-pink spinels; the 'Black Prince's ruby' in the English coronation
    regalia is a ballas ruby

attire of Cardinal Wolsey; his very shoes, says Roy, being

> " Of gold and stones precious,
>   Costing many a thousand pounds."

These were, indeed, the days when gallants

> " Wear a farm in shoe-strings edged with gold,
>   And spangled garters worth a copyhold;
>   A hose and doublet which a lordship cost,
>   A gaudy cloak three mansions' price almost;
>   A beaver hat and feather for the head,
>   Prized at the church's tithe."

Under the house of Tudor, no shoe could be fashionable that was not fastened with a full-blown rose; but in shape they were not so extravagantly long as those formerly worn.

Under Henry the Eighth, silk stockings, it is said, were first brought to England. On this subject, however, there seems to be some doubt. Planché, in his "History of British Costume," thus describes their introduction: "Hose or stockings of silk are generally supposed to have been unknown in this country before the middle of the sixteenth century; and a pair of long Spanish hose of silk were presented as a gift worthy the acceptance of a monarch, by Sir T. Gresham, to Edward the Sixth."

Howe, in the continuation to Stowe's "Chronicle," asserts that Henry the Eighth never wore any hose but such as were made of cloth. This, however, is contradicted by an entry mentioned in the inventory of his apparel, which is to be found in the Harleian Library, where we read the account of several pairs of " silk hose," " one short pair of black silk and gold

Cardinal Wolsey: circa 1457–1530
Roy: William Roy, fl. 1527; wrote "Letters & Papers of Henry VIII"
Planché: James Robinson Planché, 1796–1880
Sir T. Gresham: circa 1519–1579, English Ambassador to the Netherlands 1559–1561
Edward the Sixth: 1547–1553
Howe: John Howe of Magdalen College, Oxford, 1630–1705
Stowe: see note p. 83
Harleian Library: the collections of Robert and Edward Harley, 1st and 2nd Earls of
  Oxford, formed the basis of the British Museum library when purchased in 1753
  and combined with the collections of Sir Robert Bruce Cotton and Sir Hans Sloane

woven together ; one of purple silk and Venice gold, woven like unto a cawl [*i.e.* of open or net-work], lined with blue silver [sarcenet], edged with a passemain [lace] of purple silk and gold, wrought at Milan ; a pair of white silk and gold hose, knit ; and six pair of black silk hose, knit." And in an inventory of still earlier date, taken about the eighth year of his reign, both satin and velvet are mentioned as the materials of which his hose are composed.

But then the question arises, whether, by the word "hose," the writer of the above really meant *stockings*, or whether he intended to describe the nether garment so much worn at that time, which consisted of stockings and breeches all in one, frequently called, by old writers, "hose" and "hosen?" Shakspeare uses the word for breeches, and also for stockings : " He, being in love, could not see to garter his hose." Howe certainly intended to express stockings ; but, probably, the "embroidered and lined hose," and those made of satin and velvet, were, in fact, the coverings of the upper part of the legs, which at that time were frequently made of velvet, satin, cloth of gold, and other rich materials ; and this appears the more likely, as in another part of the same inventory we read an entry as follows : " A yard and a half of green velvet for *stocks* to a paire of *hose* for the king's grace ; " and in other parts we find various stuffs mentioned, used for " stocking the hose."

The shoes at this time were variously shaped, and richly ornamented. Buskins, slashed like the doublets, were also very fashionable. Some were of satin, some of velvet, and frequently the toes were broad and wide, and the shoe had a strap across the instep.

In the " Memoirs of the Court of Henry the Eighth," we read : " The dress of females of rank was restricted by limitations of a nature somewhat similar to those which restricted the absurdities of male attire, and was less extravagant. The gown, composed of silk or velvet, was shortened or lengthened according to the rank of the wearer. The countess was obliged by the rules of etiquette to have a train before and behind, which she hung upon her arm, or fastened in her girdle ; the baroness, and all under her degree, were prohibited from assuming that badge of distinction. The matrons were distinguished from unmarried women by the different mode of their head-attire ; the hood of the former had recently been superseded by a coif, or close bonnet, of which the pictures of Holbein give a representation ; while the youthful and the single, with characteristic simplicity, wore the hair braided with knots of riband."

Frontlets and lappets now came into fashion ; also hats and bonnets. The lappets often fell below the shoulders, and were frequently made of velvet, studded with precious stones. Some were very broad, others broad near the face, and tapering towards the ends. Sometimes they turned back, and fluttered in the breeze like streamers.

Embroidered petticoats and gowns were now much worn by the female sex. The latter were frequently made open in front, so as to shew the satin kirtle beneath ; an embroidered apron, flowered in gold and coloured silks, was also greatly admired. The bodice, or, as it was formerly called, the *surcoat*, was generally of a different colour from the rest of the dress, and had a richly ornamented stomacher. "Gowns of blew

"Memoirs of the Court of Henry the Eighth": not mentioned in the catalogue of the British Library, although letters of Henry VIII are listed in the Harleian Miscellany, 1744

velvet, cut and lined with cloth of gold, made after the fashion of Savoy," are named by a writer of the day, who also describes the dress worn by Anne of Cleves, which consisted of " a ryche gowne of cloth of gold, raised, made round, without any trayne, after the Dutch fashion."

Thanks to the observations of these old chroniclers, we are here informed of two new modes, but the latter one appears not to have pleased the English ladies, as we do not read of its being adopted.

The *partlet* and waistcoat were also invented at this time. The former, Mr. Strutt imagines, usurped the place of the *gorget* or *barbe*. In an inventory of that day we read of " partelets of Venice gold knit, two partelets of Venice gold, caul fashion, two of white thread, and two partelets of white lawn, wrought with gold about the collars." They are supposed to have resembled modern habit-shirts, and were made with or without sleeves.

Ladies' head-dresses were various : sometimes they wore a velvet cap, adorned with jewels, and a long-flowing veil ; others adopted a *caul*, a *coif*, or a French hood ; and Stowe speaks of three-cornered caps. They were, he says, white, and three-square, and the peaks full three or four inches from the head. Frontlets were also worn, before bonnets were introduced.

The gentlemen's hair, which, till this reign, had been worn long and flowing, was, by an order of this despotic monarch, condemned to be cut quite short, to the no small disgust of the gallants of that day, who, however, were a little consoled by the gracious permission of their sovereign to wear a fierce beard and

Savoy: mediæval state; now a part of France, it bordered Switzerland and Italy
Anne of Cleves: married Henry VIII in 1540
Strutt: see note p. 80
Stowe: see note p. 83

long curling moustaches.   But, alas! a sumptuary law was now passed, by which no person not of the royal family could wear fur of the black genet, and no person under the rank of a viscount fur of sable; and, still worse, no person under the degree of a knight of the garter might wear crimson or blue velvet, or embroidered apparel, brooched or guarded with goldsmith's work, except the sons and heirs of barons and knights, who were permitted to use crimson velvet and tinsel in their doublets.

Coats of various shapes were now worn; also jackets and frocks, which Hall says were jackets with skirts: waistcoats, too, were invented; and, by an inventory of Henry's own habiliments, we find numerous "trimmed shirts wrought with black and white silk, and shirtbands of silver, with ruffles to the same, whereof one is *perled* with gold."

Hall, who was very particular in describing dress, gives the following account of that of King Henry in the first year of his reign: — "A suit of short garments, little beneathe the pointes, of blew velvet and crymosyne, with long sleeves, all cut and lyned with cloth of gold, and the utter parts of the garmentes powdered with castles and sheafes of arrowes, of fyne dockett golde; the upper part of the hosen of like sewte and facion; the nether parts of scarlet, powdered with tymbrelles of fine gold.   On his head was a bonnet of damaske silver, flatte woven in the stoll, and thereupon wrought with gold, and ryche feathers in it."   Another day, Hall says the king was habited "in a *frocke*, all embroidered over with flatted gold of damaske, with small lace mixed between of the same gold, and other laces of the same going traverse-

Hall: Edward Hall, died 1547; wrote a description of life at the Court of Henry VIII and of the Field of the Cloth of Gold; see Appendix C

wise, that the ground little appeared; and about this garment was a rich guard, or border, very curiously embroidered; the sleeves and the breast were cut and lined with cloth of gold, and tied together with great buttons of diamonds, rubies, and orient pearles."

Gowns are now mentioned of all shapes,—long, short, loose, or tight; and another garment is spoken of by Hall, a *chammer* or *shamew*. Many other articles are also named in the inventories of this reign; among them are capes with buttons or points, "a paire of trunk sleeves, of redde cloth of gold, with cut workes, having twelve pair of agletes of gold, and a pair of French sleeves of green velvet, richly embroidered with flowers of damask gold, pirl of Morisco work, with knops of Venice gold, cordian raised, either sleeve having six small buttons of gold, and in every button a pearle, and the branches of the flowers set with pearles." In another part we read of a pair of sleeves "ruffed at the hande, with strawberry leaves and flowers of golde, embroidered with blacke silke."

The *chausses*, or long hose, were again *la grande mode*, and velvet caps with plumes of feathers, flat caps, and broad-brimmed hats, first appeared among the fashionables.

Chapter 6 – England, 16th Century

THE TOILETTE IN ENGLAND.

CHAPTER VI.

THE following extract from the last sermon Latimer preached before the youthful King Edward gives a good idea of the dresses of 1550, and of the rage for French fashions. Speaking of the ladies, he says: "They must wear French hoods, and I cannot tell you, I, what to call it. And, when they make them ready, and come to the covering of the heade, they will call and say, 'Give me my French hood, give me my bonnet, and my cap,' and so forth. But here is a vengeance devil; we must have our power [a name he gave to the bonnet] from Turkey of velvet. Far fette, dear bought, and, when it cometh, it is a false signe. I had rather have a true English signe than a signe from Turkey; it is a false signe when it covereth not their heads, as it should do. For if they would keep it under the *power*, as they ought to do, there should

Latimer: Hugh Latimer, circa 1485–1555; English bishop and Protestant martyr who was burned at the stake by Queen Mary I (Bloody Mary)
King Edward: Edward VI, 1547–1553

not be any such *tussocks* nor *tufts* be seen as there be, nor such laying out of the hair, nor braiding to have it open."

The gentlemen in this reign wore velvet caps, with a band round them, and a rosette of ribands and jewels on one side. The beard, too, flourished greatly. Ruffs were worn by men and women, and flat caps and jackets by the former; while, with the latter, the annexed head-dress, though of a curious shape, was a

Male & Female Head-Dresses in the Reign of Edward VI

great favourite; the ornaments on the sides of the head resemble feathers.

Let us now turn to

"The lovely rose of Bradgate's sylvan shades."

The amiable and unfortunate Queen Jane is represented in most of her pictures in a very long-waisted gown of some rich material, with a pointed stomacher and tight sleeves. Her hair is generally simply braided on the forehead, and a veil hangs down behind; but, on the day of her coronation, she was sumptuously attired in a gown of cloth of gold, raised with pearls; a stomacher blazing with jewels, and a surcoat of purple velvet edged with ermine, and embroidered in gold; her head-dress was a coif, or caul, of velvet, of

Queen Jane: Lady Jane Grey, the Queen for nine days in 1553, who was executed in 1554

the form then in fashion, and usually adorned with gold and precious stones.

At this time, gowns were made very long, the sleeves covered the arms to the waist, and but little of the neck was allowed to be seen. Sometimes the bodice was pointed, and of a different colour from the petticoat, and the hair was simply arranged.

The dress of the Duke of Northumberland, at the same date, is very splendid. His doublet was of white satin, with a kind of breast-plate of purple cloth of gold, powdered with jewels, and edged with fur. His mantle was of cloth of silver, lined with blue velvet, and festooned with a clasp of precious stones.

Stevens says that *periapts*, or charms, were worn about the neck in the sixteenth century, as preservatives from disease or danger. The first chapter of St. John's Gospel was usually inscribed upon them, as it was deemed the most effective. They were often of gold or precious stones, richly ornamented.

When we speak of the reign of Mary, we may exclaim,—

> " Here Fashion, motley goddess, changing still,
> Finds ready subjects to obey her will,
> Who laugh at Nature and her simple rules ;"

for this may well be considered the era of ruffs and farthingales, and as the fashion of both came from Spain, it is probable that the queen first wore them out of compliment to her husband. They soon became quite the rage among all classes.

At first, no doubt, the British ladies found these extraordinary modes inconvenient and unpleasant; but they remembered the adage, " Il faut souffrir

Duke of Northumberland: John Dudley, 1502-1553, father-in-law of Lady Jane Grey
Mary: Queen Mary I, 1553-1558, "Bloody Mary"
"Il faut souffrir pour être belle": One must suffer to be beautiful
Stevens: William Stevens, 1732-1807, biographer and religious writer

pour être belle," and submitted with a good grace. The queen herself had all her royal father's love of splendour, and revived much of the magnificence of apparel that had been forgotten during the reign of Edward.   Bigoted, cruel, and blood-thirsty as she was, possessing neither the majesty of him whose

" Smile was transport, and whose frown was fate,"

nor yet any of the proud beauty of her mother, she endeavoured to make up for her want of personal attractions by the aids of the toilette.   Her usual dress was a robe of coloured velvet, trimmed with costly fur and jewels, and upon her head she often wore a caul of cloth of gold, set with precious stones.

At this time long stomachers were worn, which made the waists look very small, and the farthingale, suddenly swelling out over the hips, gave the figure an appearance very different from that intended by Nature. Hanging sleeves also were invented, and open gowns, with embroidered petticoats underneath. The hair was worn quite plain, or simply curled on the temples.

After the "good Queen Bess" came to the throne, the fashions altered in a most remarkable manner. Her majesty, who was as devoted to dress as any modern votary of Fashion, possessed costumes of all countries, and is said to have left three thousand habits in her wardrobe when she died.   Her vanity and weakness on this subject have been frequently alluded to by historians; and in an old report of the presents made to her, we find that the courtiers used to give her gowns, petticoats, kirtles, doublets, or mantles, some embroidered, and adorned with jewels.

Edward: Edward VI, 1547–1553
good Queen Bess: Elizabeth I, 1558–1603

In the account of a journey to England by Paul Hentzer, we have the following description of her dress : —

"The queen had in her ears two pearls, with very rich drops ; she wore false hair, and that red ; upon her head she had a small crown ; her neck was uncovered, and she had a necklace of exceeding fine jewels. Her gown was white silk, bordered with pearls the size of beans, and over it a mantle of blush silk, shot with silver threads ; her train was very long. Instead of a chain, she had an oblong collar of gold and jewels."

During this reign, an upper dress of velvet, frequently embroidered and trimmed with ermine, was much worn. It resembled a great-coat, and was usually fastened at the throat, and open down the front to the feet, so as to display the satin kirtle and vest. This garment is thus described by Stubbs, whose pen was ever directed against the fopperies of the age : — " The women," he says, " have doublets and jerkins, as the men have, buttoned up to the chin, and made with welts, wings, and pinions on the shoulder-points, as man's apparel in all respects ; and although this be a kind of attire proper only to a man, yet they blush not to wear it."

Queen Elizabeth, whose ruffs were always of larger dimensions than those of her ladies, was much troubled to find a laundress who could undertake the difficult task of starching her cambric and lawn ruffs ; for her majesty disdained to encircle her royal throat with those made of Holland, usually worn by her subjects ; she therefore sent abroad for a Dutchwoman, whose knowledge of this art was celebrated. " There is a

Paul Hentzer: Paulus Hentzner, who published "A Journey into England in the Year 1598" the queen: Elizabeth I, 1558-1603
Stubbs: see note p. 72

certain liquid matter which they call starch, wherein the devil," says Stubbs, "hath learned them to wash and dive their ruffs, which, being dry, will then stand stiff and inflexible about their necks." He also alludes to a device made of wire, "crested for the purpose, and whipped all over either with gold, thread, silver, or silk, called a *suppertasse*, or *under-propper*."

These great ruffs, or neckerchiefs, made of lawn, Holland, cambric, and such cloth, "so fine that the thickest thread shall not be so big as the least hair that is," three or four sometimes placed under the "master devil ruff," "which was often loaded and adorned with gold, silver, and needlework," must have been most wonderful structures, particularly when they expanded like wings, as high as the head, or fell over the shoulders like flags!

"And then their gowns," exclaims the censor, "be no less famous than the rest; for some be of silk, some of velvet, some of grograin, some of taffeta, some of scarlet, and some of fine cloth, of ten, twenty, or forty shillings the yard; but if the whole garment be not of silk or velvet, then the same must be layed over with lace two or three fingers broad, all over the gowne; or, if the lace be not fine enough for them, they must be decorated with broad gardes of velvet, edged with costly lace. The fashions, too, are changing as the moon; for some be of the new fashion, and some of the olde; some with sleeves hanging down to the skirts, trailing to the ground, and cast over their shoulders like cow-tails; some have sleeves much shorter, cut up the arm, drawn out with sundry colours, and pointed with silk ribands, and very gallantly tied with love-knotts, for so they call them."

Stubbs: Phillip Stubbs, circa 1555-1610; see note p. 72

These robes frequently had deep capes of velvet or satin, "fringed about very bravely," or crested down the back "with more knacks" than can be described. "But what is more vain," he adds, "of whatever the petticoat be, yet must they have kirtles, for so they call them, of silk, velvet, grograin, taffeta, satin, or scarlet, bordered with gards, lace, fringe, and I cannot tell what." "Then they must have their silk scarfs, cast about their faces, and fluttering in the wind, with great lappels, at every end, either of gold, or silver, or silk, which they say they wear to keep them from sun-burning." Again: "Their fingers must be decked with gold, silver, or precious stones; their wrists with bracelets and annulets of gold and costly jewels; their hands covered with sweet-washed gloves, embroidered with gold and silver; and they must have looking-glasses carried with them wheresoever they go * * * and they are not ashamed to make holes in their ears, whereat they hang rings and other jewels of gold and precious stones."

The *partelet*, or habit-shirt, was sometimes worn with the ruff; at others, the latter fabric alone encircled the throat, and partially concealed the bosom, which at this period was more uncovered than it had hitherto been in the annals of fashion. But the abomination of wearing short sleeves, which once, during the reign of Henry the Eighth, astonished and shocked the fair dames of Britain, appears to have been a mode that they could not bring themselves to follow; indeed, for many years, arms "naked down from the elbows," as Hall describes them, were looked upon with horror and disgust.

Stubbs, who never spared the follies of the age in

Henry the Eighth: 1485-1509
Hall: see note p. 89
Stubbs: see note p. 72

which he lived, thus speaks of the head-dresses of ladies in 1585 : " Then," says he, " follow the trimming and tricking of their heades, in laying out their haire to shewe, which of force must be curled, frisled, and crisped, laid out (a world to see) on wreathes and borders, from one ear to the other. And least it should fall down, it is underpropped with forks, wiers, and I cannot tell what, like grim, sterne monsters rather than chaste Christian matrones. Then on the edges of their boulstred haire (for it standeth crested rounde about their frontiers, and hanging over their faces like pendices or vailes, with glass windowes on every side), there is laide great wreathes of golde and silver, curiously wrought and cunningly applied to the temple of their heads. And for feare of lacking any thing to set forth their pride withall, at their haire thus wreathed and crested, are hanged bugles (I dare not say bables), *ouches, rynges, gold, silver, glasses,* and such other childishe gewgawes."

Cauls were now very fashionable ; they had been *la mode* among the higher ranks for many years. Holinshed mentions one worn by Queen Mary, " that was so massie and ponderous with gold and jewels, that she was faine to beare up her head with her hand." Stubbs says of them : " They have also other ornaments besides these to furnishe for their ingenious heades, which they call (as I remember) *caules,* made netwise, to the end, as I think, that the cloth of gold, cloth of silver, or else tinsell (for that is worst wherewith their heades are covered and attired withall underneath their *caules*), may the better appeare and shew itself, in the bravest manner, so that a man that seeth them (their heades glister and shine in such

Holinshed: see note p. 65
Queen Mary: Mary I, 1553–1558

sorte) would think them to have golden heades ; and some weare lettice caps, with three hornes—three corners, I should say—like the forked cappes of priests, with their *perriwinkles*, chitterlings, and the like."

In Ellis's "Letters," we read, among some items relating to the wardrobe of Queen Elizabeth, under the head *Attier*, the following :—

" *Item.* One cawle of hair set with pearles in number xliij.

" *Item.* One do. set with pearle of sundry sort and bigness, with seed pearle between them chevron wise cxcj.

" *Item.* A cawle with nine trueloves of pearle, and seven buttons of gold, in each button a rubie."

From this extract we are led to suppose that the false hair was called the CAUL, but on other occasions it is certainly intended to describe a head dress : thus an old poem says :—

> " These glittering *coules* of golden plate,
> Wherewith their heads were richly dect,
> Makes them to seem an Angel mate
> The judgment of the simple sect."

And another author exclaims :—

> " Silk gownes and velvet shalt thou have,
> With hoods and *caules* fit for thy heade,
> Of goldsmiths' work a border brave,
> A chain of gold ten double spread."

French hoods were now the mode, and continued fashionable till the reign of Charles the First. "Then on toppes of their stately turrets (I mean heades)," says the indefatigable Stubbs, "(wherein is more vanitie than true philosophie now and then) stand their

Ellis's "Letters": Sir Henry Ellis edited both "Letters Illustrative of English History", 1824, and "Letters of Eminent Literary Men of the 16, 17 & 18th Centuries", 1843
Charles the First: 1625-1649
Stubbs: see note p. 72

capitall ornaments, as French *hood, hatte, cappe, kercher,* and such like; whereof some be of velvet, some of taffatie, some (but few) of wooll; some of this fashion, some of that, some of this colour, some of that, according to the variable phantasies of their serpentine minds. And to such excess is it growne, as every artificer's wife (almost) will not sticke to goe in her hatte of velvet every day; every merchant's wife and meane gentlewoman in her French hood—and every poore cottager's wife in her taffatie hatte, or else of wool at least."

A French Hood

Frontlets were now worn very broad, and frequently highly ornamented; they fell over the face, and served to protect the skin from the sun. Bonnets, too, began to be *la grande mode;* they were first brought from Italy. Hall mentions "millen bonnets of damaske gold, with lose gold, that did hang downe their backes," and "millen bonnets of crymson satten, drawn through with cloth of gold."

Elizabeth is represented in one of her portraits with a head-dress, ornamented with jewels, very nearly resembling a cushion; a richly-laced ruff, laid in close plaits, stands out on each side of her face for a considerable way, and rests upon her bosom. From the back of her gown two wings, probably of fine lawn, edged with a border of jewels, and stiffened with wire, rise in semicircular sweeps as high as the

Hall: Edward Hall, died 1547; see note p. 89
Elizabeth: Elizabeth I, 1558–1603

top of the head-dress, and turning down to the ears,
form the general shape
of a heart, with the face,
encircled with the ruff,
set in the midst. A
short, clumsy cloak, co-
vered with jewels and
embroidery, covers the
body of the gown, but
allows the small cuffs
of the sleeves, the full
ruffles, and an ornament
above the former, to be
seen. The strait and
formal stomacher gives
her majesty an im-
mensely long waist. It
is covered with jewels
and embossed gold, and her lower garment, or petticoat,
is of rich velvet.

Queen Elizabeth

In another portrait the hair is also turned over a
cushion, but without any ornament. Instead of the
immense ruff and wings mentioned above, a sort of
fan, of clear muslin, edged with rich lace, stands up
behind the neck. What this curious fabric is called,
or why worn, Fashion alone can tell; but it is frequently seen in the pictures of the time of Queen
Elizabeth. The robe is made very tight, quite plain,
long-waisted, and has tight sleeves, but the farthingale
which puffs it out over the hips gives it a very ridiculous appearance.

In general, the size of the ruffs was enormous,
probably to keep the farthingales in countenance. As

her gracious majesty is represented in almost all her portraits with the hair dressed as we have described, we may suppose that it was her favourite coiffure, and if so, it was, undoubtedly, the fashionable head-dress of her time. Sometimes she is seen with a small cap, ornamented with frills, placed on the back of her head.

It is perhaps strange that Elizabeth, hating, as she certainly did, every thing Spanish, should have adopted two of their modes, and continued partial to them for so many years.

Among the various head-dresses of this reign, we find one called the *ship tire ;* which Warburton tells us "was an open coiffure, that left the neck and shoulders exposed." Another, denominated the *tire valiant*, was, on the contrary, so closed up with kerchiefs, of various kinds, that nothing could be seen above the eyes or below the chin.

The lower class of females generally wore caps. "The men and women, also," says Malone, "had what were then called ' thrum'd hats,' they were made of a coarse kind of woollen cloth." Shakspeare mentions them and another part of female attire, when he makes Mrs. Page exclaim, " And there's her thrum'd hat, and her muffler too." The latter was, probably, a very ancient addition to dress, which concealed the lower part of the face, and not the coverings for the hands, mentioned under the same name in the early reigns of our kings.

Masks and vizors of velvet, with glasses for the eyes, were now worn ; they were kept on the face by a bead attached to the inner part, and held in the mouth of the wearer.

Warburton: John Warburton, 1682–1759; herald and antiquarian
Malone: Edmund Malone, 1741–1812

The gentlemen at this period banished the full pourpoint, and, delighting in extremes, replaced it by a tight vest, resembling a waistcoat. They also now wore more moderate-sized ruffs.

Stubbs devotes a whole chapter to the hats of this period. "Sometimes," he says, "they use them sharpe on the crowne, peaking up like the speare or shaft of a steeple, standing a quarter of yard above the crowne of the head. Some others are flatte and broade on the crowne like the battlements of a house. Another sort have round crownes, some-times with one kind of band, sometimes with another —now black, now white: now russet, now red: now green, now yellow: now this, now that; never content with one colour or fashion two days to an end. And thus they spend the Lord's treasure, consuming their golden years and silver days in wickedness and sin." Again we read: " And as the fashions be rare and strange, so is the stuffs whereof their hats be made divers also; for some are of silk, some of velvet, some of taffety, some of sarcenet, some of wool, and, which is more curious, some of a certain kind of fine hair; these they call Bever hats, of 20, 30, or 40 shillings price, fetched from beyond the seas, from whence a great sort of other vanities come besides."

In Holinshed's " Chronicle" we find the following remarks upon the dress of this time. " Nothing," says he, " is more constant in England than incon-stancy of attire. Oh, how much cost is bestowed now-a-days upon our bodies, and how little upon our souls! How many suits of apparel hath the one, and how little furniture hath the other! How long a time

Stubbs: see note p. 72
Holinshed: see note p. 98

is asked in decking up the first, and how little space
left wherein to feed the latter! How curious, how
nice, also, are a number of men and women, and how
hardly can the tailor please them in making it fit for
their bodies! How many times must it be sent back
again to him that made it! then must we put it on—
then must the long seams of our hose be set by a
plumb-line. I will say nothing of our heads, which
sometimes are polled, sometimes curled, or suffered to
grow at length, like women's locks; many times cut
off above, or under the ears round, as by a wooden
dish. Neither will I meddle with our variety of
beards, of which some are shaven from the chin like
those of Turks, not a few cut short, like to the beard
of Marquisse Otto, some made round, like a rubbing-
brush, often with *pique de vaux* (a fine fashion), or
now and then suffered to grow long, the barbers being
grown to be so cunning in this behalf as the tailors;
and, therefore, if a man have a lean and straight face,
a Marquisse Otto's cut will make it broad and large;
if it be flatter-like, a long, slender beard will make it
seem the narrower; if he be weasel-becked, then
much hair left on the cheeks will make its owner look
big, like *bowdled hen*, and so grim as a goose. If
Cornalis of Chelmsford say true, many odd men wear
no beards at all. Some lusty courtiers, also, and
gentlemen of courage, do wear either rings of gold,
stones, or pearls, in their ears, whereby they imagine
the workmanship of God not to be little amended.
But herein they rather disgrace than adorn their persons, as by their niceness in apparel, for which I say
most nations do not unjustly deride us, as also that
we do seem to imitate all nations round about us,

pique de vaux: "Van Dyke" or "Imperial" beard
Cornalis of Chelmsford: no information could be found, although he is also mentioned
    in G. W. Rhead's "Chats on Costume"

wherein we be like to the polypus or chameleon. In woman, also, it is much to be lamented that they do now far exceed the lightness of our men (who, nevertheless, are transformed from the cap even to the very shoe), and such staring attire as in time past was supposed meet for none but light housewifes only, is now become an habit for chaste and sober matrons. What should I say of their doublets, full of jags and cuts, and sleeves of sundry colours? Their galligascons to make their attire sit plum round (as they term it) about them—their *fardingales*, and diversely-coloured nether stockes of silk, and such like, whereby their bodies are rather deformed than commended. I have met with some of these in London so disguised that it hath passed my skill to discover whether they were men or women. Certes, the common wealth cannot be said to flourish when these abuses reign, but is rather oppressed by unreasonable exactions made upon rich farmers and poor tenants, wherewith to maintain the same. Neither was it ever merrier with England than when an Englishman was known abroad by his own cloth, and contented himself at home with his fine carsie hosen and a warm slop, his coat, gown, and cloak, of brown, blue, or *putre*, with some pretty furniture of velvet or fur, and a doublet of sad tawnie or black velvet, or other comely silk, without such cuts and gawrish colours as are worn in these days, and were brought in by the consent of the French, who think themselves the gayest men when they have most diversities of *iagges* and change of colours about them. Certes, of all estates our merchants do least alter their attire, and, therefore, are most to be commended ; for, albeit that which they wear be very fine and costly, yet in form and colour it representeth a great piece of the antient gravity appertaining to the citizens and burgesses.   Albeit the younger sort of their wives, both in attire and costly housekeeping, cannot tell when and how to make an end, as being women, indeed, in whom all kinds of curiosity is to be found and seen, and in far greater measure than in women of higher calling."

Stubbs tells us that the doublets were so hard-quilted, stuffed, bombasted, and sewed, that men could neither work nor yet play in them.

Stubbs: see note p. 72

Chapter 7 – England, 16th and 17th Centuries

THE TOILETTE IN ENGLAND.

CHAPTER VII.

IT was during Elizabeth's reign that Sir Thomas Gresham introduced the manufacture of pins and ribands. Knitted worsted stockings, too, were first made about the year 1565, by a London apprentice, named William Ryder, who having seen some that came from Italy, imitated a pair exactly, and presented them to William, earl of Pembroke.

In Stowe's "Chronicle" we find the following: " In the 2d yeere of Queene Elizabeth, her silk-woman, Mistress Montagu, presented her Majestie, for a new yeare's gift, a pair of black silk knit stockings, the which, after a few day's wearing, pleased her highness so well, that she sent for Mistress Montagu, and asked her where she had them, and if she could help her to any more ; who answering, said, ' I *made* them very carefully of purpose only for your Majestie, and seeing them please you so well, I will presently set more in hand.' ' Do so (quoth the queene), for indeed I like silk stockings so well, because they are pleasant, fine, and delicate, that henceforth I will wear no more

Sir Thomas Gresham: see note p. 85
Stowe's "Chronicle": 1565
2nd yeere of Queene Elizabeth: 1560

cloth stockings.'   And from that time unto her death the queene never wore any more cloth hose, but only silk stockings; for you shall understand that Henry the 8th did wear only cloth hose, or hose cut out of ell-broad taffaty, or that by great chance there came a paire of Spanish silk stockings from Spain."

From this extract it appears that silk stockings were now first *made* in England, and not first imported, as is generally supposed.

" At this day," says Stowe, " men of meane rank weare garters, and shoe roses of more than five pounds price."   Stevens also observes, that very rich garters were worn below the knee.   And Shakspeare, in " Hamlet," says, " Two Provençal roses on my razed shoes ;" probably alluding to the mode of wearing ribands made in the form of a rose, fastened to the middle of the shoe, to conceal the string.   In an old song we find—

> " Gil-de Roy was a bonny boy,
>   And roses tull his shoon."

They are, also, frequently mentioned by old dramatic authors.

Stubbs, speaking of the chaussures now in fashion, says :—" They have *puisnets*, pantoffles, and slippers, some of black velvet, some of white, some of green, and some of yellow ; some of Spanish leather, and some of English, stitched with silk, and embroidered with gold and silver all over the foot, and other gewgaws innumerable."   Of the cork shoes, we read in the same author, " They beare people up two inches or more from the ground."   The boots now worn were large, and turned back at the top.

Stowe: John Stowe, see note p. 83
Stevens: William Stevens, see note p. 93
Stubbs: Phillip Stubbs, see note p. 72

Stowe informs us that *poking sticks* were now first invented; they were made of steel, and, when heated, were used for plaiting the ruffs. Until this time, sticks of bone or wood had been employed for the same purpose.

Now, too, the English began to make costly washes and perfumes: the latter had been introduced into England by Edward Vere, earl of Oxford. He also brought Elizabeth, from Italy, a pair of embroidered gloves, scented with sweet perfume. They were trimmed with four tufts, or roses, of coloured silk, and her majesty was so much delighted with this new fashion, that in one of her pictures she is painted with them on her hands.

Wharton says that gloves were during this reign often presented to guests of distinction.

Fans, which also came from Italy, according to Stevens, in the time of Henry the Eighth, were now used both by men and women. We are informed, " that even young gentlemen carried fans of feathers in their hands, which," continues the author, " in wars our ancestors wore on their heads." The most costly were made of ostrich-feathers, fastened into handles composed of gold, silver, or ivory, curiously worked. In the Sydney papers mention is made by Wharton of a fan presented to Elizabeth, the handle of which was studded with diamonds.

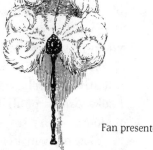

Fan presented to Queen Elizabeth

Stowe: John Stowe, see note p. 83
Edward Vere: Edward de Vere, 17th Earl of Oxford, 1550–1604, court poet and traveller
Wharton: Henry Wharton, 1664–1695
Henry the Eighth: 1509–1547
Stevens: William Stevens, see note p. 93

The bright-coloured feathers from the peacock's tail, too, were frequently formed into the same ornament, fans of painted paper and silk not being used for some years afterwards.

Perwiches (as they were then termed) were mentioned by Churchyard in one of his earlier poems, though in " Northward Hoe " we read, " There is a new trade come up for cast gentlewomen, that of perriwig-making;" and in the " Two Gentlemen of Verona " Julia exclaims, " I'll get me such a perriwig !" Warner, in his " Albion's England," is very severe upon this fashion. Stowe informs us that women's perriwigs were first brought into England at the time of the massacre of Paris, and Stubbs says that about the year 1595, when the fashion became general in England of wearing a greater quantity of hair than was ever the produce of a single head, it was dangerous for any child to wander, as nothing was more common than for women to entice such as had fine locks into out-of-the-way places, and there cut them off. The same author adds, " And if any have haire of her owne naturall growing, which is not faine ynough, then will they *die* it in divers colours."

During this reign dyeing the hair was frequently severely censured from the pulpit, and two books were published against perukes and peruke-makers.

Beards, whiskers, and moustaches, appear to have flourished greatly at this time, but the hair was worn short, curled, and parted on the forehead. In a portrait of Sir Francis Drake, painted in 1596, we find him dressed in a doublet that looks very much like

Churchyard: Thomas Churchyard, circa 1520-1604
Warner: William Warner, circa 1558-1609
Stowe: see note p. 83
Stubbs: see note p. 72
Sir Francis Drake: circa 1540-1596

the coats now worn ; it is buttoned down the front, and has a kind of collar that lies upon the breast, with a lace frill falling over it.

That distinguished statesman and accomplished gentleman, Sir Walter Raleigh, of whom it has been so truly said, "that he was one of the very chief glories of an age crowded with towering spirits," is represented, in one of his portraits, in a splendid dress. The under waistcoat, buttoned down the front, is of satin or velvet, the surcoat of dark velvet, embroidered with pearls, in rich and varied patterns, which forms a peak in front ; the back and sleeves are plain, with the exception of an ornament on the top. His ruff is large and full, his beard thick and pointed, his hair curled off the forehead, and he wears a hat with a moderate-sized crown, a broad brim, turned up all round, and adorned with a large pearl and a feather.

Sir Walter Raleigh

Sir Francis Bacon is represented in a doublet of a different shape : in front it hangs in folds, the under sleeve is tight, and of the same material as the doublet, but there is an upper one, covered with embroidery and buttons, which surrounds the arm at the top, and hangs outside the elbow. His ruff surpasses in size any yet seen, and is edged with lace, his hat much the same as the one we have given, only higher in the crown, and without ornament.

Sir Walter Raleigh: circa 1552–1618
Sir Francis Drake: 1561–1626

In Dr. N. Drake's work, entitled "Shakspeare and his Times," he remarks: "The account given of the male fashionable dress has sufficiently made out the assertion which we made at the commencement, that in extravagance and frivolity it surpassed the expenditure and caprice of the other sex." This charge was repeated by Burton at the close of this era. Exclaiming against the luxury of fine clothes, he remarks: "Women are bad, and men worse. So ridiculous are we in our attires, and for cost so excessive, that, as Hierom said of old, 'tis an ordinary thing to put a thousand oaks and an hundred oxen into a suit of apparel, to wear a whole manor on his back. What with shoe-ties, hangers, points, caps and feathers, scarfs, bands, cuffs, &c., in a short space all their patrimonies are consumed. Heliogabalus is taxed by Lampridius, and admired in his age, for wearing jewels in his shoes, a common thing in our times, not for emperors and princes, but almost for serving men and taylors; all the flowers, stars, constellations, gold and precious stones, do condescend to set out their shoes."

The dress of the citizen, indeed, was, if less elegant, equally showy, and sometimes fully as expensive as that of the man of fashion. The medium habit may, with great probability, be considered as sketched in the following humorous tale, derived from a popular pamphlet printed in 1609 : —

> "A citizen, for recreation's sake,
>   To see the country would a journey take
>   Some dozen mile, or very little more ;
>   Taking his leave with friends two months before,
>   With drinking healths, and shaking by the hand,
>   As he had travail'd to some new-found land.

Dr. N. Drake, "Shakspeare and his Times": published 1817
Burton: Robert Burton, 1577–1640
Hierom: Samuel Hierom, circa 1576–1617
Heliogabalus: 204–222; priest of the sun god at an early age, later became Roman
    Emperor Marcus Aurelius Antoninus (218–222)
Lampridius: Aelius Lampridius, Latin historian of the early 4th century

Well, taking horse, with very much ado
London he leaveth for a day or two :
And as he rideth, meets upon the way
Such as (what haste soever) bid men stay.
' Sirrah,' says one, ' stand, and your purse deliver,
I am a *taker*, thou must be a *giver*.'

Unto a wood hard by they hale him in,
And rifle him unto his very skin.
' Maisters,' quoth he, ' pray hear me ere you go ;
For you have rob'd more now than you do know.
My horse, in truth, I borrowed of my brother :
The bridle, and the saddle, of another :
The *jerkin*, and the *bases*, be a taylor's ;
The *scarfe*, I do assure you, is a saylour's :
The *falling band* is likewise none of mine,
Nor *cuffs ;* as true as this good light doth shine.
The *satin doublet*, and rays'd velvet hose
Are our church-wardens, all the parish knows.
The *boots* are John the Grocer's at the Swan :
The spurs were lent me by a serving man.
One of my rings—that with the great red stone,
In sooth I borrow'd of my gossip Jone :
Her husband knows not of it, gentlemen !
Thus stands my case :—I pray shew favor then.'

' Why,' quoth the thieves, ' thou need'st not greatly care,
Since in thy loss so many beare a share.
The world goes hard : many good folks lacke ;
Looke not, at this time, for a penny backe ;
Go, tell at London thou didst meet with foure,
That rifling *thee*, have rob'd at least a score.' "

It seems strange that Elizabeth, herself so devoted a follower of fashion, should not have permitted her subjects to please themselves, in the shape, size, and form, of their attire. On the contrary, she made more laws than any other monarch, respecting dress. She

Elizabeth: Elizabeth I

enacted that "no great ruff should be worn; nor any white colour, in doublets or hosen; nor any facing of velvet in gowns, but by such as were of the bench. That no gentlemen should walk in the streets in their cloaks, but in gowns. That no hat, or curled, or long hair, be worn, nor any gowns but such as be of a sad colour."

Dugdale remarks: "During the reign of Elizabeth several statutes were enacted for the regulation of apparel, as well as of beards, but most of them appear to relate to the members of the different inns of court. Thus we find laws against the wearing of cut or pansied hose, or bryches, and of pansied doublets, as well as against the use of light colours, of velvet caps, of scarfs, and of *wings* to the gowns, white jerkins, buskins, or velvet shoes; double ruffs to the skirts, feathers and ribbons in the caps."

The suit of armour formerly *shewn* in the Tower as Queen Elizabeth's, was composed of a helmet of *Edward the Sixth's* time, arm-pieces of the reign of *Charles the First*, and a breastplate and *garde-de-rein* of the age of *Henry the Eighth;* in short, altogether an apocryphal affair.

Dugdale: William Dugdale, 1605–1686
Elizabeth: 1558–1603
Edward the Sixth: 1547–1553
Charles the First: 1625–1649
Henry the Eighth: 1485–1509
garde–de–rein: kidney guard, a back piece of a suit of armor

Chapter 8 – England, 17th Century

THE TOILETTE IN ENGLAND.

CHAPTER VIII.

THE reign of James the First is not very fertile in fashions, and that monarch did not introduce a single new one into England. He himself cared not for adorning his person; on the contrary, a love of ease and comfort seems to have banished from his mind all wish for vain attire. His usual costume was a doublet, quilted so thick that it could resist the thrust of a dagger, and his lower garments were plaited and stuffed to the utmost extent. But when out hunting, his favourite dress much resembled modern trousers. The ruff, too, was not forgotten, and he sometimes wore a hat and feather, but was highly incensed when one of his attendants wished him to wear a Spanish hat, and also with the prevailing mode of placing roses on the shoes, which he said made him look like a "ruff-footed dove."

When James I. came to the throne, there was, in the Tower wardrobe, an immense variety of dresses

James the First: 1603–1625

of the ancient kings, but, to the great regret of persons curious in such matters, they were, on his accession, all given away.

During the reign of this monarch, the beard and whiskers were still worn ; silk garters, puffed in great knots, below the knees, yellow stockings, and embroidered cloaks, were also in vogue. Now, too, the immense ruff was sometimes superseded by a wide square collar, wired and stiffened out, but not plaited ; it was called a band. These bands, and also the ruffs, were stiffened with yellow starch, which was either invented by Mrs. Turner, or introduced from France under her auspices. She was hanged for murder in a yellow ruff.

The attire of the Princess Elizabeth when she espoused the Prince Palatine was very simple. She was habited in white vestments, her hair hung at full length down her back, and her only ornament was a diadem set in jewels. The author from whom we have obtained this account describes one of the suits intended for the lords sent as ambassadors to the court of France. " The cloak and hose," he says, " were of fine beaver, richly embroidered in silver and gold, particularly the cloak, within and without, nearly to the cape. The doublet was cloth of gold, embroidered so thick that it could not be discerned, and a white beaver hat, suitable, full of embroidery above and below."

Ruffs and farthingales were still much worn, and ladies now began to indulge a great predilection for foreign lace, a passion which has continued for two centuries. The strange fashion, also, of men wearing ear-rings, and roses stuck in their ears, was much

Princess Elizabeth: married Frederic V of Bohemia, Prince Palatine, in 1613

followed; and though Shakspeare alludes to the use of ear-rings as if censuring its folly, in one of the portraits supposed to represent him, each ear is adorned with this effeminate ornament.

If dress did not flourish during the reign of James, it resumed all its former ascendancy under Charles the First. Many great changes were now made. The hair was worn low on the forehead, and usually not divided; the king set the fashion of a "love-lock," which was a curl on the left side, considerably longer than the rest. Nothing in the annals of hair, of wigs, or of periwigs, ever caused such a commotion among quiet, staid people, as did this unfortunate "love-lock." A quarto volume was written against it by Mr. Prynne, called "The Unloveliness of Lovelocks." In it he mentions a nobleman who was dangerously ill, and who, terrified at the prospect of death, declared publicly, after his recovery, his detestation of his "effeminate, fantastic love-lock, which he then sensibly perceived to be but a cord of vanity, by which he had given the devil hold fast to lead him at his pleasure, and who would never resign his prey as long as he nourished this unlovely bush." He, therefore, ordered his barber to cut it off.

It does not appear that the eloquence of Mr. Prynne had much effect, except in this solitary instance; for love-locks were quite the rage for some years, which is, perhaps, the more remarkable, as beards were beginning to go out of fashion.

Ruffs, though worn through part of this reign, were no longer so much admired; and about the time that Vandyke came to England they almost entirely disappeared, and were replaced by falling collars of

Charles the First: 1625–1649
Mr. Prynne: William Prynne, 1600–1669
Vandyke: Sir Anthony Vandyke came to England in 1632

rich lace, or embroidered muslin, as may be seen in most of the portraits taken at this period. Doublets were worn slashed, embroidered, and richly ornamented, the sleeves slit open, and puffs of coloured satin let in ; the points, too, that formerly hung round the waist, were now worn " dangling from the knees."

But the most extraordinary singularity of dress ever seen, either in this or any other age, was the *trunk hose,* now first invented. We cannot describe these " bombasted, paned hose," better than by using the words of the " Artificial Changeling." " At the time," says he, " when trunk hose came in fashion, some young men used to stuff them so with rags and other like things, that you might find some that used such inventions to extend them in compass with certainly as great eagerness as the women of all classes did take pleasure to wear enormous, great, and stately verdingales ; for this was the same affectation, being a kind of vertingale hose."

Gentleman in the Reign of James I

Two very ridiculous stories are told of this fashion. One, that a youth so attired, and being distended with bran, whilst in deep conversation with some ladies, unluckily caught his *sack* upon a nail, when instantly all the bran escaped, and the enormous puffs became suddenly flattened. The de-

"Artificial Changeling": Bulwer, John – "Anthropometamorphosis, Man Transformed, or the Artificial Changeling, with a pedigree of the English Gallant", 1650

spair and agony of the unfortunate gallant may easily be imagined.

The other anecdote refers to the period when the law was in force against wearing " *bags stuffed in their sacks,*" and describes a person before a court of justice, who, charged by the judges with being habited contrary to the statute, convinced them that the stuffing was not composed of any prohibited article, inasmuch as it consisted merely of a pair of sheets, two tablecloths, ten napkins, four shirts, a brush, a glass, a comb, and a nightcap! Well, indeed, did these wonderful *sacks* deserve their name of *trunk hose!* In those days carpet-bags would have been quite a superfluity.

The sugar-loaf, or steeple hats, at this time much worn, were as useless as absurd. They rose into a high cone, and had a very narrow brim. Powder now, also, came into fashion, as we find from the works of John Bulwer, who gives many particulars about dress, and mentions jessamine butter as a favourite ointment for the hair. After describing other things, he says : " Our gallants' witty noddles are put into such a pure witty trim, the dislocations of every hair so exactly set, the whole bush so curiously candied, and (what is most prodigious) the natural jet of some of them so exalted into a perfect azure, that their familiar friends have much to do to own their faces·; for by their powdered heads you would take them to be mealmen."

Mr. Peck, the antiquarian, informs us that he had a whole-length portrait of Charles in the following dress. He wore " a falling band, a short green doublet, the arm-part towards the shoulders wide and slashed,

John Bulwer: fl. 1650, see note previous page
jessamine butter: jasmine-scented pomade
Mr. Peck: Francis Peck, wrote "Desiderata Curiosa or a Collection of divers, scarce
    and curious pieces relating chiefly to matters of English History", 1779
Charles: Charles I, 1625–1649

zigzag, turned-up ruffles, very long green breeches, tied far below the knee with long yellow ribbons, red stockings, great shoe-roses, and a short red cloak, lined with blue, with a star on the shoulder."

Gentleman in the Reign of Charles I

This may be considered the usual costume of gentlemen of that time, with the addition of thin, flimsy, Spanish leather boots. Some gallants, however, wore doublets and hose, richly slashed with satin, and laced with gold ; a cloak of rich velvet, lined with satin, a belt or girdle of velvet, embroidered in gold and jewels, a black beaver hat, adorned with a plume of ostrich-feathers, and coloured boots, trimmed with point lace.

The ladies of this period wore their hair low on the forehead, and parted in ringlets, or else curled like a peruke, or braided in a knot on the top of the head. " Why do they adorn themselves," says Burton, " with so many colours of herbs, fictitious flowers, curious needle-workes, quaint devices, sweet-smelling odours; with those inestimable riches of precious stones, pearls, rubies, diamonds, emeralds, &c. ? Why do they crown themselves with gold and silver, use coronets and tires of several fashions, deck themselves with pendants, bracelets, ear-rings, chains, girdles, rings, pins, spangles, embroideries, shadows, rebatoes, versicolor ribands ? Why do they make such glorious shows with their scarfs, feathers, fans, masks,

Burton: Robert Burton, 1577–1640

furs, laces, tiffanies, ruffs, falls, calls, cuffs, damasks, velvets, tinsels, cloths of gold, and silver tissue?" "It is hard," continues the same writer, to derive the abominable pedigree of cobweb lawn, yellow-starched ruffs, which so much disfigured our nation, and render them so ridiculous and fantastical."

Another fashion was forked shoes, almost as long again as the feet, not a little to the hinderance of the action of the foot; and not only so, but they proved an impediment to reverential devotions; for, as a contemporary writer notes, "one's boots and shoes are so long snouted, that we can hardly kneel in God's house."

Contrary to the custom of the preceding age, ladies now wore their gowns very long, with trains behind, and the shoulders quite bare. "Is there any thing," says Cowley, "more common than to see our ladies of quality wear such high shoes as they cannot walk in without one to lead them; and a gown as long again as their body, so that they cannot stir across the room without a page or two to hold it up?"

The peaked bodies to gowns were generally worn very long and open, the two sides laced together in front, so as to shew the satin boddice underneath. The point usually terminated with a bow of riband. The sleeves were tight, or else open and hanging, and broad bands of lace were worn round the arm and round the bust. Ear-rings, necklaces, bracelets, and indeed every description of jewels, were now in fashion; also broad-brimmed hats, with feathers, in opposition, probably, to the narrow brims worn by the gentlemen.

Some idea may be formed of the lavish profusion

Cowley: Abraham Cowley, 1618-1667

in dress during this reign by the following account of
Villiers, duke of Buckingham. " It was common with
him," says Oldys, in his " Life of Raleigh," " at an
ordinary dancing, to have his clothes trimmed with
great diamond buttons, and to have diamond hatbands, cockades, and ear-rings, to be yoked with great
and manifold ropes and knots of pearl, in short, to be
manacled, fettered, and imprisoned in jewels; insomuch that, on going to Paris in 1625, he had twenty-
five suits of clothes made, the richest that embroidery,
lace, velvet, gold, and gems could contribute ; one of
which was a white uncut velvet, set all over, both suit
and cloak, with diamonds, valued at 80,000*l*., besides
a great feather, stuck all over with diamonds, as were
also his girdle, sword, hatband, and spurs."

In the time of Oliver Cromwell, who was always
very frugal in his attire, and despised the vain follies
of the age, dress underwent a great change. The
Lord Protector himself was generally habited in black
cloth or velvet, with a scarf round his waist to support
his sword; trunk hose, long boots, and a grey hat with
a silver clasp; or else a doublet, cloak, and hose of
coarse cloth, turned up with velvet, and stockings of
grey worsted, that reached over the knees, and met
the hose. In all the portraits of him the hair is
simply arranged, without curls, but rather long
behind.

These grave and quiet habiliments, despoiled of
puffings, slashings, ribands, gold, and jewels, did not,
however, please the taste of all his followers. Sir
Thomas Fairfax, for instance, often wore a buff coat
highly ornamented with silver, open sleeves, slashed
with white satin, trunk hose trimmed with costly

Villiers, duke of Buckingham: 1592-1628
Oldys: William Oldys, 1691-1791; wrote "Life of Raleigh", 1736
Oliver Cromwell, The Lord Protector: 1653-1658
Sir Thomas Fairfax: 1612-1671

Flanders' lace, and russet leather boots. To this was added a breastplate of highly-polished steel, partly concealed by a falling collar of broad and costly lace, and a sash of silk and gold.

In those days, however strange it may appear, the military garb was frequently assumed with other rich attire, and it was a common thing to see steel corselets and breastplates overshadowed by lace and embroidery. Dark and quiet colours were, however, the fashion, particularly buff and brown, and the high-crowned beaver and drooping feather still continued in use. An old author asserts that "short cloaks, short hair, short bands, and long visages," were often observed in the portraits of the day. In a print of a fashionable man of the year 1652, we find the brim of the hat extending horizontally, and the feather drooping so much over the left side that it seems as though falling off. The hair is very long, the ruffles double and full, the doublet reaches to the waist, the trunk-hose are puffed at the knees like bladders, the boots are very short, with tops as broad as the brim of the hat, and an enormous sword is suspended to his side by a rich belt across the shoulders. Some authors distinctly assert that men wore *patches* at this time, but we find no instance of this in any old painting.

Mr. Benlowe has in his work two prints of ladies in the same year (1652). The hair of one is combed like a wig in front, the back hair braided, and fastened in a knot; her neck is covered with a handkerchief richly ornamented with deep lace, and her cuffs are trimmed the same; her sleeves are slashed with fine linen or silk, and her fan is large. The other has a sable tippet, and a large muff, which en-

Mr. Benlowe: Edward Benlowe, "Theophila or Love's Sacrifice", 1652

tirely conceals her arms, a close black hood, and a very diminutive black mask.

The Puritans, both men and women, were remarkable for an affectation of great simplicity in attire as well as manners. They wore their hair so short as scarcely to cover the ears, and thence obtained from their opponents the Royalists, or Cavaliers, the appellation of Roundheads; the former, pursuing the contrary extreme, left their hair as long as nature would permit, and those to whom flowing locks were denied, supplied their place by wearing a wig, a fashion which, after the Restoration, flourished greatly.

The Restoration: 1660

Chapter 9 – England, late 17th Century

THE TOILETTE IN ENGLAND.

CHAPTER IX.

THE enormous size to which periwigs attained during the reign of Charles II. is remarked by all writers. Curls rose above curls in regular rows, and descended upon the shoulders and back in heavy masses. The pictures of the time represent these wigs as *la grande mode*. Those who did not approve of the enormous quantity of curls, parted the hair over the forehead, and let it hang down, sometimes as low as the waist, in what were denominated *corkscrew* curls.

Noblemen, gentlemen, learned divines, military heroes, grave judges, and elderly lawyers, all followed eagerly in the steps of fashion. Some few clergymen inveighed against it in their sermons, and cut their hair as short as possible, to shew their abhorrence of the *wig mania*. But in every other profession each one tried to rival his neighbour in the size of his peruke, till at last they became quite enormous; and as if determined that the head should have all their time and care bestowed upon it alone, whiskers, beard, and moustaches, were abolished.

Charles II: 1660–1685

A facetious writer of the day supposes a field of battle strewed with wigs, as well as with the bodies of the slain; and observes, "that the king ought to be more irrate with the perukes, sporting on the breasts of his warriors, than with that wig whose curls whiffled into the eyes of the preacher, and interrupted the discourse addressed to him." Probably this censure relates to the following anecdote, which we find in Strutt's "Dress and Habits." "A letter was written by Charles II. to the University of Cambridge, forbidding the members to wear periwigs, smoke tobacco, and read their sermons; and when he was at Newmarket, Nathaniel Vincent, doctor of divinity, fellow of Clare Hall, and chaplain to his majesty, preached before him in a long periwig, and Holland sleeves, according to the fashion in use amongst gentlemen at that time. This foppery displeased the king, who commanded the Duke of Monmouth, then chancellor of the university, to cause the statutes concerning decency of apparel among the clergy to be put in execution, which was accordingly done."

When Prince Charles (afterwards Charles I.) and the Marquess of Buckingham went to Paris, on their way to Spain, a chronicler of that time relates: "That for the better veiling their visages, his highness and the marquis bought each of them a periwig, somewhat to overshadow their foreheads." This quotation proves for how long a time the prevailing fashion had endured; and, probably, to give a more dashing air to these enormous edifices of hair, hats were sometimes worn with the brims elevated on either side.

Now also appeared the garment called petticoat

Strutt's "Dress & Habits": 1796-9; see note p. 80
Nathaniel Vincent: London preacher, published extensively from 1669 on
Holland sleeves: Holland was a closely woven linen fabric; see next page
Duke of Monmouth: 1649-1685
Prince Charles and the Marquess of Buckingham: went to Paris in 1623

breeches, described by Holmes, who gives the following account of a gentleman's dress in 1659. "A short-waisted doublet, and petticoat breeches — the lining being lower than the breeches—is tied above the knees ; the breeches are ornamented with ribands up to the pocket, and half their breadth upon the thigh ; the waistband is set about with ribands, and the shirt hanging out over them."

Gentleman in the Reign of Charles I

With the usual caprice of fashion, the doublet, which latterly was so short that it scarcely came to the waist, now lengthened out wonderfully, and seemed inclined to conceal the nether garments entirely ; the sleeves, also, reached nearly to the elbows, and from under their manifold bows and puffs of riband, the shirt-sleeves, of white linen, swelled out in two or three large balloons, till at the hands they were terminated with ruffles.

Buttons appear to have been a fashionable ornament of the dress at this time.

In the " Memoirs of Lady Fanshawe," we read the following account of the costume of her husband, at an audience which he had with Philip IV., when ambassador of Charles II. at the court of Spain.

" Then came my husband," says the authoress, " in a very rich suit of clothes, of a dark phillamot brocade, laced with silver and gold lace, nine laces, every one as broad as my hand, and a little silver and gold lace

Holmes: Randle Holmes, genealogist, 1601-1659, wrote "Treason et Mort de Roy Richard" or his son, also Randle Holmes, 1627-1699
"Memoirs of Lady Fanshawe": kept by Lady Anne, 1625-1680, whose husband was Ambassador to the Court of Philip IV of Spain in 1664-1666; they were published in 1829
phillamot: filemot, corruption of "feuille mort"; name of a color resembling a dead or faded leaf

laid between them, both of very curious workmanship. His suit was trimmed with scarlet taffeta ribbands; his stockings of white silk, upon long scarlet silk ones; his shoes black, with scarlet shoe-strings, and garters. His linen very fine, laced with rich Flanders' lace. A black beaver buttoned on the left side, with a jewel of 1200*l.* value. A rich, upright, curious gold chain, made at the Indies, at which hung the king his master's picture, richly set with diamonds, and cost 300*l.*, which his majesty in his great grace and favour had been pleased to give him on his coming from Portugal. On his fingers he wore two rich rings. His gloves were trimmed with the same ribbands as his clothes, and his whole family were richly clothed, according to their several qualities."

During this reign a coat, approaching more than that garment had hitherto done to the coats of the present day, is frequently mentioned in Pepys' "Diary;" and in an inventory of the apparel of the king is named a complete suit of one material, also pantaloons, Holland drawers, and cotton trousers. Stockings were worn of leather, silk, woollen, linen, and worsted; and the rolls of silk or satin that ended the nether garments below the knee, and were called *canons*, were still in use.

Patches and paint were now as much admired as wigs, and the ladies never considered themselves *bien mises* when not following this fashion, which continued in full force through this and the succeeding reign.

Infatuated with the wish to have small, slender waists, the women wore high stays, laced so tight that they could scarcely breathe; and nothing was considered really fashionable that did not come from

Pepys' "Diary": Samuel Pepys kept a secret diary during the years 1660–1669 which covered minute details of daily life; not originally meant for publication, it was issued to the public in 1825
bien mises: well or correctly dressed

France. "We are so much addicted to strange apparel," says an old writer, "that there is scarce any thing English about us. As it was said of the courtiers of Andronicus the younger, that in respect of their hateful disguises in apparel, they seemed no longer to be Grecians, but a medley of Latins, Mysians, Toriballians, Syrians, and Phœnicians; so we have brought all nations into the wardrobe, or to act upon the garment stage. The kings of Egypt were wont to give unto their queens the tribute of the city of Antilla, to buy them girdles; and how much *girdles, gorgets, wimples, cauls, crispings, pins, veils, rails, frontlets, bonnets, bracelets, necklaces, slops, slippers, round-tires, sweet-balls, rings, ear-rings, mufflers, glasses, hoods, lawn, musks, civets, rose-powders, gessamy butter, complexion waters,* do cost in our days many a sighing husband doth know by the year's account."

Ladies now wore their hair in curls on the forehead, and sometimes braided behind, or hanging loosely down over the shoulders.

Lady in the Reign of Charles II

The gowns of the period resemble drapery more than any fixed shape, and are made exceedingly low in front and over the shoulders, with slashed sleeves and quantities of lace and jewels. The immense verdingale and stiff ruffs now disappeared, but stomachers were still the fashion.

Hoods were worn, but the most usual ornament for

Andronicus: name of three emperors of the Eastern Roman Empire: probably either Andronicus II, 1282-1328, or Andronicus III, 1328-1341
Mysians: people of an ancient country in northwestern Asia Minor

the hair was a coloured riband, or band of jewels, together with a *heart-breaker*, which was a long lock corresponding with the *love-lock* worn by the gentlemen.

Blue plush caps were now invented, cloth coats took the place of the doublet, and the hat was ornamented with coloured ribands. In the lower classes the women usually wore coloured petticoats, red or blue, grey cloth bodies, linsey-woolsey aprons, a white hood, and over it a hat. The men had cloth coats, with mixed buttons, laced cravats, and flowered waistcoats.

King Charles, in a picture by Sir Peter Lely, is represented in full armour, with an immense wig, the curls of which fall below his shoulders; a deep lace cravat, or band, is tied in front in a large bow, and the ends fall upon his breast.

Doublets of gold and silver tissue, robes of blue or crimson, interwoven with silver, and ornamented with patterns in gold—long mantles, richly adorned with chains of precious stones, and caps of velvet with plumes of feathers, form the general features of dress in this splendid age.

Every kind of costly and beautiful manufacture was brought from abroad, and seized upon with avidity at a time when dress formed one of the prevailing passions of the day; and though preachers lectured, and authors wrote against carrying this foible to too great an extent, their advice was unheeded. It is said, however, that Charles II., alarmed or disgusted with the extravagant sums lavished by his subjects on dress, towards the close of his reign made a public and solemn declaration of the fashion of the apparel he was determined to wear for the future. It was,

King Charles: probably Charles II, whose portrait by Lely hangs in the National Portrait Gallery, London
Sir Peter Lely: 1618–1680, artist who was appointed court painter in 1661

according to an old author, straight Spanish hose to the knees, tied with ribands; instead of a doublet, a long vest of velvet and satin, and above that a loose coat of velvet, trimmed with ermine, much after the Polish or Muscovite fashion, and instead of shoes and stockings he adopted boots.

Shoulder-knots and shoe-buckles were now invented, and the clerical habit as worn at present was first used. It is worthy of remark that clergymen and judges were the last to abandon the fashion of ruffs.

Samuel Pepys, in his "Memoirs," gives frequent accounts of the fashions of the time in which he lived, and the variety of changes they underwent during the reigns of Charles II. and James II. The items are so curious that we shall make extracts of several for the reader's amusement and information :—

"1659–60.—This morning put on my suit with great skirts, having not lately worn any other clothes but them.

"*Feb. 2d.*—Went home on foot to lay up my money, and change my shoes and stockings. I this day left off my great skirt suit, and put on my white suit, with silver lace coat.

"*May 24th.*—Up, and made myself as fine as I could, with the linning stockings on and wide canons that I bought the other day at Hague.

"*July 1st.*—This morning came home my fine camlett cloak, with gold buttons, and a silk suit, which cost me much money.

"*5th.*—This morning my brother Tom brought me my *Jackanapes* coat with silver buttons.

"*10th.*—This day I put on my new silk suit, the first that ever I wore in my life.

Samuel Pepys' "Memoirs": published 1690
Charles II and James II: 1660-1685 and 1685-1688
jackanapes: coxcomb, or dandy

"*August 25th.*—This night Wittever brought me home from Mr. Pims' my velvet coat and hat; the first that ever I had.

"*30th.*—This the first day that ever I saw my wife wear black patches since we married.

"1660–61, *Feb. 3d.*—This day I first began to go forth in my coate and sword, as the manner now among gentlemen is.

"*June 27th.*—This day Mr. Holden sent me a bever, which cost me 4*l.* 5*s.*

"*Oct. 29th.*—This day I put on my half-cloth black stockings, and my new coate of the fashion, which pleases me well, and with my bever I was (after office was done) ready to go to my Lord Mayor's feast, as we are all invited.

"1662, *Oct. 19th.*—Lord's Day. Put on my new lace band; and so neat it is, that I am resolved my great expence shall be lace bands, and it will set off any thing else the more.

"1663, *Oct. 30th.*—To my great sorrow find myself 43*l.* worse than I was the last month, which was then 760*l.*, and now it is but 717*l.* But it has chiefly arisen from my layings-out in clothes for myself and wife: viz. for her about 12*l.*, and for myself 55*l.* or thereabouts; having made myself a velvet cloak, two new cloth skirts, black, plain both; a new shay gown, trimmed with gold buttons and twist, with a new hat, and silk tops for my legs, and many other things, being resolved henceforward to go like myself. And also two perriwigs, one whereof cost 3*l.*, the other 40*s.*

"*Nov. 29th.*—Lord's Day. This morning I put on my best black cloth suit, trimmed with scarlett ribbon, very neat, with my cloak lined with velvett, and a new bever, which altogether is very noble, with my black knit silk canons I bought a month ago.

"1663–4.—I did give my wife's brother 20s., and a coate that I had by me, a close-bodied light-coloured cloth coat, with a gold edgeing in each seam, that was the lace off my wife's best pettycoat that she had when I married her. He is going into Holland to seek his fortune.

"1664–5, *March 6th.*—With Sir J. Minnes to St. James's, and there did our business with the duke. I saw him try on his buff coat and hat-piece covered with black velvet.

"13*th.*—This day my wife began to wear light-coloured locks, quite white almost, which, though it made her look very pretty, yet, not being natural, vexes me, that I will not have her wear them.

"1665, *Sept. 3d.*—Up, and put on my coloured silk suit very fine, and my new perriwig, bought a good while since, but durst not wear, because the plague was in Westminster when I bought it; and it is a wonder what will be the fashion after the plague is done as to perriwigs, for nobody will dare to buy any haire, for fear of the infection, that it had been cut off the heads of people dead of the plague.

"1666, *June 11th.*—Walking in the galleries at White Hall, I find the ladies of honour dressed in their riding garbs, with coats and doublets with deep skirts, just for all the world like mine, and buttoned their doublets up the breast, with periwigs and hats; so that only for a long pettycoat dragging under their men's coats, nobody could take them for women.

" *Oct. 8th.*—The king hath yesterday in council declared his resolution of setting a fashion for clothes, which he will never alter. It will be a vest, I know not well how; but it is to teach the nobility thrift, and will do good.

"14th.—This day the king begins to put on his vest; * * * being a long cassocke close to the body, of black cloth, and pinked with white silk under it, and a coat over it, and the legs ruffled with black riband like a pigeon's leg; and upon the whole I wish the king may keep it, for it is a very fine and handsome garment. Lady Carteret tells me the ladies are to go into a new fashion shortly, and that is, to wear short coats above their ankles; which she and I do not like, but conclude this long trayne to be mighty graceful.

"17th.—The court is all full of vests, only my Lord St. Alban's not pinked, but plain black; and they say the king says the pinking upon white makes them look too much like magpyes, and therefore hath bespoke one of plain velvett.

"Nov. 22d.—Mr. Batelier tells me the news, how the King of France hath, in defiance to the King of England, caused all his footmen to be put into vests, and that the noblemen of France will do the like; which, if true, is the greatest indignity ever done by one prince to another.

"May 17th.—Up, and put on my new stuff suit, with a shoulder-belt according to the new fashion, and the hands of my vest and tunique laced with silk lace of the colour of my suit.

"3Cth.—Up, and put on a new summer black bombazin suit; and being come now to an agreement with my barber to keep my periwig in good order, at 20s. a-year, I am like to go very spruce, more than I used to do.

" 1669, *May 1st.*—Up betimes.   My wife extraordinary fine with her flowered tabby gown, that she
made two years ago, now laced exceedingly pretty;
and, indeed, was fine all over."

We will now add a poetical description of a lady's
toilette, from a little poem by John Evelyn, which
gives as good an idea of female vanities as the above
extracts do of the numerous changes in gentleman's
habiliments.   Both writers lived in the same century,
and both humorously describe the follies of the age:—

> " One black gown of rich silk, which odd is,
>   Without one colour'd embroider'd boddice;
>   Three manteaux, nor can madam less
>   Provision have for due undress;
>   Nor demy sultane, spagnolet,
>   Nor fringe to sweep the matt forget;
>   Or under bodice, three neat pair,
>   Embroider'd, and of shoes as fair;
>   Short under petticoats, pure fine,
>   Some of Japan stuff, some of Chine;
>   With knee-high galoon bottomed;
>   Another quilted white and red;
>   With a broad Flanders lace below;
>   Four pair of *bas de soy* shot through
>   With silver; diamond buckles, too,
>   For garters, and as rich for shoe.
>   Twice twelve day-smocks of Holland fine,
>   With cambric sleeves, rich point to joyn
>   (For she despises Colbertine).
>   Twelve more for night, all Flanders lac'd,
>   Or else she'll think herself disgrac'd.
>   The same her night-gown must adorn,
>   With two point waistcoats for the morn:
>   Of pocket *mouchoirs*, nose to drain,
>   A dozen laced, a dozen plain:
>   Three night-gowns of rich Indian stuff;

John Evelyn: 1620-1706; wrote "Tyrannus on the Mode", 1661; father of Mary Evelyn,
    who wrote "Mundus Muliebris or the Ladies Dressing-Room Unlock'd", 1690, from
    which at least the last part of the following poem is a direct quote
bas de soy: silk stockings

Four cushion-cloths are scarce enough,
Of point and Flanders, not forget,
Slippers embroider'd on velvet:
A manteau girdle, ruby buckle,
And brilliant diamond rings for knuckle;
Fans painted and perfumed three;
Three muffs of sable, ermine, grey;
Nor reckon it among the baubles,
A palatine also of sables.
A sapphire bodkin for the hair,
Of sparkling facet diamonds there.
Three turquoise, ruby, emerauld rings,
For fingers; and such pretty things
As diamond pendants for the ears
Must needs be had; or two large pears,
Pearl neck-lace, large and Oriental,
And diamond, and of amber pale;
*   *   *   *
In pin-up ruffles now she flounts,
About her sleeves are *engageants*;
Of ribbon various *échelles*,
Gloves trimm'd, and lac'd as fine as Nell's;
Twelve dozen *martial*, whole and half,
Of jonquil, tuberose (don't laugh),
Frangissau, orange, violett,
Narcissus, jessamin, ambrett;
And some of chicken skin for night,
To keep her hands plump, soft, and white:
Mouches for pushes to be sure;
From Paris the très-fine procure
Catembuc combs in pulvil case,
To set and trim the hair and face.
And that the cheeks may both agree,
Plumpers to fill the cavity.
The *settée, cupée,* place aright,
Frélange, fontange, favorite;
Monté la haute, and *palisade,*
Sorti, flandau (great helps to trade),
Bourgoigne, jardiné, cornett.
Fridal next upper *panier* set,

engageants: deep, double wrist ruffles
échelles: stomacher laced with ribbon
martial: French perfumes
mouches: patches
catembuc: a smooth, scented wood
pulvil: powder
plumpers: thin, round balls to
    fill out the cheeks
settée: double pinner
cupée: kind of pinner
frélange: bonnet & pinner together
fontange: top-knot of ribbons, named
    for Mlle. de Fontanges
pinner: coif with two long flaps each side

favorite: locks dangling at the temples
monté la haute: wires to raise the dress
palisade: wire holding hair to the Dutch-
    ess, or first, knot
sorti: knot of ribbon peeping out between
    bonnet & pinner
flandau: kind of pinner joining the bonnet
Bourgoigne: first part of the headdress
    next to the hair
jardiné: single pinner next to the Bour-
    goigne
fridal: should be 'frilal', a border of
    ornamental ribbon
panier: should be pinner

Round which it does our ladies please
To spread the hood called *rayonnés*:
Behind the noddle every baggage
Wears bundle *choux*--in English, cabbage:
Nor *cruches* she, nor *confidents*,
Nor *passagers*, nor *bergers* wants;
And when this grace Nature denies,
An artificial *tour* supplies;
All which with *meurtriers* unite,
And *crève-cœurs*, silly fops to smite."

In Evelyn's "Diary," he also mentions King Charles's having adopted a new habit, which he thus describes: " 1666, *Oct.* 18*th*.—To court. It being the first time his majesty put himself solemnly into the Eastern fashion of vest, after the Persian mode, with girdle and straps, and shoe-strings and garters into bouckles, of which some were set with precious stones, resolving never to alter it, and to leave the French mode, which had hitherto obtained to our great expence and reproch Upon which divers courtiers and gentlemen gave his majesty gold, by way of wager, that he would not persist in this resolution."

In a note to the "Diary" it is remarked that this costume was soon laid aside, which shews how well the courtiers understood the prevalent love of French modes; and Evelyn himself, it appears, from the following paragraph, in which he predicted the change which so soon took place, was fully sensible of this: "*Oct.* 30*th*. — To London to our office; and now I had on the vest and surcoat, or tunic, as 'twas called, after his majesty had brought the whole court to it. It was a comely and manly habit, too good to hold, it being impossible for us, in good earnest, to leave the *Monsieur's* vanities long."

rayonnés: upper hood with pins in an arc like sunbeams
cruches: small circles on the forehead
confidents: small curls near the ears
passagers: a curled lock near the temple
berger: a small lock in the manner of a shepherdess

tour: an artificial dress of hair (a "rat")
meurtriers: 'murderer's knot', which, untied, loosens all the hair
crève-cœur: heart-breaker, a lock at the nape of the neck
Evelyn's "Diary": John Evelyn's "Diary" of 1666 was published in 1818

In a former part he remarks of the queen: "1662, *May 30th.*—The queene arriv'd with a traine of Portuguese ladies in their monstrous fardingals, or guard-infantas, their complexions olivader, and sufficiently unagreeable. Her majesty in the same habit, her foretop long, and turned aside very strangely." In a note to the "Diary," we are told that about the year 1640 or 1650 boys of thirteen years of age wore a coat and vest reaching nearly to the ankles. In an amusing essay, entitled "Tyrannus, or the Mode," Evelyn thus speaks of the dress in his time: "It was a fine silken thing which I spied walking th' other day through Westminster Hall, that had as much ribbon about him as would have plundered six shops, and set up twenty country pedlars; all his body was drest like a maypole, or a *Tom o' Bedlam's* cap. A fregat, newly riggd, kept not half such a clatter in a storme as this puppet's streamers did when the wind was in his shrouds; the motion was wonderfull to behold, and the well-chosen colours were red, orange, and blew, of well-gum'd sattin, which argued a happy fancy."

In another part the author inveighs bitterly against French fashions. "What," he exclaims, "have we to do with these foreign butterflies? We need no French inventions, or for the stage or for the back." He afterwards expresses a hope, that "it shall soon be as presumptuous for any foreign nation to impose upon our court, as it is, indeed, ridiculous it should, and its greatest diminution."

Randal Holmes, speaking of the coiffures of the year 1670, says: "The ladies wore false locks, set on wires, to make them stand at a distance from the

the queene: Catharine of Braganza, who married Charles II in 1662
guard-infantas: literally, princess savers (maidenhood guards), a type of farthingale
"Diary": Evelyn's, see note p. 137
"Tyrannus, or the Mode": "Tyrannus on the Mode", by John Evelyn, 1661
Tom o' Bedlam: Bethelehem (Bedlam) Hospital was the London madhouse; probably this
    was a sort of fool's hat or cap
Randal Holmes: Holmes the younger, a genealogist, 1627-1699; see note p. 127

head." In 1688, he further observes, "that the forehead was adorned with a knot of divers coloured ribbons, the head with a ruffle coif, set in corners, and
the like ribbons behind the head;" and he adds,
"all is brought again from the old, for there is nothing new under the sun, and what is now hath been
formerly."

The Spanish leather boots, introduced under
Charles I., still continued the fashion; but the immense roses on the shoes gradually declined, and were
replaced by buckles and large wide strings. The
boots were frequently trimmed with lace round the
top, like the deep ruffles on a lady's sleeve; or the
stockings, drawn up above the knees, had a wide lace
fastened to the garters.

The ribands of the shoes disappeared in the reign
of William III., when the small buckle came into
fashion. At first it was not unlike a bean in shape
and size. Since that period it has undergone every
variety of form and dimension, and, in the year
1777, buckles and buttons on the coats became so
enormous, that they gave birth to many ludicrous
caricatures. The high broad heels to the shoes were
long worn both by men and women, and a later fashion
was to have them of a red colour. Stockings of all
hues, with the clocks worked in various patterns, continued the mode for many years.

Charles I: 1625-1649
William III: 1688-1702

Chapter 10 – England, 17th and 18th Centuries

THE TOILETTE IN ENGLAND.

CHAPTER X.

PATCHING was much admired during the reign of Charles I., and for several succeeding years.   An old poem, written during the Commonwealth, thus satirizes this mode :—

> " Her patches are of every cut,
>   For pimples or for scars ;
> Here's all the wandering planett's signes,
>   And some o' the fixed starrs :
> Already gumm'd to make them stick,
>   They need no other sky,
> Nor starrs for Lilly for to view,
>   To tell your fortunes by."

As may be seen by the above lines, these patches were worn in every variety of form and shape.   Some authors think the fashion came originally from Arabia. No sooner was it brought to England and France than it became an absolute *fureur*.   In the former country, old and young, the maiden of sixteen and

Charles I: 1625–1649
Commonwealth: 1649–1660, first under Oliver Cromwell, then (1658) under his son, Richard
fureur: literally mania, thus 'all the rage'

the grey-haired grandmamma, covered their faces with these black spots, shaped like suns, moons, stars, hearts, crosses, and lozenges; and some even carried the mode to the extravagant extent of shaping the patches to represent a carriage and horses!

In a dramatic pastoral, written during the reign of Charles I., we find a humorous description of the various articles requisite for the toilette of a lady of fashion. They are equally applicable to the reign of his son, and are, it will be seen, quite different from those of Evelyn :—

> " Chains, coronets, pendans, bracelets, and ear-rings;
> Pins, girdles, spangles, embroyderies, and rings;
> Shadowes, rebatowes, ribbands, ruffs, cuffs, falls,
> Scarfes, feathers, fans, masks, muffs, laces, cauls,
> Thin tiffanies, cobweb lawn, and fardingals,
> Sweet fals, vayles, wimples, glasses, crisping pins,
> Pots of ointment, combes, with poking-sticks and bodkines,
> Coyfes, gorgets, fringes, rowles, fillets, and hair laces;
> Silks, damasks, velvets, tinsels, cloth of gold,
> Of tissues with colours of a hundred fold.
>
>   *   *   *   *   *
>
> Waters she hath to make her face to shine;
> Confections eke to clarify her skin;
> Lip salves, and clothes of a rich scarlet dye,
> She hath, which to her cheeks she doth apply;
> Ointment, wherewith she pargets o'er her face,
> And lustrifies her beauty's dying grace."

During the reign of James II. the wigs were perfectly preposterous. The coats had immensely wide cuffs, and beneath them appeared the shirt-sleeves, with their full, deep ruffles. The hats were broad-brimmed.

The ladies wore their hoods tied under the chin, and then discarded them to adopt straw hats. We

"his son": James II, 1685–1688; Evelyn had written about another son, Charles II read in Pepys : " They had pleasure in putting on straw hats, which are much worn in this country."

The *Querpo hood*, so called from the Spanish, was no longer seen, except on women of the lower classes.

Riding-habits, we find in Evelyn's " Diary," as well as in Pepy's " Memoirs," were now the fashion, and a hat and feather were worn with them. At first these dresses were much censured.

In the reigns of James, and William and Mary, dress continued much the same as it is described in that of Charles ; but the coiffures were in great variety. About this time the celebrated head-dress said to have been called the *Fontange* was introduced into England from France. But although many authors assert that *Fontange* was the name of a head-dress, we, who have dived deep into the hidden mysteries of fashion, examined, sought, and reflected upon her changes and inventions, are inclined to think that the word we allude to expresses only a knot of ribands, placed on a coiffure called the *commode*, which, in the " Lady's Dictionary," is thus described :— " Commode, a frame of wire, two or three stories high, fitted to the head, covered with tiffany, or other thin silks, being now completed into a head-dress." We are the more convinced that our opinion upon this *knotty* question is correct, from the explanation given of it in the " Dictionnaire de l'Académie," which thus describes a Fontange : " Nœud de rubans que les femmes portent sur leur coiffure, et qui tire son nom de Madame de Fontange."

In the year 1698 the high head-dress was preached

Pepys: "Memoirs", 1690
Evelyn's "Diary": (1666), published 1818
William and Mary: 1689–1702
Fontange: see note p. 136
"Lady's Dictionary": "Lady's Dictionary, being a general entertainment for the fair
    sex" by N. H., 1694; no more is known of the author
"Dictionnaire de l'Académie": Dictionary of the Académie Française, 1696
Madame de Fontange: Mlle de Fontange was Louis XIV's mistress 1661–1681
"Nœud de rubans": French translations appear in the appendix

against in the following words, by John Edwards:
" This is the pride which reigns amongst our very
ordinary women at this day, they think themselves
highly advanced by this climbing foretop. All their
rigging is nothing worth without this wagging topsail;
and in defiance of our Saviour's words, they endeavour,
as it were, to add *a cubit* to their stature. With their
exalted heads they do, as it were, attempt a superiority
over mankind; nay, their Babel builders seem, with
their lofty towers, to threaten the skies and even to
defy heaven itself."

The writers of the period frequently mention these
head-dresses with much animadversion. " Within my
own memory," says one of them, " I have known a lady's
head-dress rise and fall above thirty degrees. About
ten years ago it shot up to a very great height, insomuch
that the female part of our species were much taller
than the men. The women were of such an enormous
stature, that 'we appeared as grasshoppers before them.'"
Further on we find: " Women in all ages have taken
more pains than men to adorn the outside of their
heads; and indeed I very much admire that those female
architects, who raise such wonderful structures out of
ribbands, lace, and wire, have not been recorded for
their respective inventions. It is certain there has
been as many orders in these kinds of building, as in
those which have been made of marble. Sometimes
they rise in the shape of a pyramid, sometimes like a
tower, and sometimes like a steeple."

But these towers were not the only coiffures imported into England from France; many of which went
to the opposite extreme. Sometimes a simple bandeau
of jewels confined the tresses, at others the hair was

John Edwards: from Cambridge; author of many books
cubit: ancient measurement, generally agreed to be approximately 18-22 inches

arranged in a multitude of curls, interspersed with pearls, and the long hair was left to float in negligent profusion over the shoulders.

Lady's Head-Dress in 1700

Another head-dress, worn in the early part of 1700, was composed of pasteboard, lace, ribands, and gauze, as represented in the annexed cut.

French hoods resumed their place in the annals of fashion about the year 1711. They, as well as many other parts of the female attire, are frequently mentioned, and we find that they were worn of all colours. It appears from the following passage from a popular writer of the time, that they usurped the place of the commode : " The ladies have been for some time in a kind of moulting season, with regard to that part of their dress, having cast great quantities of ribbon, lace, and cambric, and in some measure reduced that part of the human figure to the beautiful globular form which is natural to it. We have for a great while expected what kind of ornament would be substituted in the place of those antiquated commodes. * * * * As I was standing in the hinder part of the box (at the opera) I took notice of a little cluster of women, sitting together in the prettiest-coloured hoods that I ever saw. One of them was blue, another yellow, and another philomot, the fourth was of a pink colour, and the fifth of a pale green. * * * I am informed that this fashion spreads daily, insomuch that the Whig and Tory ladies begin already to hang out different colours, and to shew their principles in their head-dress."

In No. 271 is a letter to the " Spectator," in which

philomot: filemot (corruption of feuille mort), color of dead leaves
Whig and Tory: political parties
"Spectator": famous magazine published by Addison and Steele, 1711-1712

the writer mentions an assembly of ladies, where there were thirteen different coloured hoods; and in another number occurs an advertisement from the parish vestry as follows: "All ladies who come to church in the *new-fashioned hoods*, are desired to be there before divine service begins, lest they divert the attention of the congregation."

We are further informed that the women let their hair grow to a great length, but tie it up in a knot, and cover it from being seen.

A ribbon head-dress is also spoken of as follows: "A lady of this place had some time since a box of the newest ribbons sent down by the coach. Whether it was her own malicious invention, or the wantonness of a London milliner, I am not able to inform you, but among the rest, there was one cherry-coloured ribbon, consisting of about half-a-dozen yards, made up in the figure of a small head-dress."

In 1715, we find the commode again alluded to, so that it must have reappeared; there is also a description of the feather head-dress: "I pretend not," says Addison, "to draw the single *quill* against that immense crop of plumes, which is already risen to an amazing height, and unless timely singed by the bright eyes that glitter beneath, will shortly be able to overshadow them. Lady Porcupine's commode is started at least a foot and a half since Sunday last. * * * But so long as the commodity circulates, and the outside

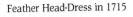

Feather Head-Dress in 1715

Addison: Joseph Addison, 1672-1719
Lady Porcupine: obviously a pun

of a fine lady's head is converted into the inside of her pillow, or, if fate so order it, to the top of her herze, there is no harm in the consumption, and the milliner, upholsterer, and undertaker, may live in an amicable correspondence, and mutual dependence on each other."

In a book of travels written about the same period, we find the following: "And now her ladyship brandishes the combs, and the powders raise clouds in the apartment. She trims up the commode, she places it ten times, unplaces it as often, without being so fortunate as to hit upon the critical point; she models it to all systems, but is pleased with none. For you must know, that some ladies fancy a vertical, others an horizontal position, others dress by the northern latitude, and others lower its point 45 degrees."

Hoops at this time swelled out the petticoats to an enormous extent, so much so that a writer of the day observes, " If the men also adopted the old fashion of trunk hose, a man and his wife would fill a whole pew in church."

In a letter to the " Spectator," we find the following account of hoops: " Since your withdrawing from this place, the fair sex are run into great extravagancies. Their petticoats, which began to heave and swell before you left us, are now blown up into a most enormous concave, and rise every day more and more. In short, sir, since our women know themselves to be out of the eye of the *Spectator*, they will be kept within no compass. You praised them a little too soon for the modesty of their head-dresses; for as the humour of a sick person is often driven out of one limb into another, their superfluity of ornaments, in-

herze: herse or hearse; the carriage for the coffin in a funeral cortège
"Spectator": see note p. 144

stead of being entirely banished, seem only fallen from their heads upon their lower parts. What they have lost in height they make up in breadth, and contrary to all rules of architecture widen the foundations at the same time that they shorten the superstructure."

A little farther on we read : "But as we do not yet hear of any particular use in this petticoat, or that it contains any thing more than what was supposed to be in those of scantier make, we are wonderfully at a loss about it. * * * * Among these various conjectures there are many of superstitious tempers, who look upon the hoop petticoat as a kind of prodigy. Some will have it that it portends the downfall of the French king, and observe that the farthingale appeared in England a little before the ruin of the Spanish monarchy."

In another letter to the "Spectator" we have the following : "I and several of your other female readers have conformed ourselves to your rules, even to our very dress. There is not one of us but has reduced our outward petticoat to its ancient sizeable circumference, though indeed we retain still the quilted one underneath ; which makes us not altogether unconformable to the fashion."

Another writer gives an amusing account of the shape and varieties of hoops: "The hoop," he observes, "has been known to expand and contract itself from the size of a butter churn to the circumference of three hogsheads ; at one time it was sloped from the waist in a pyramidal form ; at another it was bent upwards like an inverted bow, by which the two angles, when squeezed upon both sides, came in contact with the ears. At present it is nearly of an oval form, and scarce measures from end to end above twice the length of the wearer. The hoop has indeed lost much of its credit in the female world, and has suffered much from the innovation of short *sacks* and negligés."

The same writer proposes that there should be a female parliament to regulate matters relating to dress and ceremony; and after speculating upon the improvements that would be made by such judicious law-givers, he says, " And they would at least not suffer enormous hoops, to spread themselves across the whole pavement, to the detriment of all honest men going upon business along the street."

The *petticoat* of wide dimensions is also much censured : " Many are the inconveniences that accrue to her majesty's loving subjects from the same petticoats, as hurting men's shins, sweeping down the wares of industrious females in the streets," &c. &c. " The ladies among us have a superior genius to the men ; which have for some years past shot out in several exorbitant inventions, for the greater consumption of our manufacture. While the men have contented themselves with the retrenchment of the hat, or the various scallop of the pocket, the ladies have sunk the head-dress, inclosed themselves in the circumference of the hoop-petticoat; furbelows and flounces have been disposed at will, the stays have been lowered behind ; not to mention the various rolling of the sleeve, and those other nice circumstances of dress, upon which every lady employs her fancy at pleasure."

Again it is observed: "I sometimes entertained myself by observing what a large quantity of ground was hid under spreading petticoats; and what little patches of earth were covered by creatures with wigs and hats, in comparison to those spaces that were distinguished by flounces, fringes, and furbelows."

In a petition to the author of the "Tatler," is an amusing satire of these spreading petticoats, which seem to have engrossed the attention of most of the writers of the seventeenth and eighteenth centuries: "Upon the late invention of Mrs. Catherine Cross-stitch, mantua-maker, the petticoats of ladies were too wide for entering into any coach or chair, which was in use before the said invention. That, for the service of the said ladies, your petitioner has built a round chair, in the form of a lantern, six yards and a half in circumference, with a stool in the centre of it; the said vehicle being so contrived, as to receive the passenger by opening in two in the middle, and closing mathematically when she is seated. That your petitioner has also invented a coach, for the reception of one lady only, who is to be let in at the top. That the said coach, has been tried by a lady's woman in one of these *full petticoats*, who was let down from a balcony, and drawn up again by pulleys, to the great satisfaction of her lady and all who beheld her."

Patching was never more prevalent than during the reign of Queen Anne, and severely are those "*black spots*" censured by writers of the time, both French and English. A French author says: "L'usage des mouches n'est pas inconnu aux dames Françoises, mais il faut être jeune et jolie. En Angleterre, jeunes, vieilles, belles, laides, tout est *emmouché*

"Tatler": famous magazine founded by Sir Richard Steele (writing as Isaac Bickerstaff), appeared during the years 1709–1711
Mrs. Catherine Cross-Stitch: another pun
Queen Anne: 1702–1714
"L'usage des mouches": French translation appears in the appendix

jusqu'à la décrepitude; j'ai plusieurs fois compté quinze mouches et davantage, sur la noire et ridée face d'une vieille de soixante et dix ans.   Les Anglaises raffinent ainsi sur nos modes."

We have other laughable accounts of these patches : " The women look like angels, and would be more beautiful than the sun, were it not for little black spots that are apt to break out in their faces, and sometimes rise in very odd figures.   I have observed that those little blemishes wear off very soon, but when they disappear in one part of the face, they are very apt to break out in another, insomuch that I have seen a spot upon the forehead in the afternoon that was upon the chin in the morning."

" About the middle of last winter I went to see an opera at the Haymarket Theatre, where I could not but take notice of two parties of very fine women, that had placed themselves in the opposite side-boxes, and seemed drawn up in a kind of battle array one against the other.   After a short survey of them, I found they were patched differently ; the faces on one hand being spotted on the right side of the forehead, and those upon the other on the left.   I quickly perceived that they cast hostile glances one upon another; and that their patches were placed in those different situations as party-signals to distinguish friends from foes.   In the middle boxes, between these two opposite bodies, were several ladies who patched indifferently on both sides of their faces, and seemed to sit there with no other intention but to see the opera.   Upon inquiry I found that the body of Amazons on my right hand were Whigs, and those on my left Tories : and that those

Whigs and Tories: the wives of men in politics had only their costume and conversation with which to influence the course of events, but wielded or were the victims of social power to a greater extent than is seen in the modern world

who had placed themselves in the middle boxes were a neutral party. * * * Nay, I am informed that some of them adhere so steadfastly to their party, and are so far from sacrificing their zeal for the public to their passion for any particular person, that in a late draught of marriage articles, a lady has stipulated with her husband that whatever his opinions are, she shall be at liberty to patch on which side she pleases."

The absurdity is also thus attacked: " Madam, let me beg of you to take off the patches at the lower end of your left cheek, and I will allow two more under your left eye, which will contribute more to the symmetry of your face ; except you would please to remove the ten black atoms on your ladyship's chin, and wear one large patch instead of them. If so, you may properly enough retain the three patches above mentioned."

Washes for the complexion, rouge, and alabaster powder, were much used at this time, and continued fashionable for many years, but patches are said to have been finally banished towards the latter end of Anne's reign, chiefly through the censures of Addison, who waged continual war against them, and from whom many of the extracts given above have been derived.

end of Queen Anne's reign: 1714
Addison: Joseph Addison, 1672-1719

Chapter 11 – England, 18th Century

THE TOILETTE IN ENGLAND.

CHAPTER XI.

FRENCH milliners, hair-dressers, and shoemakers, were now the fashion; as well as French habiliments of every kind. In a letter to the "Spectator," we have the following remarks: "You cannot imagine, worthy sir, how ridiculously I find we have all been trussed up during the war, and how infinitely the French dress excels ours. The *mantua* has no lead in the sleeves, and I hope we are not lighter than the French ladies, so as to want that kind of ballast; the petticoat has no whalebone, but sits with an air altogether gallant and *dégagé*; the coiffure is inexpressibly pretty, and in short the whole dress has a thousand beauties in it."

In a discourse purporting to be delivered by a spinster, in defence of the woollen manufactures in the year 1719, we find the following list of the different articles of dress necessary for the attire of a lady of fashion of that year:—

	£.	s.	d.
"A smock of cambric holland about 3 ells and a half	2	2	0
Marseilles quilted petticoat 3 yards wide and 1 yard long	3	6	0

"Spectator": periodical, see note p. 144
dégagé: free, easy
ell: the English ell is 45 inches; the ell varied from country to country, sometimes
    from city to city, and was generally set by the weavers' guilds in Europe

	£.	s.	d.
An hoop-petticoat covered with tabb.	2	15	0
A French or Italian silk quilted petticoat, one yard and a quarter deep, and six yards wide	10	0	0
A mantua and petticoat of French brocade..	78	0	0
A French point or Flanders laced head, ruffles and tucker.......................	80	0	0
English stays covered with tabby..........	3	0	0
A French necklace	1	5	0
A Flanders laced handkerchief	10	0	0
French or Italian flowers for the hair	2	0	0
An Italian fan	5	0	0
English silk stockings	1	0	0
English shoes	2	10	0
French girdle	0	15	0
A cambrick pocket handkerchief..........	0	10	0
French kid gloves	0	2	6
A black French silk alamode hood	0	15	0
A black French laced hood	5	5	0
French embroidered knot and bosom knot ..	2	2	0
French garters	1	5	0
Pockets of Marseilles quilting	1	5	0
Muff	5	5	0
Sable Tippet.........................	15	0	0
Lining of Italian lutestring	8	0	0
Thread stockings	0	10	0
Turkey handkerchief	5	5	0
A hat of Leghorn	1	10	0
A beaver and feather for the forest	3	0	0
A riding suit, with embroidery of Paris	47	10	0
Three dresses for the masquerade; two from Venice	36	0	0
One from Paris, of green velvet *à la Sultanesse*, set with pearls and rubies	123	15	0

Almost all the above objects come from foreign lands. There are also other trifles, such as essences, pomatums, patches, powder, and wire, the prices of which are not given.

The muffs here spoken of were very fashionable about the year 1710 ; but their diminutive size seemed to intimate that they were invented only for fashion's sake, for they were much too small to be of any use.

The riding habit, which first appeared under the reign of Charles II., was still looked upon with animadversion even in the reign of Queen Anne, as we find by the following remarks of Addison: "Among the several female extravagancies I have already taken notice of, there is one which still keeps its ground. I mean that of the ladies who dress themselves in a hat and feather, a riding-coat and a perriwig, or at least tie up their hair in a bag or ribbon, in imitation of the smart part of the opposite sex."

This graceful writer also affords us an account of one of these equestrian ladies : " *His* hair, well curled and powdered, hung to a considerable length on his shoulders, and was tied as if by the hand of his mistress with a scarlet ribband, which played like a streamer behind him ; he had a coat and waistcoat of blue camlet trimmed and embroidered with silver, a cravat of the finest lace, and wore, in a smart cock, a little beaver hat edged with silver, and made more sprightly by a feather. * * * * As I was pitying the luxury of this young person, who appeared to me to have been only educated as an object of sight, I perceived on my nearer approach, and as I turned my eye downward, a part of the equipage I had not observed before, which was a petticoat of the same as the coat and waistcoat."

Charles II: 1660–1685
Queen Anne: 1702–1714
Addison: Joseph Addison, 1672–1719

In one of the portraits of Queen Anne, her dress is much like that worn in France under Louis XIV. Her robe, of rich brocade, is made half high, and cut square round the bosom, with a fall of lace. Her hair is drawn off the forehead, and arranged in curls to the top of the head, interspersed with pearls, and long ringlets fall gracefully down upon her shoulders; a style of coiffure much preferable to the stiff, towering head-dresses, that had been the fashion during the first years of her reign.

Fans were now very much used; ladies seldom appeared without this useful ornament in their hands. The fan was adorned with every variety of bird, beast, landscape, and figure; and even when out in a carriage or at church it was still held ready to be furled or unfurled at pleasure.

From various allusions to different parts of a lady's dress, in works printed at the beginning of the eighteenth century we find that the shape and form of attire was no longer distinguished by that modesty which had characterized it till the sixteenth century. " If," says Addison, " we survey the pictures of our great-grandmothers in Queen Elizabeth's time, we see them clothed down to the very wrists, and up to the very chin. The hands and face were the only samples they gave of their beautiful persons. The following age of females made larger discoveries of their complexion. They, first of all, tucked up their garments to the elbow, and, notwithstanding the tenderness of the sex, were content, for the information of mankind, to expose their arms to the coldness of the air and injuries of the weather."

Not long after this the petticoats were shortened,

Louis XIV: 1638–1715
Queen Elizabeth: Elizabeth I, 1558–1603

the gowns lowered to a degree that was very offensive to modesty, and altogether the dress of a lady of fashion, modelled exactly upon that of the French, was much censured by writers of the period.

Notwithstanding all that had been said, written, and preached against the hoop, which now replaced the fardingale in the toilette of the *élégantes*, it remained a favourite till the nineteenth century, when George IV. banished it altogether.

Long gloves began to be worn by the ladies in this reign.

The costume of the gentlemen, though not so preposterous as that of the ladies, still frequently fell under the reproof of rigid critics. The large, full-bottomed wigs, especially, were severely censured. In the reign of Queen Mary, Archbishop Tillotson thus speaks of this new fashion: " I can remember," he says, "since the wearing of hair below the ears was looked upon as a sin of the first magnitude; and when ministers generally, whatever their text was, did either find, or make occasion to reprove the great sin of long hair, and if they saw any one in the congregation guilty in that kind, they would point him out particularly, and let fly at him with great zeal."

These immense wigs, we are told, were named "Duvilliers," from a perruquier of that name who first invented them. Of the same family, though of much smaller dimensions, were the nightcap wigs, the campaign, major, bag, and riding wigs; and it is said that thirty pounds was not considered at all a large price for a full-sized peruke.

Hats now engaged much attention. Sometimes the brim stood straight up all round; at others the

George IV: 1820–1830
Queen Mary: Mary II (William and Mary) 1689–1694
Archbishop Tillotson: 1630–1694

right or the left sides were elevated, or, perhaps, both ; and small three-cornered hats, trimmed with gold or silver lace, and adorned with feathers, came into fashion.

The coats were of a square form, the waistcoats immensely long, with large pockets, and the stockings, though fastened below the knees with garters, were still worn pulled up far above them. The cuffs of the coats were wide, hanging, and trimmed with lace ruffles ; while the skirts, it is said, rivalled the hoop-petticoat in size, being stiffened out with wire.

The legs gloried in bright blue or red stockings, with clocks of gold and silver. The feet were encased in broad-toed shoes, with red heels, and the throat was wrapped in a lace tie.

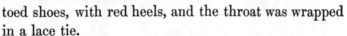

Gentleman of the Reign
of Queen Mary

To complete the costume, we must not omit to mention that the *petit-maitres* of that day wore long swords peeping from under the skirts of their coats, and had fringed gloves, also embroidered pocket-hand-kerchiefs. When the ties disappeared, *Steinkirks*, berdashes, and lastly, cravats, were worn.

In Walpole's " Anecdotes of Painting," we find that in the reign of George I. " the habits of the times were shrunk into awkward coats and waistcoats for the men ; and for the women, to tight-laced gowns, round

petit maîtres: dandies
Steinkirk: Steenkirk, a neckcloth worn by men and women, having long lace ends which
    hung free or were twisted together and passed through a loop or ring
berdash: burdash, a kind of wide cravat or sash worn originally by men at the waist
cravat: piece of lace, linen, or muslin edged with lace, worn around the neck and
    tied in a bow.
Walpole: Horace Walpole, Earl of Oxford, wrote "Anecdotes of Painting" in 1798
George I: 1714-1727

hoops, and half-a-dozen squeezed plaits of linen, to which dangled behind two unmeaning pendants, called lappets, not half covering their straight-drawn hair." To this description we may add small caps, some of which scarcely covered the top of the head, while others, frilled and puffed in small plaits, lay upon the forehead.

The hoop now underwent many important changes ;

Hoop-Dress

sometimes it projected at the sides only, or, like its ancestor the fardingale, it spread itself all round in imposing majesty, covered with a short jupe, deprived of its flowing train.

The high-heeled shoes remained. Tight sleeves with full ruffles ; small-pointed waists enclosed in whale-bone ; loose gowns called sacques ; and cloaks with hoods named cardinals, were now *la grande mode.*

Among the gentlemen's costumes the most striking novelty of this time was the *Ramilie tail*, which was a plaited tail to the wig, with an immense bow at the top, and a smaller one at the bottom. To Lord Bolingbroke the *élégantes* are indebted for the fashion of tying the hair, which hitherto had been formed into curls on the back of the neck.

Hats were of every shape. The nether garments were fastened below the knees, and the stockings no longer covered them. The following account is given of the dress of this time: "I suffered my hair," says the writer, "to grow long enough to comb back over the foretop of my wig, which, when I sallied forth to my evening amusement, I changed to a queue; I tied the collar of my shirt with half an ell of black ribbon, which appeared under my neck-cloth; the fore-corner of my hat was considerably elevated and shortened, so that it no longer resembled a spout, but the corner of a minced pye; my waist-coat was edged with narrow lace, my stockings were silk, and I never appeared without a pair of gloves."

The same writer tells us that a few years previously he wore (having cut off his hair) a brown *bob* periwig, with a single row of curls round the bottom, nicely combed and without powder. He adds that his hat was of the fashionable shape; the fore-corner projected nearly two inches further than those on each side, and was moulded into the form of a spout.

In the reign of George II. the *pigtail*, that favourite ornament of sailors in later years, first appeared, and it banished the Ramilie tail and tie. Bob-wigs followed in its train; sometimes they were powdered, and a few brave spirits actually ventured to wear their own hair curled and profusely powdered.

Lord Bolingbroke: 1678–1751
élégantes: dandies
George II: 1727–1760

A large cocked hat was now imported from Germany; it was named the *Kevenhuller*, and is thus described by a writer of the time: "It is shaped like an equilateral triangle, placed with the most mathematical precision on the head, somewhat elevated behind, and sloping on an unvarying angle downwards to the eyes, surrounded by a long, stiff, formal feather, rising from a large rosette of black riband on the dexter side."

The hoop, during the first few years of the reign of George II., appeared to have lost the favour of the fair votaries of fashion; its ascendancy visibly declined, perhaps in consequence of a pamphlet which was published against it, entitled, "The enormous abomination of the Hoop-petticoat as the fashion now is."

Caps and straw hats now flourished, and aprons were much worn even in full dress. Capuchins replaced the hoods of former reigns, and patches reappeared, though but for a very short time. A new covering for the head, too—which was neither a cap nor a bonnet—was also invented at this time: it was called a *calash*, and was made of silk, plaited closely over a wire frame.

A work published in 1753, speaks of caps the

Cap worn in 1753

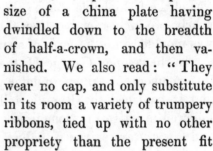

size of a china plate having dwindled down to the breadth of half-a-crown, and then vanished. We also read: "They wear no cap, and only substitute in its room a variety of trumpery ribbons, tied up with no other propriety than the present fit shall happen to direct."

George II: 1727-1760

In one of the old Norfolk journals we find the following: "Several fine ladies, who used to wear French silks, French hoops four yards wide, *tête de mouton* heads, and white satin smock petticoats, are now turned Methodists, and followers of Mr. Whitfield, whose doctrine of the new birth has so prevailed over them, that they now wear plain stuff gowns, no hoops, common night-mobs, and old plain bags."

The author of a work appearing at about the same time remarks: "Of all branches of the female dress no one has undergone more alterations than that of the head. The long lappets, the horse-shoe cap, the Brussels head, and the prudish mob, pinned under the chin, have all of them had their day. The present mode has voted out all these superfluous excrescences, and in the room of a slip of cambric, or lace, has planted a whimsical sprig of spangles, or artificial flowers. We may remember when, for a while, the hair was tortured into ringlets behind; at present it is braided into a queue. . . . . If the caps have passed through many metamorphoses, no less a change has been brought about in the other coverings contrived for the head. The diminutive high-crowned hat, the bonnet, the hive, and the milk-maid's chip hat, were rescued for a time from old women and servant-girls, to adorn the heads of the first fashion. Nor was the method of cocking hats less fluctuating, till they were at length settled to the present mode, by which it is ordained, that every hat, whether of straw or silk, whether of the chambermaid or mistress, must have their flaps turned up both before and behind. If the end of a fine lady's dress was not rather ornamental than useful, we should think it a little odd that hats,

tête de mouton: literally sheep's head, hairstyle with a profusion of small, tight curls
Mr. Whitfield: George Whitefield, 1714-1770

which seem naturally to be intended to screen their faces from the heat or severity of the weather, should be moulded into a shape that prevented their answering either of these purposes; but we must, indeed, allow it to be highly ornamental, as the present hats worn by the women are more bold and impudent than the broad-brimmed staring Kevenhullers worn a few years ago by the men.   These hats are also decorated with two waving pendants of ribbon, hanging down from the brim on the left side."

Ladies' Head-Dresses

The two head-dresses annexed were fashionable about this time.   The hair was drawn over a cushion to a great height, and surmounted by a handkerchief of lace, or fine gauze. Sometimes two ringlets were allowed to fall upon the neck, or a long, narrow strip of lace, resembling a streamer, hung from the top to the shoulders.   The cap was composed of riband and lace.

Pomatum and powder were much used by the ladies in their coiffures.   But the most extraordinary invention for the adornment of the head, of this or any other age, was that of the *capriole*.   An old poet thus speaks of this fantastical coiffure :—

> "Here, on a fair one's head-dress, sparkling sticks,
>   Swinging on silver springs, a coach and six ;
>   There, on a sprig or slop'd pourpon, you see
>   A chariot, sulky, chaise, or *vis-à-vis*."

In the same poem we read :—

> "Nelly ! where is the creature fled ?
>   Put my post-chaise upon my head."

Kevenhuller: see page 160, first paragraph
pomatum: pomade, a scented ointment in which apples (pomes) were perhaps originally
   an ingredient
sulky: light carriage for only one person, who drove him/herself
chaise: light, open carriage with (sometimes) a folding top or 'calash', see illus.
   p. 160
vis-à-vis: carriage or open cart for two passengers, who sat facing each other

In a work written about the year 1757, we read: "Be it remembered that in this year many ladies of fortune and fashion, willing to set an example of prudence and economy to their inferiors, did invent and make public, without a patent, a machine for the head, in form of a *post-chaise and horses*, and another imitating *a chair and chairmen*, which were frequently worn by persons of distinction."

We have also the following description of this fashion: "Those heads which are not able to bear a coach and six (for vehicles of this sort are very apt to crack the brain) so far act consistently as to make use of a post-chariot, or a single-horse chaise with a beau perching in the middle." The account then goes on to say: "The vehicle itself was constructed of gold threads, and was drawn by six dapple greys of blown glass, with a coachman, postilion, and gentleman within, of the same brittle manufacture. Upon further inquiry the milliner told me, with a smile, that it was difficult to give a reason for inventions so full of whim."

The prevailing fashion of powder was followed by women as well as men, so that with it and quantities of pomatum, the hair was stiffened out in large curls, or, being drawn back from the forehead, fell down *en chignon*. False hair was very generally worn, and every variety of coiffure: *French curls* that resembled eggs strung on a wire; *Italian curls*, done back from the face, and often called *scallop shells*; and German curls, which were a mixture of Italian and French. Behind, the hair was curled all over, and was called *tête de mouton*.

The quantities of powder and pomatum used at

chair and chairmen: sedan chair carried on poles by two bearers, one before and one
    behind
tête de mouton: see note p. 161
pomatum: see note p. 162

this period to build up a lady's head rendered it impossible to dress the hair every day. Frequently the coiffure remained untouched and perfect for a week, a fortnight, or even more. One indulgent writer indeed observes: " I consent, also, to the present fashion of curling the hair, so that it may stand a month without combing; though I must confess that I think three weeks, or a fortnight, might be a sufficient time. But I bar every application to those foreign artists, who advertise that they have the secret of making up a lady's head for a quarter of a year."

The gowns still continued short, and very low round the bosom and shoulders, and many writers affirm that a lady's dress was so scanty that modesty was almost banished. Hoops maintained their place; the waist was pinched in so as to be very long and slim, and laced up in front like a bodice; the sleeves were generally tight to the elbow, terminating with deep lace ruffles; the robe was ornamented with a flounce, which helped to swell out its dimensions; and an open dress was worn over it, with a train, and deep trimming of lace, or *bouffans ;* a little ornamented apron frequently finished the attire.

Hoops now reappeared, and, as if to make up for their banishment, swelled out to an immense size both to the right and left. Indeed they flourished greatly throughout the reign of George III., and were not finally banished till George IV. ascended the throne, when, with his usual good taste in every thing relating to the toilette, that monarch declared them to be cumbersome and inelegant. The opinion of so good a judge sealed their death-warrant, and the hoop disappeared, never, we may hope, to return,

bouffans: bouffant, a puffed out, full, flaring flounce
George III: 1760–1820
George IV: 1820–1830 (the Prince Regent)

at least among the British fair; though *anti-hoopists* have had cause to tremble lately, lest it should resume its place in the wardrobe of modern fashionables; for a certain *crénoline*, or horse-hair jupe, has recently astonished the world by its marked resemblance to its ancestor of famous memory.

Speaking of the *French night-cap*, a writer of the year 1762 remarks: "Our fine women have, by covering their cheeks, by this fashion put their faces into an eclipse. Each lady, when dressed in this mode, can only peep under the lace border. Perhaps they are intended, like blinds to a horse's harness, to teach ladies to look forward. It has been whispered, indeed, that this mode is an introduction to Popery; it is to bring in the veil by and by; a sort of trial to see how our English toasts will take it."

"The Ranelagh Mob is a piece of gauze mignonette, catgut, or Leicester web, which is clouted about the head, then crossed under the chin, and brought back to fasten behind, the two ends hanging down like a pair of pigeon's tails.

"The Mary Queen of Scots Cap is edged down the face with French beads; very becoming to some complexions, but as the cap is made of black gauze, and saves washing, it has too much housewifery in it to be immense taste.

"The Fly Cap is fixed upon the forehead, forming the figure of an overgrown butterfly, resting upon its head, with outstretched wings. It is much worn at present; not that it adds either to the colour or outline of the face, but as their caps are edged with garnets, topazes, or brilliants, they are very sparkling.

* * * * It is become a very interesting dispute among connoisseurs in general, whether the present turban roll, now worn round the Mecklenbourg caps, was taken from the Egyptian fillet, the Persian tiara, or the wreath round the elder Fautina's temples."

The following are some of the head-dresses of the middle of the eighteenth century :—

Ladies' Head-Dresses of the
mid-18th Century

Chapter 12 – England, 18th and 19th Centuries

THE TOILETTE IN ENGLAND.

CHAPTER XII.

THE long reign of George III. was celebrated in the annals of fashion. Hats were of every shape and size. The present round hat appeared after the French Revolution, when the three-cornered one entirely disappeared; after it came the chapeau bras and the opera-hat.

A writer of the early part of this reign is very severe upon the gentlemen for their love of adorning themselves; indeed, he attacks their costume and its appendages as poignantly as he does that of women: "The ladies," he says, "have long been severely rallied on their too great attention to finery; but, to own the truth, dress seems at present to be as much the study of the male part of the world as the female. We have gentlemen, who 'will lay a whole night (as Benedict says) carving the fashion of a new doublet.' They have their toilettes, too, as well as the ladies, set out with washes, perfumes, and cosmetics; and

George III: 1760–1820
French Revolution: began in 1789
chapeau bras: small, three-cornered flat silk hat
opera hat: man's tall, collapsible hat, a folding top hat
Benedict: a poet included in "The British Album", 1790

will spend the whole morning in scenting their linen, dressing their hair, and arching their eyebrows. Their heads (as well as the ladies') have undergone various mutations, and have worn as many different kinds of wigs as the block at the barber's. About fifty years ago they buried their heads in a bush of hair, and the beaux, as Swift says, 'lay hid beneath the penthouse of a full-bottomed perriwig.' But, as they then shewed nothing but the nose, mouth, and eyes, the fine gentlemen of our time not only oblige us with their full faces, but have drawn back the side curls quite to the tip of the ear.

From the same writer we find that gentlemen did not disdain the use of paint! "This fashion is not confined to the ladies," says another : " I am ashamed to tell you that we are indebted to Spanish wool for many of our masculine ruddy complexions. A pretty fellow lacquers his pale face with as many varnishes as a fine lady." Again: " Many of my readers will, I dare say, be hardly persuaded that this custom could have ever prevailed as a branch of male foppery; but it is too notorious that our fine gentlemen, in various other instances besides the article of paint, affect the softness and delicacy of the fair sex. The male beauty has his washes, perfumes, and cosmetics, and takes as much pains to set a gloss on his complexion as the footman in japanning his shoes. He has his dressing-room, and, (which is still more ridiculous), his toilet too."

If the hats changed after the French Revolution, the wigs felt its effects no less severely. Till about the year 1750, they became gradually smaller and

Swift: Jonathan Swift, 1667–1745
French Revolution: began in 1789

smaller; but what they lost in curls was made up by an immense bag hanging on the shoulders. Gradually that, too, dwindled down to a pigtail.

Great alterations, also, were perceived in the shape of the coats. The skirts no longer rivalled the hoop, from having their skirts stiffened with whalebone; they now assumed a modern form, and the waists were much shorter. Every colour was used for these garments—for gentlemen did not then, as at present, appear in black, dark blue, brown, or green coats; on the contrary, the *petit-maîtres* of the eighteenth century seemed to delight in every brilliant tint and shade, from the brightest scarlet to the most dazzling cerulean blue, rendered still more splendid by bindings of gold and silver lace. Cloth was the material most generally worn, but velvet was also often seen.

The waistcoats were no less brilliant than the coats. They were very long and had deep pockets, and were usually covered with embroidery and buttons. These latter ornaments to a gentleman's attire in this reign attained such a size, that they and the buckles were at last laughed out of fashion.

The nether garments, of silk, cloth, or velvet, assumed the shape of breeches, and were fastened below the knees; the stocking was gartered underneath them. Shoes were long in the quarters, broad at the toes, and had immense buckles.

After the lace tie came the white stock. This was succeeded by a muslin cravat, and shortly afterwards a shirt-collar appeared.

Subsequently coats with tails, frock-coats, short waistcoats, trousers, pantaloons, and round beaver

petit-maîtres: dandies

hats, with narrow turned-up brims, have been introduced, and have quietly maintained their place for many years with comparatively little change. Indeed, the present century is by no means so celebrated for the vagaries of fashion as most of its predecessors, at least as far as regards the costume of the gentlemen.

The following lines describe certain varieties of dress worn by the ladies in the year 1766 :—

> " Painted lawns and chequer'd shades,
> Crape that's worn by love-lorn maids,
> Watered tabbies, flowered brocades ;
> Vilets, pinks, Italian posies,
> Myrtles, jessamines, and roses ;
> Aprons, caps, and kerchiefs clean,
> Straw-built hats, and bonnets green ;
> Catgut gauzes, tippets, ruffs,
> Fans and hoods, and feathered muffs ;
> Stomachers, and Paris nets,
> Ear-rings, necklaces, aigrets,
> Rings and blondes, and mignionetts."

Ladies now wore wigs like the gentlemen, and frequently added a club, or *chignon*, behind, in imitation, probably, of the *toupées* of the other sex. Caps of every kind were also seen; some towering high in air, some equally low; some sloping down to the nose, others standing straight upwards. Mountains of lawn, muslin, net, lace, gauze, riband, flowers, and wire, assisted in composing these structures, many of which really deserved the censures of critics quite as much as those of former years.

In addition to these enormous coiffures, the fair ladies very often placed on the top of them a gipsy bonnet, surrounded with numerous bows and streamers.

blondes: blonde lace, a type of lace with a very fine réseau, or ground, of silk,
    usually worn in summer and usually, though not invariably, white or cream colored
mignionetts: mignionette, a light, fine lace
toupées: false hair or wig
gipsy bonnet: one with large side flaps

A few years later a coiffure, which certainly rivalled the commode, was very fashionable, and, in spite of caricaturists and abuse, continued so for many years. It was a perfect mountain of curls, powder, pomatum, flowers, feathers, blonde, and riband, rising one above another.

After this came the corkscrew curls, adding by their long twisted form to the ludicrous effect of the *Alps*, which towered high in air on the foreheads of our ancestors.

A work published in 1776 mentions that a parroquet, its wings and tail extended, was very often perched on the top of the powdered edifice. This rivalled the coiffures of the Chinese ladies, and their favourite head-dress of the fongwang.

Powder remained the fashion till the year 1794. After it disappeared the hair was worn in curls, which were sometimes short, at others long and straggling, falling completely over the face, so that the bright orbs beneath could with difficulty peep out from the ringlets which almost entirely concealed them.

Coiffures of 1766

pomatum: pomade, see note p. 162
blonde: blonde lace, see note p. 170

Then came the crop, that frightful coiffure, which no beauty, however youthful and graceful, could wear with impunity. Often a narrow band surrounded the head, and perhaps a rose was placed upon the forehead, or an immense feather stood up like the *panache* in a soldier's helmet, as seen in the foregoing cut.

Bonnets were equally remarkable, as will be seen by the accompanying specimens : —

 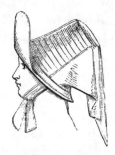

Remarkable Styles of Bonnet

After long waists had been worn for some years, extremely short ones appeared, and the petticoats of the gowns were tucked up behind, like those of many peasants of the present day. Sacques, negligées, and the far-famed great-coat, now came into fashion. The latter is celebrated for having been a favourite dress of Queen Charlotte; and Madame D'Arblay has immortalized it by the following lines, in which she alludes to her majesty's predilection for it :—

> " The garb of state she inly scorn'd,
>   Glad from its trappings to be freed;
> She saw thee humble, unadorn'd,
>   Quick of attire, a child of speed."

A little later the fashionable costume is thus described by a modern female writer: "Ladies wore cloth pelisses, formed like a man's coat, with a velvet

panache: plume; the foregoing cut referred to is at the bottom of p. 171
Queen Charlotte: 1761-1818
Madame D'Arblay: Fanny Burney, novelist, 1752-1840

collar; a round black beaver hat, silk cravat, and boots with high military heels, a sprigged black lace veil, the trousers, which peeped below the short petticoat, alone shewing the weaker sex. The driving dress usually was a box-coat and cape, a round white beaver hat, lined with green muslin, a cravat, and Hessian boots; the costume beneath the coat consisted of a cambric dress sitting close to the form, sometimes even without any plait in the skirt, and gored in such a manner as to disclose the shape of the limbs. The robe was sometimes even damped to make it sit closer. The lighter the clothing, the more fashionable."

The bust was at this period frequently enrolled in a white satin spencer. The petticoats were frightfully scanty, the shoes elaborately sandaled, the stockings of thick silk, and the pocket handkerchief had a good sempstress hem, subject to no other ornament than its neat red mark in the corner.

The Swiss petticoat and white chemisette body, was our first launch into French fashions at the early part of the present century. The writings, songs, and caricatures of the day, took up the strangeness of the attire—strange even to ourselves, much more so, probably, to the people we sought to imitate, for the very materials of Parisian apparel were then new to us. We had never seen *tulle;* we were ignorant of *satin rouleaux;* a transparent standing-up French *toque* was a thing unheard-of; neither had we seen such short waists, or the dresses open behind and in front to the very waist.

The hair was now dressed *à la Chinoise;* the broad plait surmounting the head forming a sort of basket,

Hessian boot: kind of high boot with tassels in front at the top
tulle: fine-meshed net
satin rouleaux: rolls or folds of ribbon used as piping or attached in decorative
   patterns
toque: small, close-fitting, brimless hat

which held a profusion of roses. The forehead was quite uncovered, the hair being strained up from it; and at the side fell the long distinct ringlet, emulated in length by the gold ear-ring that hung pendent beside it. Never had we seen such a head as this; we looked like so many cropped schoolboys.

The dress was equally new. A clear silk net over white satin, made very short both in the skirt and the waist, and trimmed round the petticoat with *satin rouleaux*. The morning dress of one of the first French ladies who made her appearance in England at the termination of the war, is described as having been formed of a plain English gingham, instead of silk or satin, with a beautifully worked chemisette; her hair *à la Chinoise*, without other ornament than a large Leghorn hat.

No sooner did French modes once more reach our shores than they were instantly seized upon, and the dress of the British fair changed like magic! Toques, berets, tunics, manteaux, chapeaux, bonnets, every article of attire that a French *modiste* touched with her fairy fingers, was bought with avidity. Then appeared bonnets whose shape we cannot better describe than by borrowing the words of Moore:

> "That build of bonnet, whose extent
> Should, like a doctrine of dissent,
> Puzzle church-doors to let it in—
> Nor half had reached the pitch sublime,
> To which true *toques* and berets climb;
> Leaving, like lofty Alps that throw
> O'er minor Alps their shadowy sway,
> Earth's humbler bonnets far below,
> To poke through life their fameless way."

satin rouleaux: see note p. 173
Leghorn hat: hat of fine, plaited straw; the area of Livorno, Italy (called Leghorn in English), was famous for its straw hat manufacture
Moore: Thomas Moore, 1779–1852, a fashionable Irish poet often quoted by Lady Wilton because of the Oriental scenes depicted in his work

From this period English costume is so familiar to our readers as to render any description of it quite unnecessary.

Fashionable Bonnet

THE TOILETTE IN SCOTLAND.

CHAPTER XIII.

A Highlander

N all the early annals of the Scotch, it is stated that they were a rude and hardy race of men; that they loved war; and were for the most part nearly destitute of clothing. Afterwards we find that they adopted the skins of beasts. Pitscottie, in his "Chronicles of Scotland," speaking of the ancient style of dress, says: "They be cloathed with ane mantle, with ane shirt, fachioned after the Irish manner, going bare-legged to the knie."

The author of a work on Scotland, published in 1603, writes thus: "They (the Highlanders) delight much

Piscottie: Robert Lindsay of Piscottie, 1500–1565

in marbled cloths, especially that have long stripes of sundry colours; they love chiefly purple and blue; their predecessors used short mantles, or plaids of divers colours, sundrie ways divided, and among some the same custome is observed to this day; but for the most part now they are brown, most near to the colour of the hadder, to the effect when they lye among the hadders, the bright colours of their plaids shall not bewray them, with the which, rather coloured than clad, they suffer the most cruel tempests that blow in the open fields, in such sort, that in a night of snow they sleep sound."

Pinkerton, speaking of the dress of this people, says: "The *kilt* is not ancient, but singular, and adapted to their savage life." He also adds, "that it was unknown among the Welsh and Irish, but that it was the dress of the Saxons who could not afford breeches."

The Highlander's dress consisted of the *breacon-feile*, simply a chequered covering; in original form now almost entirely in disuse. It was a plain piece of tartan, about six yards long and two yards wide. This plaid, or kilt as it was called, was so arranged that it surrounded the waist in folds, and was held firm by a leathern belt, in such a manner that the lower part fell to the middle of the knee, and then, while the plaid was in folds behind, it was doubled in front. The upper part was fastened on the left shoulder with a large brooch, or pin, so as to give it the most graceful appearance possible, and the two ends were allowed to hang down; frequently, however, that on the right side, as it was much the longest, was permitted to be tucked under the belt.

hadder: heather
Pinkerton: John Pinkerton, 1758–1826, historian and antiquarian; wrote "An Enquiry
    into the History of Scotland preceding the reign of Malcolm III, or the year 1056"
    in 1789

Thus the right arm was uncovered, except in cold weather, when the plaid being thrown loosely on, it covered all the body.

Although this plaid was peculiar to the Highlanders, it was, till the end of the last century, frequently worn by the Lowlanders also. As, of course, it had no pockets, a purse, of goat's or badger's skin, or of leather, supplied their place; it was called a *sporan*, and people of rank and wealth had it ornamented in the most gaudy manner, with a silver mouth-piece, tassels, and silver fastenings.

Formerly the Highlanders wore on their feet a piece of untanned hide, cut to the shape and size of the foot, and held fast by leathern thongs. This fashion still continues in the Shetland Isles; and to this day the Scotch dislike any covering on their feet so much, that they always go barefooted when not ashamed of being seen; and an author who wrote a century ago affirms, that he visited a well-educated laird in the north, who wore neither shoes nor stockings. At a still later period, respectable people of both sexes might be seen walking to church barefooted, carrying their shoes and stockings in a bundle; when they arrived at or near the churchyard, they quietly sat down, put them on, and, when the service was over, took them off again, and walked home without them. The stockings, generally of the same pattern as the plaid, were formerly not knitted, but cut out of the web, a custom which still prevails in some of the Highland regiments. The garters worn by the men were of rich patterns, very broad, and often ornamented with tassels.

The buskins formerely worn by the Highlanders

were of undressed deer's hide, which, as the hair was worn outwards, procured for them the title of *red-shanks ;* but the present brogue is made of untanned leather, with holes to admit and let out the water. Thus we read:

> " Speed, Malise, speed ! the dun deer's hide
>   On fleeter foot was never tied."

To finish the national costume, we must mention the bonnet, generally of blue cloth, of a round, flat shape, sometimes ornamented with an eagle's feather. A dirk, a knife and fork, a spoon, and a pair of pistols, were essential accompaniments to this garb, which, however, differed according to the rank of the wearer.

The short coat and waistcoat, which formed the dress of the wealthy, was adorned with silver buttons, tassels, embroidery, and lace, according to the fashion of the day; and it is remarked by General Stewart, that silver buttons frequently came to them from an inheritance of long descent. The reason they gave for wearing buttons of such massive silver was, that if the wearer died in battle, or at a distance from his home, their value would defray the expense of a handsome funeral.

For a great many years shirts were unknown among this people; and it is an old saying among them, that shirts and rheumatism came together.

It is asserted by many authors, that of all national garbs there is not one that can be compared to the Highland costume for beauty and gracefulness. Certainly in these peaceful times its utility may be ques-

dirk: dagger
General Stewart: John Stewart, 1749–1822, known as "the Walking Stewart"

tioned; but at the time when it was used it would have been impossible to invent a more suitable one for activity and freedom of limb, although the old ballad, on the "Battle of the Bridge of Dee," does say:

> "The Highlandmen are pretty men
> For target and claymore;
> But yet they are but naked men,
> To face the cannon's roar."

The antiquity of the tartan is supposed to be very great. It is dyed, and the colours arranged with the greatest nicety, so as to preserve the patterns, or *sets*, as they are called, each of which represents a different clan, tribe, family, or district. Thus a Stuart, a Macdonald, a Campbell, &c. &c., was known by the colour and pattern of his plaid; and the Athole, Glenorchy, and other colours of different districts, were easily distinguished. These plaids are now made of the finest wool, and form dresses of the most beautiful texture, being soft, light, and very warm.

It is said that there were formerly different modes of wearing the plaid: one when on a peaceful journey, another when danger was apprehended; one way of enveloping themselves in it for repose, and another which enabled the wearer to start up, sword in hand, ready for the conflict, like the warriors of Roderick Dhu:

> "Instant, through copse and heath, arose
> Bonnets, and spears, and bended bows;
> On right, on left, above, below,
> Sprung up at once the lurking foe:
> From shingles grey their lances start,
> The bracken bush sends forth the dart,

"Battle of the Bridge of Dee": 19 June 1639
Roderick Dhu: 'Black Roderick' in Sir Walter Scott's "Lady of the Lake", who was defeated by James V of Scotland (1513-1542)

The rushes and the willow wand
Are bristling into axe and brand,
And every tuft of broom gives life
To plaided warrior armed for strife."

The dress of the Highland women was no less characteristic than that of the men. Until they married they always wore a riband, or, as it was called, a *snood*, with which alone they were allowed to ornament their hair; after they married they exchanged the snood for a *curch*, *toy*, or coif of linen, tied under the chin. Martin, in his observations on their dress, says: "The women wore sleeves of scarlet cloth, closed at the end as men's vests, with gold lace round them, having plate buttons set with fine stones. The head-dress was a kerchief of fine linen, strait about the head. The plaid was tied before on the breast, with a buckle of silver, or brass, according to the quality of the person. I have seen some of the former, of one hundred merks value, the whole curiously engraved with various animals. There was a lesser buckle, which was worn in the middle of the larger; it had in the centre a large piece of crystal, or some fine stone, of a lesser size."

A Highland Lady

Pennant, in his Tour through Scotland, about the year 1769, remarks that, " the Highland women drew the *tonnag*, or plaid, over their heads in bad weather, or during the church service ;" though by an edict made

Martin: Martin Martin, died 1719
Pennant: Thomas Penant, 1726–1798

by James II., in 1457, this habit of concealing the face, either at kirk or at market, was expressly prohibited. From a passage in the same statute, it appears that about that time Scotch head-dresses had risen to the height fashionable in other countries, for the edict goes on to say: " The wives and daughters are to wear on their heads little curchs with hoods; and as to their gowns, no woman is to wear fur of Martin skin, or lace, or *tails* of an unfit length, or furred, except on a holyday."

The snood, plaid, and brooch, were formerly worn by all women, whether of high or low degree. The material used by the higher orders, instead of wool, was silk or satin, and the brooch of a more precious metal than those worn by the lower classes. Thus we find in the beautiful description of Ellen:—

" A chieftain's daughter seem'd the maid ;
Her satin snood, her silken plaid,
Her golden brooch, such birth betray'd."

The plaid was formerly worn hanging from the neck nearly to the feet; it was tied round the waist, and was usually white, with stripes of red, black, or blue. The snood formed the only difference in dress between the matron and the young maiden; for bonnets were quite unknown among the Highland women, and a veil, though worn by women of almost every other nation, appears never to have made part of their costume.

The higher classes, in the sixteenth century, seem to have followed the English fashions. Sir Walter Scott, aware of this fact, in the " Lay of the Last

James II: 1437–1460
kirk: church
Sir Walter Scott: 1771–1832

Minstrel," describes Margaret as wearing the following dress :—

> " Of sable velvet her array ;
>   And on her head a crimson hood,
> With pearls embroidered and entwined ;
> Guarded with gold, with ermine lined,
> A merlin sat upon her wrist,
> Held by a leash of silken twist."

And, before the battle of Flodden, represents King James in the following splendid attire :—

> " An easy task it was, I trow,
>   King James's manly form to know,
>   Although, his courtesy to show,
>   He doffed, to Marmion bending low,
>   His broidered cap and plume.
>   For royal were his garb and mien,
>   His cloak, of crimson velvet piled,
>   Trimmed with the fur of marten wild ;
>   His vest, of changeful satin sheen,
>   The dazzled eye beguiled ;
>   His gorgeous collar hung adown,
>   Wrought with the badge of Scotland's crown,
>   The thistle brave, of old renown ;
>   His trusty blade, Toledo right,
>   Descended from a baldric bright ;
>   White were his buskins, on the heel
>   His spurs inlaid of gold and steel ;
>   His bonnet, all of crimson fair,
>   Was buttoned with a ruby rare."

In the same poem occurs the description of the Scottish soldiers and their chiefs, giving their Highland dress as then worn :—

> " Just then the chiefs their tribes arrayed,
>   And wild and garish semblance made,

"Lay of the Last Minstrel": published 1805
Battle of Flodden: 1513
King James: James IV, 1488–1513
Marmion: fictitious character, supposedly a favorite of Henry VIII

The chequered trews, and belted plaid,
And varying notes the war-pipes brayed
　　To every varying clan;
Wild through their red, or sable hair,
Looked out their eyes, with savage stare,
　　On Marmion as he passed;
Their legs above the knee were bare;
Their frame was sinewy, short, and spare,
　　And hardened to the blast;
Of taller race, the chiefs they own
Were by the eagle's plumage known.
The hunted red deer's undressed hide
Their hairy buskins well supplied;
The graceful bonnet decked their head;
Back from their shoulders hung the plaid."

The dress of the unfortunate Mary queen of Scots is thus described in a letter to Lord Burghley: " Hir borrowed haire borne hir attire on hir head, was on this manner: she had a dressing of lawne, edged with bone lace; a pomander chaine, with an Agnus Dei about the neck; a crucifix in her hand; a payer of beads at her girdle, with a goulding crosse at the end of it; a vaile of lawne fastened to her carole, with a bowed out wire, and edged round about with a bone lace; hir gowne of black sattin prynted, with a trayne and long sleffes to the gownd, set with a range of buttons, of jett trimed with pearle, and short sleffes of purple velvet hole under them; her kirtle hole of figured sattin black; her pettycote upper body, unlaced in the back, of crymsen satten; her pettycote scirtes of crymson velvett; hir shooes of Spanysh lether, with the rough side outward; a payer of green silk garters; her nether stockings worsted coloured water set, clocked with silver; and next her legg a payer of Jarsey hose whit."

Marmion: see note p. 183
Mary, Queen of Scots: reigned 1542–1567, executed 1587
Lord Burghley: William Cecil, 1st Baron Burghley, 1520–1598

The attachment of the Highlanders to their national costume rendered it a bond of union, often dangerous to the government, and many efforts were made by the legislature after the rebellion in 1715, to disarm and oblige them to conform to Lowland dresses. Shoe-buckles were unknown among them till within the last 150 years; neckcloths, also, have only latterly been adopted, and they still retain a great affection for the ancient attire of their country.

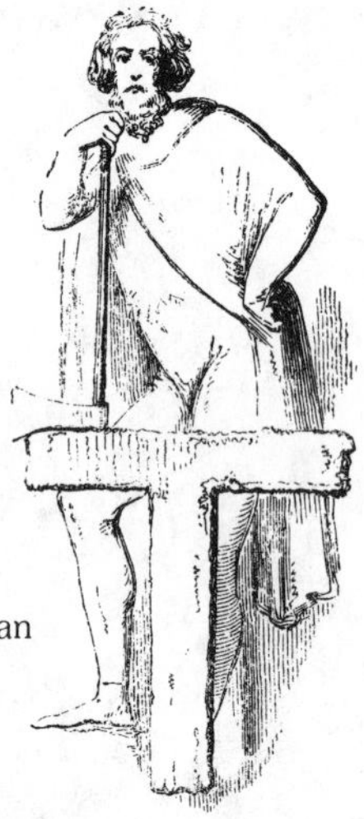

Ancient Dress of an Irish man

THE

TOILETTE IN IRELAND.

CHAPTER XIV.

HE ancient dress of the Irish appears to be but little known till the twelfth century, when it is said to have been much the same as that worn by the southern Britons. After the garments of skins were discarded, the Irish adopted breeches, a cota, and a mantle, fastened, as usual, with a brooch or bodkin. Armillæ and torques were favourite ornaments among them. Giraldus Cambriensis says of the Irish in the twelfth century: "They wear their woollen clothes mostly black, because the sheep in Ireland are in general of that colour; the dress itself is of a barbarous fashion. They

Giraldus Cambriensis: Gerald of Cambridge, scholar-monk, circa 1146–1220, wrote "Topographica Hibernica" in 1186

wear moderate close-hooded or cowled mantles, which spread over their shoulders and reach down to the elbow, composed of small pieces of cloth, of different kinds and colours, for the most part sewed together ; beneath which they have woollen *phalinges*, instead of a cloak, or breeches and stockings in one piece, and these generally dyed of some colour."

Man's Costume in the 12th Century

The mantle and brogues are two well known parts of an Irish costume. Froissart, in Richard the Second's reign, mentions the four Irish kings who swore allegiance to that monarch, and says that linen drawers were ordered to be made for them, and houpelands of silk, trimmed with miniver and gris. " For," adds the chronicler, " formerly these Irish kings were thought to be well dressed if wrapped up in an Irish mantle." The dress of the females up to this time is but little known, but it is supposed that they wore mantles, bodkins in their hair, and various ornaments of jewels ; they are said to have been very partial to long hair, and allowed it to grow lank and rough and to fall over their ears.

Fine cloth, silks, and cloth of gold, it is said, were worn by the higher ranks in the sixteenth century, and worsted and canvas materials by the lower orders. In the reign of Henry the Eighth an act was passed to prevent the Irish wearing clothes dyed of their favourite

phalinges: breeches and stockings all in one
brogue: a rude shoe of untanned hide
Froissart: Jean Froissart, chronicler, 1337–1410
houpeland: robe, worn tucked up under a belt
miniver: white ermine, fur used for lining and trim
gris: a kind of grey fur, generally squirrel
Henry the Eighth: 1509–1547

colour, saffron ; the number of yards also allowed for
their garments is specified, and women are ordered
not to wear dresses of the Irish fashion. This edict
leads us to suppose that they had a form and shape
for their garments peculiar to themselves. The yellow,
or saffron colour, is often mentioned as being a very
favourite hue, and one which they usually employed in
dyeing their habits.

Spenser greatly censured the ancient Irish dress.
He considered the cloak " a fit house for an outlaw,
a meet bed for a rebel, and an apt cloke for a thief."
He also strongly objects to the custom of women
wearing mantles, and mentions several articles of their
dress : " a linen roll which they sometimes wear upon
their heads, a thick linen shirt, a long-sleeved smock,
a half-sleeved coat, and silken fillet." And Camden
informs us that when in Queen Elizabeth's reign the
Prince of Ulster came to the English court, with his
attendants, they all wore " their hair flowing in long
locks upon their shoulders, and had shirts dyed with
saffron ; their sleeves were large, their tunics short,
and their mantles jagged."

A writer of the reign of James I. says :—
" Touching the mean or wild Irish, it may be truly
said of them, which of old was spoken of the Germans,—namely, that they wander slovenly and naked.
The gentlemen, or lords of counties, wear close
breeches and stockings, of the same piece of cloth,
of red, or such light colour, and a loose coat, and a
cloak, or a three-cornered mantle, of coarse light
stuff, made at home, and their linen is coarse ; and,"
adds the writer, " their shirts, before the last rebellion, were made of twenty or thirty ells, folded in

Spenser: Edmond Spenser, poet and author of "The Faery Queen", circa 1552–1599
Camden: William Camden, 1551–1623
Queen Elizabeth: Elizabeth I, 1558–1603
Prince of Ulster: Shane O'Neal, Prince of Ulster, went to the Court of Queen
    Elizabeth in 1562
James I: James VI & I, 1603–1625
ells: the English ell was 45 inches

wrinkles, and coloured with saffron. * * * The women," he goes on to say, "living among the English, wear linen, a gown, and a mantle, and cover their heads in the Turkish fashion, with many ells of linen, only the Turkish turban is more round at the top, while that worn by the Irish is flatter and broader." Speed also speaks of wide-sleeved linen shirts, stained yellow, the mantles, and the skeins, and says:—

"The women wore their hair plaited in a curious manner, hanging down their backs and shoulders, from under the folden wreaths of fine linen rolled about their heads."

From the time of Charles II. the gentlemen in Ireland are said to have gradually abandoned the national costume, and to have adopted the English fashions. The lower orders, however, retained their dress to a much later period, and even now the brogues and mantles are constantly seen, and still oftener the feet unencumbered with shoes or stockings.

Female of the Lower Class

ells: English ell was a length of 45 inches
Speed: John Speed, antiquarian and cartographer, 1552–1629, wrote "A History of Great
    Britain" in 1611
Charles II: 1660–1685

THE

TOILETTE IN WALES.

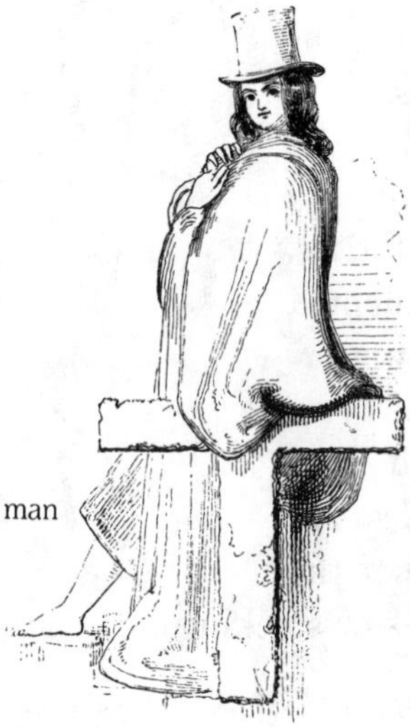

Ancient Dress of a Welsh man

CHAPTER XV.

HE ancient costume of Wales greatly resembled that of Ireland; cloaks or mantles were always worn, and the feet were generally naked. The Rev. W. Bingley, speaking of this country, says:—"The women wear long blue cloaks, that descend almost to the feet; they are seldom to be seen without them. In North Wales they all have hats similar to those of the men, and blue stockings, without any feet to them, which they keep down by a kind of loop, that is put round one of the toes. In the unfrequented parts they seldom wear any shoes except on Sundays."

Rev. W. Bingley: William Bingley, who wrote "North Wales" in 1804, and "Excursion in North Wales" in 1838

In Warrington's " History of Wales," we read that the ancient Welsh "had no expensive riches in their cloaths. The same garb that the people were used to wear in the day, served them also in the night; and this consisted of a thin mantle, and a garment or shirt worn next to the skin. They either went with their feet entirely bare, or they used boots of raw leather, instead of shoes, sewed together with raw skin."

Warrington: Rev. William Warrington's "History of Wales" appeared in 1786

THE TOILETTE IN FRANCE.

CHAPTER XVI.

O France is universally conceded the palm in the race of fashion ; and she is unwearied in her exertions to retain the distinction.

The dress of the ancient Gauls was, we are told, very simple, and, like that of most other European nations, consisted of skins, formed into a rude kind of tunic, and in winter a cloak of the same, fastened on one shoulder, and descending to the heel. Though these garments could not well fetter their movements when they went to battle, still we find that, either for lightness or bravado, when in the presence of an enemy, the Gauls divested themselves of all covering as far as the waist. On the head they usually wore a skin cap, of a very primitive shape: and even these few garments were simple in form and coarse in texture. The dress of the women only differed from that of the men in having the tunic longer, and the cap shaped like a triangle.

But though habited in so simple a manner, the love of ornament which has characterised the French in later times, appears, even at the early period of which we speak, to have been remarkable. They covered themselves with chains, rings, necklaces, and bracelets. In the " Æneis," we read :—

" The approaching Gauls,
Obscure in night, ascend and seize the walls.
The gold, dissembled well their golden hair :
And golden chains on their white necks they wear."

There are still extant many monuments of the Gauls ; one of the most ancient was dug up in the cathedral church of Paris in 1711 ; it represents six figures, all dressed in tunics, with sleeves reaching to the wrist ; over this is worn a *saye*, which is exactly the same as the Roman *sagum*, whence its name, only it has sleeves. The heads of these figures are covered with caps, which bend forward much like the Phrygian bonnet. Considerable difference as to the lesser details of dress is frequently met with in these statues, and no doubt various fashions were employed, both for forming and ornamenting the habiliments of the Gauls, even though their attire is described as so simple. Long garments, adorned with a border of sable, ermine, or miniver, formed, during several ages, the dress of persons of distinction.

"Æneis": Virgil's "Æneid; Virgil lived circa 70-19 B.C.
sagum: Roman military cloak; the Gauls' cloaks were woollen
Phrygian bonnet: soft conical cap with the peak turned over in front, now identified
    with the cap of liberty (see illus. p. 387, top)

King Clovis
and
Queen Clothilde

Clovis and his successors for many generations wore a tunic, and a mantle resembling the Greek *chlamyde*. On the door of the church of St. Germain des Prés, are to be seen figures of most of the ancient French kings. There stands Clovis, and by his side Clotilde, his queen. The former has a long beard, moustaches, and short hair; his dress is a tunic and chlamyde, and his shoes are very *échancré*. Clotilde wears a crown, her tunic resembles the *côte-hardi* of later years; it fits tight to the shape as far as the throat, where it is confined by a broad band of jewels, another band encircles her waist, and a third forms the pointed shape of the *côte-hardi* to below the waist, where it seems joined to a petticoat with numerous folds. The girdle is ornamented with jewels, and from it hangs a long cord also ornamented with jewels. The chlamyde falls nearly to the ground, and a broad jewelled band encircles the waist.

Montfaucon in his " Mon. Fran." gives drawings of several old statues of Clovis, and other royal personages. He has copied two or three of the

Clovis: Clovis I, King of the Franks, circa 466–511
échancré: slashed
Clotilde: Queen Clotilde, circa 475–545
Montfaucon: Bernard de Montfaucon, 1655–1741; also wrote "Travels of Father Montfaucon from Paris through Italy (in the years 1698–1699–1700)" which was published 1712
"Mon. Fran.": "Monumens de la Monarchie Française", published 1767

most ancient from the cathedral of Chartres; they all have long hanging sleeves, an upper tunic, with a petti-coat underneath. The ladies' hair falls in long plaits, while that of the men is short, and they have neither beard nor moustache. Several others are given from the abbey of St. Denis. It is supposed they were executed about the time of Clovis, but the dress is much changed from the description we have given above. One of the kings (said to be Clovis) has a long mantle reach-ing to his feet, falling back from his shoulders, and fastened in front; his tunic has tight sleeves, and is confined at the throat by a band of jewels and a brooch. Round his waist is a girdle, apparently of leather, from which is suspended an *escarcelle*. The tunic and mantle are jagged round the bottom. The shoes are very neat, and are open in front, with a latchet over the instep. Several other figures are represented with the tunic and chlamyde.

For many years the same dress appears to have been worn by the ancient French. The first change in the costume which we meet with is visible in two statues of Charlemagne, copied by Montfaucon. The first has moustaches, but neither beard nor whiskers, a very short tunic, that does not reach to the knees, and a chlamyde, fastened on the right shoulder, and ornamented with a broad border; the legs are wrapped with fillets, bound crosswise, called *lingettes*. The other statue is habited in a garment that very much resembles a modern surtout. It has large wide sleeves, with deep cuffs, turned back, and a square collar. But the most remarkable part of this dress is that it is trimmed down the front with large round buttons. This is very extraordinary, as buttons are supposed to

escarcelle: small purse or pouch worn, by men, hanging from the belt
Charlemagne: Charles the Great, Charles I of France, 768–814
lingettes: linen tapes, flat; used for lacing and binding stockings

have been unknown in these early days, and are not seen on any other statues of the same period.

There is a portrait of Charles the Bald, in which that monarch is dressed in a blue tunic, embroidered in gold, a purple chlamyde, adorned with jewels, and a red cap under the crown. By his side is his wife, habited in a red tunic, ornamented with a gold band; her hair is concealed under a large blue veil, that falls upon the back and shoulders, but leaves the face exposed.

The two attendants have the short tunic and chlamyde, and their heads are bare. On a statue of the same king we find a shoe which is very curious, being barred in a lozenge pattern.

Shoe of Charles the Bald

The French appear from the earliest ages to have understood the art of shoemaking, for as soon as shoes were worn their shape was very good, at least those we perceive on the statues of the men; the women's long tunics completely conceal their feet.

Girdles also appear to have been generally worn: those of the women were richly ornamented, and had long ends falling to the feet.

Cuff of the Countess de Dreux

The dress of the French continued much as we have described it for many years. The first novelty that we meet with in head-dresses is the capuchon of Charles le Bon, which has no cape, and the tippet is bound tight like a cord, and twisted round the head. The hanging cuff which appears in the reign

Capuchon of Charles le Bon

Charles the Bald: Charles II, 840–877
his wife: he married Ermentrude d'Orléans (died 869), then Richilde de Lorraine
Charles le Bon: Charles the Good, Count of Flanders, circa 1083–1127

of Louis VII. continued in fashion for many years. The Comtesse de Dreux, from a portrait of whom we have copied it, wears a robe like a chemise, and a hood. Veils were much worn at this time, and were called *couvrechefs*.

In the same reign the fashion of emblazoning the robes was first invented. Louis appears in a tunic and mantle, covered with fleur-de-lis. Geoffrey Comte de Maine is strangely habited. His cap resembles the Phrygian bonnet, the point being bent forwards ; he wears an embroidered tunic, with tight sleeves, and a vest which reaches to the knees, confined at the waist by a broad girdle. The mantle is splendid, and lined with vair.

In the illuminations of the reign of St. Louis, his sons appear in variously shaped habits. This gives reason to suppose that Fashion was now beginning to exert her power. Prince John has hanging sleeves over the tight ones of his tunic, and he holds a glove in his hand. Another of the princes has a cap upon his head, and wears a garment like a surtout, laid back in front so as to shew the vest underneath. A third appears in a hat of quite a modern form, and his emblazoned robe is trimmed round the bottom with a deep fringe.

The costume of the daughters of this king also presents various novelties in form and shape. The robes are so immensely long all round, that they lie in large folds at their feet. Under sleeves, tight to the wrist, are seen, with wider ones over them. The capuchons have more the shape

Costume of a Princess

Louis VII: 1137–1180
couvrechefs: literally, cover heads; kerchiefs
Maine: ancient province of France, bordering on Brittany, Normandy and Anjou
St. Louis: Louis IX of France, 1226–1270
Prince John: John Tristan, Count of Valois, 1250–1270, a son of Louis IX

of caps, being confined by a narrow band across the forehead, and a *côte-hardi* of ermine is first seen. The shoes of both men and women are excessively pointed at this period.

St. Louis himself is represented as habited in a tunic, which leaves his throat quite bare, and over it a super-totus, with long sleeves, trimmed with fur. This upper robe is brown, embroidered with red flowers. The hair is quite short, the face closely shaven, and a red velvet cap is placed on the top of the head. In another picture his majesty has red stockings and black shoes; the sleeves of the furred robe hang to his knees, and have a slit down the front part, through which the arms, covered with tight sleeves, are passed. Across the shoulders is a deep cape of fur, gradually narrowing to the front, which is ornamented with fur, sewn on to resemble deep fringe.

Lady's Coiffure in the Reign of Philip the Bold

The coiffure of a lady in the reign of Philip the Bold is curious. Her capuchon is formed like a plate on the top of the head, and the veil, as usual, falls in folds over the cheeks and back. Wimples, which were wrapped round the head and throat, were much worn; and in this reign a gorget, or *cheve-sail*, first appears. Women of the middle and lower classes now wore grey shoes, whence it is said is derived the word *grisette*. Some authors assert that the pointed caps came into fashion in this reign, but Montfaucon does not mention them for some years later.

The ladies continued to wear their long shapeless

St. Louis: Louis IX of France, 1226–1270
Philip the Bold: Philip III, 1270–1285
grisette: working girl in the fashion trade, a seamstress, embroiderer, etc.
Montfaucon: Bernard de Montfaucon, 1655–1741

garments, pendent sleeves, hoods, and gorgets, through this reign. The only exception is that of a lady, who astonishes us with a small waist and a kind of pointed tippet, the ends of which fall much below the waist. The cuffs of the under sleeves are now frequently ornamented with buttons, and the long cuffs, instead of hanging from the wrist as before described, are made like a long narrow bag, slit open from the elbow to the shoulder, where they are fastened into the robe; the arm passes through the opening, and the rest of the sleeve falls to the ground, and even trails upon it. The frightful gorgets concealed every thing but the eyes, nose, and mouth, and the hood fell over them. The men still wore long or short tunics, capuchons, and shoes, tied across the instep; the face was shaven, and the hair fell scarcely as low as the ears.

The capuchon of Jeanne, Comtesse de Champagne, is remarkable for its form, being pointed in front, with a jewel hanging upon the forehead. Instead of enveloping the face so as to conceal the hair, the ends merely hang down behind, and curls are seen beneath the folds.

Capuchon of Jeanne, Comtesse de Champagne

In the reign of Philip of Valois, we find the dress much altered. The men appear in chaussées and doublets,—some with long, some with very short skirts, scarcely reaching below the waist. The sleeves are generally rather larger, the shoes very pointed, and the hats much like those now worn. Red, blue, and green, were the prevailing colours for the garments. A curious appendage to the hats is a long piece of black stuff, which is fastened to one side of the hat, the other end being

Jeanne, Comtesse de Champagne: Jeanne of Navarre, who married Philip IV in 1286 and
    died in 1305
Philip of Valois: Philip VI, 1328–1350
chaussées: chausses, stockings

thrown over the left shoulder. This band was frequently held in the hand, and the hat
was allowed to fall from the head
upon the back. The capuchons varied in shape and size according to
the taste of the wearer.

Fashionable Capuchon

The materials of which the dresses
were formed were splendid; silk,
velvet, cloth of gold, and cloth of
silver, with jewels of various kinds, were generally
worn by the noblesse; and in this respect the French
equalled, if they did not surpass, the English. The
hood of Philip of Valois rather more resembles a hat
than those usually seen. The coiffure of Jeanne de
Sancerre will not excite the admiration of
my fair readers; it completely envelopes
the head, joining the wimple, having a
sort of ears standing out, which give it
a very strange appearance.

Capuchon of Jeanne de Sancerre

Great extravagance in everything belonging to the toilette was very apparent
in France about the year 1357. Gold and silver glittered on the garments, and precious stones became
very costly, from the immense demand there was for
them. The *côte-hardi* was usually embroidered; the
under sleeves quite tight, and the upper ones long
and narrow. A feather is now for the first time seen
to grace the cap of a gentleman, and the taste in
bonnets, as they were called, was very various,—some
were pointed, some broad, some with brims, some
without; in short, the variety was quite endless.

About the year 1367 we first find the French
ladies allowing their hair to ornament their heads,

Philip of Valois: Philip VI, 1328–1350

without the addition of cap, bonnet, or hood. It was arranged in one large curl, or plait, on each side of the face, and only a small wreath of flowers or jewels interspersed with it.

Now, too, the trains of the gowns became very long, and they were held up by pages. The shape of the robe in other respects remained the same; but when Queen Isabella of Bavaria came to reign in France, great changes took place in the empire of fashion. Charles VI. and his court, prodigal as they are represented to have been in every thing relating to dress, were still far behind the splendid magnificence introduced by the new queen, of whom Brantome says: " On donne le los à la Reyne, Isabelle de Baviere, femme du Roy Charles Sixième, d'avoir apporté en France les pompes, et les gorgiasetez, pour bien habiller superbement et gorgiasement les dames."

Cap and Coiffures in the Reign of Charles VI

The form of cap given above was soon followed by the sugar-loaf; but the capuchons, frightful as they were — sometimes like cushions, sometimes like horns, stuffed out and ornamented with a *couvre-chef* thrown over the top — still continued *la mode* with those who had not courage to wear a tower. The

Queen Isabella of Bavaria: married Charles VI in 1385, was crowned in 1389
Charles VI: Charles the Mad, 1368–1472
"On donne le los": French translation appears in the appendix
Brantôme: Pierre de Bourdeilles, writer, circa 1534–1614
couvre-chef: see note p. 197

gentlemen, too, seemed to amuse their fancy in inventing new coiffures, each one more ugly and clumsy than
the other. The change
must have been great
in these head-dresses
when Isabella exerted
her genius and power
to remodel the toilette
of her subjects. Gowns
soon became lower in
the body, the *côte-hardi*
was adorned with er-
mine and jewels, the
petticoat was splen-
didly emblazoned, the
mantle was magnifi-
cent, and the shoes were
pointed. The hair, per-
haps out of compliment
to the queen, was con-
cealed; and before the
end of the reign, we
read that a deep flounce
ornamented the jupe of
one of the fair dames
of the court.

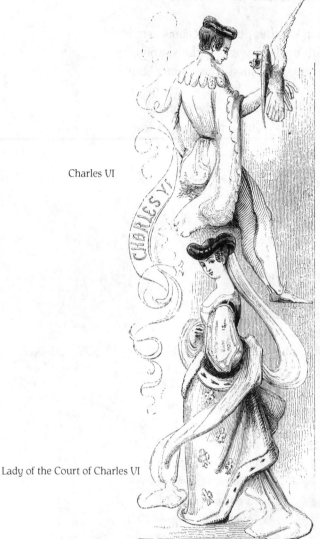

Charles VI

Lady of the Court of Charles VI

The gentlemen shone
in velvet, gold, and
jewels; their chaussées
were tight, their shoes
ridiculously pointed;
their doublets full,
short, and embroidered, the under sleeves tight, the

Isabella: Queen Isabelle, 1389-1472
chaussées: chausses, stockings

upper ones immensely long, open, pointed, and jagged. The hair was curled, and a kind of jewelled cushion was laid upon it; indeed, the coiffure of both ladies and gentlemen was not dissimilar.

The *bipartite* habit, introduced into France and England towards the close of the 13th century, was now falling into disuse amongst the higher classes; but in a journal of this time we find it recorded, "that in October 1409, the Sieur Jean de Montague was conducted from the châtelet to the halle, being seated high in a cart, and dressed in a garment half red and half white, and a hood of the same, with a red buskin and a white one, and gilt spurs upon his heel."

The reign of Charles VII. shews a great change in fashion. The sleeves of the doublet appear to be wadded upon the point of the shoulders, so as to raise them—a mode that we perceive in the ladies' gowns in the reign of our Queen Elizabeth. Bottines appear to be worn, and jewelled collars and girdles. In short, every thing that riches could procure, or the inventive genius of man and woman conceive, was visible in the costume of the French nation.

In one portrait of Charles VII. the monarch is represented in a garment similar to a blouse; his hat is of a modern form, but has a pattern of lozenges worked upon it. In another picture he wears a full green *casaque*, reaching half way to his knees; it is edged with a fringe; the sleeves approach to the gigot form, the stockings meet the nether garments, which, unlike the usual fashion, are turned back. No hair is visible. A short time afterwards, we see gentlemen with vests covered with embroidery, and sleeves of a different shape, not very wide till they reach the

bipartite: garments half in one color or pattern, half in another
Sieur Jean de Montague: was Treasurer of the Church of Beauvais, Bishop of Chartres among other preferments
Charles VII: 1403–1461
Queen Elizabeth: Elizabeth I of England, 1558–1603
gigot: leg of mutton, a sleeve shape revived from time to time

hands, when they stretch out amazingly, ending in a point edged with fur. Chaussées of blue or red were the mode, and pointed shoes. Ladies, too, appear in vests reaching to the hips, made so tight as to shew the figure.

Petticoats, or jupons, were richly emblazoned, the sleeves quite tight, and the upper part of the *côte-hardi*, or surcoat, was now made much lower across the bosom, a fashion that perhaps induced the chroniclers and writers of that time to stigmatise ladies' dresses as offensive to modesty.

A Curious Coiffure

Curious coiffures, of a different shape, were now often seen, but the hair, as usual, was concealed. The trains of the gowns were so long, that the fair dames carried the front part over the arm. A little later they became much shorter. The gentlemen's caps and hoods were of all shapes and sizes — round, pointed, or square, and some had a single long feather in front. Their sleeves became wide at the top, but tight at the wrist; and the short pourpoint, embroidered and made in folds, was held in at the waist by a girdle. The shoes *à la poulaine* were the fashion at this period. Ladies' gowns now appear shorter, so much so as to shew the feet in front; but behind they still continued long; and on one we find an ornament very much resembling a flounce.

In ancient works upon the French nation, its customs, laws, and ordonnances, we find it recorded, that the early French had a particular law concerning the hair of members of the royal family; viz. that such as

chaussées: stockings
à la poulaine: long, narrow shoes; perhaps derived from poule, or chicken, because
   the toes were long and narrow like a hen's

were chosen kings by the people, or were of the royal family, should preserve their hair, and wear it parted from the forehead, on both sides of the head, and anointed with sweet oil, as an ornament and a peculiar mark of their being of the royal family; whilst all other persons, how nobly born soever, had no right to wear a large head of hair. This privilege is treated at large in Hottoman's " Franco Gallia." To cut off the hair of a son of a king of France under the first race of kings, was to declare him excluded from the succession.

French historians affirm that Charlemagne wore his hair very short; his son, shorter. Charles the Bald had none at all, as his sobriquet denotes. Under Hugh Capet it appeared again; but the clergy excommunicated all who let it grow. Charles the Young cut off his hair to please Peter Lombard, and for many generations his successors wore it very short. This custom may perhaps account for the many strange coiffures worn by Frenchmen in the early ages.

In the " Mémoire de l'Histoire de Lyon," we find the following account of French head-dresses at this period : —

" La mutation et variété d'habits a tousieurs esté naturelle aux François, plus qu'autre nation; en quoy ils reçoivent plus de réputation et d'inconstance que de profit. Car en ceste année mille quatre cens soixante un, les dames de Lyon qui auparavant portoyent les longues queues en leurs robbes, changèrent, et mirent aux bords de robbes, de grands et large pans, les uns des gris de laitices, les autres de martres, les autres des autres semblables choses, chacun selon son estat, et possible passoyent aucunes plus outre; et en

Hottoman's "Franco Gallia": François Hotman wrote "Franco Gallia, or an Account of the
    Ancient Free State of France" in 1711
Charlemagne: Charles I, 768–814
his son: Louis I, 813–840
Charles the Bald: Charles II, 840–877
Hugh Capet: 987–996
Charles the Young: in fact, it was Louis the Young, Louis VII, 1121–1180, who cut his
    hair
Peter Lombard: 1100–1164, was created Bishop of Paris in 1159
"Mémoire de l'Histoire de Lyon": written by Guillaume Paradin, 1573
"La mutation": French translation appears in the appendix

leurs testes chargèrent certains bourrelets pointus come clochiers, la plus part de la hauteur de demie aulne, ou trois quartiers ; et estoyent nommés par aucuns les grands papillons, parcequ'il y avait deux larges ailes deça delà, comme sont aisles de papillons, et estait ce haut bonnet couvert d'un grand crespe trainant jusques en terre, lequel la plupart portoyent autour de leur bras. Il y en avait d'autres, que portoyent un accoustrement de teste, qui estait parti de drap de laine, parti de drap de soye meslé, et avait deux cornes, comme deux donjons, et était cette coiffure découpée et chiquettée, comme un chapeau d'Allemant, ou crespée comme un ventre de veau ; et elles portoyent des robbes ayans des manches tres étroites depuis les épaules jusque vers les mains, qu'elles s'élargissoyent et decouppées à undes. Les dames médiocre maison portoyent des chaperons de drap, faits de plusieurs larges lais, ou bandes entortillées autour de la teste, et deux ailes aux cotés, comme oreilles d'asne. Il y en avait aussi d'autres des grandes maisons, qui portoyent des chaperons de veloux noir, de la hauteur d'une couldée, lesquels bon trouverait maintenant fort laid et estrange. L'on ne pourrait bonnement monstrer ces diverses façons d'accoustremens de dames, en les escrivant, et seroit besoin qu'un peintre les representa. L'on en voit plusieurs façons exprimées, en tapisseries à Lyon, et aux verrières des Eglises, faites de ce tems là. Au surplus les filles, depuis qu'elles estoyent fiancées, jusqu'après un an entier des leur noces, portoyent un ornement de teste, qu'on nommait a Lyon *Floccard*, lesquels elles laissoyent estat l'année, revolve et prennent les chaperons susdits."

The extraordinary head-dresses above mentioned

are probably those which were so much reprobated in England, but which nevertheless remained more or less the fashion for two centuries. In French illustrated works of that time, we frequently meet with drawings of these " horned caps." The ecclesiastics preached against them, and severely censured the extravagance displayed in the immense quantities of fine linen and other materials used in the formation of so high a fabric; but their fair auditors turned a deaf ear to their remonstrances.

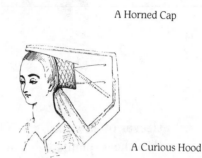

A Horned Cap

A Curious Hood

Black hoods and capuchons were also much worn, and the hair seldom peeped from beneath the mass of linen that enveloped the head. Sometimes a fret-work of gold was placed on the back of the head, and two wings of gauze, or fine lawn, spread out from it: these hoods were fashionable for many years. Some of them looked like black handkerchiefs thrown carelessly over the head, without any attention to shape or grace. Gowns now had the long upper sleeves, and the under ones tight, as usual, but with this difference, that the cuffs turned back up the arm.

Louis XI. is said to have invented *l'habit court*. He is represented as wearing a short casaque, or sur-

Louis XI: 1461-1483
l'habit court: short coat

tout, of crimson velvet, with a deep cape hanging in a point down his back, the sleeves being moderately tight, with deep cuffs; his chausses are of a deep blue colour, and his head covered with a cap of crimson velvet, having a coif underneath it.

Louis XI

Long tunics or gowns for men were now banished. Fur was much used as a trimming, and collars of precious stones were frequently seen. A vest with gigot sleeves often appears. The hair continues short, and the shoes pointed. The ladies' costume differs but little from that of the preceding reign. Very tall sugar-loaf caps are often seen, and, opposed to them, some equally flat. The one we give is curious; it is ornamented with jewels. The gowns were embroidered and made *en cœur*, the sleeves tight.

Lady's Coiffure in the Reign of Louis XI

Necklaces of jewels were much worn; no hair visible under the caps; black head-dresses were still *la grande mode;* and ladies' feet quite concealed by the immense length of their dresses.

The towering caps, exactly like extinguishers, were most extraordinary, and must have been exceedingly uncomfortable, as every puff of wind would be

en cœur: heart-shaped neckline

apt to blow them away. The long veil, which usually hung from the point, would look like a streamer floating in the breeze. The common people at this time wore hoods of black cloth, some square, some pointed.

Chapter 17 – France, 15th and 16th Centuries

THE TOILETTE IN FRANCE.

CHAPTER XVII.

DURING the reign of Charles VIII. it is recorded that head-dresses were lowered considerably; but in the portrait of Mary of Burgundy, we find that she still wears the favourite towering cap, that had now been fashionable for two hundred years: the veil hangs to the ground, and the cap is edged in front with jewels, and has a square piece which lies upon the neck and shoulders.

The veils attached to these coiffures, like the trains of the gowns in England under Henry VIII., described the rank of the wearers. Thus, a woman of the lower order had a veil that reached only half way down the back; a lady of the middle class wore her veil down to the waist; and a *dame de haut rang* was permitted to allow it to trail upon the ground.

The upper garment of the Princess Mary is splendidly embroidered in gold and flowers, with a very deep border; the surcoat is of ermine, the under garment also ornamented, and the sleeves quite tight, without any cuffs; the surcoat is fastened in

Charles VIII: 1483–1498
Mary of Burgundy: 1457–1482
Henry VIII: 1491–1547
dame de haut rang: lady of high rank
Princess Mary: Mary of Burgundy; this probably refers to the portrait showing her
    marriage to Maxmillian of Austria in 1477

front, and ornamented round the top, with splendid jewels.

It is curious that the French ladies, till this period, appear to have had a great repugnance to long hair; or at least, if they permitted it to grow, they carefully concealed it under their coiffure. The men, too, seem to have had the same dislike to a beard and whiskers.

Every thing belonging to the toilette in France now began to be rich and splendid in the extreme. Velvets, satins, cloth of gold, and silver; rich gems, embroidery, and plumes,—all were united to satisfy the love of splendour, so prevalent in this age. Velvet cloaks, lined with ermine, again became *la mode;* and pointed shoes gave place to a triangular-topped chaussure. Buttons were much used as ornaments, and bracelets appear to have been worn in great profusion.

When Louis XII. married the beautiful and accomplished Anne of Brittany, she had her hair simply arranged, without any ornament, and wore a white satin robe. At no period of French history were the dresses of both men and women so sumptuous, as at the time of which we now write. The robes, or gowns, were generally composed of cloth of gold, or velvet trimmed with ermine. Over this was worn a tunic of different coloured velvet, covered with embroidery; round the bust, and down the front of the tunic, was usually a profusion of jewels and gold ornaments. Sometimes the upper robe was open down each side, so as to shew a petticoat of gold or silver tissue, adorned with jewels.

Long hanging sleeves, trimmed with gold or fringe,

Louis XII: 1499–1514
Anne of Brittany: 1477–1514; they married in 1499, after Louis' accession

and lined with rich satin, were worn ; or sleeves of the same shape, made of muslin, sprigged with gold or silver.   Sometimes the sleeves were looped up with jewels ; and often a velvet *sous jupe* was worn under a white satin robe, beautifully embroidered ; a velvet head-dress and gold veil, and the whole body of the dress and coiffure sparkling with jewels. Sleeves were often worn slashed with velvet and satin, and a veil was an indispensable part of the toilette, though evidently worn only as an ornament, for it was always fastened to the back of the head, and fell in folds to the ground, never being drawn over the face.   The tunic, fitting close to the shape, was well calculated to shew the elegance of the form ; and the long open sleeve, even when, as frequently was the case, a tight one was placed under it, gave great grace to the robe. When the bottoms of these sleeves were not trimmed with ermine, they usually had a broad velvet cuff. The girdle and *cordelière* were always worn.

The quantity of ermine and all kinds of furs now worn, must have made the dresses heavy and very hot; but fashion could reconcile *les belles Fran-çaises* to any thing. The upper robes, when open down the front, were frequently of velvet, lined with rich satin, and had long trains —the under garment being of satin of a different colour.

The head-dress of Anne of Brittany, in many of her portraits, is very curious, and forms a strong contrast to the towers worn during the preceding reigns. Sometimes it seems to be merely

Anne of Brittany

sous jupe: underskirt
cordelière: type of hanging belt, see page 213, second paragraph
les belles Françaises: French beauties
Anne of Brittany: see note p. 211

a square hood of black velvet, lying flat on the top of the head and hanging down the back; at others, it takes the shape of the head, being square to the ears, with a long piece behind, while underneath the ermine, which forms the border, appears a plaited cap frill. The hair is drawn back from the face, so that only the roots of it are visible on the forehead. All the attendants of Anne are in exactly the same dress; so that we may suppose it to have been the fashionable costume of 1509.

This queen, who was much beloved by the French nation for her virtues and accomplishments, appears to have preferred very rich habiliments, but not many bracelets or necklaces; for, in her time, jewels were usually sewn on to the sleeves and stomachers, and, except as a cross, rarely ornamented the neck or arms. The order of the *Cordelière*, founded by her, probably gave the name to the long chain pendant from the waist so called; it was often of gold, but was sometimes formed of large beads, and ended with a tassel. The gowns were always cut quite square across the bosom, and the sleeves are represented to have sometimes reached to the ground.

The costume of the gentlemen at this period very much resembled that of England under Henry VIII., excepting the sleeves, which were nearly as wide and long as those of the ladies. The dress usually consisted of a tunic, with sleeves, the former fastened round the throat by a narrow collar; a surcoat richly embroidered, the body tight to the shape as far as the girdle, from whence it hung in rich folds half way to the knee. The sleeves of the tunic were

Anne: Anne of Brittany
Henry VIII: 1491-1547

slashed near the wrist, and had a deep frill that fell
over the back of the hand, and was held in by a band.
The girdle was often of gold and jewels, supporting a
rapier with a thick tassel hanging from it.   The
nether garment then the fashion, which formed drawers and stockings all in one piece, was usually of red
or blue silk, and very tight; the shoes were no longer
pointed, but quite square and clumsy-looking, fastened
with a strap across the foot.   They were sometimes
richly ornamented, and boots of black satin, turned
up with velvet and edged with gold, were also often
worn.   Indeed, much of the elegance of the costume
of the period consisted in having the chaussure richly
embroidered in gold, on satin or velvet.

The cap usually worn was of velvet, either red,
blue, or black, studded with jewels and ornamented
with several ostrich-feathers.   When a cloak was
added to the above costume, it was frequently of
cloth of gold, lined with embroidered white satin,
and trimmed with miniver; it seldom reached lower
than half way down the leg, and was very wide and
without a collar, having a long slit in either side
to allow the arms to pass through.   Sometimes, but
not very frequently, the nether garment, or hosen,
were striped in two colours; and the cloak often had
large sleeves trimmed with fur.   Occasionally the
tunic was cut so low in front, that it much resembled
a lady's gown.   Jewels were used in great profusion
to ornament every part of this dress, which was rich
and splendid in the extreme.

The hair was worn considerably longer than in the
preceding reigns.

Never was the love of splendour and magnificence more fully displayed, than at the period we are now approaching; viz. the time of the *Champ d'Or*, which has been long celebrated in the annals of the toilette. In the reign of Francis I., dress in England and in France was much alike; the same splendour and extravagance were displayed by both nations, for each seemed anxious to surpass the other in the richness and magnificence of their attire. Never was there such a display of silks, satins, velvets, cloth of gold and silver, feathers, laces, and jewels witnessed, as on the far-famed " Field of the Cloth of Gold," where the two monarchs and their respective courts met as friends.

Lady in the Reign of Francis I

Francis I

From this time the faces of the French noblesse were no longer shaven; beards, whiskers, and mous-

Champ d'Or: Field of the Cloth of Gold", the famous meeting in 1520 between Henry VIII, 1491–1547, and Francis I of France, 1515–1547; see Appendix C

taches, were allowed to grow. Some writers account for this change by asserting that Francis was wounded in the face in battle, and allowed his whiskers to grow to hide the scar. Certainly his subjects eagerly followed the fashion set them by royalty; and, in a few years, beards, whiskers, and moustaches, flourished in all their glory.

The doublets were now slashed with satin, and reached nearly to the knee. Stockings were fastened with rich jewelled garters; and full trunk-hose, puffed with satin, joined the stockings, and were ornamented with large bows of riband. Frequently, so bizarre were the fashions of the time that one stocking was white while the other was striped with blue and white. When the full doublet was not worn, the stockings and pantaloons met, and the former were clasped with a jewelled band. The pantaloons were often slashed with puffs of satin, and the surcoat also and sleeves to correspond. The body of the surcoat fitted tight to the shape, and was made square across the neck, so that the throat remained uncovered; the surcoat and the bottom of the sleeves were usually trimmed with broad lace.

The cloak was worn very short and wide, and was usually composed of velvet or cloth of gold, lined with satin, and ornamented with gold or miniver. A velvet cap, with feathers, and a jewelled band, and satin or velvet shoes, completed the costume. The cloak was considered rather as an addition to the elegance than to the utility of the costume; it was worn in the house, and formed part of the attire even in the ball-room. It was seldom, if ever, used for warmth or for the walking-dress. For these latter purposes, a habit not unlike a wagoner's frock was worn. Its shape was singular; it had a deep square collar of fur, short, full sleeves that reached to the elbows, trimmed likewise with fur; and the coat itself did not quite cover the knees, while the legs were protected by long black boots, similar to those worn by many of the military at this day. Shoes at this period were of a singular shape, very square, and cut low, almost down to the toes.

At the far-famed " Field of the Cloth of Gold," the dress of Francis is thus described by Hall :— " His garment was a chesnew of cloth of silver, culponed with cloth of gold, of damask cantelwise, and guarded on the borders with Burgon bands. Over that he had a cloak of broached satin, with gold of purple colour, wrapped about his body, traverse-beded from the hip to the waist, fastened in the loupe of the first folde; this said cloak was richly set with pearls and pretious stones. The French king had on his head a *coif* of damask gold set with diamonds, and his courser that he rode was covered with a trapping of tissue, bordered with device, cut in fashion mantell-wise; the skirts were embowed and fret with frized work, and knit with corbelles and buttons tasseled of Turkie, making raines and headstall answering to the same work."

At this same magnificent display of beauty, rank, and splendour, our national chronicler reluctantly admits, that the ladies of France surpassed their fair rivals in the richness and elegance of their habiliments; and this was no doubt felt by Queen Catherine and her attendants, as we mentioned, in the reign of Henry VIII., that the English ladies at that time

Hall: Edward Hall, died 1547
chesnew, etc.: divided between silver and gold damask slantwise
traverse-beded: beaded from side to side
embowed and fret: bent and interlace with raised or twisted work
corbelles: ornamental projections or bobbles
Turkie: looped or pile fabric
raines and headstall: reins and bridle or halter
Queen Catherine: Catherine of Aragon, married Henry VIII in 1509, was divorced by him
   in 1533

were devoted to French *modes*. Queen Claude certainly seems quite to have abandoned the strait sleeves and grave costume usually worn by Anne of Brittany; for we find her and her ladies wearing sumptuous apparel, and she is celebrated for introducing from Spain the fashion of wearing a hoop, or, as it was called by the French, a *vertugadin*. This curious machine swelled the petticoats out to an immense size at the bottom of the dress, while the waist, being much compressed, and ending in a long point, gave the figure a strange appearance. The whalebones, of which this pannier was composed, formed a small circle near the top, and gradually enlarged, till the lower hoop spread the petticoat out to its fullest extent.

Over this was worn a satin garment, richly embroidered, and an open gown of velvet, worked in patterns of gold and silver, trimmed with fringe. This robe met at the point of the waist, but gradually became more open, till, at the bottom of the dress, from the size of the hoop, it spread out on each side, giving a full view of the embroidered satin petticoat. The waist was quite tight, and finished at the bosom with a chemisette of fine lace, so that the neck was covered almost to the throat.

Under-sleeves of satin were worn slashed, or else embroidered, to match the petticoat, and had full cuffs at the wrists; over them were tight velvet sleeves like the robe, finished at the elbows with an immense deep sort of manche of fur, that hung from each arm nearly to the ground. Round the waist was a girdle of jewels and a splendid *cordelière*, that terminated at the bottom of the petticoat with a large brooch.

The hair was plain on the forehead, and over it

Queen Claude: married to Francis I 1515–1524
Anne of Brittany: 1477–1514
chemisette: under-bodice
cordelière: see note p. 212

was worn the favourite black velvet cap, hanging down the back, and embroidered in jewels. In compliment, perhaps, to the gentlemen, who now allowed their beards to grow, the ladies permitted more of their tresses to be seen; and though the "hyacinthine flow" of the curl was still unknown among them, the little they ventured to display was still a great improvement.

Some *élégantes* wore a cap much resembling a saucer, that fitted quite tight to the head. The arms were always covered down to the wrists. Sometimes the bodice was made of ermine or minever, and the upper sleeves resembled two small cloaks, being attached to the dress at the top, and from thence hanging loosely down, every part being embroidered either in silk or jewels. The cap we have described still continued in fashion, and gold and silver veils, chains, ear-rings, and *cordelières*, were much worn; also shoes with high heels, which were brought from Spain, and much admired.

élégantes: dandies
minever: white ermine (winter coat) fur

Chapter 18 – France, 16th and 17th Centuries

THE TOILETTE IN FRANCE.

CHAPTER XVIII.

UNDER the reign of Henry II. curls first began to appear. Ladies arranged their hair in ringlets on each side of the head, or raised it up in a *toupet*. *Toques* of velvet, not unlike the caps worn by the men, were much the fashion; also velvet *cauls*, adorned with jewels, the same shape as the one given in the reign of Lady Jane Grey.

The hoop and open robe were still worn; also large ruffs. Henry himself was the first person in France who wore silk stockings; they were presented to him when his sister married Philibert of Savoy. The trunk hose, large doublet, and short cloak, with tight silk hose, continued to be the fashionable attire; the doublet, however, instead of being open, reached to the throat, and a lace collar fell over it.

Ermine, jewels, cloth of gold, and embroidery, were still to be seen in great profusion. Through this and the succeeding reigns also, beards, whiskers, and curled hair. The ruffs of the ladies bore some proportion to their immense hoops. Lace handker-

Henry II: 1547–1559
toupet: forelock or mass of hair
toques: small, close-fitting, brimless hat
caul: network or netted cap

Lady Jane Grey: 1537–1554
sister of Henry: Margaret of France, married in 1559
Philibert of Savoy: Emmanuel Philibert, Duke of Savoy, 1553–1580

chiefs were worn over the neck, and curious sleeves, like small gigots, but padded, so as to give a most ungraceful appearance to the shoulders. Embroidered gloves and feather fans now came into fashion.

During the three following reigns little alteration took place in dress. The hoops and ruffs were worn very large, the gowns perfectly laden with jewels, and the ladies' hair was no longer concealed under a capuchon, or towering cap, but was allowed to appear in curls, turned back from the forehead and adorned with jewels and flowers. The stomachers of the gowns were long and pointed, the waists very small, the sleeves large, hanging, and usually ornamented with deep fur, or with velvet. The under-sleeve was tight and slashed, or adorned with *bouffettes* of satin, and bows of riband, or knots of pearls. When no *fichu* was worn, it was frequently the fashion to veil the neck and bosom by large squares of pearls or precious stones.

Many of the gowns in the reign of Henry III. were so laden with puffs of satin in every part, that it was difficult to distinguish the shape. Some were made like our riding-habits of the present day, and covered with bows, buttons, and jewels, till the real material of the robe was hardly visible.

In the reign of Henry III., the hoop that swelled out from the hips also first came into fashion; it was quite different from those that had been worn previously, as the immense size began from the waist, and did not increase, as with the others, to the bottom of the petticoat. While this hoop was in fashion, only one robe was worn, but the waist had as long a point as could be made, by which means the hips looked

Francis II: 1559–1560   Charles IX: 1560–1574   Henry III: 1574–1589
boufettes: bows or tassels
fichu: draped scarf or shawl

quite preposterous; and if the fair wearer took it into her head to wear tight sleeves, and, as was frequently the case, an enormous ruff, the effect of the *tout ensemble* must have been most extraordinary.

Lady in the Reign of Henry III

Henry III

Charles IX

The tall caps, which would in some degree have counterbalanced the size of the hoop and ruff, were banished by all true *élégantes*, and were replaced by very small velvet caps, poised on the back of the head, and ornamented in front with an aigrette, or small feather. Sometimes, instead of the ruff, ladies wore two wings of lace or gauze, that were fastened to the gown behind the head, and stood up as high as the forehead. These strange appendages, from which not unfrequently a splendid veil fell to the ground, do not appear to have been

tout ensemble: the whole thing, or entire costume
élégantes: elegant women

brought into fashion till the reign of Henry III. Under his successor the hoop really became so enormous, that the marvel is how ladies ever got into carriages, or through doors. The fan of lace also stretched out to the top of the head, and the puffings, slashings, and ornaments, far exceeded any extravagance of that kind previously seen. Marguerite de Valois is represented in this dress, with her hair curled all over her head, powdered, and ornamented with a large diamond star.

Though the gowns are made lower at this time, the arms are still carefully covered, and the petticoats quite plain, but, as of course was necessary with a hoop, immensely full. One picture of that time represents a lady in a tight velvet dress, with a boa thrown over her shoulders. The *pianelles*, or low embroidered shoes, with flat heels, now superseded the *pattins*, with their immense heels often a foot high, and silk stockings began to be worn by ladies of fashion.

Although the sleeves in this reign were usually rather tight than otherwise, still some *élégantes* preserved the fashion of the long open sleeve over the under one. When this was the case, the upper one was open from the shoulder, and fell to the ground in a point. Large ruffs were worn at the wrists.

Frequently the dress was such a mass of jewels, that the weight must have been very great. When Mary of Scotland married Francis, the chronicler relates, that the blaze of her diamonds made her too dazzling to look upon. Brantôme, describing the appearance of Marguerite, wife of Henry of Navarre, at the celebrated festin given at Lyons in honour of

Henry III: 1574-1589
Marguerite de Valois: 1553-1615, Queen of Navarre, noted for her beauty and loose
    living; married Henry IV of France 1589-1599
Mary of Scotland: married Francis II in 1558
Brantôme: Pierre de Bourdeilles, circa 1534-1614
Marguerite: Marguerite de Valois (above)

the arrival of Henry III., says : " Her head was adorned with a quantity of large pearls and precious stones, and, above all, diamonds of immense value placed amidst her glossy hair, in the form of stars ; her graceful form, of commanding height, was arrayed in a robe so rich and heavy with its gorgeous ornaments, that none but one so majestic and perfectly made in all proportions could have ventured to appear in it, as it would have overpowered and crushed those of ordinary size or figure. The stuff which composed it had been a present from the Grand Signior to the Queen of Navarre. It was of cloth of gold, covered with raised work, of different tinted gold from its ground, and embroidered in borders with pearls and gems of every colour, in flowers and leaves. The fringes were resplendent, and the whole costume such as surpassed in costliness any thing that had ever been before seen in France. It was thought a *chef-d'œuvre* of art ; and the quantity used for the robe was fifteen ells, each ell being worth a hundred crowns of gold."

The empire of dress was certainly never more triumphant than at this period. Catherine of Medicis feeling the necessity of amusing the minds of the people, to prevent their paying attention to the affairs of the nation, was continually promoting the most splendid balls, fêtes, and entertainments ; and nothing could exceed the extravagant luxury displayed in the dresses worn on these occasions by the lords of the creation, as well as by their fair partners. Nor can it be wondered at that the duties of the toilette should now be considered as most important, when it is remembered that the sovereign himself would spend

Henry III: 1574-1589
Grand Signior: Sultan of Turkey
Queen of Navarre: Marguerite de Valois, see note p. 223
chef-d'œuvre: masterpiece
Catherine of Medicis: 1519-1589; married Prince Henry (later Henry II), second son
    of Francis I, and became queen in 1547

whole days in devising new fashions; that he would
cut out his wife's robes, as well as perform the office
of hairdresser to her and his effeminate courtiers,
who, following his example, were often to be seen
winding silk, stringing beads, and embroidering. It
is affirmed, that Henry III. divided his time between
the adornment of his beautiful wife and the care of
his own person. His hands were covered every night
with gloves, and a cloth dipped in essences was laid
over his face, in order to improve the delicacy of his
complexion; his hair was always curled with the
greatest care, and dyed of a beautiful black; whole
hours were passed in giving the proper shade to the
red and white of his cheeks, and painting his eyebrows. His dress, on any great occasion, was always
so covered with pearls, precious stones, and embroidery, as almost to conceal the cloth of gold of which
it was generally formed; and, as at this period nobody
was permitted to appear at more than one fête in the
same costume, the enormous sums lavished upon dress
are quite incalculable.

The garments worn by gentlemen consisted generally of a doublet of velvet, slashed with satin, and
worked

> "In emerald tuffs, flow'rs purpled, blue and white,
>   Like sapphire, pearl, in rich embroidery;"

with light silk hose, and a cloak. Some of the latter
had large sleeves, and were lined with ermine. The
immense trunk hose, which seem in almost all countries to have accompanied the hoop, were now quite
the fashion; when they were worn the doublet was
tight like a jacket, and only reached to the waist,

Henry III: 1574–1589

the sleeves were narrow, and ornamented with a deep frill at the hand. Some of the trunk hose reached to the knees, and swelled out like two balloons; others were much shorter. On the field of battle they must have had a very strange effect, yet it appears they were frequently worn there.

People who did not approve of this preposterous mode had slashed breeches, reaching to below the knee, where they were fastened by richly jewelled garters, large rosettes of riband, or gold bands. The doublet was frequently made in a point from the waist, like a lady's gown, and the body was often of one material, and the sleeves of another. Thus we are told that a gentleman of the court of Charles IX. had a scarlet doublet with white sleeves, slashed with blue, trunk hose and stockings of blue, and a red cloak lined with satin and ermine.

It was very much the fashion at this period for ladies to wear small black masks when they went abroad, not for the sake of concealing their faces, but to preserve their complexions, as we find by the following lines :—

> " Since she did neglect her looking-glass,
>   And throw her sun-expelling *mask* away,
>   The air hath starv'd the roses in her cheeks,
>   And pitch'd the lily tincture of her face."

Embroidered pocket-handkerchiefs were much in fashion at this glittering epoch. Under Henry IV. (*dit* Le Grand) the full doublet nearly disappeared, and gave place to a tight pourpoint; trunk hose were superseded by breeches, and the cloak became smaller. The fashion of wearing blue or red stockings, however,

Charles IX: 1560-1574
Henry IV (dit Le Grand): Henry of Navarre, called "the Great", became Henry IV,
    reigned 1589-1610; husband of Marguerite de Valois

continued, and the ruffs at the throat and wrists maintained their place; large roses also were worn upon the shoes.

Henry IV. particularly admired small velvet caps, and generally wore one adorned with a white feather, which served as a rallying point to his followers on the field of battle, and soon became so celebrated that a velvet cap with a *panache blanc* is still termed, *à la Henri Quatre*.

In this reign the beard was shortened: it was now worn only three fingers in length, in the shape of a fan, rounded, and set off with two long moustaches; afterwards the whiskers only were retained, with a little *toupée* of hair in the middle, and quite round the under lip. Maréchal Bassompierre said, that the only alteration he found in the world after twelve years' imprisonment was that the men had lost their beards and the horses their tails. Whilst the fan-beards were in vogue they were kept in that form with preparations of wax, which gave the hair an agreeable smell, and the colour that was desired. The beard was dressed over night, and that it might not get out of order it was enclosed in a *bigotelle*, or kind of bag, made for the purpose.

Shaking off their effeminacy, under the banner of this warlike prince, the French no longer devoted themselves to fashion, or wore their hair turned over a comb like women, as some of the minions of the court of Henry III. are said to have done; but became in their dress, as well as in their character and manners, more worthy the name of French men, and of subjects of so great a king. Magnificence and extravagance, however, still reigned, though effeminacy

Henry IV: 1589-1610
panache blanc: white plume
à la Henri Quatre: in the style of Henry IV
Maréchal Bassompierre: François de Bassompierre; his memoirs were published 1665
Henry III: 1574-1589

was banished; and the annals of the period speak in raptures of the cloth of gold and silver, embroidery, and jewels. The hair of the men remained short, but a gradual increase in its length might be perceived. Beards were large and pointed.

Towards the end of this reign hoops decreased perceptibly. Ladies wore their hair curled, and frequently adorned their heads with a coiffure that somewhat resembled a *cawl*, only it was pointed, and came very forward on the forehead, falling back behind, and very narrow on the ears, so as to shew all the side of the head.

The *collaso monté*, which at this period eclipsed the ruff, was a curious invention. It stood round the back of the robe like an immense fan, and sometimes rose as high as the top of the head; frequently the edges were fringed, and ornamented with lace. It was usually made of gauze, which was stiffened and thickly plaited. At times, according to the fancy of the wearer, the *collaso* stood up or was laid down, round the back of the robe; but it was very rarely brought more forward than the top of the shoulders.

During the reign of Louis XIII. the bell-hoops ceased to be worn, but the upper robe was raised behind, and on the sides, to admit of the under garment being seen. The sleeves were slashed, or had *bouffans* all along the arm; some hung down nearly to the ground, and others were held up with knots of pearls. In " France Painted to the Life," by Dr. Heylin, who visited it in 1625, we read of the dames de Paris: " Their habit, in which they differ from the rest of France, is the attire of their heads, which hangeth down their backs in fashion of a veil."

Louis XIII: 1610–1643
bouffans: bouffant puffs
Dr. Heylin: Peter Heylin, 1600–1662

Another head-dress of this period seems very strange at the present day, though when worn it was much admired. The front hair was turned back over

two cushions, the back roll being the highest, and ornamented with knots and bows of riband. A long veil, which was generally the most admired part of a French *élégante*'s coiffure at the time of which we are writing, hung in graceful folds down the back.

Head-Dress in the Reign of Louis XIII

It appears, however, to have been worn for ornament only, as it is never seen drawn over the face; and, indeed, the height of the head-dress would have rendered it inconvenient.

Under this king great changes took place in the manner of wearing hair. Beards disappeared; "la barbe pointue," so much admired by all fashionables in the three preceding reigns, was banished, and a small tuft of hair, termed an "imperial," was all that "la Mode" permitted to grace the chins of her followers. Moustaches, however, grew longer, and were shaped at the ends into a most insinuating twist. The head was now adorned with long curls, which soon gave place to enormous perukes.

Gentleman in the Reign of Louis XIII

la barbe pointue: pointed beard, note illustration; a longer, more assertive style of beard than the Imperial, which is short and more blunt in cut

Ruffs vanished, and were replaced by falling collars of costly lace ; while ruffles, tied with ribands, ornamented the sleeves of the doublets at the wrists, and either lay back upon the arm, or fell over the hand : they, also, were of lace.

Chapter 19 – France, 17th and 18th Centuries

THE TOILETTE IN FRANCE.

CHAPTER XIX.

Louis XIV, on Horseback

WE now arrive at the reign of Louis XIV., an epoch in the annals of fashion celebrated for the variety of its coiffures, and also for the magnificence and splendour of its habiliments. Madame de Sevigné, in a letter to her daughter, says, speaking of the head-dress then much the fashion, of which we give the sketch: " Imaginez vous une tête partagée à la

Louis XIV: 1643–1715
Madame de Sevigné: 1626–1696
"Imaginez vous": French translation appears in the appendix

paisanne jusqu'à deux doigts du bourlet; on coupe ces cheveux de chaque côté, d'étage en étage dont

Lady's Head-Dress in the
Reign of Louis XIII

on fait de grosse boucles, rondes et négligées, qui ne viennent point plus bas qu'un doigt, au-dessous de l'oreille; cela fait quelque chose de fort jeune et de fort joli, et comme deux gros bouquets de cheveux de chaque côté. Il ne faut pas couper les cheveux trop courts; mais comme il les faut friser *naturellement*, les boucles qui en emportent beaucoup, on a attrapé plusieurs dames, dont l'exemple doit faire trembler les autres. On met les rubans comme à l'ordinaire, et une grosse boucle entre le bourlet et la coëffure; quelquefois on la laisse traîner jusques sur la gorge." Of the dress called *hurlu bielu*, we find in another letter from the same lady, "Ces coëffures m'ont fort divertie : il y en a que l'on voudrait souffleter."

She also mentions *coëffes* and *cornettes* as being then the fashion. The latter seem to have been worn *en déshabille*, for in speaking of a visit which she paid to a lady, Madame de Sevigné thus describes her dress : "Je la trouvai fort négligée ; pas un cheveu ; une *cornette* de vieux point de Vénise, un mouchoir noir, un manteau gris effacé, une vieille juppe." In another letter the same writer says : "Votre belle-sœur a une *souris* qui fait fort bien dans ses cheveux noirs ; la plaisante folie !" But what it was, whether a head-dress or only an ornament, she does not mention. In speaking of another fashion of that period she gives the following description : "Vous avez donc eu peur de ces pauvres petites *chouettes noires ;*

coëffes: coifs, close-fitting caps
cornettes: lady's headdress, see translation in appendix
en déshabille: undressed, i.e., informal or casual
"Je la trouvai": French translation appears in the appendix
"Votre belle-sœur"; "Vous avez donc": French translations in appendix

je m'en doutai, et j'en ris en moi-même : vous trouvez qu'elles ont l'air triste ; mais au moins elles ne sont point rechignées ; elles n'ont point *une voix de Megere ;* et quand vous verrez ce qu'elles sçavent faire, vous trouverez qu'au lieu d'être de mauvais augure, elles font la beauté, au moins, de la coëffure." In a letter from Vichy, Madame de Sevigné writes : " Je voudrois que vous eussiez vu jusqu'à quel excès la présence de Termes et de Flamarens fait monter la coëffure et l'ajustement de deux ou trois belles de ce pays : enfin, dès six heures du matin tout est en l'air, *coëffure, hurlupée, poudrée, frisée ; bonnet à la Bascule, rouge, mouches, petite coëffe qui pend, évantail, corps de juppe long et serré ;* c'est pour pâmer de rire."

At intervals during this reign, a very becoming mode of dressing the hair was the fashion. Curls were raised in rows from the forehead to the top of the head, each row divided with a string of pearls, and an ornament of jewellery, termed a *Sevigné,* was placed in the uppermost curl, this being finished with great care though apparent negligence. The long hair from the back of the head

Mode of Dressing a Lady's Hair

was arranged in large curls upon the neck and shoulders, the longest falling quite to the waist, and with jewels peeping out here and there, as if dropped accidentally. The hair arranged in this manner left the forehead quite bare.

This appears to have been the era of wonderful head-dresses. One known in England by the name of com-

"Je voudrois": French translation in appendix
Sevigné: named for Madame de Sevigné, 1626-1696

mode, was formed like two cones or spires, and stood so high on each side of the head that a woman who was of low stature without her head-dress became a giantess on assuming it. The name of Fontange, by which this coiffure was known during the latter years of the reign of Louis XIV., had a singular origin. Madame de Fontanges, at a hunting party at Vincennes, had her head-dress disarranged by a gust of wind, and in order to keep it in its place she took one of her garters and tied it up with that. Louis thought she looked so pretty in this fashion that he begged her to continue to wear her head-dress so arranged. Next day the ladies of the court made their appearance with a riband, or top-knot, which assumed the name of Fontange.

Horace Walpole remarks that, about the year 1714, Louis XIV., being struck by the elegant and tasteful appearance of two English ladies in low head-dresses, requested the ladies of his court to follow that *mode ;* but, from the following quotation, it would appear that the lofty coiffures had disappeared previously to this period : " They received fresh advice that the French king had forbid the wearing of gold lace, and that all below a countess lay under a prohibition ; that he had clipt *commodes*, and taken the sex a story lower ; that the Duchess of Burgundy immediately undrest, and appeared in a fontange of the new standard, and his majesty had a design against all topknots."

For a description of the petticoats in fashion during this reign, we must again apply to Madame de Sevigné : " Avez-vous oüi parler des transparens ? Ce sont des habits entiers des plus beaux brocards d'or

Madame de Fontanges: was Louis XIV's mistress, 1661–1681
Louis XIV: 1643–1715
Horace Walpole: 4th Earl of Oxford, 1717–1797
Duchess of Burgundy: Marie Adelaide of Savoy, 1685–1712
Madame de Sevigné: 1626–1696
"Avez-vous oüi parler": French translation appears in the appendix

et d'azur qu'on puisse voir, et par-dessus des robes
noires transparentes, ou de bel dentelle d'Angleterre,
ou de chenilles veloutées sur un tissu, comme ces dentelles d'hyver, que vous avez vues : cela compose un
transparent, qui est un habit noir, et un habit tout
d'or ou d'argent ou de couleur, comme on veut ; et
voilà la mode."

" Monsieur de Langlée a donné à Madame de
Montespan une robe d'or sur or, rebrodé d'or, rebordé
d'or, et par-dessus un or frisé rebroché d'un or mêlé
avec un certain or, qui fait la plus divine étoffe qui
ait jamais été imaginée : ce sont les fées qui ont fait
en sécret cet ouvrage ; âme vivante n'en avoit con-
noissance. On la voulut donner aussi mystérieuse-
ment qu'elle étoit fabriquée : le tailleur de Madame
de Montespan lui apporta l'habit qu'elle avoit or-
donné ; il en fit le corps sur des mesures ridicules :
voilà des cris et des gronderies, comme vous pouvez
penser ; le tailleur dit en tremblant, Madame, comme
le temps presse, voyez si cet autre habit que voilà ne
pourroit point vous accommoder, faute d'autre. On
découvre l'habit ; ha, la belle chose ! ha, quelle étoffe !
vient-elle du ciel ? il n'y en a point de pareille sur la
terre : on essaye le corps ; il est à peindre. Le Roi
arrive ; le tailleur dit, Madame, il est fait pour vous :
on comprend que c'est une galanterie ; mais, qui peut
l'avoir faite ? C'est Langlée, dit le roi ; C'est Langlée
assurément, dit Madame de Montespan ; personne que
lui ne peut avoir imaginé une telle magnificence : c'est
Langlée, c'est Langlée. Tout le monde répète, C'est
Langlée ; les échos en demeurent d'accord, et disent,
C'est Langlée, et moi, ma fille, je vous dis pour être
à la mode, C'est Langlée."

"Monsieur de Langlée a donné": translation appears in appendix
Madame de Montespan: 1641-1707, a marquise, she was Louis XIV's mistress for a number
    of years before retiring to a convent

In another letter we find : " Madame de Coësquen a fait faire une juppe de velours noir, avec de grosses broderies d'or et d'argent, et un manteau de tissu couleur de feu, or, et argent : cet habit coute infiniment ; et quand elle a été bien resplendissante, on là trouvée comme une comédienne."

Patches were worn in France at this period, but only by ladies, and not, as some assert was the case in England, by both sexes. It seems to have been only the young and handsome who ventured to follow this strange fashion in France. These *mouches*, as they were called, had each a separate appellation. When placed at the corner of the eye, the *mouche* was called *passionnée ;* in the centre of the forehead it became a *majestueuse ;* on the corner of the mouth it received the denomination of *baiseuse ;* in the middle of the cheek it was a *galante;* on the fold formed by the mouth when it laughs, an *enjouée ;* on the nose, an *effronter ;* and on the lips, a *coquette.*

During the reign of Louis XIV. ladies wore stockings of one colour, with clocks of another. About the year 1712 a doll was sent over from France as a model for the fashions ; it had been dressed with the greatest care by the most celebrated tire-women in Paris, and we find the following account of it : " The puppet was dressed in a cherry-coloured gown and petticoat, with a short working apron over it, which discovered her shape to the most advantage. Her hair was cut and divided very prettily, with several ribands stuck up and down in it. The milliner assured me that her complexion was such as was worn by all the ladies of the best fashion in Paris. Her head was extremely high : I was also offended at a small patch

---

Madame de Coësquen: the Marquise de Coetquen, who was not one of Louis XIV's mistresses
Louis XIV: 1643–1715
tire-women: ladies' maids or dressers
"Madame de Coësquen a fait faire": translation appears in the appendix

passionée: passionate
majestueuse: majestic
baiseuse: kiss patch
galante: gallant
enjouée: playful
effronter: impudent
coquette: a flirt

she wore on her breast,   *   *   *   Her necklace was of an immoderate length, being tied before, in such a manner that the two ends hung down to her girdle."

The dress of the gentlemen underwent many and striking changes. The head, particularly, instead of being covered with short hair, or, at most, curls reaching to the shoulders, now gloried in an enormous curled, frizzed, and pomatumed peruke, with short ring-  lets upon the forehead, longer ones upon the shoulders, and others, longer still, hanging down the back nearly to the waist.

Mode of Dressing a Gentleman's Hair

The invention of these immense bushes of hair has been attributed to the devotion of the courtiers of the youthful monarch for every thing his majesty wore, said, or did. Louis, while still a young boy, had a head of most beautiful and luxuriant hair, which fell in long waving ringlets upon his shoulders; but, as none of his attendants could boast such tresses, the aid of the perruquier was called in, and soon the whole court of *la Grande Monarque* appeared in perukes, which mode speedily travelled to other countries.

In Madame de Sevigné's letters, we find great complaints of the length of the sleeves sometimes worn by gentlemen. In one letter she says: " Les manches du chevàlier font un bel effet à table; quoiqu'elles entraînent tout, je doute qu'elles m'entraînent aussi; quelque faiblesse que j'aie pour les modes, j'ai une grande aversion pour cette saleté." And again:

la Grande Monarque: Louis XIV, 1643–1715, called "the Great" and the "Sun King"
Madame de Sevigné: 1626–1696
"Les manches du chevalier": translation appears in the appendix

" J'ai vû des manches comme celles du chevalier. Ha, qu'elles sont belles dans le potage, et sur les salades ! "

In Evelyn's " Diary," we find the following account of Louis XIV., when he went to open his first parliament in the year 1651. It gives an excellent idea of the profusion and magnificence displayed in the dress and equipages of that day : —

" *7th Sept.*—I went to visit Mr. Hobbs, the famous philosopher of Malmsbury, with whom I had a long acquaintance. From his window we saw the whole equipage and glorious cavalcade of the young French monarch, Lewis XIV., passing to Parliament, when first he tooke the kingly government on him, now being in his 14th yeare, out of his minority and the Queene Regent's pupillage. First came the captaine of the King's aydes, at the head of 50 richly liveried ; next the Queene Mother's light horse, an hundred, the lieutenant being all over covered with embroidery and ribbons, having before him 4 trumpets habited in black velvet, full of lace and casaques of the same ; then the King's light horse, 200, richly habited, with 4 trumpets in blue velvet embrodred with gold, before whom rode the Count d'Olone, cornet, whose belt was set with pearle ; next went the grand Provost's company on foote with the Provost on horseback ; after them the Swiss in black velvet toques, led by two gallant cavaliers habited in scarlet-colour'd sattin after their country fashion, which is very fantastic,—he had in his cap a pannach of heron with a band of diamonds, and about him 12 little Swisse boyes with halberds ; then came the *Aydes des Cérémonies ;* next the grandees of court, governors of places, and

"J'ai vû des manches": translation appears in appendix
Evelyn's "Diary": John Evelyn, 1620-1706; the diary was published in 1818
Louis XIV: 1643-1715
Mr. Hobbs: Thomas Hobbes, 1588-1679, philosopher and writer
Queene Regent: Anne of Austria; the power was actually held by Cardinal Mazarin
    until his death in 1661

lieutenants gen¹ of provinces, magnificently habited and mounted, among whom I must not forget the Chevalier Paul, famous for many sea-fights and signal exploits there, because 'tis said he had never been an academist, and yet govern'd a very unruly horse, and besides his rich suite, his Malta Cross was esteem'd at 10,000 crownes; these were headed by 2 trumpets, and the whole troup cover'd with gold, jewels, and rich caparisons, were follow'd by 6 trumpets in blew velvet also, preceeding as many heralds in blew velvet *semée* with *fleurs de lys*, caduces in their hands and caps on their heads; behind them came one of the mast^rs of the ceremonies; then divers marishalls and many of the nobility, exceeding splendid; behind them Count d'Harcourt, grand escuyer, alone, carrying the King's sword in a scarf, wch he held up in a blew sheath studded w^th *fleurs de lys ;* his horse had for reines 2 scarfs of black taffata: then came abundance of footmen and pages of the King, new liveried with white and red feathers; next the guards de corps and other officers; and lastly appear'd the King himself on an Isabella Barb, on wch a houssing *semée* with crosses of the Order of the Holy Ghost, and *fleurs de lys ;* the King himselfe, like a young Apollo, was in a sute so cover'd with embrodery, that one could perceive nothing of the stuff under it; he went almost the whole way with his hat in hand, saluting the ladys and acclamators who fill'd the windows with their beauty, and the aire w^th *Vive le Roy.* He seem'd a prince of a grave yet sweete countenance. After the King follow'd divers greate persons of the Court, exceeding splendid."

The falling-collar, which came into fashion in the

semée: seeded
caduces: caduceus, or herald's wand
Isabella Barb: war horse from the Barbary Coast (Morocco); "Isabella" was a greyish yellow or buff color
Apollo: Greek sun god
Vive le Roy: Long Live the King

preceding reign, was now superseded by bands of very broad and rich lace, the long ends of which fell down upon the breast. From the journal of an English gentleman, who visited France in 1690, we give the following account of the dress then generally worn :— " A hat about two inches broad, a peruke very thick of hairs, a coat fully plaited all round with short cuffs, the quarters of the shoes not above an inch broad, a small neckcloth tucked within the coat, with a very full cravat-string tied upon the same."

The petticoat breeches, or full-plaited doublets, were the fashion in this reign ; they reached nearly to the knees, and were made of silk, satin, velvet, or any costly material, richly embroidered. The following description, also from Madame de Sevigné, of the marriage of M. le Prince de Conti, gives a good idea of the splendour of the dresses worn during this reign. It would appear that this gentleman was not remarkable for his submission to the laws of fashion, for it begins : " Je vous dirai une nouvelle la plus grande et la plus extraordinaire que vous puissiez apprendre, c'est que M. le Prince fit faire hier sa barbe ; il étoit rasé, ce n'est point une illusion, ni de ces choses que l'on dit en l'air, c'est une vérité : toute sa cour en fut témoin, et Madame de Langeron prenant son temps qu'il avoit les pattes croisées comme le Lion, lui fit mettre un juste-au-corps avec des boutonnières de diamans ; un valet de chambre abusant aussi de sa patience, le frisa, lui mit de la poudre, et le réduisit enfin à être l'homme de la cour de la meilleure mine, et une tête qui effaçoit toutes les perruques ; voilà le prodige de la nôce : l'habit de M. le Prince de Conti étoit inestimable, c'étoit une broderie de diamans fort

preceding reign: Louis XIII, 1610–1643
Madame de Sevigné: 1626–1696
marriage of M. le Prince de Conti: probably François-Louis III (1664–1709) who married, in 1688, Marie Thérèse de Bourbon (Conti). The Conti and Condé families form interlocking collateral branches of the French Bourbons, frequently marrying among themselves
"Je vous dirai une nouvelle": French translation appears in the appendix

gros, qui suivoit les compartimens d'un velouté noir, sur un fond de couleur de paille, on dit que la couleur de paille ne réussissoit pas et que Madame de Langeron, qui est l'âme de toute la parure de l'hôtel de Condé, en a été malade ; en effet, voilà de ces sortes de choses dont on ne doit point se consoler. M. le Duc, Madame la Duchesse, et Mademoiselle de Bourbon, avoient trois habits garnis de pierreries, différentes pour les trois jours ; mais j'oublois le meilleur, c'est que l'épée de M. le Prince étoit garni de diamans,—

> ' La famosa spada
> Cui valore ogni vittòria é certa.'

La doublure du manteau du Prince de Conti étoit d'un satin noir, piqué de diamans, comme de la moucheture."

Mademoiselle de Bourbon: the bride, see p. 240

Chapter 20 – France, 18th and 19th Centuries

THE TOILETTE IN FRANCE.

CHAPTER XX.

In the " Mémoires de la Duchesse d'Abrantès," we read of the reign of Louis XV.: " Jamais les Français n'avaient été plus créateurs qu'à cette époque ; jamais les sensualités de tous genres ne s'étaient autant multipliées pour entourer une femme de leur élégance recherchée. Le service d'une femme comme il faut n'était jamais composé de moins de deux femmes de chambre, et presque toujours d'un valet de chambre se mêlant du service intérieur. Une salle de bain était de rigueur, car une femme élégante ne passait pas deux jours sans se baigner ; et puis des parfums en abondance ; les batistes, les toiles les plus fines, les dentelles les plus précieuses, pour chaque saison, étaient sur la toilette, dans les sultans, les corbeilles ambrées, garnies de peaux d'Espagne, qui recevaient les objets nécessaires, en premier ressort, à la toilette d'une femme riche."

It was during the reign of Louis XV. that a most celebrated but extraordinary *procès* was held in the highest court of judicature,—a *procès* that none but Frenchmen would ever have undertaken, for it was

Mémoires de la Duchesse d'Abrantès: Madame Junot, 1784-1838; see note p. 252
Louis XV: called the Well-Beloved, 1715-1774
procès: law suit
"Jamais les Français": French translation appears in appendix

between the *coiffeurs des dames de Paris*, against the corporation of master *barbers and hairdressers*. In the speech of one of the *avocats*, it was declared that dressing ladies' hair was a liberal art, and it was compared to that of the poet, the painter, and the statuary. In another part, the *coiffeur des dames* is made to say, " If the arrangement of the hair, and the various colours we give the locks, do not answer our expectations, we have under our hand all the treasures of the mines of Golconda. To us belongs the happy disposition of the diamonds, the placing the pearl pins, and the suspending the feathers." A great deal more, in the same flowery strain, follows ; but the grave tribunal before whom the case was tried ordered it to be suppressed, as unworthy the majesty of the judges and the court. But the coiffeurs gained their cause against the perruquiers, and the decision was hailed with rapturous applause by the brilliant conclave of Parisian beauties, who looked upon this *procès* as one of national importance. During the researches and inquiries which were made, it was discovered that there were actually 1200 *coiffeurs des dames* in Paris.

At this time dress was in the zenith of its splendour. Every thing that art could produce or riches procure was swiftly borne to the temple of fashion. New manufactures were introduced, distant lands ransacked of their treasures, and every invention that could add to the charms of youth and beauty, or restore lost graces to the face and form of age, were united in the capital of France ; and having been transformed by the magic fingers and fertile genius of the handmaids of fashion into robes, bonnets, chapeaux, and ornaments of every kind, were then distributed

coîffeurs des dames de Paris: hairdressers to the ladies of Paris
avocat: lawyer, barrister
mines of Golconda: city in India so famed for its wealth that it became a byword for unlimited riches
perruquiers: literally, wigmakers; in this case, the barbers and hairdressers

over Europe, the name of *mode Parisienne* stamping them with every grace, beauty, and elegance.

Ladies' gowns were now usually embroidered, and an open petticoat of rich velvet or satin was worn over it. The corsage was pointed, and ornamented round the bosom with lace; the sleeves were bouffante, and terminated with deep ruffles at the elbow. The hair was often parted on the forehead, and hung in rich

curls upon the neck, adorned with bandeaux of pearls and precious stones. At other times the upper robe sloped away from the waist, and terminated in a long train; the sleeves, wide and hanging, were looped up with jewels, and the hair, powdered and pomatumed, was drawn over a cushion to a great height, and adorned with feathers, ribands, or lace.

Ladies' Head-Dresses in the Reign of Louis XV

From the sketches we now give, which are all of the time of Louis XV., it appears that high head-

dresses were the most fashionable, for even the head with curls assumes the same towering height as the others.

mode Parisienne: Parisian fashion
Louis XV: 1715–1774

The commode of which we spoke in our notice of the toilette in England, was much in vogue during the whole of this reign ; and one variety was shaped somewhat like a modern cap, with an ornament resembling a fan rising up from the forehead, and two streamers floating behind.

The Commode, or Cap

In Thunberg's account of Paris in the year 1771, we read : " In rainy weather the streets are scarcely passable for umbrellas, which are indispensably necessary in a city where all the world follows the Japanese fashion of going bareheaded." The same author also mentions that very small muffs were worn at this time in Paris by men as well as women.

Wraxall, in his " History of France," compares the eighteenth with the sixteenth century ; and says, in point of dress, there was a striking similarity, as will be seen by the following description : " The petticoat was made very long, so as to conceal the feet entirely in walking, but as a sort of compensation for this mark of modesty and bashfulness, the ladies displayed their necks in an immoderate degree. To Margaret of Valois was due the introduction of this mode, which she continued, in defiance of the admonitions and reprehensions levelled at her from the pulpit." It excites entertainment to know that inventions for increasing the size of the female figure behind, as well as for augmenting it before, and both of which have been renewed in the present age, were common under the last princes of Valois. As early as 1563 treatises were written, and satires composed, on the

commode: tall headdress
Thunberg: Carl Peter Thunberg, wrote "Travels in Europe, Africa & Asia 1770–1779"
Wraxall: Sir Nathaniel Wraxall, 1751–1831, wrote "Memoirs of the Kings of France of the Race of Valois, with a Tour through the Western, Southern and Interior Provinces of France", 1777
Margaret of Valois: 1553–1615, see note p. 223; she had problems with the Church because of her loose living and her marriage to Henry IV was dissolved by the Pope in 1599; she wrote her mémoirs, which were not published until 1628
last princess of Valois: this was Margaret, as the line died with her

" Basquines" and " Vertugalles," the two articles of dress destined to the above-mentioned purposes.

The " Guardian" says : " France may as properly be called the 'fountain of dress,' as Greece was of literature.   French ladies have been celebrated in all ages for the fruitful genius they have displayed in the ever-varying form of petticoats and head-dresses, and never more so than during the reign of Louis XV., when every succeeding hour gave birth to some fresh mode, and new words had to be invented to express the thousand elegancies daily added to the mystic wonders of the toilette-table."

Hoops, which had failed to secure the good graces of the fair ladies of the court of Louis XIV., again shone forth in all their glory during the reign of his successor ; while ruffles, plumes, ribands, laces, satins, brocades, and jewels, acquired a more important station in the wardrobe than at any former period. Waists were worn very long and pointed, bodies generally open, and laced across ; sleeves reaching to the elbow, where they terminated with a rich lace ruffle ; and the upper petticoat open, and forming a kind of train, while the under one was covered with embroidery and flounces.

Long, square-cut coats, without collars, and with large pockets, seem to have been generally worn during this reign ; they were often ornamented with gold or silver lace, and had very large buttons.   The gayest colours and most expensive materials were frequently employed in their manufacture, as well as in that of the waistcoat, which had long flaps, and was almost always embroidered.   Breeches were still worn, as well as ruffles, lace neckcloths, and high-heeled shoes.

Basquines: rich outer petticoats, originally worn by Basque and Spanish peasant women
Vertugalles: Spanish farthingales
the "Guardian": "The Manchester Guardian", which was the local paper for the authoress
Louis XV: 1715–1774
Louis XIV: 1643–1715

Wigs, of various forms and denominations, preserved their ascendancy in the toilette of men of fashion; three-cornered hats were generally worn, and a sword still formed an indispensable part of a man's attire.

High head-dresses appear to have continued the fashion with ladies during the reign of Louis XVI. In the one of which we give a sketch, the hair is stiffly pomatumed and powdered, and drawn from the forehead in two points, to which are added several bows of hair, a plume of ostrich feathers, and another of  marabouts set in jewels. High caps, with lappets, were also much worn at this period, the gowns were made *en fourreau lacé*, with sleeves to the elbow *en sabot*, and lace ruffles.

Lady's Head-Dress in the Reign of Louis XVI

The Duchesse d' Abrantès' account of M. de Caulaincourt gives a good idea of the dress of gentlemen in the time of Louis XVI. " Ancien officier de cavalerie, il avait conservé, en dépit du temps, de la reforme et de la révolution, les grandes bottes à l'écuyer et à manchettes, le toupet en vergette, les faces courtes, et la queue bien serrée; les culottes courtes, l'habit à grands boutons de métal, et le gilet à effilé. Audessous de cet effilé pendaient deux immense chaînes de montre, avec une telle collection de breloques que, lorsque je n'entendais pas le bruit accoutumé que faisaient son cheval et lui, m'avertissait dès qu'il montait l'escalier."

Previously to the opening of the Etats Généraux in 1789, it was decided that a distinct dress should be

Louis XVI: 1774–1792
pomatumed: pomaded
marabout: marabou feathers, from a large stork or heron
en fourreau lacé: laced sheaths, that is, tight to the body like a sword sheath
en sabot: in the shape of a horse's hoof
Duchesse d'Abrantès: Madame Junot, 1784–1838, see note p. 252
M. de Caulaincourt: Marquis de Caulaincourt, who was Napoleon's aide de camp, circa
    1773–1827
"Ancien officier": French translation appears in appendix
Etats Généraux: "Estates General", comprising the three classes: clergy, nobility,
    and commons

worn by the three orders or ranks; ancient records were consulted, and the archives of the reign of Louis XIII. searched, to find models for the garments to be worn by the nobility and the tiers-état. At length it was decided that the nobles should represent the barons of the time of Philippe le Bel, and the tiers-état the clercs, baillis, and échevins of former days. Dulaure, however, in his work on the French revolution, gives the following description of these costumes; which shews that the nobles eventually assumed the dress not of barons of the time of Philippe le Bel, but of chevaliers of the time of Henri Quatre :—

"La noblesse devait être vêtue de la manière suivante : habit noir, avec veste et paremens d'or, manteau de soie, cravate de dentelle, et chapeau à plumes retroussé à la Henri IV. Le clergé devait paraître en soutane, grand manteau, bonnet carré ; les évêques se distinguaient par la robe violette et le rochet. Quant au tiers-état, sa parure était des plus modestes. On l'avait condamné à l'habit de laine noire, au simple manteau de soie noire, à la cravate de batiste, et au chapeau rabattu, sans ganse ni bouton."

During the Revolution the Athenian mode of attire was adopted. A French lady of that time gives the following account of it: "A simple piece of linen, slightly laced before, while it leaves the waist uncompressed, serves the purpose of a corset. If a robe is worn which is not open in front, petticoats are altogether dispensed with, the cambric chemise having the semblance of one, from its skirt being trimmed with lace. When attired for a ball, those who dance commonly put on a tunic, and then a petticoat becomes a matter of necessity rather than of choice. Pockets,

Louis XIII: 1610-1643
Phillipe le Bel: Philip IV, 1285-1314
tiers-état: third estate (lowest)
clercs: clerks and scholars
baillis: bailiffs (administrators and officers)
échevins: sheriffs
Dulaure: Jacque Antoine Dulaure, late 18th-early 19th century writer
chevaliers: knights
Henri Quatre: Henry IV, 1589-1610
"La noblesse devait être": French translation appears in the appendix

being deemed an incumbrance, are not worn; what money is required is carried in a small purse, which is concealed in the centre of the bosom, this is also occasionally the receptacle of a small gold watch, or other trinket, which is suspended to the neck by a collar of hair, decorated with various ornaments. In dancing the fan is introduced into the zone or girdle."

Riding-habits seem to have been worn by ladies even when not on horseback. Madame Tallien, one of the most celebrated beauties of this period, is described as having worn one of deep blue casimir, with yellow buttons, and a collar and trimming of red velvet, at a great meeting which she attended at Bordeaux. Her beautiful black hair was cut *à la* Titus, and curled round her head, on which was placed, a little on one side, a small scarlet velvet cap, edged with fur.

A dress in which this lady appeared at a great ball at Paris is represented as having been most graceful. It consisted of a simple white India muslin drapée à l'antique, and fastened at the shoulders with two cameos; she wore a gold belt, also clasped with a cameo, and a large gold armlet held in the sleeve, which was very short: her hair, which was curled all over her head, was without ornament, and round her shoulders was gracefully thrown a superb scarlet cashmere shawl.

The Duchesse d'Abrantès, in her Memoirs, gives an account of an elegant costume worn by one of Buonaparte's sisters. She says: "Madame Leclerc était coiffée ce jour-là, avec des bandelettes d'une fourrure très précieuse, dont j'ignore le nom, mais d'un poil très ras, d'une peau très souple et par-

Madame Tallien: 1773–1835, a woman of fashion, she initiated the neo–Greek styles of the Directoire period (1795–1799)
Titus: Roman Emperor, 79–81 A.D.; the hairstyle à la Titus is worn by Mme. Recamier in the famous portrait of her by David, although men wore the style, also
drapée à l'antique: draped in the Grecian style; in French, "à l'antique" refers specifically to ancient Grecian modes in art and dress
Duchesse d'Abrantès: Madame Junot, 1784–1838, see note p. 252
"Madame LeClerc": Maria Paolina, 1780–1825, married Charles Leclerc 1797; translation appears in the appendix

semée de petites taches tigrées. Ces bandelettes étaient surmontées de grappes de raisin en or, mais sans que la coiffure fût élevée comme le sont les coiffures d'aujourd' hui. Une robe de mousseline de l'Inde, d'une excessive finesse, avait au bas une broderie en lames d'or, de la hauteur de quatre à cinq doigts, représentant une guirlande de pampre. Une tunique de la forme grecque la plus pure, se drapait sur sa jolie taille, et avait également au bord une broderie semblable à celle de la robe. La tunique était arrêtée sur les épaules par des camées du plus grand prix. Les manches, extrêmement courtes, et légèrement plissées, avaient un petit poignet et étaient également retenues par des camées. La ceinture mise au-dessous du sein, comme nous le voyons dans les statues, était formée par une bande d'or bruni, dont le cadenas était une superbe pierre graveé à l'antique."

The same writer also mentions a costume worn at that time by ladies, which consisted solely of a cambric chemise, and a muslin gown perfectly *collante*.

"Au nombre des folies du temps," adds Madame Junot, "les perruques jouaient un rôle important. Rien ne peut-être comparé à l'absurdité de cette mode. Une femme brune devait avoir une perruque blonde ; une femme blonde, une brune. Enfin une perruque devenait partie nécessaire d'un trousseau. J'en ai vue qui coûtaient jusqu'à huit et dix mille francs, mais *en assignats,* ce qui revenait à cent cinquante ou deux cents francs en argent."

Dulaure, whom we have before quoted, says : "Les vêtemens se ressentirent des changemens politiques. Le bon ton consistait à être vêtu en *carmagnole,* c'est-

---

collante: form-fitting
Madame Junot: Duchesse d'Abrantès, 1784–1838, see note p. 252
Dulaure: Jacque Antoine Dulaure, see note p. 248
"Au nombre des folies"––"Les vêtemens": translations appear in the appendix

à-dire, à porter des pantalons et une veste de chasse. Ceux qui observaient strictement le costume, avaient pour chaussure des sabots ; au lieu de canne, un bâton noueux. Ils étaient coiffés en cheveux ronds et en bonnet rouge, avec cocarde ; on a vu des millionnaires dans cet équipage. Le 22 Novembre, dans le conseil de la commune de Paris, il s'éleva une discussion assez vive sur la question de savoir si les membres des autorités constituées seraient seuls décorés du bonnet rouge, ou si l'on laisserait à chacun la liberté de s'en coiffer ; il fut décidé que chacun pourrait se coiffer à sa guise. La veille, ce conseil avait pris un arrêté qui proscrivait les perruques noires *à la Jacobite*. Les femmes, dans leur habillement, ne portaient rien d'extraordinaire si ce n'est la cocarde tricolore à leurs bonnets, ou à leurs chapeaux, dont la forme présentait un cône tronqué. Leur chevelure éparse sur leurs épaules, et taillée sur le devant, couvrait la moitié de leur front."

The *Muscadins*, says Madame Junot, "portaient des redingotes grises, avec des collets noirs, des cravates vertes ; et leurs cheveux, au lieu d'être à la Titus, comme ceux de la plupart des jeunes gens, étaient nattés, poudrés, et relevés, avec un peigne, tandis que de chaque côté de la figure, descendait une longue face appelée, en style du temps, *oreilles de chien*."

The mania of republicanism seems to have extended even to dress, for many young men, anxious to imitate the Greeks in every thing, were now habited, *sans-culottes*, in tunics and cloaks, or rather ample togas.

Madame Junot describes the *incroyable* of a year or two later, with his "cadenettes relevées" and long

Muscadins: literally, musk-comfits; applied pejoratively after 1794 in Parisian
    slang to a type of perfumed fop, dandy, or exquisite of the upper middle class
Madame Junot: Duchesse d'Abrantès, 1784-1838, see note p. 252
"portaient des redingotes": French translation appears in the appendix
sans-culottes: literally, without breeches
incroyable: literally, unbelievable; an extreme form of fashion akin to the Macaronis
cadenettes relevées: the hair was divided into two simple or braided strands and fas-
    tened with bows over the ears, hanging in loops along the sides of the face

The Incroyable

corkscrew curls, as wearing a hat so very small as to be kept with difficulty on the head; an immense cravat, containing at least two yards of muslin, a short coat or jacket, scarcely reaching to the hips, and a pair of pantaloons of immense width, which gave him the appearance almost of a woman.

The Greek style of dress continued the fashion during the Consulate; most of the coiffures were copied from ancient statues. A few caps and turbans occasionally made their appearance, but the usual head-

Ladies' Head-Dresses during the Consulate

dress, at least for young unmarried women, consisted of a crop adorned with a wreath of flowers.

Madame Junot gives the following account of her trousseau, and the dress that was the fashion for a bride in 1800:—" D'une immense corbeille, ou plutôt une malle en gros de Naples rose brodée en chenille noire, portant mon chiffre, et fortement parfumée de peaux d'Espagne, étaient sortis une quantité immense de petits paquets noués avec des faveurs roses ou bleues. C'étaient des chemises à manches gauffrées, brodées, et brodées comme brodait Mademoiselle l'Olive; des mouchoirs, des jupons, des canesous du

Consulate: 1799–1804

Madame Junot: Duchesse d'Abrantès, 1784–1838; born Laure Permon, she was the wife of an ambassador to Portugal, and wrote "Souvenirs Historiques sur Napoléon, la Révolution, le Directoire, l'Empire et la Restauration"

"D'une immense corbeille": translated in the appendix

matin, des peignoirs de mousseline de l'Inde, des ca-
misolles de nuit, des bonnets de nuit, des bonnets du
matin de toutes les couleurs, de toutes les formes, et
tout cela brodé, garni de valenciennes ou de malines,
ou de point d'Angleterre.   A cette époque on n'avait
pas encore la très-bonne coutume de ne point donner
de *corbeille ;* c'était dans une corbeille que se trou-
vaient les châles de cachemire, les voiles de point
d'Angleterre, les garnitures de robes en point à
l'aiguille, et en point de Bruxelles, ainsi qu'en blonde
pour l'été.   Il y avait aussi des robes de blonde
blanche, et de dentelle noire ; des pièces de mousseline de l'Inde, des pièces de velours en étoffe turques,
que le Général avait rapportées d'Egypte, des robes
de bal pour une mariée ; ma robe de *présentation ;* *
des robes de mousseline de l'Inde brodées en lames
d'argent, et puis des fleurs de chez Madame Roux ;
des rubans de toutes les largeurs, de toutes les couleurs ; des sacs, des éventails, des gants, des essences
de Fargeon, de Riban, des sachets de peau d'Espagne,
et d'herbes de Montpellier ; enfin rien n'avait été
oublié. * * * *   Le matin, à peine neuf heures
furent-elles sonnées, que l'on commença la toilette
demi-habillée, que je devais faire pour aller à la mairie.
J'avais une robe de mousseline de l'Inde brodée au
plumetis, et en points à jour, comme c'était alors la

* " Cette robe avait cela de curieux, que, comme on ne portait
pas encore un costume spécial pour le château, ce qui n'arriva que
sous l'empire, Madame Germon s'était cependant cru obligée, sur ce
mot *robe de représentation* qu'avait dit ma mère de faire une robe
différente des autres.   Cette robe était à queue, cela n'était pas extraordinaire alors, on les portait toujours ainsi le soir.   Mais elle était
de la même forme que les robes qu'on portait sur la scène.   Elle était
ouverte et laissait voir une jupe de crêpe lamée en argent ; la robe était
d'une riche étoffe de Lyon imitant le brocart d'argent de l'Orient."

mode. Cette robe était à queue, montante, et avec de longues manches ; le lis de devant entièrement brodé, ainsi que le tour, le corsage, et le bout des manches, qu'on appelait alors amadis. La fraise était en magnifique point à l'aiguille. Sur ma tête j'avais un bonnet en point de Bruxelles, monté par Mademoiselle Despaux ; au sommet du bonnet était attachée une petite couronne de fleurs d'orangers, d'où partait un long voile en point d'Angleterre, qui tombait à mes pieds, et dont je pouvais presque m'envelopper. Cette toilette, qui était celle adoptée pour les jeunes mariées, et qui ne différait que par le plus ou moins de richesse, d'une fiancée à une autre, avait, selon moi, bien plus de charme et d'élégance que celle d'aujourd'hui."

The French court, during the Empire, was the most sumptuous, the most brilliant, and the most elegant ever witnessed in Europe. Buonaparte passed a sumptuary law to regulate the dress of the ladies of the court, of which Madame Junot gives the following description : " Ce costume était alors à-peu-près ce qu'il est encore aujourd'hui ; *la chérusque,** qu'on retrencha très-promptement, allait pourtant fort bien ; le manteau et la jupe étaient comme nous les portons toujours, avec cette différence, que dans l'origine la bordure du manteau ne pouvait excéder quatre pouces ; les princesses seules, avaient le droit de porter le manteau brodé en plein. Tels furent d'abord les ordres de l'empereur. C'était, avait-il dit à Junot, à nous à donner l'exemple de la modération, et à ne pas écraser, par un faste ridicule, la femme d'un officier sans fortune ou d'un savant respectable."

---

* " Fraise gothique à longues dents, en tulle bordé d'or ou d'argent comme l'habit."

Empire: 1804-1815
Buonaparte: Napoleon Bonaparte, 1796-1821
Madame Junot: see note p. 252
"Ce costume": translated in the appendix

This law was, however, soon disregarded, and the Empress herself took the part of the youthful beauties, whose love of splendour and magnificence could not be restrained. A dress, worn by the beautiful Josephine, is thus recorded by Madame Junot: " La toilette de l'impératrice était admirable de bon goût et de fraicheur ; elle avait une robe de mousseline de l'Inde, de ces mousselines qu'on peut appeler un tissu d'air, que, cependant, malgré sa finesse, on avait brodée au plumetis d'un semis de petites étoiles, dont le milieu était rempli par un point de dentelle fait à l'aiguille. La robe était montante, et faite comme une redingote ; tout autour était une magnifique Angleterre de la hauteur de deux mains, et abondamment froncée ; le tour du col et le devant de la robe en avait également ; de distance en distance, étaient des nœuds de ruban de satin bleu, si frais, si pur de nuance, bleu turquoise, que jamais on ne vit rien de si charmant ; le dessous de la robe était en satin du même bleu que les rubans ; sur sa tête, l'impératrice avait un bonnet dont les *papillons* étaient en Angleterre du même dessin, mais encore plus fine que celle de la robe, et gracieusement posé et coupé par des touffes de ce ruban bleu auquel ne venait se mêler aucune fleur."

The Empress Josephine was remarkable for the taste she displayed in every thing relating to dress. The following *costume de cour*, which she occasionally wore, must have been very elegant: " La jupe et le manteau étaient pareils ; tous deux en tulle brodé en lames d'or, mais avec une délicatesse infinie. C'était un carreau pris dans un autre, et pris pas ses quatre côtés, ce qui formait, non pas un tissu d'or, mais un réseau admirablement fait. Une petite frange bordait

Empress Josephine: married Napoleon 1796, was divorced in 1809
Madame Junot: see note p. 252
"La toilette de l'impératrice": translation in the appendix
costume de cour: Court costume
"La jupe": translation in the appendix

le manteau et la robe. Puis le tour du corsage, les manches, la ceinture, tout était brodé en émeraudes entourées de diamans. Le diadème, le peigne, les boucles d'oreilles . . . . tout en émeraudes."

The Emperor, not satisfied with arranging the toilette of the ladies, ordered a particular court-dress for the gentlemen also. It consisted of an embroidered coat and ruffles, and shirt frills in *point* d'Angleterre. Powder was no longer worn in the hair, which, instead of hanging down the back in a queue, was cut short, like the present fashion.

In Lady Morgan's " France" is a curious and amusing account of the trousseau of the Duchesse de Berri; and it shews the importance with which such matters are regarded in France : " At last," says the authoress, " after full two hours' efforts, and more suffering from heat and apprehension than I ever endured, we passed the last barrier, and arrived at the palladium of the royal toilette. A long suite of beautiful rooms were thrown open, whose lofty walls were thickly covered with robes of every hue, tint, web, and texture, from the imperial drapery of coronation splendour, to the simple *robe-de-chambre* of British lace and British muslin; from the diamond coronet to the *bonnet-de-nuit* ; while platforms, or counters, surrounding each room, were guarded off from the unhallowed touch of plebeian curiosity by silken cords, and placed under the surveillance of the priests and priestesses of the toilette, in grand pontificals. These formed the sanctuary of all the minor attributes of the royal wardrobe. Every article of female dress, from the most necessary to the most superfluous, was here arranged, not by dozens, but by hundreds. Here

Emperor: Napoleon I, 1796–1821
point d'Angleterre: English (bobbin or pillow) lace
Lady Morgan: Lady Sydney Morgan, circa 1783–1859, Irish woman of letters, wrote many
    books of which her
"France": was published in 1817
Duchesse de Berri: Marie Caroline of Naples, 1798–1870, married in 1816
robe-de-chambre: dressing gown
bonnet-de-nuit: night cap

the Queen of Sheba might have died of envy ; here the treasures of the ' forty thieves,' or the ' cave of Baba Abdalla,' were rivalled or surpassed, not only in splendour but extent. The life of the old Countess of Dumont would have been too short, though spent in dressing, to exhaust such a wardrobe as here presented itself ; and if such were the sumptuous provision to be made for the future daughters of France, it may be truly said that ' Solomon, in all his glory, was not arrayed like one of these.' "

Before concluding the annals of the toilette of *la belle France*, we must add, that many of the coiffures worn in that country, during the last twenty years, were quite as extravagant for size and height as those censured by Paradin and Jean de Meun. The giraffe was a tower of bows, ribands, combs, and feathers ; while the casque head-dress was much narrower, though nearly as high, having the hair drawn up from the forehead into a bow and plait on the summit of the head.

The Giraffe Head-Dress

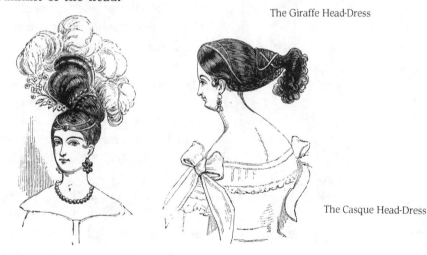

The Casque Head-Dress

Baba Abdalla: Ali Baba
Paradin: Guillaume Paradin wrote "Mémoire de l'Histoire de Lyon", 1573
Jean de Meun: wrote the "Roman de la Rose", 1275

Chapter 21 – France, Regional Folk Dress

THE TOILETTE IN FRANCE.

CHAPTER XXI.

" It is a curious fact," writes a French author, when speaking of Brittany, " that here we still find the traditions, manners, language, nay, even the costume, of the old Celtic race."

When we reflect that the inhabitants of this province are descended from those warriors who once possessed by far the greater portion, if not the whole, of western Europe, every incident belonging to them becomes of the greatest interest, and their costume particularly; since, though belonging to the chief temple of Fashion—*la belle France*—have still resisted the blandishments of the goddess, and retain their ancient dress in spite of all her attempted innovations.

Mrs. Stothard, in her " Tour through Normandy in 1818," says : " The common people in some parts of Brittany wear a goat-skin dress, and look not unlike Defoe's description of Robinson Crusoe. The furry part of the dress is worn outside ; it is made with long sleeves, and falls nearly below the knees. Their long, shaggy hair, hangs dishevelled about their

Costume of a Peasant in Brittany

Brittany: the region of France that juts into the Atlantic below the Channel; also
    known as Less Britain, to distinguish it from Great Britain
Mrs. Stothard: Anna Eliza Bray, 1790–1883
"Tour Through Normandy": "A Tour Through Normandy and Brittany", published 1818
Defoe: Daniel Defoe, 1660–1731

shoulders, the head being covered by a broad-flapped straw or beaver hat. Some few of the Bretons go without shoes or stockings; but the generality wear sabots (wooden shoes), and thrust straw into them, to prevent the foot being rubbed by the pressure of the wood.

"The usual costume of the pea-sants of Brittany is a broad-flapped hat, from beneath which the hair floats down loosely on the shoul-ders; a coat, lined with scarlet, generally of a dark mulberry co-lour; a white waistcoat, also lined with scarlet, and a broad belt corresponding in colour with the lining, or else plaided, like a Scotch tartan. The most singular feature of their dress is the taste and ca-price displayed in the coat, which, instead of being of a uniform colour, has the skirts often of quite a dif-ferent shade from the upper part. The goat-skin dress is also commonly worn, particularly in Bas Bre-tagne. Very few go barefooted, wooden shoes being generally used by men, women, and children. The women are invariably dressed in the peculiar costume I have described above; however, it sometimes varies a little in some of the districts."

Costume of a Female Peasant in Brittany

A *paysanne* of Bignan is thus described: "She was dressed in a petticoat or skirt of white flannel, bordered with a scarlet band above the hem. This skirt is sewed to the body in large full plaits; the body, or jacket, was made of scarlet cloth, tight to the shape, and reached nearly up to the throat; the

Bretons: people of Brittany
Bas Bretagne: (lower) western Brittany
paysanne: countrywoman, peasant
Bignan: an area of Brittany

sleeves were of the same colour, sitting close to the
arm, and turned up at the wrist, with a deep cuff;
both the body and sleeves being turned with a braiding, composed of a black velvet riband, embroidered
with coloured worsteds. Her apron was of a deep
mulberry colour, fastened with an ornamented sash,
tied in a bow at the side; her cap of white linen sat
quite tight upon her head, and was covered with another cap, that served the purpose of a bonnet. This
last was made of a coarse starched cloth, like brown
Holland, the form conical, with two long flaps hanging
down her back, or sometimes pinned up, at the pleasure of the wearer. Her necklace was of amber and
black beads; she wore also, suspended by a velvet
string, a little ebony crucifix, wrought in pure gold;
her brooch, that fastened her shift in front, was made
of white bugles and green glass-beads tastefully arranged."

The dress in the district of the Léonais is, like its
wearers, grave and formal; it is generally made of
black cloth or serge, which gives it a most sombre
appearance. The coat is cut quite square, but sometimes reaches half way to the knee; at others,
it is only like a long jacket. The waistcoat is very
long. The breeches of the better farmers are very
large, and tied in at the knees; the poorer peasants
have them not nearly so wide. The stockings are
black, and a blue scarf encircles the waist: the hair
always hangs at its full length over the back and
shoulders; the hat is of immense size, and the shoe-
buckle enormous. Those peasants who cannot afford
to wear cloth clothes have them made of linen, and
wear straw hats, with a black cotton rosette.

Léonais: an area of Brittany

" Unlike the Léonards," says the author of the " Summer in Brittany," " the inhabitants of the hills delight in the most gay and contrasted colours. Violet is a very favourite colour for the coat, which is usually adorned with crimson trimmings and buttons. Gaiters, or leggings rather, for they do not cover any part of the foot, are worn of the same hue, and similarly ornamented with crimson. The ' *bragon bas*,' or enormous breeches, are almost always of linen, or of a coarse brown woollen cloth. The coats and waistcoats of the richer farmers, and the boddices and petticoats of their wives, are usually made of a coarse cloth ; those of the poorer classes, of a woollen material they call '*gainé*,' which is full of little knots, and resembles the sort of stuff of which greatcoats are sometimes made. The poorer classes are dressed entirely in linen, or else in a sort of coarse brown thick flannel. The hats in Cornouaille are broad-brimmed, but not so immensely large as those of the Léonards ; and, instead of the simple broad band of black velvet, which is used by the latter, they are ornamented with two or three circles of string, prepared with the gayest and most varied colours, for the purpose, in the same manner that the handles of church bell-ropes are made. Between these variegated strings the Kernewote, or Cornouaille man, puts a circle or two of silver thread, and all the various strings are united into a tassel, which hangs down behind."

It is a curious fact, that the peasants of each district retain the costume of their native village, even when they move to a different part of the country. Thus it is easy to know whence they come ; and the

Léonards: people of Léonais
"Summer in Brittany": by T. A. Trollope, 1840
Cornouaille: literally, Cornwall; probably Concorneau, a town near Quimper

variety of dress forms a pleasing contrast. In the neighbourhood of St. Pol de Léon the peasants wear flannel jackets and violet-coloured breeches; men from near Brest appear in red coats and breeches, and white waistcoats with crimson buttons, very different from the mourning habiliments of the Léonards. On the western coast a blue cloak, with a falling cape, distinguishes the native peasant from those of other districts. The Roscovites, too, have close green jackets, white trousers, and crimson belts; while the men from the remote villages of the northern shore wear small, close, blue caps, dingy woollen jackets, and short linen trousers. They do not even adopt the sabot, but leave the feet and legs bare.

The dress of the peasants at Quimper is very singular; they have the large broad-brimmed hat before mentioned, the crown of which is ornamented with two bands of gold, a long blue waistcoat, a jacket made so tight that only the lower button can be fastened, thus leaving it very open, to shew the waistcoat to advantage. On the edges of the jacket and round the throat is a band of gold, or gold-coloured lace. The " bragon bas " are immense in size, and made of white linen; the stockings brown, large sabots on the feet, and a broad brown leather belt round the waist, fastened with a large buckle. The hair of these " exquisites " hangs in long curls half-way down their backs.

The costume of the women also is diversified, but more in colour than shape. Most of them wear a jacket laced up in front, with tight sleeves, that reach only to the elbows: under these are white sleeves, fastened round the wrist. The petticoat is often white,

St. Pol de Léon: port in the northwest of Brittany
Brest: seaport at the western tip of Brittany
Roscovites: from Roscoff, seaport near St. Pol de Léon
Quimper: port on the southwest coast
"bragon bas": loose, wide breeches
"exquisites": fops or men of fashion

and very full and short, to shew to perfection the gold buckles in the shoes. Sometimes the jacket and gown are blue, trimmed with gaudy gold and red lace; half the sleeves are blue, then pink, and lastly, near the hands, white, tied with yellow or red ribands. The chemise reaches to the throat, where it is fastened with a collar of various colours. An orange-tinted apron finishes this gaudy dress.

In another part of this province—in the department of Morbihan—the men wear short square-cut coats, of white cloth, or drugget; the edges of the coat, the buttons and button-holes, also the flaps of the large pockets (which latter are Vandyked), are all trimmed with crimson cloth; and on the breast of the coat is frequently embroidered the date of the year in which it was made. The women here wear close caps, or hoods, of a violet or green colour.

The variety in the shape of the women's caps is a great peculiarity of dress in this province. Some of these coiffures look like folds of linen laid one upon another, others are immensely high, and some closely encircle the face, but have long lappets hanging down the back. Their hair, unlike the custom with the men, is never seen, even from infancy; and this may account for their strange want of vanity in this ornament of female beauty, for, in many parts of Brittany, they actually part with their tresses at the fairs to regular hair-merchants, who buy for a few sous what they afterwards sell in other towns for large prices, when curled and made into perukes. We have frequently described ladies, who, not content with Nature's beauty in this respect, have added borrowed ringlets to their own; but these are the first people we have

Morbihan: a state surrounding the Gulf of Morbihan, whose main port is Vannes
Vandyked: with ragged or deeply pinked edges

met with who part with their beautiful long hair for " filthy lucre," and allow their heads to be shorn like sheep.

Ladies' Head-Dresses in Morbihan

The costume of the Norman peasants, in many respects, differs from those of Brittany. The men frequently wear no hats; and when they do, they are of every shape, form, and colour; sometimes without brims, at other times the brims are very broad; and often the only covering for the head is a cotton white or red night-cap. They seldom wear neckcloths; and both men and women have wooden sabots, fastened to the feet by leathern straps. Their coats are often long, and made of a dark-coloured cloth; and if they wear a hat, they frequently have a cap also underneath it.

In Mrs. Stothard's " Tour" the costume of the women is thus described : " It looks singular at the first view, but, when the eye is accustomed to it, appears by no means unbecoming. It generally consists

Norman: from Normandy, an area of northwest France on the English Channel
sabots: wooden shoes
Mrs. Stothard's "Tour": see note p. 258

of a woollen petticoat, striped with a variety of colours, as red, blue, &c., and an apron also of red or blue. The jacket of the gown is most commonly made of maroon, white, black, or red worsted, the long sleeves of which being sometimes, perhaps, of maroon, as far as the elbow, and the lower half of a scarlet colour. A little shawl (white or coloured), with a fringe round it, pinned in plaits upon the back, covers the shoulders. The head-dress, called the *bourgoin*, is the most remarkable and conspicuous part of their attire. It is formed of white, stiffly-starched muslin, that covers a pasteboard shape, and rises a great height above the head, frequently diminishing in size towards the top, where it finishes in a circular form; two long lappets depend from either side towards the back, and these are often composed of the finest lace. Some of the women have a piece of velvet, which fastens their head-dress under the chin, and others a riband, that crosses the forehead from the cap. Several paysannes, on Sundays or holydays, appear clothed entirely in white instead of in this costume; but they still retain their *bourgoin*, which, on such occasions, is always composed of fine muslin and lace."

Bourgoin Head-Dresses

The back hair is usually worn *en chignon*, that is, allowed to fall at full length down the back, then turned back and the ends fastened under the cap, so as to form an immense thick club of hair on the shoulders.

paysannes: peasants, countrywomen
en chignon: caught up in a bun

The *bourgoins* throughout all Normandy are not alike : that of the Pays de Caux deserves to be described.   The part which surrounds the face is of scarlet velvet ; from underneath it peep some curls on

Bourgoin Head-Dress of the Pays de Caux

the temples ; the upper part is of blue pasteboard, covered with tiny flowers in gold tinsel, and greatly resembles an ancient casque. At the top, which is much elevated above the head, is an immense ruff of muslin, edged with lace, from which hang two streamers, that reach nearly to the ground, falling over the *chignon*. This towering edifice is kept in its place by a string passing under the chin, and is much like the caps worn in England in the fifteenth century. When travelling in Normandy, I was shewn one of these coiffures, belonging to the wife of a rich peasant ; it had descended from mother to daughter for several generations, and was looked upon with as much reverence as a box of family diamonds would be among the higher classes. It very much resembled the one we have already described, only it was more laden with tinsel and lace, and the weight was quite extraordinary.

The Normandes, unlike their neighbours in some parts of Brittany, almost always curl their hair, and seem to regard it as an addition to their personal charms. Not unfrequently they wear low gowns, and a ruff round the throat. In their ordinary dress they have pockets, made of a different-coloured stuff to the petticoat, hanging outside it. They are also very fond of silver or gilt ornaments, such as chains, ear-

Pays de Caux: region near Dieppe

rings, brooches, and crosses; and very frequently, when a fête-day permits their indulging in the luxury of wearing shoes, they are adorned with huge paste buckles.

In the southern parts of France the dress approaches more nearly to that of the Spanish peasant. In Bearn it is very curious. The men have flat woollen caps, and cloaks of a brown colour, the latter being sufficiently wide not only to cover themselves, but also the tail of the animals they ride. The hood belonging to this cloak is very convenient, as in rain it completely shelters the head, though it gives a very grotesque appearance to the wearer.

The paysannes when they ride to market very frequently wear trousers and spurs, which but ill agree with their neatly frilled caps and collars. Sometimes, however, they have hoods of a striped cloth, and long aprons, which serve for riding-habits. "Their usual head-dress," says the author of "A Summer in the Pyrenees," "is a handkerchief made of a manufacture of the country, which never fades or crumples. The middle is usually brown, drab, or fawn colour, with a broad border to suit. It is adjusted so as to give a Grecian contour to the head and face, and I suspect, notwithstanding its appearance of artless simplicity, that there are degrees of coquetry by which it is arranged so as best to suit the appearance of the wearer. Beneath this head-dress we see soft bands of dark hair, carefully parted on the forehead, and placed against the cheek, so as to contrast in the best manner with a complexion at once glowing and delicate, healthy and pure. Add to this the neatest little collar round the neck, the universal shawl pinned

Bearn: Béarn, region in the south of France in the Basque country
"A Summer in the Pyrenees": actually "A Summer and Winter in the Pyrenees", by Mrs.
    Sarah Stickney Ellis, 1841

down in front, over which the hands, in curiously
coloured mittens, are closely folded.   The peasant
women, besides the handkerchief above described, wear
a hood called a *capulet,* made of white or scarlet cloth,
of the finest texture, often bordered with black velvet,
and has a striking effect, whether hanging loosely
from the head to the shoulders, over which it extends,
or folded thick and flat on the head, as we see in
Italian pictures.   When at church they wear a cloak
of black or blue stuff, lined with red.

"The rest of the dress is of the simplest description : usually a thick woollen petticoat of brown or
blue, with a stripe of a different colour, a blue cloth
jacket, tight to the waist, and a cotton shawl or handkerchief pinned over it.   This dress being dark and
durable, and exactly suited to their occupation, never
looks shabby or dirty ; nor is there such a thing as a
ragged garment to be seen, even upon the poorest or
the most infirm.   With regard to shoes and stockings,
they are not particular, and we often see the women
stopping to put them on before they enter the towns.
The peasants and mountaineers wear, universally,
rudely shaped shoes of wood, immensely thick, turned
up with a pointed toe."

In the Pays des Landes the costume of the men
consists of long trousers, a kind of garment between a
jacket and a spenser, and a worsted cap, stuck on the
back of the head like a Scotchman's bonnet.   Their
hair, which they allow to grow thick and bushy, falls
in masses below it.   The paysannes' dress generally
resembles that above given of Bearn.

The female peasants at Aubagne, near Marseilles,
have broad black hats, adorned with little scraps of

Pays des Landes: region along the Atlantic coast southwest of Bordeaux silver lace, smart spensers, and gorgeous petticoats; while their male companions, on their part, by the display of their gayest stockings and vests, seemed determined not to be outdone in finery. The women at Drappo, near Nice, wear their hair bound together with a silk fillet or net, which is fastened above their heads with a long pin. The men wear short vests, blue belts and stockings, and their hair tied up behind.

From an old French work printed in 1727, and entitled " Histoire de la Provence d'Alsace," par le Père Laguille, we copy the annexed print of an Alsatian belle. Her dress is very curious; her robe appears to be of two different materials, half the petticoat being laid in very fine close plaits, the other half in larger plaits, and the bottom all round escalloped. The body is made with an immensely long pointed stomacher, trimmed with lace and jewels; over it is a lace handkerchief, with long pointed ends, apparently of black silk, trimmed with black lace. The sleeves are full, puffed, short, and open, being much longer at the under than the upper part of the arm; the long gloves meet them, scrupulously concealing the fair skin beneath. Several rows of jewels and a cross adorn the neck, and the shoes very much resemble those worn in England during the reign of Charles II. being very pointed, with immense heels and large rosettes.

But the coiffure quite eclipses the rest of this singular dress, and is more *outré* than any other we have met with. It is an enormous three-cornered edifice of satin, lace, and jewels, stretching out on

Alsace, Alsatian: the region around Strasbourg, on the German border
Charles II: 1660–1685
outré: outrageous, exaggerated

each side, far beyond the width of the figure, and standing up in a point of front. The hair is turned back from the forehead, and hangs in a very long plait, which the fair lady carries over her arm.

An Alsatian Belle

THE TOILETTE IN GERMANY.

Dress of a Lady

CHAPTER XXII.

ASHION seems to have been more than usually capricious in the fancies she has displayed in the adornment of the natives of Germany, and singular are the descriptions given by old travellers of their curious and often splendid attire.

On the column of Antoninus, which commemorates the victories gained by Marc Aurelius over several of the German nations, we find this people represented with the long close trousers (the *bracchæ*) then almost universally worn ; shoes much resembling those now in use ; and a cloak (the *sagum Germanicum* mentioned by Tacitus), fastened on the shoulder by a buckle.

Ancient Male Costume

column of Antoninus: column in the Piazza Colonna, Rome, commemorating Marcus Aurelius Antonius's victory over the Germans in 167
Tacitus: Cornelius Tacitus, 55-117, historian, wrote "The Annales, The Description of Germanie"

Pomponius Mela, in his " Description of the ancient Germans," iii. 17, says : " The rich wore a garment, not flowing loose, as the Sarmatians and Parthians, but girt close, and shewing the shape of every limb; they also wore the skins of wild beasts; those bordering on the Rhine without choice or nicety, those in the interior parts were more curious in the selection, as not having acquired by commerce a taste for other apparel. They chose particular beasts, and having stripped off the furs, variegated them with spots and pieces of the skins of marine animals, which the exterior parts of the ocean and seas, unknown to the Romans, produced. The dress of the women was not different from that of the men, except that the women frequently wore linen robes, and variegated them with purple, not extending part of the upper garment into sleeves, but leaving the whole arms and part of the bosom bare."

Lewis, Emperor of Germany, made a solemn declaration, forbidding the introduction of all foreign apparel into his country. Subsequently, however, the people in the higher ranks, like those of all European nations, followed the fashions of France; still, however, retaining their love of splendour, which was, and still is, displayed in the profusion of jewels, rich furs, and gold and silver lace, with which they adorn themselves.

In Montfaucon's " Monarchie Française," is a splendid print of Isabelle of Bavaria, wife of Charles VI. She is represented as being very fond of rich and costly attire, and is accused by Brantome of teaching the French ladies great extravagance in dress. Certainly, in the picture to which we

Pomponius Mela, "Description of the ancient Germans": a 1st century chronicle
Sarmatians: buffer people living along the Danube who allied with Rome against the Germans
Parthians: a Persian tribal people, defeated by Rome and scattered among the other Persians
Lewis: Lewis II, circa 804-876
Montfaucon: Bernard de Montfaucon, 1655-1740, author of "Monumens de la Monarchie Française" which was published 1767
Isabelle of Bavaria: 1370-1435, married Charles VI of France, 1385
Brantôme: Pierre de Bourdeilles, 1534-1614

allude, her majesty is magnificently habited, covered with a profusion of jewels, and wearing the tall head-dress which was the fashion in France for so many after years, and was called a horned cap. The robe worn by Isabelle is adorned with embroidery and jewels; as is also her train, which is immensely long, trimmed with ermine, and supported by two ladies, whose heads are also covered with immense caps, still higher than the queen's. No hair is visible, and her majesty's coiffure is surmounted by a crown; her shoes are long and very pointed.

Isabelle of Bavaria

The two heads given beneath are copied from the "Nuremberg Chronicle" of the year 1493:

Coiffures of the Women of Nuremberg

"Nuremberg Chronicle": early printed history by Hartman Schedel, illustrated with 2,000 woodcuts

The inhabitants of Nuremberg, says a traveller in Germany in the year 1786, aped the Venetians in every thing, even to their pointed hats and monstrous bushy ruffs. In some parts the paysannes set off their blonde complexions and light hair with becoming, little, black velvet hats, and have a very variegated costume, their blue aprons being flowered with white, their stockings red or blue, their cloaks green, and their petticoats of an immense width, reaching just below the knee.

Reisbec, in his account of Vienna in the eighteenth century, says: " French fashions prevail here universally; all the women are painted up to the eyes and ears, as at Paris." On the introduction of the modes and loose garments of their neighbours across the Rhine, the clergy of Germany declaimed most loudly against them from the pulpit, and the emperor issued a prohibition to abolish the use of the French dress called a *sack*, in which many ladies appeared of a morning at church, without stays, or hardly any other covering.

The dress of the German ladies previous to the adoption of these foreign fashions was very splendid: robes made of the richest velvets, lined with the most costly furs, and trimmed with lace and jewels, were in common use, whilst the head was adorned by a small but high velvet cap, with a plume of feathers, a bunch of flowers, or an aigrette of jewels. Wraxall, in his " Memoirs," says, speaking of Vienna: " Here they follow the absurd fashion of dressing little girls like women, with the high-powdered head and the hoop ;" whilst Lady Wortley Montagu represents the dress of the Austrian ladies of her time, 1716, as very disfiguring.

Nuremberg: city in mid-Bavaria
Reisbec: Johann Caspar Risbeck, wrote "Travels through Germany", 1787
Wraxall: Sir Nathaniel Wraxall, 1751-1831, wrote "Memoirs of the Courts of Berlin, Dresdin, Warsaw & Vienna, 1777-1779"
Lady Wortley Montagu: 1689-1762, wrote "Letters from the East" among other works

The peasants of Germany are celebrated for wearing gay-coloured petticoats, exceedingly full and short, strange-looking head-dresses, and blue, red, or pink stockings. Their coiffures have been long celebrated for their immense height and grotesque appearance. The horned cap, for so many years *la grande mode* in France and England, was imported from Germany; small skull-caps, which entirely conceal the hair, are very generally worn to the present day.

"At Saltzburg," says a modern traveller, "the women dress in the most grotesque gowns, with the waist between the shoulders, and immense broad-brimmed men's hats." The German peasantry generally weave the cloth of which their garments are made, it is of a dark grey colour, and their shoes and stockings are of the same hue.

Near Radstade the women wear large straw hats, that serve equally as a protection from the sun and from the rain. Their garments are short and wide, and their legs and feet are seldom fettered with shoes and stockings.

In Mr. Planché's work, entitled the "Descent of the Danube," we read that, in the neighbourhood of Ratisbon the peasantry are in many places wealthy, exceedingly proud, and fond of all kinds of finery. "The finest Swiss and Dutch linen, silk and satin kerchiefs of the gayest colours, Brabant lace, and gold and silver stuffs of all descriptions, are in constant requisition. The men wear gold rings, and generally two gold watches. The black velvet, or embroidered silk boddices of the women, are laced with massive silver chains, from which hang a pro-

Saltzburg: city on the Austrian border of Bavaria
Radstade: Austrian town south of Salzburg
Planché: James Robinson Planché, 1796–1880, wrote "Descent of the Danube from Ratisbon to Vienna, during the Autumn of 1827" as well as works on English costume
Ratisbon: the old name of Regensburg, city in Eastern Bavaria, on the Danube

fusion of gold and silver trinkets, hearts, crosses, coins, and medals."

In the neighbourhood of Bamberg and Augsburg the peasants have a pretty dress. The chemise has short sleeves, and fits close to the throat, with a small collar, not unlike a modern habit-shirt. The boddice fits tight to the shape, and is ornamented with buttons or gilt beads. The petticoat reaches just below the knees, it is very wide, and of a different-coloured stuff from the boddice; the stockings are white or blue, with scarlet clocks. The shoes have buckles. A riband often encircles the waist, and is tied in front. The women arrange their hair flat on the forehead, or roll it back in front, and allow it to hang in a short chignon on the neck. Some wear a close neat cap, much like a nightcap; others a coiffure resembling a caul, that fits the head, and ties under the chin. A good deal of the back hair is seen, and long ribands hang from it.

The better class of peasants have curiously-shaped

Curious Head-Dresses

caps, some of black satin or velvet, others of lace or muslin, plaited and stiffened like wings; the upper

Bamberg: town in Bavaria, near Bayreuth
Augsburg: town in Bavaria, near Munich

part, of coloured silk, resembles a skull-cap, and is ornamented behind with two large bows. The hair, when these head-dresses are worn, is quite flat upon the forehead, but when the skull-cap is used without the two wings underneath, curls adorn the forehead. The gowns are high up to the throat, which is frequently encircled with a broad necklace or band. The women are fond of gaudy colours, and often wear dark blue or scarlet shoes.

The men in this district have black hats, turned up behind, and surrounded with a gold-coloured band, scarlet waistcoats, long blue coats, black breeches, and shoes with large buckles.

Near Coblentz the costume of the men is much the same as we have just described. The women's dress, too, varies but little; but instead of the caps mentioned above, they plait their back hair, tie it with bows of riband, and let it hang down behind to below the waist. Sometimes, however, they comb it flat on the forehead, and make a broad plait on the top of the head, which they ornament with two large gold pins or gold arrows, while the middle of the head is covered with a crimson or blue velvet caul, that comes as low as the ears, and is ornamented with gold.

In the district of Baden the lower class of peasants are gaily attired: the men wear a broad-brimmed black hat, a coat of lilac or blue, lined with scarlet, a vest of scarlet, striped with green, black breeches, blue stockings, and shoes bound with red. The women comb back all the hair from the forehead, and plait it into one large tress, which hangs down the back; or else cover the head with a straw hat, tied

Coblentz: city in western middle Germany, on the Rhine
Baden: city in southwest Germany

under the chin with a black riband. Their shift has full sleeves to the elbow; the boddice of crimson, black, or blue, is usually laced across, striped, and adorned with some other bright colour. The petticoat is often green, the apron purple, and the stockings frequently scarlet; so that the *mélange* of colours has a very gay and lively effect. Frequently, however, the peasants instead of stockings wear linen or cloth leggings, which leave the ankles and feet uncovered.

Near Frieburg they have little velvet caps, white petticoats, black jackets, laced with crimson, white stockings, and black shoes with crimson rosettes. The men in some of the provinces tie their hats on to their heads with a broad riband, and wear wide riband neckcloths, knotted in large bows. Frequently, too, they draw their white stockings above the knees, and fasten them with broad black garters.

In Wirtemberg a black jacket is generally worn over the laced boddice. It has long sleeves to the wrist, and is often left open to the waist, so as to shew the bright-coloured vest beneath. The petticoats scarcely hang over the knees; they are very full, and have a coloured border round the bottom. The chemise is often tied at the throat with a broad riband; sometimes it has long sleeves, and a worked corsage. The boddice is usually scarlet, laced over a blue stomacher with yellow, and the wide petticoat is white, with a broad border of blue and yellow. Stockings are worn of all colours, also girdles or belts. The coiffures are various; sometimes a little black skull-cap is seen, with a bow at the top, or the hair hangs in long plaits behind, and a large gilt comb ornaments

Frieburg: Freiburg, city in the extreme southwest of Germany, near Basel, Switzerland
Wirtemberg: Wurttemberg, province and city in the southwest of Germany

the top of the head; frequently, however, an immense cap of black lace is worn, and forms a fan that

Head-Dress of the Women of Wirtemberg

Fan-shaped Head-Dress

stretches far beyond the face; the crown is merely two rolls of scarlet silk, with ribands hanging from it.

The men wear either broad-brimmed or three-cornered hats, and dark clothes, except on holidays, when they may be seen in white coats, lined with blue, scarlet waistcoats, and leather nether garments.

Near Frankfort the peasants are not dressed in such gaudy colours as many of those already described. The women have full petticoats, frequently of black, brown, or some dark colour. The boddice is laced with crimson, so as to shew the chemise beneath, and ornamented with silver buttons. The shift-sleeves are tied in at the elbow. A coloured handkerchief covers the neck, a crimson sash hangs from the girdle, and a little blue cap conceals all the hair except the chignon behind. The men wear striped night-caps, with a tassel at the end, not unlike those used by the French fishermen. They have dark blue jackets, trimmed with gilt buttons, pale blue waistcoats, ornamented with silver ones, short nether leather garments, white stockings, pulled up over the knee,

Frankfort: Frankfurt, city in central Germany

and fastened beneath with wide black garters, the shoes are made with a broad piece of leather, which lies upon the instep, and are clasped with immense buckles.

A Peasant of Frankfort

A very singular-shaped, high, flat cap, which somewhat resembles a plate set up on its edge, is peculiar to the women of this district.

Near Pfalz the women generally wear blue petticoats, coloured handkerchiefs, and small tight-fitting caps. The hair is flat on the forehead, and arranged in a chignon behind. The men have large hats turned up at one side, blue jackets, dark vests and nether garments, white stockings, and large shoe-buckles.

The Saxon peasants in the neighbourhood of Dresden have a curious and variegated costume. The women wear dark petticoats, white jackets, sleeves, and aprons, and a scarlet handkerchief pinned over the neck, the ends hanging down from under the jacket. No hair is visible. Frequently the coiffure is a tight cap of crimson, with a white border round the face. An immense frill, like a ruff, surrounds the neck; in front it is tied with a large blue bow, and the cap behind is adorned with one equally immense of crimson. Another coiffure is a coloured handkerchief, tightly pinned round the head, and ornamented at the back with large bows.

A Saxon Peasant

Coloured shoes, or slippers, are often seen. The costume of the men is much like that of the English farmer.

Near Altenburg, the dress of the Saxons is quite

Pfalz: town in northern Bavaria
Dresden: city in East Germany, between Poland and Czechoslovakia; at that time it was
    a princely Court
Altenburg: town in Saxony near Czechoslovakia

different. The little short petticoat of the women, almost like a kilt, with its coloured border, scarcely conceals the knees, which are covered with white stockings, and ornamented with gay-looking garters of black and scarlet. The stomacher, which reaches nearly to the throat, is of bright blue, the jacket black, laced with crimson, and laid back in front so as to shew its crimson lining; the collar stands up round the neck, and the chemise is tied at the throat with a very broad black riband, made into an immense bow, with ends hanging down over the breast. A corresponding bow, of still larger dimensions, adorns the waist, and with the neat white stockings are worn green or blue shoes, edged with scarlet, and having a strap of the same colour across the instep.

Often a stone-coloured stuff, or cloth cloak, that just reaches to the knees, conceals the rest of the costume; it has a deep cape and full collar, and the stockings not unfrequently match it in colour, but are rendered more gay by scarlet clocks and slippers.

The coiffure is very singular. First of all, a broad band encircles the forehead, nearly touching the nose; thence rises a long black funnel covered with silk or velvet, gradually tapering to the point, which is small, and ornamented with a frill. No ribands adorn this coiffure, but a broad black band holds it firmly upon the head, and passing under the chin, leaving only the nose, eyes, and mouth visible, is fastened with an enormous rosette of large bows, also black.

Singular Coiffure

This head-dress is probably the remains of the

German fashion in coiffures, which were formerly so celebrated for their height and extraordinary shape. When abroad, the women often tie a gay-coloured handkerchief, or shawl, over the cap, and let the ends hang down behind. Altogether this costume is the most curious of any in Germany; the excessive shortness of the petticoats, the bright colours composing the dress, and the high caps, form a *tout ensemble* that is very remarkable to foreigners. The men frequently wear loose nether garments, stockings, and shoes of black cloth, short coloured jackets, gay waistcoats, and large bows in the place of a neckcloth. The hair falls upon the neck, and is adorned with a tiny hat, set on the crown of the head.

Near Hamburgh the peasants wear little round straw hats, nearly as flat as plates, with a tight cap of linen under them. A short gown of black or brown stuff, tucked up so as to shew the bright red petticoat beneath; blue stockings, a coloured handkerchief over the neck, and a blue stomacher. Some have short red petticoats, white gowns, and blue jackets. The men have large hats, gaudy waistcoats, short coats trimmed with a profusion of silver buttons, wide nether garments, dark stockings, and buckles in the shoes.

The Bohemian women often wear little jackets trimmed with fur, scarlet stomachers, black petticoats, scarlet stockings, and have on their heads a tight band of linen, with a red crown and long ribands hanging from it. The chemise is never seen; a black handkerchief covers the neck, and a black cloak is often worn, lined with scarlet and carelessly hanging from the shoulders. When a cap is not worn, the

tout ensemble: total costume
Hamburgh: Hamburg, German port and trading city on the Elbe near the North Sea
Bohemian women: Bohemia is now part of western Czechoslovakia

hair is arranged quite flat on the forehead; a velvet band, ornamented with silver, encircles the head, and the back part is ornamented with coloured ribands. The men have long coats, with waistcoats of scarlet or blue, adorned profusely with silver lace and buttons; the shirt is seen above, tied with a black riband. The nether garments are large and wide, the stockings blue, and the shoes black, edged with scarlet.

In Bavaria, near Munich, the peasants wear broad felt hats, or bonnets, with a knob on the crown the size of a walnut, or a droll little silver turban, with two peaks behind, which is fastened on the very back of the head. Both men and women also have broad-brimmed hats of black felt, with scarlet or yellow bands round them, bunches of riband suspended from the crown, and, not unfrequently, a tall feather. The dark petticoats of the women are very short; and the boddice, which resembles a cuirass, is made quite stiff with silver buttons, chains, and ornaments, which shine brightly upon the scarlet or blue stuff of which the body is made. The sleeves are white and short, the stockings usually of a bright blue, with long stripes and clocks of scarlet and white. The men have nether garments that scarcely reach to the knees, which are usually bare, for the blue and white stockings are gartered underneath; their waistcoats are green or blue, their jackets black and very short; and those who can afford it ornament their vests, like the women's boddices, with every kind of silver trinket.

The costume in the Tyrol is very gay. The women have coloured stomachers, either yellow or red, dark boddices, and nine or ten full petticoats, of different bright tints, and very short; aprons with

Bavaria: princely state in southeastern German mountains
cuirass: breastplate of a suit of armor
Tyrol: region in the mountains of western Austria

coloured borders, and black handkerchiefs pinned over the bosom within the stomacher, or crossed over the lacing of the boddice, which has a frill round the waist behind. The sleeves are frequently trimmed at the hands with fur; sometimes, however, they are short, and have a white frill at the elbows, and the lower part of the arms is covered with neat knitted mittens, generally black, with coloured patterns. The hair is drawn from the face, plaited and twisted round the back of the head, where it is held firm by gold pins of a great length. On their heads they wear immense caps, with plaited crowns, sometimes ornamented with a feather or a bunch of flowers, often weighing six or seven pounds. Their shoes are of black leather, and their legs are wrapped in short stockings, or rather leggings, for they do not cover the foot, but reach from the knee to the ankle, leaving the instep quite bare. The men wear these leggings of linen or cotton, very large and loose, tied round the ankle, and looped up to the nether garments behind the knee, which is always uncovered.

The jackets of the men resemble short coats, and are lined and bordered with some gay colour. Their vests seem made in imitation of the boddices of the women, being of every shade of scarlet, green, and yellow, with black and white stripes. The throat is generally bare, or a large black neckcloth is tied loosely round it. The nether garments are ornamented with patterns in white thread, and are so

Costume of the Tyrolese Men

short that the knees are quite uncovered. The hats, usually of green felt, are shaped like a cone, have narrow brims, and a feather or bunch of ribands stuck on one side, which gives them a gay and lively appearance.

In Prussia, as in many other countries, French modes and fashions completely effaced all remains of national costume, so much so, that even patching was adopted by the fair sex; and an author of the last century, speaking of that country, says: " This practice has been followed here. The damsels frequently cut their patches in the shape of flies, beetles, hares, asses, bears, sheep, oxen, and hogs; so that the French have not devised any thing, be it ever so silly and absurd, that the Germans have not made still more silly and absurd in the imitation."

In " Frederic the Great and his Times," we have the following account of the wedding-dress of the daughter of Frederick I. in 1709: " The jewels worn by the bride were valued at four millions of dollars. She had a coronet, set with diamonds and pear-shaped pearls, which alone was estimated at one million; her train was borne by six maids of honour, who, on account of the great weight of the precious stones with which it was garnished, had two pages to assist them. The total weight of the bridal attire is said to have been nearly a hundred pounds." The dress of the king, in 1713, is thus described:—

" The dress of the king was simple. He appeared in a large flowing wig, for the last time, at the funeral of his father. The king, we are told by Pollnitz, had the finest hair in the world—of a light brown—but he had it cut off, and for a long time wore a wig with

Prussia: state in northeast Germany
"Frederick the Great and his Times": "Frederick the Great, his Court and Time" was
    written by Thomas Campbell, published 1842
Frederick I's daughter: Princess Louise, 1680–1705, child of his first wife Eliza-
    beth Henrietta of Hesse-Cassel, married in 1700, not 1709, Frederick I, Land-
    grave of Hesse-Cassel, 1676–1751; the double association with the House of
    Hesse-Cassel obviously provided the opportunity for a grand and elaborate wedding
Pollnitz: Karl Ludwig Freiherr von Pöllnitz, 1692–1775, wrote "Memoirs of and Tra-
    vels in Prussia, Germany, Italy ...", published 1737

a tail; but in the latter years of his life he had close and almost white wigs, in which, though they were ill made, he looked extremely well.   Till 1719 he dressed sometimes in plain clothes, sometimes in uniform; but in the following years he was scarcely ever seen but in the uniform of colonel of the Potsdam Grenadiers, blue turned up with red, yellow waistcoat and breeches, white linen gaiters with brass buttons, and square-toed shoes.   Every thing was made to fit very tight. His hat was three-cornered, with a narrow gold lace, gilt button without loop, and a band of gold thread with two small gold tassels.   When not in uniform, the king wore a brown coat and red waistcoat, with a narrow gold border.   He was so saving of a good coat, that, when engaged in his cabinet, he would put on linen sleeves and an apron.   He was a decided enemy to gaudy dresses and new fashions; and as, while yet a boy, he had vowed vengeance against French wigs and gold brocade dresses, so they still continued to be the objects of his displeasure.   He observed, with indignation, that the large laced hats and bags, in which Count Rothenburg and his retinue appeared in public, found admirers at court.   To prevent imitation, he ordered, at the great review held at Tempelhoff, near Berlin, in 1719, that the regimental provosts, who, like the executioners and skinners, are reputed infamous, should appear in the new French costume, only with the brims of the hats and the bags enlarged to an extravagant size.   Paint was prohibited.'

In Moore's " France," we find the wardrobe-roll of Frederick of Prussia.   Its contents are not a little different, in number and simplicity, from the extrava-

Potsdam Grenadiers: armed company from the city of Potsdam, near Berlin
Count Rothenburg: the Rothenburgs are a large family of the old German nobility
Moore: Dr. John Moore, 1729–1802, wrote "A View of Society & Manners in France,
    Switzerland & Germany ...", published in 1779
Frederick of Prussia: Frederick II, 1740–1786

gance and splendour of many of the monarchs whom we have mentioned in this little work. " The whole wardrobe consisted of two blue coats, faced with red, the lining of one a little torn ; two yellow waistcoats, three pair of yellow breeches, and a suit of blue velvet, embroidered with silver, for great occasions."

THE TOILETTE IN SPAIN.

CHAPTER XXIII.

A Spanish Lady

THE dresses worn by the inhabitants of Spain are varied and tasteful, and in some respects totally different from those belonging to other nations. In a work entitled " A Summer in Andalusia," we find the following remarks upon the dress of this country :—

" The mysterious mantilla is always black or white, the former being the prevalent colour, and invariably worn in winter; the white has a very pretty effect, especially if the wearer be a *rubia*, or of fair complexion. The white are always of lace, but the black are of all materials; from the rich lace of the upper ranks, the silk with a wide border of lace of the

"A Summer in Andalusia": written by George Dennis, published 1839
Andalusia: region in southern Spain

tradesmen's wives, or edged with velvet, a grade lower, to the coarse mantilla of *punto* of the lowest classes."

The *basquina* of Cadiz is pretty much like a modern English gown, with full sleeves, though these are short, and do not cover the arms. It was formerly adorned with deep flounces, and trimmed with a profusion of braid ; but such are now rarely seen except on the stage or in the interior of the country. Though in winter the basquina, as well as the mantilla, is usually black—the ancient and genuine hue of the whole costume—still in summer gowns of other colours are worn ; either white, or of some dark shade of purple, crimson, brown, or green. The legs and feet are cased in networked stockings and sandalled slippers.

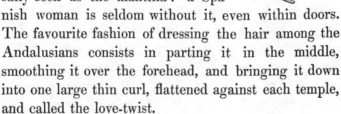

Basquina of Cadiz

One peculiarity in the dress of the ladies of Spain consists in wearing fresh flowers in the hair, which form a beautiful contrast with the dark complexions and mantillas. The comb worn in the hair is generally about the size of those used in this country. The fan is as universally seen as the mantilla : a Spanish woman is seldom without it, even within doors. The favourite fashion of dressing the hair among the Andalusians consists in parting it in the middle, smoothing it over the forehead, and bringing it down into one large thin curl, flattened against each temple, and called the love-twist.

punto: "point" or lace
Cadiz: southwestern coastal port of Spain

The most important part of the Spaniard's costume is the *capa*, or cloak. The lower orders wear it of a dark chocolate colour, faced with crimson plush, or cotton velvet; while that worn by the higher classes is of blue or black cloth, faced with rich black silk velvet, and frequently lined throughout with taffety. The cloak is not a winter garment alone; in the hottest days of summer it is often worn, as in obedience to the proverb:

Capa, or Cloak

" However hot the sun,
        Keep thy cloak on."

The rest of the costume consists of a short round jacket, with an upright collar. It is sometimes of dyed sheep-skin, with the wool outwards, but more commonly of coarse cloth or velvet—brown, green, blue, or black—adorned with tags on the breasts, trimmed with braid and velvet, and lined with silk. It often has silk epaulettes in addition. Two handkerchiefs, red and white, or red and yellow, are thrust into small side-pockets, with their ends depending. The waistcoat on fête-days is generally of bright silk, gaily figured, and often with representations of bull-fights. It is adorned with basket-buttons, and trimmed with braid like the jacket, and is worn very open to display the well-worked shirt, the collars of which are invariably turned down, leaving the throat exposed. Round the neck is worn a silk scarf, tied in a slip knot, and descending on the bosom. It is generally crimson, pink, or canary-coloured, but ought always to correspond in hue with the lining of the jacket, and with the sash or *faga*, which is a narrow strip of silk or worsted, girded round the waist with several turns. One end is often sewn up into a pouch, which serves as a purse, and bag for tobacco. A large clasp-knife is a never-failing inmate of the faga.

Tight breeches of blue, green, or chocolate plush, or *punto*, reach below the knee, where they are tied with cords, terminating in tassels of the same colour. The outer seams are adorned with rows of dangling basket-buttons, plaited or gilt, and sometimes with broad stripes of dark braid. The legs are cased in spatterdashes or *botines* of calf-skin, fastened with leather loops on the outer sides of the leg, but left open at the calf, so as always to give the appearance of a full and handsome limb. They are made with the rough side outwards—when new of a beautiful light colour—and are tastefully worked on the front and back with flowers of darker leather, or are sometimes stitched with silk of various colours.

The shoes (*zapatos*), which are partially covered by the *botines*, are of similar leather, so that together they appear like high boots. The botines of Seville are most in fashion, and a handsome pair costs not less than four or five dollars. I have seen them, though rarely, of black tanned leather, studded with brass tacks. Those who cannot afford botines wear *alpergatas*, sandals of *Esparto* rush, beaten and bound together, and fastened to the foot by thongs or strings; but these are only the poorest peasants, and

punto: "point" or lace
Seville: city in Andalusia, southern Spain

there is a saying, that " every low fellow wears spatterdashes."

Over the head is a bright silk
handkerchief, folded diagonally,
and tied with a knot behind, —
a fashion bequeathed by the
Moors. Over this is a broad-
brimmed sugar-loaf hat of black
felt.

The muleteer's costume is
very becoming. It consists of a
jacket and breeches, of dark
coffee-coloured cloth, plentifully
garnished with buttons, a crimson sash, in which is stuck a
cuchillo, or knife, blue stockings, and red garters at
the knees, shoes of brown leather, a striped handkerchief rolled round the head, and the whole surmounted
by a huge sombrero.

Muleteer's Costume

The costume of the peasants varies considerably.
The inhabitants of Rondo and the mountainous districts dress very differently from those who live on the
plains. Not only the shape and form of their garments, but also the materials of which they are composed, suit better with the colder air of the hills.

In the streets the women wear veils instead of
caps or hats : these veils, very unlike the gossamer
texture of those worn by ladies of most other nations,
are made of blue or pink flannel. This, with a black
petticoat of stuff, forms the principal part of the costume. The men wear no hats, but instead of them
montero caps, made of silk or black velvet, and most
abundantly ornamented with fringe and tassels. Their

Rondo: Ronda, town near Málaga, in the southern coastal mountains

short jackets, adorned with gold and silver buttons, and covered with embroidery, are worn sufficiently open to enable them to display a splendid waistcoat. The breeches are of black leather or velvet, and they wear gaiters. The *tout-ensemble* of this costume is exceedingly picturesque.

The Catalonian ladies are great *élégantes ;* they wore, a few years since, a black silk petticoat, with a small hoop. The body of the dress was made so low in front that the shoulders were quite uncovered, and the veil so stiffened out with wire that it formed two arches, one on either side of the head.

The muleteers in this province wear their hair in a net, and their broad silver-laced hat, squeezed quite flat, hangs with a coquettish air on one side of the head. A handkerchief is thrown loosely round the neck, the waistcoat is striped, and over it they wear a red jacket, with large silver buttons like bells. A belt of blue, edged with yellow, is bound round the waist. On the left shoulder hangs a blue great-coat, embroidered with white thread. Their breeches are striped with blue and white, their stockings are rolled below the knee, gartered and fastened with an enormous buckle, and a bunch of black ribands reaches nearly to the ankle, round which they tie some blue fillets, to keep on their packthread sandals, which scarcely cover the toes. The sailors of this province are known throughout all Spain by wearing a red woollen cap, like that of the ancient Phrygians. The middle classes are habited in hats and dark clothes, with a half-wide coat thrown carelessly over the shoulders.

In Valencia the peasant's costume is a white linen waistcoat, trousers which reach to the knee, net caps,

tout-ensemble: entire outfit
Catalonia: region on the northeast coast of Spain
Phrygian cap: or liberty cap, see illus. p. 387, top
Valencia: city on the Mediterranean coast of Spain

and sandals made of cord.   The women have no caps:
they plait their hair in a spiral form, and fasten it
with a large silver pin.   Swinburne says : "The men
in this province strut about all day in monstrous hats
and dark brown cloaks."   In the town of Salamanca
the lower classes wear large hats—some black, some
white; slit sleeves, broad leather belts, and sandals
made of cords.

The Biscayan women, who are usually very handsome, wear a neat pastoral garb.   The hair falls down
the back in long plaits, and on the head is worn a
sort of white cap or hood, with a bow in front.   The
boddice is laced up the front, and has lappets hanging
from the waist; the petticoat is rather short, the
sleeves full, and reaching to the elbow; its colour on
Sundays or holidays of pure white, and then tied with
rose-coloured ribands.

"The most singular thing in the dress of the
men," says Swinburne, "is the covering of their legs;
they wrap a piece of coarse grey, or black woollen
cloth, round them, and fasten it with many turns of
tape; it answers precisely to the idea I have of
Malvolio's cross-gartering in the Twelfth Night."   The
same author relates the dress of the innkeeper's
daughter at Lorea: "Her hair was tied in a club
with a bunch of scarlet ribands, large drops hung
from her ears, and on her breast she wore a load of
relics and hallowed medals; the sleeves of her gown
were fastened together behind by a long blue riband,
that hung to the ground."

In Castile the women have large clumsy sabots,
a dark gown thrown back, and tied behind, an apron
of blue and white, and a large veil fastened to the

sandals made of cord: the forerunners of our modern espadrilles
Biscayan women: the Bay of Biscay is on the north coast of Spain in Navarre
Swinburne: Henry Swinburne, late 18th century traveller and writer, see note p. 318
Castile: province of central Spain

head with streamers of blue riband. The montero caps of the men are frequently faced and ornamented with red or blue.

The women of Burgos, who, unlike the other Spanish peasants, are not in general handsome, do not improve their beauty by their coiffure, which is particularly ugly, and not unlike that worn by some of the Tartar tribes. They wear a black periwig, faced all round with the wool of a black lamb, ending behind in two long plaits, which hang half way to the ground.

In the neighbourhood of Irun the man's costume is a brown jacket, a small round hat, and sandals, or an old slipper tied on with a riband. Some of the inhabitants wear a handkerchief round the head, and over it a small cap, chocolate-coloured jackets and trousers are worn, while a red sash encircles the waist. The women's hair, which is of a beautiful black, is tied in long tresses.

In Bilbao the dress of the women is very becoming. It consists of a black silk petticoat, a black or a white jacket, and a large silk capuchon, the ends of which hang down in front like a shawl.

The ever-varying modes of France have long crept across the Pyrenees; French clothes, French fashions, and French colours, have quite superseded the ancient costume of the country among the higher classes.

Spain is famous in the annals of fashion for having invented two additions to dress, which have been worn, admired, and followed by most of the European nations—we mean ruffs and fardingales. Most writers agree that to Spain they owe their birth, and certainly the inventive genius who first imagined them is worthy of renown.

Burgos: city in north central Navarre, Spain
Irun: Basque city in the northwest of Spain, near the French border
Bilbao: port city in the Basque region of Navarre
Pyrenees: the mountain range dividing Spain and France

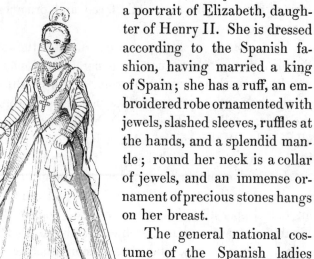

Elizabeth, daughter of Henry II

In Montfaucon's " Monarchie Française," we find a portrait of Elizabeth, daughter of Henry II. She is dressed according to the Spanish fashion, having married a king of Spain; she has a ruff, an embroidered robe ornamented with jewels, slashed sleeves, ruffles at the hands, and a splendid mantle; round her neck is a collar of jewels, and an immense ornament of precious stones hangs on her breast.

The general national costume of the Spanish ladies when *en grande tenue*, was formerly a petticoat of rich satin, embroidered in gold and colours; a jacket of velvet trimmed with jewels, the sleeves slashed and bordered with gold, and finished at the wrists with ruffles; a girdle, and cordelière of jewels. Frequently the robes were trimmed with ermine and the most costly furs, and were made of brocade or gold and silver tissue. The head-dresses were generally formed of jewels, and a veil was usually added to the coiffure, which gave it much grace and elegance.

Montfaucon's "Monarchie Française": see note p. 272
Elizabeth: Elizabeth de Valois married Phillip II of Spain in 1560
Henry II of France: 1547–59
en grande tenue: in full formal attire, full evening dress

THE TOILETTE IN PORTUGAL.

CHAPTER XXIV.

Broad-brimmed Hat

N this smiling and sunny land the common dress of the lower class of men is the cloak and large broad-brimmed hat so frequently met with in Spain. They have loose breeches and a coat, bound round the waist with a girdle of leather. The sleeves are tight, and open part of the way up the arm, so as to shew the shirt; the throat is uncovered.

Ornaments, such as gold and silver lace, and embroidery, are not allowed to be worn on the garments of the Portuguese; but the higher classes, when they do not follow the French fashions, pay no attention to these rules, but adorn their silk dresses with embroidery and precious stones.

The women among the peasantry seldom wear caps, but have a very becoming way of dressing the hair, and tying it in a net of silk, not unlike a large purse, with a long tassel hanging down the back, and a bow on the forehead. This coiffure they call *redecilla*, and the men also frequently adopt it. Their gowns usually have a boddice, and short sleeves reaching the elbow, of a different material from the jupe; this boddice is made with a long pointed stomacher, and is cut round at the bosom. Beneath it is worn an under-dress, with long sleeves and a body, that fastens round the throat. White dresses are much worn, ornamented with coloured ribands.

Mode of Dressing the Hair

The Portuguese ladies wear very large heavy ear-rings, and in their hair they are fond of placing quantities of precious stones, which are generally set in the form of butterflies and other insects. Sometimes feathers and coloured ribands are placed among their tresses. No young woman ever conceals her hair under a lace or muslin head-dress. Elderly ladies wear a cap shaped like a caul, of very fine clear muslin.

Their gowns, of which they sometimes wear two or three, one over the other, are richly embriodered; the upper one forms a long train, which sweeps along the ground, and is of black stuff. Their hoops are quite enormous, and their sleeves immensely wide. Instead of a girdle, they encircle their small waists with a string of relics; the ends hang to the ground, and have knots of diamonds in them. Their shoes are of Spanish leather, without any heels, but when they go out they put on pattens, or silk sandals fastened with gold clasps, by which they are raised several inches from the ground. They wear paint, not only on the cheeks, but on the shoulders also.

It is said by many authors that the manners and customs of the Jews and Moors are still, to a certain degree, retained in this country. Perhaps from them they derive their love of jewels; even the fishwomen wear gold necklaces and bracelets. The women who sell fruit frequently wear boots instead of shoes or sandals, and black conical caps.

The higher orders of the Portuguese do not appear to admire gaudy colours; black is almost universally worn, ornamented with fringes of gold and colours.

In the Memoirs of Madame Junot are many amusing descriptions of the dress of the Portuguese court. A hoop was there considered an indispensable part of the toilette of Madame l'Ambassadrice; and she thus describes her dress, which was arranged according to the fashion of Portugal: " Je mis par-dessus cette monstrueuse montagne dont j'étais flan-quée de chaque côté, une belle robe de moire blanche brodée en lames d'or, et rattachée sur les côtés avec de gros glonds d'or, absolument comme aurait pu l'être une draperie de croisée. Je mis sur ma tête une toque avec six grandes plumes blanches retenues par une agrafe de diamants, et le fond de la toque était brodé avec des épis de diamants; j'en avais au cou, aux oreilles; et ainsi harnachée, je partis pour Quelus."

The same writer then describes the dress of the Princess of Brazil. Her gown was of white India

Madame Junot: née Laure Permon, she married the Duc d'Abrantès, who was French Ambas-
    sador to the Court of Portugal in 1804-5; thus, Madame l'Ambassadrice
"Je mis pardessus": translation appears in the appendix
Princess of Brazil: Maria I, 1737-1816

muslin, embroidered in gold and silver; the sleeves were very short, and the robe was fastened on the shoulders with large diamond clasps. Her hair was dressed in large puffs and plaits, interspersed with splendid diamonds and pearls; her ear-rings and *girandoles* were quite magnificent.

In another part of this work we read of the following coiffure worn by an old Portuguese lady: " Elle avait ses cheveux blancs relevés sur le bout de sa tête avec un ruban, comme on le voit encore dans quelques tableaux." And, in a note, we find: " Il y a encore beaucoup de Portugaises de haut rang qui restent ainsi coiffées chez elles. Dès qu'elles sortent, elles se mettent à la Française; mais, par exemple, dans l'intérieur des provinces, j'en ai vu qui ne portent jamais d'autre coiffeur."

The costume of *les dames du Palais* is thus described: " C'était la plus étrange mascarade qu'on puisse imaginer de faire revêtir à des femmes Chrétiennes. C'était une jupe de taffetas bien fort, bien épais, d'une couleur bleu foncé, avec une large broderie en or au bas, et puis ensuite une queue, une robe, je ne sais quel morceau d'étoffe d'un rouge éclatant qui leur pendait en manière de traine derrière elles. Les plus âgées, comme le camariera-môr, portaient un petit toquet, une façon de bonnet assez serré à la tête (c'étaient je crois, les veuves) et sur ce bonnet était une fleur gros bleu, comme la jupe."

Speaking of the ancient dress of Spain and Portugal, Appian says: " We know that the Hispanians and Lusitanians wore the *saie*, fastened with a buckle or brooch; but we are ignorant of its form, and no remains of antiquity have yet been found to explain

girandoles: pendants generally composed of a central stone surrounded by smaller ones
"Elle avait", "Il y a encore", "C'était la plus étrange": translations in the appendix
les dames du Palais: the ladies of the Palace
Appian: Appianus, Roman historian of the 2nd century
Hispanians and Lusitanians: Spanish and Portuguese
saie: the sagum, Roman military cloak

it." Strabo, too, mentions this garment being in use with the Lusitanians. He also says: "That the Moors wore their hair *frizzed* and curled, and that they combed their beards."

When Isabella of Portugal went to France to marry the Duke of Burgundy, she wore a tabard, or stomacher of ermine, a robe of splendid embroidery, tight sleeves, a cloak reaching to the ground behind, but so narrow that it only fell over the shoulders, and a curious head-dress of white muslin. She had no ornaments of any kind.

Female Peasant

Strabo: Greek historian and geographer, circa 63 B.C.–24 A.D.
Isabella of Portugal: married the Duke of Burgundy in 1429; the Order of the Golden Fleece was founded in honor of the wedding

THE TOILETTE IN SWITZERLAND.

CHAPTER XXV.

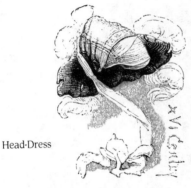

Head-Dress

HE dress of the Swiss peasantry is admired by all who visit their country. It varies considerably in most of the cantons, and each separate district is easily distinguished by the colour and shape of the garments worn by its inhabitants. Laws relating to dress have, however, been found necessary, even among these simple people, to restrain a wanton extravagance and luxury of attire, which spreads so rapidly when once allowed a free indulgence.

The dress of the higher ranks is usually very plain. Black is the colour invariably worn for full dress. On Sundays the women dress in black in the morning, and in colours in the evening.   In the arrangement of their hair they follow the French modes.

Of all the numerous costumes seen in this country, that of the canton of Berne is the most admired.   The men wear immense broad-brimmed straw hats, brown jackets, and large breeches.   The women plait their hair in long tresses with ribands, and let it hang down their backs.   They have a very becoming straw hat, a jacket without sleeves, a black or blue petticoat, edged with red or white, red stockings with black clocks, and no heels to their shoes.   The shift, or under garment, has short full sleeves, and reaches to the throat,

Costume of the Women of Berne

where it is fastened with a broad black collar ornamented with red: they frequently have silver ornaments passed between the shoulders and under the arms. On fête days they often wear a black lace cap, of large size, almost like a fan, tied under the chin, and long green gloves.

Dress on Gala-Days

The costume of the canton of Lucerne is described as extremely becoming for the young, to whom the gay colours of which it is composed impart a charm of appropriate interest.   The paysanne's dress consists of a large flat straw hat, decorated round the

Berne: city in west central Switzerland
Lucerne: city in north central Switzerland
paysanne: peasant or countrywoman

Paysanne's Dress in Lucerne

crown with four large bows of ribands of different colours, and also a bunch of flowers; the hair, which is drawn back from the forehead, falls behind in two long braids. The jupe is exceedingly short,—sometimes even the garter is visible; it is usually of two, but not unfrequently of three colours, and very full. The chemise, or under garment, reaches to the throat, and has full round sleeves. The boddice of the jupe is so covered with lace, embroidery, chains, and buttons of brass and silver, that the real material of which it is composed is scarcely perceptible. Frequently, too, the throat is surrounded with a broad frill, lying flat upon the bosom, not unlike the bands worn in England in the reign of Charles II. The stockings are always white and fine, and the shoes neat.

In Schaffhausen the men dress very much in the antique mode, with large puffed breeches. Silk, lace, and many other luxuries of the toilette, are here prohibited; but the women repay themselves for these deprivations by the gaudiness of their costume. The short petticoat is often blue, the boddice scarlet, embroidered in various colours, the collar round the neck black and red, edged with white, the stockings scarlet, the shoes black, with large buckles; the apron and sleeves, which are

Man of Schaffhausen

jupe: skirt
Charles II: 1660–1685
Schaffhausen: Swiss city and canton, in the north near the German border

not so short as in many of the other cantons, are of a pure white, and the hair hangs in two long plaits, tied with pink ribands, down to the waist, but in front instead of behind; frequently a bunch of flowers is placed in one of the braids, which looks very gay and becoming.

The women of Soleure are distinguished by a neat and elegant straw hat, fastened on to the head with a frill of black lace. Their hair is curled in front, and they frequently have a black handkerchief round the throat; a black petticoat, a green and scarlet boddice, and scarlet ribands in their

Woman of Soleure

shoes. The upper jupe is often black, with a red border round the bottom; it just reaches to the knees, and below it is seen about two inches of a white under-petticoat, edged with pink. The white stockings are gartered with coloured ribands, with long ends; the sleeves of the shift are full, and cover the arms to the elbows. A large white muslin cap, with a plaited border, is often worn.

Near Bâle the only head-dress is a frill of black lace, pinned into the plait of hair which surrounds the head. The petticoats are longer, and of a dark colour, with a gaily striped boddice and handkerchief.

In the Grisons the paysannes wear becoming black lace caps, which are pointed upon the forehead, but allow the hair on the temples to be seen, and are tied under the chin. They often have red stockings with white clocks, an orange boddice laced with green over a blue stomacher, a purple cloth petticoat bordered

Soleure: Solothurn, Swiss city and canton in the northeast of the country
Bâle: Basel, city and canton on the northwest border, near France and Germany
Grisons: the canton of Graubünden, in the southeast near Austria
Paysannes: peasant women

with green, a striped handkerchief and apron, and long white sleeves.

In the small canton of St. Gall the head is frequently uncovered, the hair being made into one large plait on the back of the head, and adorned with long

Woman of St. Gall

gold or silver pins. On Sundays, a pretty little cap made of white muslin, lined with green silk and with a small crimson crown, is frequently worn; it has a neat and becoming appearance. The hair is arranged quite flat upon the temples, and very little of it is allowed to be seen. The top of the chemise is often finished round the neck with a full frill, not unlike a ruff. On fête days a neat little short jacket is worn; it is quite open in front, so as to shew the stomacher, and is bordered with coloured ribands.

In Uri the hair is worn in ringlets, and a pretty little straw hat, decked with bows of coloured ribands, is coquettishly perched on one side of the head. The striped petticoats are long, the boddice without a stomacher and adorned with a silver chain, the stockings scarlet, and large buckles in the shoes.

In Zurich a white chemisette, which meets the boddice and is finished at the throat with a frill, and the sleeves of which form three large puffs, is worn; the hair, which is plaited, hangs down the back, and has black lace entwined with it.

In Unterwalden the hair is drawn back from the forehead, leaving it quite bare; behind, it is formed into a broad plait, adorned with several gold pins,

St. Gall: St. Gallen, city and canton in the northeast, near Germany
Uri: canton in central Switzerland
Zurich: city and canton in the northeast, on Lake Zurich
chemisette: undergarment or blouse of fine muslin or lace which fills in the front of women's bodices
Unterwalden: canton in central Switzerland

that stand round the head like stars.   The rest of the dress resembles that in most of the other cantons.

In Zug the hair is curled in front, and a large straw hat is placed on the top of the head. A large white frill lies flat over the bosom, and the petticoat is frequently black for half its length, while the other half is blue or red; the stockings are coloured, and the boddice gaily embroidered.

In Fribourg the boddice is replaced by a long apron of white linen, which covers the front of the body of the dress; the petticoat is very long, the sleeves white, and above the top of the apron is seen a black and scarlet neckcloth, with a rosette in front. The hair is arranged in two plaits down the sides of the face, and the head is covered with a large straw hat, trimmed with black velvet.

In Appensell the boddice boasts every variety of colour, and the petticoat is generally bright scarlet, with white stockings and black shoes. Beneath the stomacher and boddice is a kind of brown vest, fastened round the throat with a necklace. The hair hangs in small curls on the temples and neck, and a cap of black velvet adorns the head; the crown fits quite tight, and two black lace wings rise from the sides, and are supported by a crimson riband passed through them.

Woman of Appensell

Near Thurgovia the paysannes' cap is very simple, being a tight caul of coloured silk, with a frill of black lace round it: the hair is

Zug: city and canton in northeast/central Switzerland
Fribourg: city and canton, west central region
Appensell: Appenzell, city and canton in the extreme northeast, near Austria
Thurgovia: Thurgau, canton in the northeast

curled. The little brown jacket, with its blue stomacher and yellow boddice laced with scarlet, has a
very pretty effect, which is increased by a yellow
petticoat and a red *sous jupe*, bordered with black or
green.

At Tessin a long brown great-coat is frequently
worn by the women; the broad-brimmed hat is tied
on with a coloured handkerchief, the petticoat is ornamented with fringe, and not unfrequently the paysannes are seen with bare feet and ankles.

At Oberhasli straw hats are worn, with very long
petticoats, shoes trimmed with scarlet, gay boddices,
and coloured aprons.

Near Gouggisberg the head is adorned with a
coloured handkerchief, twisted round it like a turban.
The little black jupe, bordered with scarlet, does not
reach to the knees, which are uncovered, the stockings
being gartered below them. The shoes have large
red rosettes, the boddice is scarlet; above it the
chemise reaches to the throat, where it is fastened
with a black and scarlet collar; over this is worn
a brown jacket with long sleeves, and a white apron.

In the Valais the usual mixture of gay colours is
seen in the costume, but the petti-
coat is larger than in most of the
other cantons, while the neat white
sleeves, which are full and short,
and the snow-white stockings and
black shoes, give a picturesque appearance to the dress, which is height-
ened by the curiously shaped little
straw hat, decorated with flowers

Woman of the Valais

and ribands, and placed so as to shew a broad plait

sous jupe: underskirt
Tessin: Ticino, Italian-speaking area of southern Switzerland
Oberhasli: town in the area of Berne
Gouggisberg: Guggisberg, city near Berne
Valais: canton in the southwest

of the hair which peeps from beneath it. Sometimes the hat is nearly as flat as a plate, surrounded with bows of riband and edged with black velvet.

At Neufchâtel and Geneva, probably from the visits of numerous foreigners, the paysannes have abandoned their national costume, and generally appear in gowns, caps, and shawls, of a French make.

In the Pays de Vaux the boddice is worn without a stomacher; it is often green, the jupe striped in white, scarlet, and blue, the apron of snowy linen, fastened with a pink riband, and a pink fiche over the neck completes the dress. The large straw hat is placed on one side, and within it is a cap of black lace, which sets off the complexion most becomingly. The crown of the hat is curiously shaped.

Woman of the Pays de Vaux

In Moore's "Travels in France" we find the following description: " At Murat the Swiss peasant's dress is peculiar. They wear little round hats, like those worn by Dutch skippers; their coats and waistcoats are all of a coarse black cloth, their breeches of coarse linen, like sailors' trousers, but drawn together in plaits below the knees, and the stockings are of the same stuff. The women wear short jackets, with a great superfluity of buttons. The unmarried pride themselves on the length of their hair, which they separate into two divisions, and allow to hang at full

Neufchâtel: city and canton in the west, near France
Geneva: city and canton in the southwest, near France
Pays de Vaux: the canton of Vaud, of which Lausanne is the capital
Moore: John Moore, 1729-1802, wrote "A View of Society and Manners in France, Switzerland & Germany, etc.", published 1779
Murat: Murten, town on the Lake of Neuchatel

length. When married they twist the hair round the head in spiral lines, and fix it to the crown with silver pins; wear straw hats and black ribands. They fix their petticoats so high as to leave hardly any waist."

THE TOILETTE IN HOLLAND.

Ancient Dutch Costume

CHAPTER XXVI.

H E merchants and better classes of the Dutch nation all follow the French modes, with this difference, that they have not, as in that country, a dress suited to each varying season of the year.

The costume of the Dutch peasants is but little affected by fashion. The men's coats have little shape, and are made tight, without any fulness, and with very high, large pockets. Their breeches are immense, their waistcoats long; they wear a kind of round hat or bonnet, and stockings and shoes of a clumsy form.

A Dutch Peasant

The costume of the Dutch women is singular;

their petticoats are very full, and exceedingly short, the sleeves long and tight, and the bod-dice laced in front, with a handkerchief pinned over the neck.   An apron always forms part of this dress.   The stock-ings and shoes are neat.   They hardly ever wear any head-dress, simply tying up their hair, and binding it with knots of black riband, or covering it with a hood. The Dutch paysannes are generally very large and unwieldly, and the elderly women formerly wore hoops to increase their size.   The ladies preferred what is called the bell-hoop, or pannier, but the maid-servants, who always used them on great fête days, were only allowed the hoop that spreads out at the hips.

Female Costume

In the province of Guelderland the richer of the peasantry are very smart.   The coat and waistcoat are adorned with gold and silver buttons, which are placed close together all down the front; the waist-band of the trousers is ornamented also with immense buttons; the shoes glitter with large silver buckles. A silver clasp is also worn at the throat, and silver buckles at the knees.   This costume looks exceed-ingly gay and brilliant.   The women of this province ornament their dress with gold; they place gold in their hair, and have golden trinkets hung about them on every part of their garments.

For the amusement of our readers we will add the description of the attire of an Amsterdam belle of the last century, in holiday guise.   " To begin with her head : it is covered with a small muslin cap, and a tiny round black silk hat, which is balanced upon the

paysannes: peasant women
Guelderland: province in east central Holland, the capital is Arnheim
Amsterdam: capital city of Holland

back of the head. A neat white handkerchief is fastened across the bosom with a pin, and carefully pinned underneath the arm; round her neck, upon the handkerchief, hangs a necklace, made of rows of gold beads. Her upper garment is a short, striped cotton bedgown; the body is laced before, the gown part reaching just below the hips, which are swelled out to a large size by her hoop; the sleeves of this garment are tight, and do not fall beyond the elbow; the petticoat, which reaches to the ankles, is of a red or green stuff, spread out to the size of a barrel, forming a strange contrast to the small head; the feet are encased in black shoes, with red heels and enormous buckles."

The following is the costume of a beau of that period: " The hair is rolled up above the ears, the hat is three-cornered, and in size about three-quarters of a yard from corner to corner; the white waistcoat is very long, the coat closely buttoned, and the shoes ornamented with Brobdignag buckles."

" The Dutch burgomaster always dresses in black. His lady appears in a bell-hoop, and a lace head-dress worth 100*l*.; but the daughter not unfrequently walks between this antiquated couple tricked out in all the 'bravery' of the last Paris fashions."

The dress of the peasants of French Flanders resembles that of the Burgundians. The women wear a kind of nightcap, with a plaited border, gold ear-rings, a gold cross hanging from the neck, a jacket, petticoat, and slippers. The petticoat is short and full, and the jacket is laced up the front. A black bib, and short black cloak, are also occasionally worn. No hats are ever seen in this part of the country; the

Brobdignag: immense, taken from Swift's "Gulliver's Travels"
French Flanders: what is now the French-speaking part of Belgium
Burgundian: from Burgundy, area in east central France which includes the city of Dijon

common people when they go out throw over their heads a kind of thick veil, formed of three or four yards of stuff, and the better class of women wear camlet hoods; the latter also wear long cloaks of the same material.

The dress of the men consists of a long jacket, shaped much like those worn by the fishermen in many parts of England, breeches, shoes, and a small, square, flat cap.

The dresses anciently worn in the Netherlands seem to have been very splendid; for we read that when Jane, queen of France, the wife of Philippe le Bel, visited Bruges in the year 1301, she was much struck by the pomp and magnificence displayed by the inhabitants, particularly the ladies, and exclaimed: "What do I see! I thought I alone was queen, but here I find them by whole hundreds!"

The women of Alckmaer (which may almost be called the capital of North Holland) dress in white, and have a singular head-dress, but one that is very characteristic. A bandeau of lace is placed on the forehead, a thin plate of gold confines the hair in a semicircle at the back of the head, and terminates at each temple with a hook, which holds the curls. Over this horse-shoe coiffure is a transparent lace cap, with long lappets, which hang gracefully down the neck.

Jane: queen of Philip IV, 1285–1314
Bruges: city in western Belgium
Alckmaer: Alkmaar, city north of Amsterdam near the coast

THE TOILETTE IN ITALY.

CHAPTER XXVII.

An Italian Lady

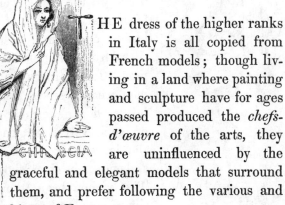

THE dress of the higher ranks in Italy is all copied from French models; though living in a land where painting and sculpture have for ages passed produced the *chefs-d'œuvre* of the arts, they are uninfluenced by the graceful and elegant models that surround them, and prefer following the various and volatile fashions of France.

The Roman peasant's dress is usually of a dark

chefs-d'œuvre: masterpieces
Roman: of the area around Rome

colour; the petticoat is long, the boddice laced across the bosom, the sleeves nearly tight from the shoulders to the wrist, a handkerchief pinned across the bosom, immense earrings, and a curious head-dress of white linen, which lies quite flat upon the head, and the ends hanging down upon the shoulders and back. The boddice is frequently gaily ornamented, and usually of some bright colour, different from the robe or petticoat. The hair hangs in long tresses, and the shoes have immense silver buckles.

Female Peasant

The love of finery is very great among the Roman women, and those that can afford such ornaments usually wear necklaces, chains, and crosses. The dress of the Trasteverini, who form a large portion of the population of Rome, distinguishes them from the rest of the Romans. Lady Morgan says: "The men wear a silken net on their heads, *à l'Espagnole*, a jacket of black velvet thrown on their shoulders, a broad crimson sash, and enormous silver shoe-buckles. The women braid their hair in silken nets, and ornament it with silver bodkins; and in their gala habit appear in vel-

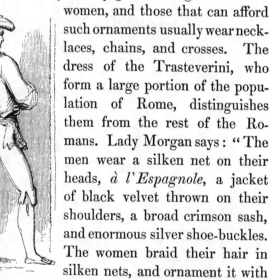

Dress of the Trasteverini

Trasteverini: Romans who live across (tras or trans) the Tiber (Tevero), on the
    Right Bank, traditionally a very poor area
Lady Morgan: Lady Sydney Morgan, 1783–1859, woman of letters, see notes p. 256

vet boddices, laced with gold, silken petticoats, white and coloured (which discover feet shining with large, showy, silver buckles), and scarlet aprons.

The Massari, or rural stewards of the Roman princes, present a very picturesque appearance. The Roman ferrainolo, or mantle, is thrown over their gaunt figures with great effect; their broad hats are flapped over their eyes, and they carry a gun slung at the side, and a hunting-spear in the hand, which give them, according to Lady Morgan, an air rather military than pastoral.

The female peasantry of Terni wear a singular cuffa (a veil of embroidered linen, projected like a shade over the eyes by a piece of whalebone), showy scarlet jackets, and coloured petticoats.

Female Peasant of Terni

Lady Morgan mentions the great resemblance between the dress of the peasantry in parts of the pontifical states to that of the common Irish, the men being muffled to their chins in dark and ragged mantles. To use her own words: " It is remarkable that some of the women of this district wear a head-kerchief precisely like that worn in the remote parts of Ireland; and that others had on the Irish mantle, a piece of bias-cut cloth drawn over the head, almost always of a dingy red. The Irish mantle is, in fact, the Roman cloak, so universally worn by all ranks. Another point of resemblance was that almost all the women were bare-legged, and frequently bare-footed."

Lady Morgan: Lady Sydney Morgan, see note p. 256, wrote many travel books
Terni: town in Umbria between Perugia and Rome

Evelyn, in his "Diary," mentions that when he visited Rome in 1645, all the Jews who inhabited that city wore yellow hats.

Lady Morgan states that the female peasants in the neighbourhood of Rome wear white Isis-like head-dresses.

At Mola di Gaeta the women roll their long tresses, mingled with silken bands, round their heads, with an antique grace; and the vessels with which they are often seen fetching water from the fountain are generally of a graceful Etruscan form, which adds to the elegance of their appearance.

Lady Morgan, speaking of the magnificence of the dresses of Naples, says that they might be supposed to be the "plunder of a sultan's warbrobe."

Swinburn tells us that " At Naples the women are also very splendid on those days of show; but their hair is then bound up in tissue caps and scarlet nets, a fashion much less becoming than their every-day simple method. Citizens and lawyers are plain enough in their apparel, but the female part of their family vies with the first court ladies in expensive dress, and all the vanities of modish fopperies. Luxury has of late advanced with gigantic strides in Naples. Forty years ago the Neapolitan ladies wore nets and ribbons on their heads, as the Spanish women do to this day, and not twenty of them were possessed of a cap; but hair plainly dressed is a mode now confined to the lowest order of inhabitants, and all distinctions of dress between the wife of a nobleman and of a citizen are entirely laid aside. Among the paysannes may be seen almost every mode of hair-

Evelyn: John Evelyn, 1620–1706
Lady Morgan: see note p. 256 and p. 317
Mola di Gaeta: seaport south of Rome
Naples: city on the southern coast; it was a separate kingdom during the 11th–19th
    centuries
Swinburn: Henry Swinburne wrote "Travels in the Two Sicilies in the Years 1777–80"

dressing found on the Roman and Grecian coins. The coiffure of the younger Faustina, with the coil of hair plaited upon the crown of the head, occurs frequently in the old town; that with the coil lower down, which may more properly be styled Lucilla's head-dress, is common among the younger part of the sex in the Chiaia; and Plautina's among the women more advanced in years. * * * Very little suffices to clothe the lazaro, except on holidays, and then he is indeed tawdrily decked out, with laced jacket and flame-coloured stockings; his buckles are of enormous magnitude, and seem to be the prototype of those with which our present men of *mode* load their insteps."

Neapolitan Peasant

A curious anecdote is related respecting the queue, which, at the revolution in Naples, in the year 1799, was a most important addition to the heads of the gentlemen, inasmuch as, in many cases, it actually saved the heads it served to ornament. The royalists seized all those whom they suspected of being inimical to their party; but instead of questioning their captives, they adopted a novel and summary way of discovering their political sentiments—they merely looked whether ther heads gloried in queues or not. If they possessed this appendage, which was considered as strictly *loyal*, they were instantly liberated; but woe to those whose love of French modes had persuaded them to drop their pigtails! Words, entreaties, prayers,

Faustina: wife of Marcus Aurelius, 125–176
lazarro: old English term for dock worker or lascar
Naples: see note p. 318

were unavailing; the test of royalty was not there, and the queueless Neapolitans fell victims to their adoption of the new fashion, and met the deaths of traitors, rebels, and insurgents. So deeply did those who had been saved by their coiffure feel the obligation, and also the safeguard it had proved to them, that many are said to have worn their queues concealed under their coat-collars years after all fear of revolutions had been banished; and when at last the king cut off his pigtail, the news caused a sensation of dismay and astonishment throughout the whole town.

" At Avellino," says Swinburn, " the women are handsome, and take great pains to deck out their persons to advantage. Once a-week they wash their hair with a lye of wood-ashes, that changes it from a dark brown colour to a flaxen yellow, of many different tints in the same head of hair. This I take to be the true *flava cæsaries* of the Latin poets."

The costume of the Tuscan peasantry varies much according to the district they inhabit. In Florence, the out-of-doors dress of the middle classes is generally black. The Tuscans, on Sundays and fête days, wear their hair becomingly ornamented with a very small hat, elegantly poised over the left ear, while the hair on the opposite side is interwoven with a string of pearls, or adorned with a shining comb. They have ear-rings formed of several drops of pearl, set in gold, and necklaces composed of two rows of pearls and coral. Their feet are enclosed in black velvet slippers, and in their hands are to be seen gaudily ornamented fans. They have jackets without sleeves, laced with riband. When at work, or market,

Avellino: town in the interior, east of Naples
Swinburn: Henry Swinburne, see note p. 318
flava cæsaries: yellow of the cæsars
Tuscan: Tuscany is the area around Florence

they confine their hair in a net of crimson, scarlet, or blue silk, tied by two strings, and ornamented by tassels, which are often of gold or silver. They are also often seen with the hair drawn into a knot on the top of the head, and a veil hanging down behind.

A Tuscan Lady

The Venetians dress their heads in a curious manner. They wear a little rose-coloured hat, trimmed with blonde, placed over the right ear; and over the left a bunch of artificial flowers, the hair behind tied with a riband. "A custom here prevails," says Lady Millar, "of wearing no rouge, and increasing the native paleness of the face by lightly wiping a white powder over the face."

Mrs. Piozzi gives the following account of their morning dress in her time: "It consists of a black silk petticoat sloped, just to train on the ground a little, flounced with black gauze. On their heads they have a skeleton wire, like what is used for making up hats; over it they throw a large piece of black mode or

A Venetian Lady

Venetians: from Venice and the surrounding area
Lady Millar: Lady Anne Miller wrote "Letters from Italy, describing the Manners and
    Customs, Antiquities, etc....1770-1771"
Mrs. Piozzi: Hester Lynch Piozzi, 1741-1821, wrote "Observations and Reflections
    Made in the Course of a Journey through France, Italy and Germany" 1789

persian, so as to shade the face like a curtain.   The
front is trimmed with deep black lace, or soufflet
gauze, very becoming.   The thin ends of silk they
roll back, and fasten in a puff before on the stomacher;
then once more rolling it back from the shape, tie
it gracefully behind, and let it hang in two ends.
The evening coiffure is a silk hat, shaped like a
man's, with a white or worked lining, and sometimes
one feather; a great black silk cloak, lined with
white, and perhaps a narrow border down before,
with a very heavy round handkerchief of black lace,
which lies over the neck and shoulders, and conceals
the shape completely.   Here is surely little appearance of art! no creping, no frizzing the hair, which
is flat at the top, all of one length, and hanging in
long curls about the back and sides, as it happens.
No brown powder, no rouge at all."

Lady Millar thus describes a Venetian wedding:
" All the ladies, except the bride, were dressed in
their black silk gowns with large hoops; the gowns
were straight-bodied, with very long trains, the trains
tucked up on one side of the hoop with a prodigious
large tassel of diamonds.   Their sleeves were covered
up to their shoulders with falls of the finest Brussels
lace, a drawn tucker of the same round the bosom,
adorned with rows of the finest pearls, each the size
of a gooseberry, till the rows descended below the top
of the stomacher; then two rows of pearls, which
came from the back of the neck, were caught up at
the left side of the stomacher, and finished in two fine
tassels.   Their heads were dressed prodigiously high,
in a vast number of buckles, and two long drop curls
in the neck.   A great number of diamond pins and

Lady Millar: see note p. 321

strings of pearls adorned their heads, with large *sultanes*, or feathers, on one side, and magnificent diamond ear-rings. The bride was dressed in cloth of silver, made in the same fashion, and decorated in the same manner, but her brow was quite bare, and she had a fine diamond necklace and an enormous bouquet. Her hair was dressed as high as the others, with this difference, that it had curls behind and before. These curls had a singular appearance, but not near so good an effect as the other ladies', whose hair was plaited in large folds, and appeared much more graceful. Her diamonds were very fine, and in great profusion."

Keysler says : " There is a college at Venice, to whose care the regulation of dress is committed by the republic. All the *nobili* wear black, and foreign cloth is prohibited."

Formerly it was requisite that a noble Venetian should have eight cloaks ; three for the masks, one of which was for the spring fête of the Ascension, when the Doge married the sea ; one for the autumn, for the ridotto and theatre ; one for winter, for the Carnival. These three were called *baceta*. In addition to these, they had two for summer, of white taffeta ; one of blue cloth for winter ; one of white cloth for great occasions ; one of scarlet cloth for the great church-ceremony days.

The following is said to be the origin of the cross in front of the ducal coronet worn by the Doge. The father of Laurentius Celsus, who was elected Doge in 1361, thinking it beneath his dignity to pull off his cap to his own son, went, from the moment of his election, on all occasions and in all weathers, with his head uncovered. The Doge, being solicitous for his

sultanes: plumes of the porphyrio, or purple gallinule, a sea-bird
Keysler: Johann Georg Keysler wrote "Travels through Germany, Bohemia, Hungary, Switzerland, Italy and Lorrain" 1756
nobili: nobles, nobility
Doge: the elected Leader of Venice

health, and finding it impossible to change his opinion, suggested an expedient, which had the desired effect: he placed a cross on his ducal coronet. The old man's piety got the better of his pride, and he resumed his cap to testify his respect to the cross.

In Evelyn's "Diary" we find the following amusing description of the dress of the Venetians: "It was now Ascension Weeke, and the great Mart or Faire of the whole yeare was now kept, every body at liberty and jollie. The noblemen stalking with their ladys on *choppines ;* these are high-heel'd shoes, particularly affected by these proude dames, or, as some say, invented to keepe them at home, it being very difficult to walke with them ; whence one being asked how he liked the Venetian dames, replied, that they were mezzo carne, mezzo legno, half flesh, half wood, and he would have none of them. The truth is, their garb is very odd, as seeming allwayes in masquerade ; their other habits also totally different from all nations. They weare very long crisped haire, of severall strakes and colours, which they make so by a wash, dischevelling it on the brims of a brocade hat that has no head, but an hole to put out their heads by ; they drie them in the sunn, as one may see them at their windows. In their tire they set silk flowers and sparkling stones, their peticoates coming from their very arme-pits, so that they are neere three quarters and an half apron ; their sleeves are made exceeding wide, under which their shift sleeves as wide, and commonly tucked up to the shoulder, shewing their naked armes, thro' false sleeves of tiffany, girt with a bracelet or two, with knots of points richly tagged about their shoulders and other places of their body,

Evelyn: John Evelyn, 1620–1706

which they usually cover with a kind of yellow vaile of lawne very transparent. Thus attir'd they set their hands on the heads of two matron-like servants or old women, to support them, who are mumbling their beades. 'Tis ridiculous to see how these ladys crawle in and out of their *gondolas* by reason of their *choppines*, and what dwarfs they appeare when taken down from their wooden scaffolds; of these I saw near thirty together, stalking halfe as high again as the rest of the world, for the citizens may not weare *choppines*, but cover their bodies and faces with a vaile of a certaine glittering taffeta or lustrèe, out of which they now and then dart a glaunce of their eye, the whole face being otherwise entirely hid with it. To the corners of these virgin-vailes hang broad but flat tossells of curious point de Venize. The married women go in black vailes. The nobility weare the same colour, but of fine cloth lin'd with taffeta in summer, with fur of the bellies of squirrels in the winter, which all put on at a certaine day, girt with a girdle emboss'd with silver; the vest not much different from what our Bachelors of Arts weare in Oxford, and a hood of cloth made like a sack, cast over their left shoulder, and a round cloth black cap fring'd with wool which is not so comely; they also weare their collar open, to shew the diamond button of the stock of their shirt. I have never seen pearle for colour and bignesse comparable to what the ladys weare, most of the noble families being very rich in jewels, especialy pearles, which are always left to the son or brother who is destined to marry, which the eldest seldome do. The Doge's vest is of crimson velvet; the Procurator's, &c. of damasc, very stately."

point de Venize: Venice point or lace

The costume of the Doge's lady is represented in the accompanying engraving.

The Dogarissa

The inhabitants of the skirts of the Apennines differ much from those of the valleys. The women, according to Lady Morgan, resemble the peasantry of Wales: "Tight in their dress, and universally wearing little, round, black beaver hats with high crowns, and a stiff plume of black feathers. Their gala dress is principally characterised by a profusion of ribbons floating from their shoulders, their waists, and their sleeves. The beaver hat is then replaced by combs and bodkins; and at all times their necks are encircled with pearl and coral—usually an heir-loom of many generations' descent, but occasionally the purchase of years of labour, and the most rigid economy."

skirts of the Apennines: foothills of the central Italian mountain spine
Lady Morgan: Lady Sydney Morgan, see note p. 256
bodkin: pin for the hair

Of Bologna the same author says : " The costume appears to belong to other ages. Spangled fans, silver combs, coral necklaces, and every sort of gaudy finery, are as indispensable to the toilette of the Bolognese peasant as to that of the same class in other Italian provinces. The French toilette prevailed in Bologna among the higher classes nearly a century ago. The females of the lower ranks still wear the becoming *zendada*, a scarf or veil, which falls from the head, and which they drape prettily enough round their shoulders. Their hair is ingeniously plaited, and set off with showy combs or bodkins ; and coral, mock or real, is abundantly and universally worn."

The women of Lombardy are remarkable for the tawdriness of their ornaments, and for the large black and gold German fans which they parade on festivals in the streets of Turin; yet many of both sexes go bare-legged, and some even bare-footed. A love for costly personal decorations of gold and silver is very general : the peasantry vest all their savings in valuable ornaments. The younger females display much classic taste in the braiding of their luxuriant tresses, which are sometimes confined by a shining comb, and sometimes fastened by a glittering bodkin; even the elder dames wear a square linen veil, not ungracefully disposed, which forms a great contrast to their tattered petticoats and bare legs. Bright and gaudy colours are much admired.

In the " Notes of a Wanderer" we read : " In Genoa the women were all gracefully dressed, without bonnets, wearing merely a white muslin scarf, fastened to the crown of the head by its centre, and the ends hanging down over the shoulders."

Bologna: city in north central Italy, center of culture and great cuisine
Lombardy: area in northern Italy centering on the Po Valley and Milan
Turin: city which is not in Lombardy, but in Piedmont, farther west
"Notes of a Wanderer": "Notes of a Wanderer in search of Health through Italy, Egypt,
    Greece ... " written by William Fullarton Cumming, 1839
Genoa: seaport in northwest Italy, formerly a city-state with an elected Doge like
    Venice

Gray, in his "Germany," says of the women of Genoa: "The painted linen veil which they wear, called *mezzaro*, is not unbecoming, though it resembles a flowered gown thrown over the head and hooded."

From Lady Morgan's account of Genoa we take the following: " The women's heads are ornamented by a quantity of silver bodkins, forming a sort of coronet or star at the back, and confining a profusion of plaited tresses. Many of the elder women wear square linen veils, embroidered and trimmed with coarse lace. Dresses are here considered as heir-looms. Many a silken vest and quilted boddice, many a chain of gold and of coral, purchased in the days of Genoa's prosperity, still remain to deceive the eye with the appearance of rural and commercial wealth. The shops at Genoa display a profusion of gold and silver filagree work, clasps, rings, ear-rings, chains, combs of coral, and even of costly gems, all destined for the peasantry. The nobility were, in the latter times of the republic, prohibited from wearing such sumptuous ornaments; and the lower classes are still, as formerly, the sole purchasers of the old-fashioned jewellery of the Genoese goldsmiths. The fullest dress allowed to the ladies by the sumptuary laws was a black velvet, trimmed with coloured ribbons and point lace. The women of Genoa are covered, even on working days, with gold and silver ornaments; on holydays they add a profusion of pearl and coral to their ordinary decorations, and a female peasant, when making her marriage trousseau, thinks seven or eight hundred francs a very moderate price for a necklace or chain."

From Veryard's " Travels in Italy in 1682," we

Gray: Thomas Gray, 1716–1771, wrote "Letters of Thomas Gray" and travelled on the
    Continent in 1739–1740
Genoa: see note p. 327
Lady Morgan: see note p. 256
Veryard: Ellis Veryard wrote "An Account of Diverse Choice Remarks ... taken in a
    journey through the Low Countries, France, Italy ...", published 1701

learn that the women of every rank at Genoa, as well as at Monacha, affected many of the customs of the Spaniards. He says: " They wore fardingals like the Spanish ladies, which are circles of whalebone about their waist, bearing out their petticoats on all sides as far as they can well reach, insomuch that when two meet in a narrow street they find much difficulty to pass."

Evelyn also says: " The inhabitants of this city are much affected to the Spanish mode and stately garbe." And Lasselles describes them as wearing " broad hats without hatbands, broad leather girdles with steel buckles, narrow britches, with long waisted doublets and hanging sleeves. The great ladies go in *guard infantas;* that is, in horrible overgrown vertingals of whalebone, which being put about the waiste of the lady, and full as broad on both sides as she can reach with her hands, bear out her coats in such a manner that she appears to be as broad as long. The men look like tumblers that leap through hoops, and the women like those that anciently danced the Hobby-horse in country mummings."

The dress worn at Ancona, according to Nisson, is very singular. On fête-days, he says, " they wear black clothes lined with green, blue stockings, shoes whitened with chalk, and tied with coloured ribbons; their waistcoats unbuttoned, the cuffs of their coats embroidered; their shirt-sleeves hang over their hands. The women wear head-dresses, with long fringes over their faces; jackets of red or yellow silk, laced with seams of gold or silver lace, and short petticoats of a hundred colours."

Evelyn says, that at Lucca he bought, in 1645,

Monacha: Monaco, which was under Spanish protection 1524-1641, was ruled by a Genovese family, the Grimaldis; the current ruler, Rainier III, descends from a French family, the Goyon-Matignons, who took the name and arms of Grimaldi when they succeeded to the title by marriage in 1731
Evelyn: John Evelyn, 1620-1706
Lasselles: Richard Lassels' "The Voyage of Italy" was published in 1670
guard infantas: see note p. 138
Ancona: seaport on the central east coast
Nisson: actually Maxmilian Misson whose "A New Voyage to Italy ..." was published 1695
Lucca: city in northern Tuscany, near Pisa

gloves and embroidered stomachers, the same as those
" usually worn by gentlemen in these countries."

The annexed cut represents the costume of a lady
of Florence.

A Lady of Florence

" The dress of the inhabitants of Sardinia," says
Pinkerton, " is a vest of white or scarlet woollen,
covered with a long coat, or a short jacket, made out
of four sheep-skins ; this garment is without sleeves.
The woman's dress has nothing peculiar."

Florence: city in Tuscany
Sardinia: large island west of Italy
Pinkerton: John Pinkerton, 1758–1826, wrote several books such as "A General Collec-
    tion of the best and most interesting Voyages and Travels in all parts of the
    World", which was published 1808

THE

TOILETTE IN SICILY AND MALTA.

CHAPTER XXVIII.

Dress of the Maltese

MARTIN thus describes the dress of the Maltese : " They are clothed in a loose cotton shirt, over which is a wide vest or jacket, with silver, sometimes gold buttons ; a long twisted scarf wound several times round the body, with very often a sheathed knife placed therein ; loose trousers, leaving the legs bare from nearly the knees downwards ; and very peculiar shoes, called *korch*, which is a leathern sole fastened with strings or thongs to the foot and leg, nearly like the old Roman sandal. The head in winter is covered with a

Martin: Selina Martin's "Narrative of a Three Years' Residence in Italy 1819-22" was published 1828
Maltese: Malta is a small island republic between Sicily and Africa

woollen cap of different colours, having a hood attached, and falling down on the back ; in summer large straw hats are worn.   The women are attached to their primitive dress, consisting of a short cotton shift, a petticoat generally of a blue colour, and upper robe opening at the sides, and a corset without sleeves."

The Faldetta

The higher classes among the Maltese follow the French and English fashions ; but we must not omit to mention the *faldetta*, a black silk veil, their usual coiffure when abroad, which almost rivals in grace and elegance the much‑admired mantilla of the Spanish.

Denon, in his " Travels in Sicily and Malta," in the year 1787, says : " Large breeches, a shirt of blue linen, a broad sash, and the arms and feet left naked, form the whole description of the light dress and or‑naments of the Maltese."   Speaking of the women, he remarks : " Their dresses display more of coquetry than magnificence ; elegance and neatness constitute their luxury."

The accounts given by old authors of the magni‑ficence of the ancient inhabitants of Sicily, are truly amazing.   Plato, when he visited this island, was so struck with the luxury of Agrigentum, that he ex‑claimed, " They build as if they were never to die, and eat as if they had not an hour to live."   Diodorus also, speaking of the riches of this island, mentions one of the citizens returning victorious from the Olympic games, and entering his city attended by

Denon: Baron Dominique Vivant Denon, 1748-1825, whose "Travels in Sicily and Malta" was published 1789
Sicily: very large island off the "toe" of Italy; formerly a Greek colony, held by the Arabs, part of Spain, part of the Kingdom of Naples, now part of Italy
Plato: circa 427-348 B.C., Greek philosopher
Agrigentum: now Agrigento, town in the middle south coast of Sicily
Diodorus: Siculus Diodorus, historian in the latter half of the first century B.C.

three hundred chariots, each drawn by four white horses, richly caparisoned; and gives many other instances of their profusion and luxury.

Brydone, in his "Tour through Sicily and Malta," says of the ladies of Palermo, "The ladies here have remarkably fine hair, and they understand how to dress and adorn it to the greatest advantage. It is now only used as an embellishment, but in former times, we are told that, like that of Samson, it was found to be the strength and protection of the country. Their historians relate (in whose reign, I believe, is rather dubious), that this city had suffered a long siege from the Saracens, and was greatly reduced by famine; but what distressed them still more, there were no materials to be found for making bowstrings, and they were on the point of surrendering. In this dilemma a patriotic dame stepped forth, and proposed to the women that the whole of them should cut off their hair, and twist it into bowstrings: this was immediately complied with. The besieged, animated by this gallant sacrifice of the fair, renewed their defence with so much vigour, that the assailants were beat off; and a reinforcement soon after arriving, the city was saved. The ladies still value themselves on this story. 'The hair of our ladies,' says one of their quaint poets, 'is still employed in the same office; but now it discharges no other shafts but those of Cupid; and the only cords it forms are the cords of love."

In Denon's "Travels" we read: "Historians relate, that the ancient Argyrians cut off their hair to sacrifice it to Hercules, in token of gratitude for the water with which that hero furnished them, Argyrium

Brydone: Patrick Brydone's "Tour through Sicily and Malta" was published 1773
Palermo: capital city, on the northwest coast
Saracens: Arabs, they held Sicily in the 9th-11th centuries
Denon: see note p. 332
Argyrians: classical reference to an untraceable people
Argyrium: could perhaps be Agira, in the east central area

before being totally destitute of water.   Whether it be from tradition, or for their greater convenience, the modern inhabitants still cut their hair almost entirely off, preserving only two locks on the temples."

Brydone mentions some statues, which, though of marble, gave a good idea of the dresses worn in the last century, for they were formed of pieces of different colours.   The shoes were black, the stockings red, and the garments of blue, green, and almost every hue, ornamented with a rich lace of *giall' antique.* The periwigs of the men, as well as the head-dresses of the ladies, were white, and the flowing ruffles were of the same colour.

In this island is found a fish called *Pinna marina,* from which is extracted a fine thread, much resembling silk, which the inhabitants make into beautiful gloves and stockings.

Brydone: see note p. 333
giall' antique: giallo antico, "ancient yellow", named from the rich yellow marble
    found in Italy

THE TOILETTE IN ANCIENT ROME.

CHAPTER XXIX.

Roman Toga

THE Romans, like the Greeks, had a distinguishing feature of dress which was different from that of all other nations — the *toga* — and it corresponded with the *pallium* of the Greeks. It was a robe of peace, and was chiefly worn in the city. The toga worn by the early Romans, when they had no other dress, was narrow and close, covering the arms and hanging down to the feet. Afterwards, however, it was a very loose flowing robe, closed at the bottom, but open from the top as far as the waist, and made without any sleeves. The right arm was always bare, and the left supported a part of the drapery, which, being thrown back over the shoul-

der, formed a sort of cavity or pocket. The toga usually worn by rich people was large, wide, and made of fine materials, and the Romans took much pains in adjusting the folds, so as to make it sit gracefully. These folds were sometimes collected in a knot. Thus we read in the "Æneid:"

> " Bare were her knees, and knots her
>   garments bind,
>   Loose was her hair and wanton'd in
>   the wind."

Women formerly wore the toga, but afterwards they adopted a different robe called a *stola ;* it had a broad border reaching to the feet, and when they went abroad they threw over it a kind of mantle called *palla.*

There are, however, various opinions on this subject ; some learned authors assert that the toga and the stola were the same garment as to shape and form, the only difference between them being that the latter had a border or fringe ; others repudiate this idea, and declare that they were in every way different.

The usual colour for the toga was white, but when

Another Style of the Roman Toga

The Robe called "Stola"

Æneid: epic poem written by Virgil to glorify the origins of Rome as having come out of the Trojan War

persons were in mourning they wore it of a black or dark colour. Magistrates and some of the priests added a purple border, and generals, when they were victorious, had the toga splendidly embroidered. Thus we read in the " Æneid : "

> " The leaders are distinguished from the rest,
>   The victor honoured with a nobler vest ;
>   Where gold and purple strive in equal rows,
>   And needlework its happy cost bestows."

Young men, till they were considered of an age to be freed from the constraint of guardians and teachers, and also unmarried women, wore a toga edged with purple. When the former were old enough to assume the manly robe, many ceremonies were observed, and the youth was formally invested with a toga of pure white. Underneath this garment was worn another made of white woollen stuffs, called a tunic ; it reached to the knees in front, and to the middle of the legs behind. When first invented it had no sleeves ; afterwards, however, sleeves were worn with fringes at the hands. A girdle or belt confined the tunic round the waist.

> " A golden belt shall gird his manly side,
>   Which with a sparkling diamond shall be tied."—*Æneid.*

The women's tunic reached to the feet and had long sleeves ; they also wore a girdle.

Tunics were often presented to foreign princes as presents ; Virgil says :

> " And rich embroidered vests for presents bear."

Æneid: see note p. 336
Virgil: Publius Vergilius Haro, 70–19 B.C., famous poet

And Æneas presents embroidered garments to the Queen of Carthage :

> " A robe of tissue, stiff with golden wire,
> An upper vest, once Helen's rich attire ;
> From Argos by the famed adultress brought,
> With golden flowers and winding foliage wrought."

Linen clothes were not worn by the Romans till the emperors introduced them from Egypt, but they had woollen shirts, and the women vests or shifts.   In later ages a kind of great-coat was thrown over the rest of the dress ; it was open in front, and fastened with clasps or buckles, and was called *lacerna*.   The materials of which it was made were various ; sometimes it was made of many colours, and in later ages it usurped the place of the toga to such a degree, that ancient writers relate that Augustus one day from his tribunal seeing a number of citizens dressed in the lacerna, gave orders to his officers not to allow any one wearing that garment to enter the Forum or Circus.

The Romans had another great-coat called *penula*, which was shorter and narrower than the one we have just described ; it had a hood, and was worn on journeys and in the army.   It was used by men and women, and was often made of skins.

Their coverings for the feet were various ; they had neither stockings nor breeches, but wrapped their limbs with pieces of cloth.   They had a kind of shoe called *calceus*, which covered the whole foot, and was tied with a latchet ; also sandals, which projected the sole only.   The calcei were worn with the

Æneas: Trojan hero of the "Æneid"
Queen of Carthage: Dido, queen of the city in what is modern Tunisia
Augustus: Cæsar Augustus, 44 B.C.–14 A.D.

toga when a person went abroad, but the sandals were generally used on a journey.

The patrician senator's shoes reached as high as the middle of the leg, and had a gold or silver crescent on the top of the foot. The ordinary shoes were black, but some were scarlet or red, and others were ornamented with gold, silver, and precious stones; those worn by the Roman women were usually white, but often red, scarlet, purple, and yellow, and adorned with pearls and embroidery. A senator was known by having four latchets to his shoe, instead of one, like ordinary people. The shoes were of unwrought leather. Sometimes they had socks of wool or goat's-hair.

Many writers imagine that the Romans had no gloves, but they are mentioned both by Greek and Roman authors, and also mittens.

We see by the ancient coins and medals that the ancient Romans were bareheaded, except at sacred rites, games, festivals, and when at war. Baldness was looked upon as such a deformity that Cæsar, who had no hair on his head, is said to have prized the honour of wearing a laurel crown above all the other dignities conferred on him by the senate, because it served to conceal his baldness. In the city, to screen themselves from the heat, rain, or wind, the Romans frequently threw the folds of their robe over their heads; but if they met any one to whom they owed respect, they immediately let the folds drop and remained bareheaded. At all sacred rites but those of Saturn, and in any grief, danger, or despair, they veiled their heads. At festivals they had a woollen cap or bonnet, and on a journey a round cap like a helmet, or a cap of un-

Cæsar: Julius Cæsar, 100 B.C.–44 B.C.
Saturn: a reference to the Saturnalia, a ritual celebration that fell in December and gradually, because of the excess associated with it, became synonymous with debauched merrymaking

wrought leather; but this last was more frequently worn by warriors.

Men and women, but particularly the latter, wore quantities of false hair, often arranged in the shape of a helmet. The head-dresses of the Roman women frequently changed, but when they went abroad they at all times covered their faces with a veil. They were particularly addicted to frizzling and curling their hair, and raising it into stories of curls, some of a great height. Ancient writers say that the lofty pile of false hair they wore upon their heads resembled a building. They used long hair-pins to fix their curls. Thus Virgil says:

> "his frizzled hair to soil,
> Hot with the vexing iron, and smeared with fragrant oil."

Mode of Dressing the Hair

Arranging the hair was a matter of grave importance; slaves frizzled and adjusted it, and a number of females learned in the art of the coiffeur attended to see to the proper arrangement of the locks, while the fair dame herself watched the growing edifice of curls, gold, pearls, precious stones, crowns, or chaplets of flowers, in a mirror made of polished steel or brass, of tin, or of silver.

Ribands, or fillets, were a very general head-dress. Thus Virgil says:

> "In perfect view their hair with fillets ty'd."

An embroidered, or golden net or caul, was fre-

Virgil: see note p. 337

quently used to enclose the hair. We find in the
" Æneid :"

> " Her head with ringlets of her hair is crown'd,
> And in a golden caul the curls are bound."

The caul appears, also, to have been used to enclose the tresses of a corpse; for in describing the
preparations for the funeral of Pallas, after the account of the vests in which the body was arrayed, we
read :

> " One vest array'd the corpse, and one they spread,
> O'er his closed eyes, and wrapp'd around his head :
> That when the yellow hair in flame should fall,
> The catching fire might burn the golden caul."

The priests who offered up sacrifices for the fertility of the ground had a woollen bandage, tied with
ribands, round the head.   To this custom, probably,
Virgil alludes :

> " His hoary locks with purple fillets bound."

Others of the ministers of religion wore wreaths of
oak-leaves, or vervain, around their brows.   Thus in
the " Æneid :"

> " In purest white the priests their heads attire ;
> *   *   *   *   *
> And o'er their linen hoods, and shaded hair,
> Long twisted wreaths of twisted vervain wear."

Suppliants, also, and warriors wore fillets of purple
or of gold.   Æneas is thus described :

> " Green wreaths of bays his length of hair enclose,
> A golden fillet binds his awful brows."

Æneid: see note p. 336
Pallas: character in the Æneid, the son of Evander
Æneas: hero of the Æneid

Cosmetics, washes, paint, and perfumes, were much used among the Roman women. White lead, to whiten the skin, and vermilion to make it red, were constantly employed by both sexes. The wife of Nero invented a pomatum said to have preserved her beauty. But not content with paints and ointments, the women wore patches also, and stained their eyelids and eyebrows with black powder or soot. They also wore massive ear-rings, sometimes three or four in each ear, of immense value, bracelets, necklaces, armlets, brooches, and clasps. Men wore a twisted chain, or a circular plate of gold.

> " Some at their backs their gilded quivers bore,
> Their chains of burnished gold hung down before."—*Æneid.*

Roman matrons wore an ornament peculiar to themselves, called *segmentum*. Some authors suppose it to have been a necklace, others imagine it was an embroidered riband or fringe, sewn upon the robe. Women of all ages also had a boddice, formed of a broad riband, which served for modern stays, and they wore a clasp or buckle on the left shoulder, also a muffler or handkerchief round the neck.

No ornament was so much cherished and worn by men and women of all ranks as rings of gold, silver, and baser metals. They were frequently set with precious stones, on which were usually engraved the images of some of their friends, or the representation of some great event. These rings were used for sealing letters and papers. When at the point of death a Roman usually presented his ring, as a token of esteem, to his dearest friend.

wife of Nero: Octavia, daughter of Claudius, 42–62 A.D.

Young boys wore an ornament hung round their necks, which was supposed to prompt them to wisdom : it was called *bulla*, and was a hollow golden ball or boss.

The beard among the ancient Romans was allowed to grow, shaving it off being quite unknown among them till about the year of the city 454, when some barbers came from Sicily, and introduced the fashion of *smooth chins.* Beards, however, were allowed to sprout again under Hadrian, who, having some deformity on the face, revived the custom, but it was soon abandoned again.

Man wearing the Ornament called "Bulla"

The Romans usually cut their hair very short, and in the later ages they devoted much time to the arrangement of it ; they dyed and perfumed it, and wore false hair and perukes. The men frequently consecrated their beard and hair to some deity : Nero devoted his, enclosed in a golden box, to Jupiter Capitolinus. Philosophers always wore long beards, to give them an air of gravity and learning. In sorrow and mourning the Romans, unlike the Greeks, allowed their beards to grow, and both men and women let their hair hang dishevelled. Thus Virgil says :

" Her beauteous breast she beat, and rent her flowing hair."

And again :

" In mournful guise the matrons walk around :
   With baleful cypress, and blue fillets crown'd,
   With eyes dejected, and with hair unbound."

Hadrian: Emperor, 117–138
Nero: Emperor, 54–68
Jupiter Capitolinus: Roman god
Virgil: see note p. 340

The garments of the Romans, which in the early ages were composed of coarse materials, gradually, as civilisation and arts increased, became splendid in the extreme. Silk was brought from India towards the end of the republic, and fine linen at an earlier period from Egypt and Tyre, whence also came the dye so celebrated in ancient times, and known under the name of Tyrian purple.

Silk robes were first worn by Heliogabalus. Till his time the silk, when brought from India, was unravelled, and wove anew with linen or woollen yarn, forming a thin and nearly transparent material. The Emperor Aurelian is said to have refused his wife a robe of pure silk, on account of the immense expense.

Ancient writers frequently allude to the rich embroidery worn by the Romans, and to the vests dyed with purple. In Virgil we read :

"And vests embroidered of the Tyrian dye."

And in another verse :

"Your vests embroider'd with rich purple shine."

The ornamenting these garments in gold was very frequent :

"Then two fair vests of wondrous work and cost,
Of purple woven and with gold emboss'd."

Even when arrayed in armour splendid robes were still worn, and the purple colour was the mark of royalty. Virgil says :

"By his purple known
A Tuscan prince, and by his regal crown."

Cæsar prohibited the wearing a particular kind of

Tyre: city-state on the coast of Lebanon famous for making Tyrian dye, a brilliant
    purple derived from certain shellfish
Heliogabalus: Emperor 218-222
Emperor Aurelian: 270-275
Virgil: see note p. 340
Tuscan: from Tuscany, region around Florence
Cæsar: Julius Cæsar, 100 B.C.-44 B.C.

purple, except on certain days, and by persons of a certain rank and age. Many sumptuary laws were also made by the Romans against extravagance in dress. One issued by Numa ordered that no woman should have in her dress above half an ounce of gold, nor wear a garment of different colours. But these edicts were soon forgotten, and splendour of attire, gold, silver, embroidery, and jewels, shone around.

A Roman bride on her wedding-day was always covered with a flamen, or red veil.

Numa: Pompilius Numa, King of Rome 715-673 B.C.

THE TOILETTE IN NORWAY.

Ancient Dress of a Peasant

CHAPTER XXX.

HE ancient dress of the Norwegian peasants was made of the reindeer's skin. From what old authors say, it seems to have consisted of a cloak or mantle; but we find that about the middle of the eleventh century, when King Oluf Haraldren founded the city of Bergen, he brought thither a great many foreign merchants, who carried their fashions with them. In the Norwegian Chronicles we read: " Then the Norwegians took up many foreign customs and dresses, such as fine-laced hose, golden plates buckled round their legs, high-heeled shoes, stitched with silk, and covered with tissue of gold, jackets that

King Oluf Haraldren: Olaf Haroldson, 1066–1093
Bergen: port, directly west of Oslo; Norway's second most important city
Norwegian Chronicles: "Norlandz Chronika ...", 1670

buttoned on the side, with sleeves ten feet long, very narrow, and plaited up to the shoulders."

By this account we may imagine that the Norwegians were eager followers of fashion, and that at the time of which Snoro Sturlesen writes, they dressed like other European nations. We find, however, in another part of the same work, that the long garments were not quite discarded in Norway till about the year 1100, and then King Magnus Olufsen introduced short clothes and bare legs.

The lower order of peasants rarely trouble themselves about Fashion's vagaries; and the natives of this foreign clime still retain the costume that has descended to them from father to son. Some wear breeches and stockings all in one, and waistcoats of the same, and, if they wish to be very smart, they cover the seams with cloth of a different colour.

The Hardanger peasants always wear black clothes edged with red; the Vaasserne wear all black; the Strite, white, edged with black; and those near Soynefiord prefer black and yellow; so that almost every parish has its own colour.

They wear on their heads a broad-brimmed hat, or else a grey, brown, or black cap. Their shoes are without heels, and consist of two pieces of leather; the upper part sits close to the foot, and the other is joined to it in folds. In winter they have laced half-boots, but when on the ice they put on skates, about ten feet long, covered with seal-skin. The peasants never wear a neckcloth, but leave their throats and necks entirely uncovered. Sometimes they fasten a leathern belt round the body, to hold their knives and other implements.

Snoro Sturlesen: Snorri Sturluson, 1178–1241, historian
King Magnus Olufsen: Magnus III, the Barefoot, 1073–1102
Hardanger: southwest of Bergen, on a fjord
Vaasserne, Strite: we could not identify these peoples
Soynefiord: Sognefjorden, on the west coast, above Bergen

Costume of the Woman

At church and on holydays the Norwegian women wear laced jackets and leathern girdles, adorned with silver. They are also fond of a chain, which they put three or four times round their necks, and hang a gilt ornament at the end of it. Their handkerchiefs and caps are covered with plates of silver, brass, and tin, buttons, and rings; and of the latter they wear quantities on their fingers. The young women plait their hair, and while employed in their household affairs they wear a shift and a petticoat; the collar of the former reaches to the throat, and they have a sack, generally of a black colour, twisted round the waist. The linen they wear is very fine, and this simple costume is said to be very becoming.

In some parts of Norway the men wear coats of stone-coloured cloth, the button-holes being sewn with scarlet, and the buttons formed of white metal: this has a very gay appearance.

THE TOILETTE IN SWEDEN.

CHAPTER XXXI.

Ancient Swedish Dress

THE inhabitants of this northern clime are distinguished from those that dwell in southern lands by having a national dress, which was established in 1777, doubtless with the wise intention of repressing or totally preventing those extravagancies and luxuries of clothing so prevalent among other nations. "The monster Fashion," says Swinton, in his travels, "created for a scourge for mankind, has occasioned every evil that infests the age." Gustavus III. of Sweden has shewn that he participated in this opinion, for his sumptuary laws regarding dress are very determined and exact.

By the edict on this subject, settled in 1777, the

Swinton: Andrew Swinton wrote "Travels into Norway, Denmark, Russia in the Years 1788–1791" and "Letters from Scandmare on the past and present state of the Northern Nations of Europe", the latter published 1796
Gustavus III: 1771–1792

men are ordered to wear a close coat, very wide breeches, strings in their shoes, a girdle, a round hat, and a cloak. The usual colour for all these articles of dress is black on ordinary days, but on court-days they must assume a singular appearance, for they are enjoined to wear the cloak, buttons, girdle, and shoestrings, of *flame colour*. The women are obliged to wear a black gown, with puffed gauze sleeves, and a coloured sash and ribands; those, however, who go to court are allowed white gauze sleeves.

The higher classes on great occasions appear in a blue satin suit, lined throughout with white, and splendidly ornamented with rich lace. The women are allowed a white satin robe, with coloured ribands.

Coxe, in his Travels, gives a more detailed account of this costume. The dress of the men, he says, resembles the old Spanish; and consists of a short coat, or rather jacket, a waistcoat, a cloak, a hat, with a feather *à la Henri IV.*, a sash round the waist, a sword, large and full breeches, and roses in the shoes. The cloak is of black cloth, edged with red satin, the coat, or jacket and breeches, are also ornamented with red stripes and buttons; the waistcoat, sash, pinks at the knees, and roses for the shoes, are of red satin. This costume, however, is only for such persons as have been presented at court: those who have not been permitted this distinction are not allowed to ornament their habits with red satin.

The Swedish gentlemen wear neither beards nor whiskers. The ladies turn their hair back over a cushion, and leave two large curls to hang down at the back of the neck. They were formerly exceedingly

Coxe: William Coxe's "Travels into Poland, Russia, Sweden and Denmark" was published 1784

à la Henri IV: panache or plume in the style of Henry IV of France (1399–1413)

prodigal in their dress, and followed all the extremes of the French fashions, until the legislature interfered to restrain such a love of expense and finery. In winter they wear dresses lined and trimmed with costly furs.

The Swedish peasants are generally well clothed and protected from the inclemency of the weather. The men wear long cloth coats, warmly lined with sheep-skins, and the women a striped woollen stuff of many colours, chiefly green, white, and red.

Male Peasant

Female Peasant

THE TOILETTE IN DENMARK.

CHAPTER XXXII.

National Dress of the Men

THE ancient kingdom of Denmark still preserves an old national habit among its peasants, but the higher classes were almost the first of these northern nations to admire and follow the French fashions; so that if you would know the dress of a Danish belle, look in the " Magasin des Modes," and there you will find her gown, shawl, bonnet, and coiffure. The toilette of the gentlemen also strictly follows Parisian fashions.

The old costume of Denmark is not unlike the habit of the Quakers, and consists of, for the men, broad-brimmed hats, black jackets, and full, glazed, black breeches, left quite loose at the knees, and fastened round the waist with a girdle.

The women wear black jackets and red petticoats, and their only head-dress is a piece of blue glazed cloth bound round the head.

"Magasin des Modes": "Storehouse of Fashion", literally; a famous French fashion
  periodical of the mid-Victorian period

In a work entitled "Eirik's Rauda Saga," we find described the dress of a woman, which appears much like that of our gipsies. "She had on a blue vest, spangled all over with stones, a necklace of glass beads, and a cap made of the skin of a black lamb, lined with white cat-skin. She leaned on a staff adorned with brass, with a round head set with stones, and was girt with an Hunlandish belt, at which hung her pouch full of magical instruments. Her buskins were of rough calf-skin, bound on with thongs studded with knobs of brass, and her gloves of white cat-skin, the fur turned inwards."

Swinburne says that "the dress of the Danish men is after the German fashion; but what appears ridiculous to strangers is, that many of them, even during their hot summers, wear great-coats." "The ordinary women, in their Sunday clothes, appear exceedingly awkward," says the same author, "and their finery is put off to the best advantage, or the worst, with starch and beads, till they seem to be enclosed in a coat of mail."

In Otto Sperling's Observations, there is a passage which shews that this warlike people formerly gave fashions in dress to those very southern nations who now govern their taste on this subject.

The shoes worn in some parts of Denmark, and other of the extreme northern nations, for travelling over

Ancient Danish Warrior

"Eirik's Rauda Saga": also known as "Eiriks Saga Rauda" and "Thorfinn Karlsefnes Saga", the edition of this work in the British Library is dated 1838
Hunlandish: a reference to the Huns, followers of Attila the Hun, considered a byword for primitiveness and crudeness
Swinburne: Henry Swinburne's "Courts of Europe at the Close of the Last Century" was published 1841
Otto Sperling: Otto Sperling the Younger's "Altes und Neus von Gelehrtan Sachen aus Dännenmark" was published 1768

the snow, are very curious. They are formed of cane, with a place in the centre for the heel, and are from three to four feet long, and from nine to twelve inches wide. From presenting such a broad surface they do not readily sink in the snow; but, according to travellers who have used them, they are not at all agreeable, for they rub the skin off the heel. Franklin says he might have been traced for miles by the blood which flowed from his feet occasioned by the friction of this chaussure.

Snow-Shoe

Franklin: Sir John Franklin, 1786-1847, was an explorer
chaussure: shoe

THE TOILETTE IN HUNGARY.

CHAPTER XXXIII.

Hungarian Military Dress

THE dress worn by the better classes in most of the courts of Europe, is swayed by the fashions of France and England; but the national costume of Hungary is well known to the lovers of the fancy-ball, who often array themselves in its sable dress, with sleeves straight to the arms, and stays fastened in front with gold, pearl, or diamond buttons.

Lady Wortley Montague, in her " Letters," says : " The Hungarian lady's dress is beautiful; a gown of scarlet velvet lined and faced with sables, made exactly to fit her shape, the skirt falling to the feet. The sleeves are straight, the stays buttoned before with two rows

Lady Wortley Montague: 1689-1762, her "Letters Written during Her Travels in Europe, Asia and Africa" were published 1763 of little buttons of gold, pearl, or diamonds.   On their heads they wear a tassel of gold, that hangs low on one side, lined with sable or some other fine fur."

Dress of a Female Peasant

The dress of the female peasants is not so becoming. The hair in front is plaited tight, and joined to the back, which is likewise plaited, and hangs down behind, in the same manner as that of the Swiss peasants. The neck is covered with a white handkerchief, and a variegated body and petticoat, with a white apron, forms the rest of the dress. The petti-coat is worn short, to shew the yellow leather boots, with low iron heels.

The men have thick stout blue jackets, strong thick boots without much shape, lank, uncombed hair, and a broad-brimmed hat with a low crown.

The costume of the better classes is much admired. It consists of a hussar jacket and pantaloons, the former girded round the waist with a sash of some rich manu-facture. Over this jacket they throw a cloak, or mantle, which buttons under the arm, so as to leave the right hand at liberty. The ornaments of their dress are usually black lace, but sometimes a profusion of gold lace also is used in the adornment of their attire, particularly the pelisse, which is generally crossed by a gold cord. The boots are long, and have a tassel of black cord or gold bullion in front. On the head is worn a *kalpac*, or cap of fur, with a falling top of crimson cloth, and sometimes a plume of fea-thers. Spurs on the heels are indispensable to the costume.

The *guba*, a manufacture peculiar to Hungary, is also employed for the garments of the lower orders: it can only be made from long-woolled sheep, and exactly resembles a sheep-skin. This cloth is only a yard in width; but its great peculiarity, which distinguishes it from other kinds of cloth, is that, after every four threads, a small lock of the long wool of the Hungarian sheep is put in with the fingers.

When the guba is finished weaving, it is sent to be washed in the hot springs at Gross Wardein. It is then dyed, generally of a black colour, to make greatcoats for the poorer classes, and is most comfortable for those who are exposed to the inclemency of the weather. A finer kind of guba is made from the wool of lambs. When dyed blue, it looks very well, and is used in winter instead of fur.

The Morlacchi, though belonging to Hungary, differ much in manners and appearance from the inhabitants of that country. The dress of the women is very remarkable. The unmarried females are very whimsical in respect to the ornaments of the head, but when married, they are not allowed to wear anything but a handkerchief tied round it. The girls wear a scarlet cap, to which they generally fasten a veil, which falls back over the shoulders; strings of silver coins, glass beads, shells, feathers, and artificial flowers, as well as tremulous plumes of glass, are all employed to ornament these caps, which, though singular in their appearance, are often not devoid of elegance. Their holiday shifts are embroidered with red silk, and sometimes with gold; these they work for themselves, while tending their flocks, and it is wonderful how well they are executed.

Gross Wardein: famous springs in eastern Hungary, near Transylvania
Morlacchi: probably the Moravians in northwest Hungary, an area now part of Czechoslovakia

The use of stays is unknown, nor do they put whalebone or iron in their stomachers. A woollen girdle sustains the petticoat, which is commonly decked with shells, and of a blue colour, whence it derives the name of *modrina*. The gown, which is made of serge, reaches to the ankle, and is bordered with red; it is called *sadak*. In summer the modrina is not worn, only the sadak without sleeves, and the shift. The girls always wear red stockings, and their shoes or *opanke*, which somewhat resemble the *cothurnus* of the ancients, are made of undressed leather, and fasten with knotted thongs above the ankles. The unmarried women, even of the richest families, are not permitted to wear any other sort of shoe, but after marriage they are allowed to replace it by the Turkish slipper.

The girls keep their hair concealed under their caps, but the women wear it falling on their shoulders. Sometimes they tie it under the chin, and always have beads and coins twisted among it, in the Tartar fashion.

Both old and young women wear round their necks strings of various sized beads, and rings of silver, brass, and tin, on their fingers; they have bracelets of leather covered with wrought tin or silver, and they embroider their stomachers or adorn them with beads and shells.

The dress of the men is much plainer than that of the women. It consists of breeches of coarse white serge, which they draw tight round the waist by means of a woollen string; a shirt, and a short doublet, called *jacerma*. In winter they add a short cloak, made of coarse red cloth, called *rabiniza*. On their heads they wear a red cloth cap, and above it the sheep-skin kalpac of the Tartars.   They bind their waist with a fillet of silk or wool, in which they carry pistols, a tobacco pipe, a horn with powder and shot, a bag to hold their money and tinder-box, and a large knife with a brass handle set with false stones.

Tartars: people of central Asia (originally from Mongolia); the name is commonly used to refer to Asian tribal peoples indiscriminately

THE TOILETTE IN POLAND.

CHAPTER XXXIV.

Male Costume

MEN of all ranks in Poland, whether gentle or simple, formerly shaved off their hair, leaving only one or two ringlets on the crown of the head. They seem, however, to have admired large whiskers and long moustaches, which looked very fierce so long as the nearly bald pate was not seen ; but when the bonnet was removed, the face and head formed a singular contrast.

The vest of the peasants reaches down to the middle of the leg, and the sleeves fit quite tight to the arms. Over this is worn a gown lined with fur, and confined round the waist by a sash ; but in summer they only wear a shirt and drawers of coarse linen, without any shoes and stockings. They wrap the rind of trees round their legs and feet in winter, and cover their bodies with sheep-skin cloaks; they have neither neckcloth nor stock, and wear on their heads a fur cap or bonnet.

The lower orders cover their heads with a piece of linen, from under which the hair hangs in long plaits. Many add to this another long piece of linen, which, hanging on each side of the face, and reaching down to the knees, makes them look as if they were doing penance in a white sheet.

The costume of the higher classes is very elegant and becoming, and much admired by all nations. Their waistcoat has sleeves, and over it is worn an upper vest of a different colour, which reaches to below the knee: the sleeves in warm weather are

Female of the Lower Class

tied behind the shoulders. The sash, or girdle, is generally rich and ornamented; a sabre is suspended from it, and is a badge of nobility. Their robes are very rich. In summer they are made of silk, in winter of cloth, stuff, or velvet, ornamented and lined with the most expensive furs. Their boots are of yellow turkey leather, very thin, and plated with iron heels, made in the shape of a half-moon; their caps and bonnets are of the finest furs, and their cloaks, when on horseback, are of sable, or of the skins of tigers or leopards. Some of the Polish nobles have as many as

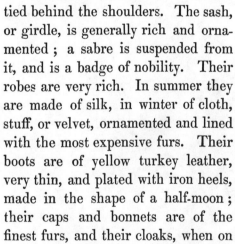

Gentleman of the Higher Class

fifty suits of the richest vests, which descend from father to son.

A Polish Lady

An old author asserts that Charles II. of England thought of introducing this costume into his court, and after his restoration he himself wore it for two years; not, however, so much from admiration of its elegance, as from the patriotic wish of encouraging the manufacture of broad-cloth.

The habit of the ladies is a long rich robe, ornamented and lined with fur, called a *polonaise*.

Charles II: 1660–1685

THE TOILETTE IN RUSSIA.

CHAPTER XXXV.

Ancient Male Costume

URN we now to snowy mountains and glittering icebergs,—to the land of the czars, the cold and dreary clime of the north.

As may be supposed, in so severe and frozen a country as Russia, skins and furs form two of the principal articles of clothing. The ancient dress of the men was a kind of swaddling coat of skins, or of coarse linen, lined with skins, furs, or cloth. Round their waists they twisted a coloured shawl; they wore trousers and boots, and allowed their beards to grow very long. Of later years the men, however, have adopted the dress usual among the other nations of Europe, and beards are but rarely seen.   Their clothes are generally made of the richest materials they can afford to procure.

The ancient dress of the women, the reverse of that of the men, was as short and as tight as decency would allow, and it continues much the same among the lower classes to this day.   In some respects it resembles the costume of the Highland women, and is as gaudy as possible, and much ornamented.   The petticoat is of striped plaid, very scanty in width and length ; the jacket is usually of a different colour, and the head is adorned with a white cloth, which is wrapped round it.   All, however, who can afford it ornament their dress with gold lace and jewels.

During the season of festivals in Russia, in spite of snow, ice, and severe cold, the wives of the wealthy tradesmen drive about in droskies, with riches upon their persons " enough," as Rodrigo says, " to corrupt a votarist."   Their caps are manufactured of matted gold, pearls, and other precious stones : and the richest Turkish and Persian shawls, and most brilliant diamond ear-rings, are often seen.   But, however costly the materials, they endeavour, to a certain degree, to preserve the national costume, of which the jacket forms a principal feature.   The shawl is worn in a peculiar and very graceful manner ; it is thrown over the head-dress, and falls in elegant folds down to the feet.

The ladies of high rank follow the French and English fashions, and wear a profusion of ornaments.

The czar and grandees formerly dressed in the most splendid Asiatic costumes ; and, before the days of Peter the Great, the court was said to be the most magnificent in the world.   The Earl of Carlisle,

Highland women: refers to the Scots
Rodrigo: Roderigo, a Venetian gentleman, Act IV, Scene 2, of Othello
Peter the Great: 1672-1725
Earl of Carlisle: Charles Howard, 1629-1685, who wrote "The Earl of Carlisle's Rela-
    tion of three Embassies from his Majesty Charles II to the Duke of Muscovy, the
    King of Sweden, and the King of Denmark, in 1663 and 1664"

when ambassador in Russia, said that he could see nothing but gold and precious stones in the robes of the czar and his courtiers. Peter the Great, however, forced the higher classes of his subjects to discard their long robes, and to dress after the European fashion; he obliged them also to cut off their beards, which, till his accession to the throne, they had regarded almost with veneration.

Furs constitute a principal article of dress among the upper orders, and the most expensive are the most admired. The lower ranks are of course obliged to content themselves with the skin of any animal they can procure, and envelop their persons in them merely as a defence against the inclemency of the weather.

The manner in which the lower orders clothe their feet and legs indicates great simplicity and antiquity; their shoes are made of the matted bark of trees, and their legs covered with bandages of woollen cloth, bound on with ligatures of the same material, very similar to sandals. These thongs, however, do not, of course, add to the beauty of the ankle, and it is probably in consequence of these numerous bandages (which are, perhaps, necessary to defend the legs and feet from the cold) that many writers remark the large size and clumsy shape of the limbs of the Russian peasants, male and female.

It may not be uninteresting to our readers to add the costume of a people that inhabit a small hamlet in Siberia; the account is taken from the travels of M. l'Abbé Chappe d'Auteroche. "The dress of the women of this tribe" (the Wotiaks), says the writer, " is most singular. They wear a shift of coarse linen,

ambassador: the Earl of Carlisle was the English Ambassador 1663-1664
Peter the Great: 1672-1725
M. l'Abbé Chappe d'Auteroche: 1722-1769, his "A Journey into Siberia made by the order of the King of France" was published 1761
Wotiaks: a people living in Siberian Udmurt, Finno-Permians in origin; the capital of their district is Izheusk

slit in front like a man's shirt, and hemmed up each
side of the opening with thread or worsted of different
colours ; there is also a little ornament of a triangular
figure wrought on the right side of the shift.   Their
gown is woollen, and bears a great resemblance to
the habit of the Jesuits in college ; the sleeves of the
upper gown are slit in the middle, to give passage to
the arms, and the lower part generally hangs down.
This gown, which reaches to the legs, is fastened
merely by a girdle, curiously wrought.   They wear,
also, coarse cloth stockings and sandals, like the
Russians.   Their head-dress is very remarkable : they
first wrap their heads in a towel, over which they
fasten, with two strings, a kind of helmet, made of
the bark of a tree, and ornamented in front with a
piece of cloth and with copecs ; the helmet is then
covered with a handkerchief, wrought with thread or

Head-Dresses of the Wotiaks

worsted of various colours, and edged with a fringe.
This head-dress is above a foot high.   The hair is

divided into two tresses, which fall down upon the shoulders, with a necklace like that worn by the Tartars."

The Kamtschatkians, though belonging to Russia, have a different dress; and being a very uncivilised people, residing in a wretched, dreary country, destitute of culture, their costume is more fitted for warmth and comfort than for the display of elegance, variety, or taste. They still wear the skins of dogs, deer, sea and land animals, and even the skins of birds. Very often all these are sewn together, forming a *tout-ensemble* as ugly as it is extraordinary. Their upper garments are made in two ways. Sometimes the skins of which they are formed are of an equal length, at others they are left long behind, like

Costume of the Kamtschatkians

a train, with wide sleeves that reach to the knees, and a hood, which in bad weather they put underneath their caps; there is an opening in this dress just large enough to pass the head through, and round it they sew the skins of dogs' feet, with which to protect their faces in cold weather. The skirts and sleeves of this dress are ornamented with a border of white dog-skins, and others of different colours, sewn together in patterns. They generally wear two coats, the under one with the hair inwards, the other side dyed with alder, and the outer one with the hair uppermost. For this latter

Tartars: Mongols who settled in parts of Russia
Kamtschatkians: peninsular people on the Siberian Pacific coast, probably the Koryak
tout-ensemble: entire outfit

garment they use black, white, or speckled skins, the hair of which is much esteemed.

This is the upper garment of both men and women; but the latter also wear very wide and short trousers, and a waistcoat tied round the body. Their hats are made of birch, bark, or plaited grass. The women use a white paint, made of rotten wood, and a red paint, made from a sea plant boiled in seal's fat, which they rub over their faces; they also were formerly much addicted to the wearing of perukes, some weighing ten pounds each.

A veil is often thrown over their faces when they go abroad; and though both men and women wrap their feet and legs in bark, both the Cossac and Kamtschatkian *petit-maîtres*, when in their best dress, wear buskins of peculiar elegance; and if an unmarried man appears in them when visiting his friends, it is immediately concluded that he is about paying his addresses to some fur-clad maiden. The sole of these buskins is of white seal-skin, the upper part of fine white leather, made from white dog-skins; and the part which adorns the legs is of dressed leather or dyed seal-skin, beautifully embroidered.

The inhabitants of Kasan, another province of Russia, wear a dress that somewhat resembles that of the Russians. The Tartars who live in Kasan have a woollen jacket, which is bound round the waist with a girdle; over this is a long flowing outer robe. They always have boots on their feet, and they shave their heads, except on one place on the back part, which they cover with a small piece of leather. They wear a cap edged with fur.

Cossac: Cossack, military/peasant class of people in the Ukraine along the Dniepper and Don Rivers
Kamtshatkan: see note p. 367
petit maîtres: dandies
Kasan: probably the Chuvash people
Tartars: live along the Upper Volga River in Kazan

The women's dress is much the same as the above, only they place the girdle above the robe; their cap is shaped like a sugar-loaf, and covered with glass beads, which they consider as precious as we do jewels. A large piece of cloth, also ornamented with beads, is fastened to the back of the cap, and hangs down below the waist. The young girls are not allowed to wear caps; they only bind their hair with a fillet of riband.

Female Costume in Russia

The Kalmuc Tartars wear a round bonnet with a border of fur, in the Polish fashion, and a kind of loose coat of sheep-skin, which reaches to the middle of the leg. The great people wear garments made of silk, which they procure from the neighbouring nations.

Female Costume of the Kalmuck Tartars

Clarke, in his " Travels in Europe," says : " The dress of the Tartar noblemen displays as much taste as can be shewn by a habit necessarily decorated with gold and silver lace ; it is neither heavily laden with ornament, nor are the colours tawdry. They sometimes delight in strong contrast, by opposing silver lace to black velvet for their caps ; scarlet or rose-coloured silk to dark cloth, for their vests or pelisses ; but, in general, the dress of a Tartar of dis-

Kalmuc Tartars: Kalmyk is at the mouth of the Volga River where it enters the Caspian Sea

Clarke: Edward Daniel Clarke's "Travels in Various Countries of Europe, Asia and Africa" was published 1810

tinction is remarkable for its simple elegance as well as cleanliness. Their favourite colour in cloth is drab; and the grey or white wool for their winter caps is, of all other ornaments, most in esteem."

Costume of a Mordvine Woman

The costume of many of the Tartar tribes belonging to Russia is very picturesque. The Mordvine women, when married, wear a high stuffed cap, sewed with many variously-coloured threads, with a flap hanging down the back, to which are attached chains and other ornaments. Their linen petticoats they adorn gaily with red and blue needlework; they wear an apron hanging from their girdle, but instead of being in front, as with most other people, it hangs behind, and is curiously embroidered and bordered with fringes, tassels, and beads. Those who can afford it have a wide ornamented linen gown, with very short sleeves, generally dyed a bright yellow. It is fastened closely round the throat with a small pin, and across the bosom with a larger one, from which hang such a quantity of corals, copper buttons, chains, medals, coins, bells, and indeed any thing that makes a jingling sound, that the dress of a Mordvine *élégante*, in holyday costume, is of a very great weight. Ear-rings are always worn; but when they intend to be very smart, they also have bracelets, twisted several times round the arm, like those used in India.

The young women have fewer ornaments, but their dress is the same as we have described above; they,

Tartar tribes: Mongols who settled in various parts of Russia
Mordvine: people scattered around the Upper Volga River

however, wear their hair braided, like the Russians, in a long tail, with knots of riband and fringes tied to it. Formerly they plaited the hair in eight or nine small tresses, those behind the ears being larger than the others. To these tresses they tied ornaments of various kinds, and fastened them through the girdle; some even plaited sheep's-wool with their hair, till it resembled a large tail, and fell to the knees. The men belonging to this tribe wear the Russian dress, except that their shirts are curiously embroidered.

The Mohschonian costume is not devoid of elegance. The women's caps are not very high, and are worked with a needle; many wear a band of linen over the head, with long ends, which hang down the back. Round the neck they have a collar of network, formed of glass beads; from the girdle is suspended an apron covered with embroidery, glass beads, tassels, and Indian shells. Their hair is curled and frizzed upon short sticks, and sometimes braided into small tresses; their feet are bound with leathern thongs.

The inhabitants of a village called Tscherask wear a costume greatly resembling that of the Scotch. The women, over the shift, have a petticoat of plaided callimanco; their caps are of various colours, bound with ribands, gaudily worked, which hang down behind their backs. Young girls braid their tresses, and wind them with much grace round the head: across the forehead they place a parti-coloured riband, or *bandeau* of coral beads.

We will take leave of these singular people, by giving the dress of the Kirguise. The men wear an under-garment of cotton, and an upper one of blue

Mohschonian: Muscovite, from Moscow
Tscherask: European spelling which we were not able to trace in Russia
callimanco: calamanco, a woolen twill
Kirguise: Kirghiz, the Kirghiz Steppe borders the Caspian Sea on the northeast

linen, open before, but tied across the body with a cotton belt. Over this they have a leathern belt, in which they place their guns, shot-bags, and powder-horns. Their summer-caps are of felt, covered with stuff, embroidered in silks of various colours, and lined with velvet: the top of this cap is conical, and has two flaps, one on each side, which either hang on the cheeks or are fastened back. The winter-caps are made of fur. The men shave their heads, but have moustaches on the upper lip, a pointed beard, and a small tuft of hair at each corner of the mouth. When not abroad, they cover their bare skulls with a round cap of black cloth, ornamented in colours. Their boots are very clumsy, and made of asses'-skin, the soles full of large points, and edged with iron. When out on a hunting-party they wear immense trousers, fastened under their arm-pits, which, when on horse-back, give them a shapeless and frightful appearance.

The women's ordinary costume is a blue shift, a pair of trousers, bands to wrap round the legs and feet, and a veil of parti-coloured linen. Their head-dress requires no little time and care to arrange: they first lay a piece of stuff, three or four yards long, upon the head, bringing the ends down the sides of the face, after which they braid their hair in two tresses; the ends of the stuff are then crossed under the chin and carried up over the head, whence they fall down again over the ears. This done, they wind a narrow strip of some other stuff, four or five yards long, round and round the head many times, till it forms a turban.

The better classes make this head-dress of fine striped stuffs, and they also wear an upper robe of silk ornamented with artificial flowers, then a tippet to match the turban, and over the whole another open garment : their necks are covered with worked handkerchiefs.

Another gala head-dress, which is considered very ornamental, consists of two lappets of flowered muslin, fastened to the back of the head under the turban ; above these fall two more lappets, covered with velvet and black fringe. Married women bring the latter over the shoulders, but young girls allow it to hang down their backs. " Princesses," says Tooke, " and the daughters of illustrious persons, are distinguished by the necks of herons, which they wear in their hair, raised up in an ornament upon the head in the shape of a horn, and the plumage is very beautiful." They also wear silk clothes or rich stuffs, or fine cloth set off with gold lace and loops, or faced with fur ; and even velvets are very common among them.

The dress of the Scythians, or ancient Tartars, resembled that of the Persians. Like them they wore tiaras, and stockings and breeches all in one piece. On the column of Theodosius, at Constantinople, is seen the most ancient representation to be found of them. They appear to have worn a tunic down to the heels, and a chlamyde, which was sometimes raised at the back of the neck, so as to cover the head.

Tooke: Rev. William Tooke's "A View of the Russian Empire during the Reign of Catherine III, and to 1798" was published 1799
Scythians: Indo-Iranic people, fl. 8th-4th century B.C.; definitely not Tartars
Theodosius: Theodosius I, 346-394

THE

TOILETTE IN TURKEY, WALLACHIA,

ETC.

CHAPTER XXXVI.

Vignette, Female Figure

ET us now transport our readers to the shores of the East—the land of the Sultan—the far-famed city of Stamboul. Here, within the closely-guarded chambers of the harem, mid the perfume of thousands of flowers, the soft rippling of fountains, and the sweet melody of voices, "Fashion" still holds undisputed sway. Within the gorgeous chamber, secluded from the gaze of all but her immediate attendants, sits the Eastern beauty, the Rose of the Garden, the Pearl of the Ocean. Paintings and gildings adorn the walls, carpets of the richest dyes are laid over the floors, silken sofas and couches, whose softness invite repose, are scattered around, and near them lie cushions, glittering in satin, velvet, brocade, and embroidery, and tassels and fringes of gold and silver. To describe her beauty, and the

Stamboul: Istanbul/Constantinople

dress of Eastern ladies, let me borrow the gifted pen of Lady Wortley Montague.

"On a sofa, raised three steps, and covered with Persian carpets, sat the kihàya's lady, leaning on cushions of white satin embroidered; and at her feet sat two young girls about twelve years old, lovely as angels, dressed perfectly rich, and almost covered with jewels. But they were hardly seen near the fair Fatima, so much her beauty effaced every thing I have seen; nay, all that has been called lovely in England or Germany. She was dressed in a caftan* of gold brocade, flowered with silver, very well fitted to her shape, and shewing to admiration the beauty of her bosom, only shaded by the thin gauze of her shift. Her drawers were pale pink, her waistcoat green and silver, her slippers white satin, finely embroidered, her lovely arms adorned with bracelets of diamonds, and her broad girdle set with diamonds. Upon her head a rich Turkish handkerchief of pink and silver, her own fine black hair hanging a great length, in various tresses, and on one side of her head some bodkins of jewels."

Such was the dress of the lady of the deputy to the grand vizier, above one hundred years since, and such is still the dress of the Eastern women; for though fashion frequently changes the colour of their garments, and the materials of which they are composed,—now bidding the fair recluse array herself in pale blue silk, now in deep crimson, then again in white muslin, fine as the spider's web, pure as the untrodden snow, still the form of the garments never changes, and has been the same for hundreds of years.

* A kind of vest.

Lady Wortley Montague: 1689-1762; her husband was English Ambassador to Turkey in 1716; see note p. 355

Lady Wortley Montague, who while residing in the East adopted the costume of the country, thus describes her own dress in a letter to her sister then in England:

" The first part of my dress is a pair of drawers, very full, that reach to my shoes, and conceal the legs more modestly than your petticoats ; they are of a thin rose-coloured damask, brocaded with silver flowers. My shoes are of white kid leather, embroidered with gold. Over this hangs my smock, of a fine white silk gauze, edged with embroidery. This smock has wide sleeves, hanging half-way down the arm, and is closed at the neck with a diamond button. The antery is a waistcoat, made close to the shape, of white and gold damask, with very long sleeves falling back, and fringed with deep gold fringe, and should have diamond or pearl buttons. My caftan, of the same stuff as my drawers, is a robe exactly fitted to my shape, and reaching to my feet, with very long, straight, falling sleeves. Over this is my girdle, of about four inches broad, which all that can afford it have entirely of diamonds or other precious stones ; it must be fastened before with a clasp of diamonds. The curdee is a loose robe they throw off or put on according to the weather, being of a rich brocade (mine is green and gold), either lined with sable or ermine ; the sleeves reach very little below the shoulders. The head-dress is composed of a cap called *talpack*, which in winter is of fine velvet, embroidered with pearls and diamonds, and in summer of a light silver stuff ; this is fixed on one side of the head, hanging a little way down, with a gold tassel, and bound on either with a circle of diamonds (as I have seen several) or a rich embroidered handker-

Lady Wortley Montague : see notes p. 355, 375

chief. On the other side of the head the hair is flat,
and here the ladies are at liberty to shew their fancies;
some putting flowers, others a plume of heron's feathers,
and, in short, what they please. But the most general
fashion is a large bouquet of jewels, made like natural
flowers; that is, the buds of pearl, the roses of different
coloured rubies, the jessamines of diamonds, the jonquil of topazes, &c., and so well set and enamelled
'tis hard to imagine any thing of that kind so beautiful.
The hair hangs at full length behind, divided into
tresses braided with pearl and ribbon, which is always
in great quantity."

The above is considered a perfect description of
the in-door costume of an Eastern lady of quality;
but when they go abroad they are all obliged to wear

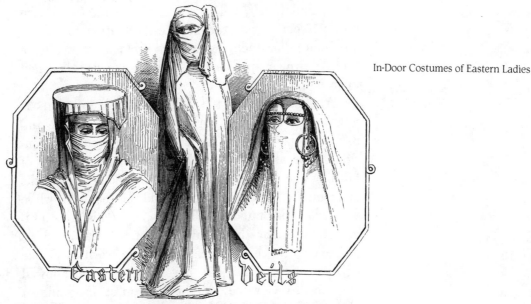

In-Door Costumes of Eastern Ladies

two dresses, called murlins; these form a complete
disguise, one covering all the face, except the eyes,

the other quite concealing the head-dress. Besides these a *ferigee* is worn to hide the figure; it has straight sleeves, reaching to the ends of the fingers, and, wrapping round them, perfectly conceals the dress and shape.

All Eastern women, whether of high or low degree, wear drawers: indeed the poorer classes only wear these and a shirt. Yet, though half naked, no one is ever seen without a veil; which, even from the time of Rebecca, has been considered a necessary part of female dress; and all but the very poorest contrive to possess some jewels, for ear-rings, bracelets, and necklaces.

Although there is a chapter in the Koran which strictly prohibits adorning of the person with gold, silver, and jewels, silks, and costly robes, the Turks do not seem to pay the slightest attention to the admonition; for men, as well as women, only esteem their attire in proportion to the expense lavished upon it.

Any alteration in the fashion of their garments is unknown among the Turks, although from time immemorial points of dress appear to have been considered of almost as much importance as points of faith. The long sleeve still worn among the Turks is mentioned by both Strabo and Herodotus; while the turban is stated by Pliny to be in his time universally worn by the inhabitants of the East, and, as at present, the high turban was then worn by people of distinction, while the lower classes were allowed one not so elevated. Thus the most insignificant objects of dress in this country are of real importance: for rank and privilege are here designated

Rebecca: Old Testament figure, Genesis 24:60
Strabo: Roman historian, circa 63 B.C.
Herodotus: Greek historian, circa 480-425 B.C.
Pliny: Pliny the Younger, 62-113, Roman Pro-Consul in Pontus (Bithynia, now a part of Turkey)

by the height of a turban and the colour of a slipper.

The fair imprisoned inmate of the harem, whose life glides away in all the dull monotony of seclusion, whose only means of cheating the lagging hours is by employing them in embroidery, or in watching the graceful movements of the dancing girls, may be pardoned for devoting so much time to the amusements of the toilette.

Inmate of the Harem

Shaping the eyelashes with antimony, increasing the lustre of the eyes by drawing between the lids a fine pencil dipped in kohol, and dyeing the nails and ends of the fingers with the leaves of henna, require much attention and time; so also does arranging the folds of the dress as to give a graceful and elegant *tournure;* placing the turban skilfully in the exact position; braiding the tresses in the proper number of plaits; selecting the jewels that match the colour of the dress; and, lastly, throwing over the head the light and snowy veil.

Neither do the lordly Osmanlis disdain to bow their proud and turbaned heads at the footstool of " Fashion." Let me here borrow the words of the author of " Anastasius," who thus describes a Turkish *petit-maître:* " His turban attracted the eye less even by its costliness of texture than by its elegance of

kohol: kohl, powdered antimony used to outline the eyes and darken the lids
tournure: literally, the turning or drape of a garment, also used to refer to the bustle
Osmanlis: Ottoman Turks, from Osman I (1259–1326), founder of the Ottoman dynasty
"Anastasius": Thomas Hope's "Anastasius" was published 1819
petit maître: dandy

form. A band of green and gold tissue, diagonally crossing the forehead, was made, with studious ease, completely to conceal one ear, and as completely to display the other. From its fringed extremity always hung, suspended like a tassel, a rose or a carnation, which, while it kept caressing the wearer's broad and muscular throat, sent up its fragrance to his disdainful nostril. An hour every day was the shortest time allotted to the culture of his adored moustaches, and to the various rites which these idols of his vainglorious heart demanded; such as changing their hue from a bright flaxen to a jetty black, perfuming them with rose and amber, smoothing their straggling hairs, and giving their taper ends a smart and graceful curve. Another hour was spent in refreshing the scarlet dye of his lips, and tinting the dark shade of his eyelids, as well as in practising the most fascinating smile and the archest leer which the Terzhana could display. His dress, of the finest broadcloth and velvet, made after the most dashing Barbary cut, was covered all over with embroidery of gold, so thickly embossed as to appear almost massive. His chest uncovered down to the girdle, and his arms bared up to the shoulders, displayed all the bright polish of his skin. His capote was draped so as, with infinite grace, to break the too formal symmetry of his costume. In short, his hanjar with its gilt handle, his watch with its concealed miniature, his tobacco-pouch of knitted gold, his pipe mounted in opaque amber, and his pistols with diamond-cut hilt, all were in the style of the most consummate *petit-maître.*"

This splendid costume is that of, more or less, all the grandees in Turkey. We will now describe that

Terzhana: probably a title
Barbary: Barbary Coast, North Africa; at that time the word was used approvingly to indicate richness and delicacy
capote: long cape
hanjar: a type of dagger

of the lower classes. Their ordinary dress consists first of a shirt, with very wide sleeves, drawers made of linen, which join their stockings,—these latter being formed of the same material,—cloth breeches or short trousers, a vest which reaches to the knees, or a jacket ornamented in gold or silk twist, a robe which falls down to the feet, and over this a kind of great-coat, with short sleeves, and on the feet scarlet slippers.

The Turks of better rank always wear the long dress, and over it robes of fine cloth, or pelisses of the most costly furs, while their poniards and yatagans are studded with silver and precious stones. When in-doors they wear a *mestler*, which is a thin shoe without any sole; when they go abroad it is thrust into the papoosh, or slipper.

Costume of a Turkish Gentleman

In a work entitled the " Turks and the Russians," we read the following description of the dress of the Turks : " Trousers very loose to the calf, thence tight to the ankle; a close waistcoat, open at the neck, and covered below by a shawl tied round the waist; a jacket, with very full and short sleeves, shewing the equally loose sleeves of the shirt; a turban on his head, and yellow boots or slippers on his feet, form the usual and very becoming dress of a Turk : the trousers, waistcoat, and jacket, are of various colours, and ornamented with embroidery; and the turban is white, green, or otherwise, according to the rank and privileges of the wearer."

"Turks and the Russians": T. B. Armstrong's "Journal of Travels in the seat of war during the last two campaigns of Russia and Turkey" was published 1831

Emirs or shirrefs (descendants of Mohammed's daughter) are alone allowed the high honour of adorning their heads with green turbans; and the Turks allow none but themselves to appear in yellow slippers. The men of high rank are in the habit of carrying in their hands a *tespi*, or, as Moore calls it, a "ruby rosary," which is used as much for amusement as devotion. Gloves are never worn by the Turks.

All the attendants of the sultan wear splendid garments, particularly on days of ceremony, when they appear in dresses of the most gaudy colours, till at a distance they resemble a garden of tulips.

The immense width of the Turkish garments may be accounted for by the prevailing custom of sitting cross-legged.

In Bulgaria the women wear on their heads a cap somewhat resembling a mitre, ornamented with pieces of money; it covers the forehead, and the hair, plaited with shells, hangs down the back. The robe is long, and fastened round the waist by a girdle; the surcoat, which closes tightly round the throat, with a bow of riband in front, is curiously embroidered, and often adorned with jewels. Over this garment is worn a loose robe, not unlike a great-coat; it is shorter than the under vest, and has long sleeves, which, though wide at the top, become tight below the elbow to the wrist: this garment is open underneath the arms as far as the bottom, and the sides are united with large bows of riband, placed at distances from each other. The slippers are very low in the quarters, and made high upon the instep.

The men wear round fur caps, a long robe that reaches to the knees, and shews the full trousers that

Moore: John Moore, 1729–1802; his "A New and Complete Collection of Voyages and Travels" was published 1780

meet the stockings, which terminate below the knee; this robe is quite open, and a shawl, twisted round the waist *à la Turque*, retains it in its place. Over this is worn a much longer garment, also open, with large wide sleeves. The legs are covered with bands of linen, which give them a clumsy appearance, and the feet are inclosed in sandals, or rather open shoes, laced across from the toes to the instep.

In Wallachia the women of high rank wear splendid silk or satin robes, often embroidered or brocaded in gold and silver. The upper garment is full and long, with long tight sleeves: it is not confined at the waist, but hangs quite loose; it is open at the bosom, and shews a splendid jewelled stomacher, and is generally trimmed all round with fur. Beneath it is an embroidered vest, with a collar of precious stones and velvet encircling the throat. On the head is a cap of fur, made something in the shape of a turban.

Lady of Wallachia

The young girls wear their hair flat on the temples, and twisted in a broad plait behind, interspersed with flowers. The silk jupe reaches to the feet, the boddice is sufficiently open to shew an ornamented stomacher, the sleeves are tight to the hands, and a coloured scarf, after circling the waist, falls to the feet. As stays are unknown in these countries a slim waist is never seen, and a French *élégante* would be

jupe: skirt

shocked at the clumsy tournure of a Wallachian *belle*.

In Lady Craven's "Journal" we have an account of her reception at the Wallachian court. She says: "In the corner sat the prince, dressed and attended *à la Turque ;* over his head were ranged the horses' tails, the great helmet and feather, the magnificent sabre, and other arms with which I had seen him parade the streets at Constantinople. * * * * I was then summoned to an audience with the princess: she was sitting *à la Turque,* with three of her daughters by her. There were twenty ladies in the room, one of whom, instead of a turban, had a high cap of sable put behind her hair, that was combed up straight over a kind of roll : this head-dress was far from being ugly or unbecoming. The princess told me that it was a lady of Wallachia, and that the cap was the head-dress of the country."

The men wear a long robe that reaches to the feet, and a shawl round the waist ; over this is an upper garment with long tight sleeves, lined throughout with fur. The head is covered with a fur cap ; no beard is worn, only moustaches ; the shoes have very high heels.

In Macfarlane's "Armenia" we find the following description of the dress of an Armenian bride : " Her figure was enveloped in a robe, that, but for the costly material of which it was composed, might have been called a sack. Under the hand and the needle of an Armenian priest's wife, this wrapper concealed every member of the body, not permitting even the loose purple *mestler* and *papooshes*—no, not so much as the toe of the latter to be visible. The same matron

tournure: drape of the gown; sometimes used to refer to the bustle
Wallachian: Roumanian
Lady Craven: Baroness Elizabeth Craven's "A Journey through the Crimea to Constantinople ... " was published 1789
Macfarlane: Charles Macfarlane wrote "The Armenians", published 1830, describing the peoples living in northeastern Turkey, and parts of Iran and Russia
mestler: foot covering, see page 381, second paragraph
papoosh: slipper

had bound round her head a linen veil, called a *perkem*, so thick that it entirely concealed what it covered, and had placed over this an additional veil, composed of tinsel and thin lamina of gold sewed together, that fell from her crown down to her neck, like some extraordinary head of hair. The *perkem*, or linen veil, reached below the breast in front, and below the shoulders behind; beyond it projected and floated the ample folds, not of her tinsel locks, but of her own luxuriant coal-black hair, which, had she stood, might have fallen lower than her knees, and, as if the natural were not long enough, *des grosses tresses* — a thick mass of false hair — was attached to it, that looked, as it lay huddled in a heap on the sofa, like the unpowdered wig of a judge."

In another part we read: " The khenna, or well-known drug used by ladies throughout the East for painting the nails red, was produced with great solemnity, and it was part of the functions of the chief Armenian priest's wife to dye the bridal fingers. When both right and left hand were of the proper hue, the other presents that always accompany the khenna were brought forth from their costly envelopes of silk and gold tissue. These were, a broad piece of cloth entirely to wrap up the person of the bride, a *feridji*, or outer cloak, an ample *yasmack*, a pair of papooshes or morocco slippers, and a large wax torch." " The family of the maiden sent to the bridegroom, on the part of themselves and daughter, a gauze silk shirt, a pair of drawers, two sashes or stripes of fine linen cloth, embroidered in gold, to close and support the drawers; a towel, richly embroidered at the four corners in worsted and tinsel; a pocket-handkerchief,

C C

khenna: henna
yasmack: yashmak, a double veil covering the face from the bridge of the nose to below
   the chin

worked all over with different coloured silks into the forms of doves, flames, and hearts; stuff of mixed silk and cotton, for an *enterré* or long close robe worn under the *beneesh*." The bridegroom's dress, consisting of an *enterré*, a shawl, a *calpack*, and a *beneesh*, was put on after his having been shaved; and we are told that his mother-in-law hung a tress or lock of tinsel to his calpack, an example which was followed by the other relatives, till, " by adding fresh strings of tinsel and gold thread, his capacious balloon-shaped hat shewed like a globe with a reversed glory, or rather like a cooling comet with its tail still radiant."

" The Armenian women," says a modern traveller, " cover themselves when they go from home with a large white veil from head to foot. In the house they still wear the *nose-band*, which is never laid aside even in bed. Their dress consists of a silk shift, a pair of silk trousers which reach to the ankles, a close garment that fastens at the throat with silver clasps, and an outer garment generally made of padded chintz, and open in front. They wear a silver girdle, which rests upon the hips, and is generally curiously wrought; their feet are naked, and some of them have silver rings round their ankles; no hair is seen except a long plaited tail, that hangs over the back to the ground. On their heads they place a species of cushion, which expands at the top." The same writer also says, that the Armenian women do not wear so entire a veil as the Mahomedan; it leaves the eyes at full liberty, and just encloses the nose, by which some general idea may be formed of the features and expression.

The column of Trajan gives a very correct notion

calpack: kalpak, a fur cap
beneesh: probably the over-jacket shown in many illustrations of Armenian wedding
    couples but not described here
nose-band: a short veil covering the nose
column of Trajan: stands in the Forum of Trajan, in Rome; it celebrates his victories
    over the Armenians and others in the area; he was Emperor of Rome 98–117

of the dress of the ancient inhabitants of Turkey and the neighbouring states. We there see that they wore tunics reaching to the knees, and also the garment met with amongst most nations, which formed breeches and stockings all in one piece. Their shoes were much like those of the moderns; their chlamyde, or cloak, was sometimes ornamented with a fringe all round the bottom, and was fastened upon one shoulder. Those who had the head covered wore a Phrygian cap, with the front bending over.

Phrygian Cap

Among the "reforms" carried into effect by the late sultan Mahmoud, and sanctioned and maintained by his son and successor the present sultan, is one which has changed the whole character and appearance of Turkish costume. We allude to the substitution of the *fez* for the turban. The fez is a small cap of felted wool, dyed of a crimson colour, without edge of any kind, fitting close to the head, and having a long tassel of blue silk threads hanging from the centre of the top. It is now universally worn in place of the turban.

Turkish Man's Costume

Mahmoud: Mahmud II, 1808–1839

THE TOILETTE IN GREECE.

CHAPTER XXXVII.

Implements of Warfare

HE distinguishing feature of Grecian dress in ancient times was the *pallium*, whence the people were frequently called *Palliati*. This garment, which was shaped somewhat like a modern cloak, was very wide and long, so that its ample dimensions enabled it to be wound several times round the body ; the edges were sometimes cut out to resemble fringe. The pallium had no collar, and was worn over the chlamyde.

Ancient Female Costume

The *chlamyde* is a garment about which authors greatly differ. Some affirm that it resembled the Roman toga, but the greater number reject this opinion; whatever its exact shape and dimensions may have been is therefore uncertain, but it was usually fastened on the shoulder by a brooch.

The *phelone,* a dress often mentioned by Greek writers, differed from the chlamyde only in the quality of the material of which it was formed, the former being usually made of a coarse manufacture fit for wearing in the country.

The under-garments of the Greeks, which generally were of white woollen stuff, bore the name of *tunics —*

" A vest and tunic o'er me next she threw."—*Odyssey.*

The tunics were of different kinds, and varied in name according to their shape and texture; they were worn equally by men and women, the only difference being that the latter always had the petticoat and sleeves long, while the common tunic of the men generally descended no lower than the calf of the leg, and the sleeves were short and very narrow. Thus, in the " Odyssey," we read of Ulysses :

" The goddess with a radiant tunic dress'd
My limbs, and o'er me cast a silken vest."

The *exomide* was a tunic without sleeves, generally worn by servants, and often also by philosophers, who, to mark their contempt of luxury, sometimes clothed themselves in the most unostentatious manner.

The *calasiris* was another tunic made of linen,

Odyssey: Homer's epic poem on the travels of Odysseus after the Trojan War
Ulysses: Odysseus

and with a fringe at the bottom. The richest tunics were made of silk, and they were fastened at the waist by a girdle or belt.

The upper-garment worn by Grecian women was called *ampechone*; it was a kind of light cloak.

The Grecian matrons were, like the ladies of most other nations, fond of dress and ornament, and also of perfumes. The following description of the goddess Saturnia, given by Homer, is applicable to them :

Ancient Female Costume

" Swift to her bright apartment she repairs,
Sacred to dress and beauty's pleasing cares.

*   *   *

Here first she bathes, and round her body pours
Soft oils of fragrance and ambrosial showers.

*   *   *

Her artful hands the radiant tresses ty'd ;
Part on her head in shining ringlets roll'd,
Part o'er her shoulders wav'd like melted gold.
Around her next a heavenly mantle flow'd,
That rich with Pallas' labour'd colours glow'd ;
Large clasps of gold the foldings gather'd round,
A golden zone her swelling bosom bound ;
Ear-beaming pendants tremble in her ear,
Each gem illumin'd with a triple star.
Then o'er her head she casts a veil, more white
Than new-fall'n snow, and dazzling as the light.
Last her fair feet celestial sandals grace."

The principal occupations and amusements of wo-

Saturnia: another name for Demeter, goddess of the harvest
Homer: famous Greek poet of unknown date who wrote the "Iliad" and the "Odyssey"

men in the earlier ages seem to have consisted in spinning, weaving, and embroidering. The Grecian ladies, in particular, were very celebrated for their skill in all kinds of needlework. At some of the religious festivals it was the custom to offer, to the god or goddess in whose honour it was instituted, a garment wove and embroidered for that purpose. Thus, at the Athenian fête in honour of Minerva, a robe was carried in the procession; it was of a white colour, without sleeves, and embroidered with gold: upon it were described the achievements of the goddess. Jupiter also, and the heroes, had their effigies in it. Hence, men of courage and bravery are said to be worthy to be portrayed in Minerva's sacred garment, as in Aristophanes:

"We will our fathers treat with high esteem,
Whose brave exploits are worthy Attica,
Fit to be portrayed in Minerva's vest."

The garments worn by the Grecian priests were very costly and magnificent; they differed according to the gods in whose honour they were officiating. Those who sacrificed to the celestial gods wore purple, to the infernal gods they sacrificed in black, and to Ceres in white garments.

The ancient Greeks generally went bareheaded; they had nevertheless a kind of hat, which they called *sciadion*, which signifies parasol. Their hair was an object of great importance, and they devoted much time and attention to it. The custom of dedicating the hair to one of their deities, and shaving off some of their locks for that purpose, seems to have been general both with the men and women of ancient

Minerva: Athena
Aristophanes: Greek playwright, circa 448-380 B.C.
Ceres: Demeter, goddess of the harvest and of fertility

Greece. In Euripides, when Pentheus threatens Bacchus to shave his hair, the young god tells him it would be an impious action, because he designed it as an offering to some deity:

> " This lock is sacred, this I do preserve
> As some choice votive off'ring for the god."

The ancient Athenians, says Ælian, curled their hair, and dressed it with small golden ornaments shaped like grashoppers, in token of their being sons of the earth. Virgil mentions this custom in his poem entitled " Circis :"

> " Wherefore she did, as was her constant care,
> With grashoppers adorn her comely hair,
> Brac'd with a golden buckle Attick wise."

Fashion seems to have exercised as much influence over the head-dresses of the ladies, in the ancient days of Greece, as she does at the present time ; gold, pearls, precious stones, flowers, and ribands, were employed to ornament the tresses. One of their coif-

Ancient Head-Dresses

fures is described as an immense tower of bows and curls, and appears to have served as a model for the

Euripides: Greek tragic playwright, 5th century B.C.
Pentheus: King of Thebes in the "Bacchæ"
Bacchus: Dionysus, god of wine and fertility
Ælian: Claudius Adiames Ælian, Roman writer of the 3rd century B.C.
Virgil: famous Roman poet, 70–19 B.C.

commode already mentioned. False hair seems also to have been very generally used, and in great quantities, both curled and frizzled.

In Greece, married women were distinguished from the unmarried by the manner in which the hair was parted in front.

It seems to have been the custom for women always to cover their faces with a veil when they went out, or appeared in public, as we read of Penelope:

> " Then from her lodgings went the beauteous dame,
> And to her much-expecting courtiers came;
> There veil'd before the door she stood."

A veil seems also to have been worn as an emblem of mourning by the ancient Greeks:

> " Her face wrap'd in a veil declar'd her woes."

Nor does this fashion appear to have belonged to women only, for Theseus thus addressed Adrastus, when he came to him after his loss at Thebes:

> " Speak out, unfold your head, restrain your tears."

No part of the dress of the ancients has given rise to more discussions and disputes than their chaussure, and the passages we find relating to this subject in different authors are not sufficiently explicit to throw much light upon it. The ancient statues enable us to judge of the shape, but do not enlighten us as to the colour of the boots and sandals. Pythagoras ordered his disciples to wear sandals made of the bark of trees. Strabo tells us that, these sandals being found too thin to protect the feet, they were sometimes made with copper soles; he also mentions that Phi-

Penelope: faithful wife of Odysseus, who had many suitors during his long absence
Theseus: King of Athens
Adrastus: King of Argos who led the Seven Against Thebes
Pythagoras: Greek philosopher, circa 582–507 B.C.
Strabo: historian and geographer, fl. 63 B.C.

lotas, a poet, who lived in the island of Cos, being so very thin and light that he was afraid of being carried away by the wind, had the soles of his sandals made of lead!

The *cothurnus,* or *buskin,* worn by the Greeks of both sexes, is said by some to have been invented by Thespis, a native of Attica, and the first tragic author. Others assert that Sophocles was the first who introduced it upon the stage, where its high heels were of much service to those who undertook the part of heroes. It usually reached up the leg, and was fastened under the knee. Some were richly ornamented, and they were frequently of a purple colour.

Soccus, which is often used to express a comic style, as *cothurnus* does a tragic, was also Greek. Terence speaks of it, in one of his tragedies, as an outside covering for the feet: " Uncertain as to what I should do, I seated myself, and my slaves came to to take off my *soccus.*" Gradually, as the love of ornament and display advanced, sandals, which at first were only made of the skins of animals, assumed a different appearance, and soon no part of dress was more remarkable for splendour and magnificence; gold, precious stones, and embroidery, were all employed to adorn them. Thus, Homer says:

" And on his foot the golden sandal shone."

" Clasp'd on his feet th' embroider'd sandals shine."

The *phasia* was a kind of shoe. Appianus, the Greek historian, mentions that they were made of white leather, and were worn by the Athenian priests when they offered sacrifices.

Cos: Kos, second largest of the Dodecanese Islands
Thespis: fl. 534 B.C., after whom actors are now sometimes called Thespians
Attica: the province and plains around Athens
Sophocles: Greek tragedian, 496–406 B.C.
Terence: circa 190–159 B.C., Roman comic poet
Appianus: Appian, an Alexandrian-born Greek who wrote in Rome, 2nd century A.D.

Some think that the ancients were unacquainted with the use of gloves, but we find them mentioned by Homer in his description of Laertes, king of Ithaca:

"—— and gloves against the thorn."

Among the ornaments worn by the Greeks, the brooch bore a distinguished place; it was a necessary as well as an ornamental part of their attire, being used to fasten the tunics and the chlamydes. It was of various shapes and materials. Bracelets, which were worn both by men and women, appear to have served as a mark of honour as well as of slavery, for we find them presented to warriors as a recompense for valour, at a period when they are mentioned by the historian Suetonius as being worn by slaves, in token of their servitude. The ordinary kinds were made of copper or iron, the more elegant of ivory, silver, gold, and precious stones. Homer thus describes the bracelet presented by Eurymachus to Penelope:

"A bracelet rich with gold, with amber gay,
That shot effulgence like the solar ray."

Necklaces and bracelets also seem to have been awarded as the prize of courage both in real and mimic warfare. Homer speaks of "orient necklaces" —necklaces strung with pearls, and others worked with art, whence we may infer that the ancients were skilful in their manufacture. Ear-rings appear to have been worn only by women and boys: immense sums were expended upon these ornaments. Seneca observes that a single pair was often worth the revenue of a rich man.

Laertes: father of Odysseus
Suetonius: biographer of the Cæsars, circa 140–69 B.C.
Eurmachus: one of Penelope's many suitors, see note p. 393
Seneca: Lucius Annæus Seneca, Roman philosopher and poet, circa 4 B.C.–65 A.D.

Rings were worn both by men and women; they were made of plain gold, or of some of the inferior metals; at others they were set with precious stones, and often had an image engraved upon them. These latter were used for sealing letters and papers, and were called signet rings.

Dieararchus describes the ancient Theban women as veiled from head to foot, leaving nothing visible but the eyes, which peered through two holes in the drapery that covered their faces. This account corresponds exactly with the dress they now wear.

The dress of the modern Grecians differs much in various parts of the country. The matrons of Athens wear garments made of red or blue cloth, with very short waists, and petticoats falling in folds to the ground. Over the head and shoulders they throw a thin flowing veil of white muslin, ornamented with a gold border. The attire of a maiden of the same city consists of a long red vest, with a square yellow satin cape hanging down behind; they walk with their hands concealed in the pocket-holes at the sides of their gowns, and their faces muffled.

Chandler, in his "Travels in Greece," gives the following elegant description of a Grecian virgin in her secluded apartment: "There the girl, like Thetis, treading on a soft carpet, has her white and delicate feet naked, the nails tinged with red. Her trousers, which in winter are of red cloth, and in summer of fine calico or thin gauze, descend from the hips to the ankle, hanging loosely about her limbs, the lower portion embroidered with flowers, and appearing beneath the shift, which has the sleeves wide and open,

Theban: citizen of Thebes, ancient rival of Athens
Chandler: Richard Chandler's "Travels in Asia Minor and Greece" was published 1817
Thetis: mother of Achilles

and the seams and edges curiously adorned with needlework. Her vest is of silk, exactly fitted to the form of the bosom and the shape of the body, which it rather covers than conceals, and is shorter than the shift. The sleeves button occasionally at the hand, and are lined with red or yellow satin. A rich zone encompasses her waist, and is fastened before by clasps of silver gilded, or of gold set with precious stones. Over the vest is a robe, in summer lined with ermine, and in cold weather with fur of a

warmer kind. The head-dress is a skull-cap, red or green, with pearls, a stay under the chin, and a yellow forehead cloth. She has bracelets of gold on her wrists, and, like Aurora, is *rosy-fingered*, the tips being stained. Her necklace is a string of zeckins, a species of gold coin, or the pieces called Byzantines. At her cheek is a lock of hair, made to curl towards the face;

Grecian Maiden

and down her back falls a profusion of tresses, spreading over her shoulders. Much time is consumed in combing and braiding the hair after bathing; and, at the greater festivals, in enriching and powdering it with small bits of silver, gilded, and resembling a violin in shape, and woven in at regular distances. She is painted blue round the eyes, and the insides of the

Aurora: Eos, goddess of the dawn
zeckins, Byzantines: gold coins are still worn as head-dress decorations and necklaces as part of a bride's dowry

sockets, with the edges on which the lashes grow, are tinged with black."

The men on the continent of Greece are usually seen with large blue trousers, naked legs, and red slippers; a red sash, sometimes of silk, girding their waist, and a jacket of cloth, made in the Venetian fashion, with seams of guimp. Whiskers are universally worn: beards only by priests. The elder men shave the head and cover it with a fez, or cloth skull-cap, and a blue turban; the younger have their hair full, and turned under a bonnet of scarlet cloth, which hangs down on one side.

The usual dress of a Greek lady we find described by a recent traveller, as follows: "The dress of the Grecian ladies of rank and wealth, except at Smyrna, Constantinople, and a few other large commercial towns, does not differ very materially from that worn by the Turkish ladies. When out of doors, however, the two classes are easily distinguishable; the Turks muffle up and cover their faces in muslin, and wear yellow morocco slippers; the Greeks show their faces, and are obliged to wear slippers of a dingier hue; besides which there are other points of difference between their promenade dresses. The usual costume is a scarlet cloth skull-cap on the head, more or less richly worked in gold, with pearls, &c.; an open and flowing gown, with very full sleeves, mostly made of silk, richly embroidered; an inner vest, also richly worked, and setting to the body almost as closely as a man's waistcoat; very wide muslin drawers, tied above the ankle, and concealed by the gown; morocco bottines, without soles, thrust into well-soled morocco slippers, or coloured silk

Smyrna: now Izmir, city in Turkey

stockings and loose shoes; a long and rich veil, put on with singular gracefulness, and the cestus, or zone or girdle (a beautiful shawl), which rests upon the hips, and is kept down in front by two silver clasps or bosses. This zone is altogether distinct from the waist, which is formed by the foldings of the dress below the bosom; it is, in short, a second waist, and though very classical, and the image of the ancient cestus, is one of the few things at once classical and Greek that strike us as ungraceful. In cold weather a short satin pelisse or spenser, trimmed and lined with furs, is worn over the dress."

We find a great variety in the dress of the inhabitants of the Grecian islands. Their peculiar customs, infinitely various as they are in what relates to dress, are scrupulously retained by the social islanders; whilst the continental Greeks are but in a small degree to be discriminated from each other.

The costume of the inhabitants of these sunny climes is beautiful, various, and elegant. "The higher classes," says a modern author, "have adopted the Venetian or Italian dress, and some have even ventured upon the English and French modes; but the lower ranks still retain their own picturesque costume. The hair is worn very long, and floats upon the shoulders; some use the small red Albanian skull-cap, which just covers the crown of the head; others wear a cap of white, red, or blue cotton, which hangs in a bag behind, or on one side; this is the common head-dress of the men, particularly the peasants. A double-breasted waistcoat, usually made of velvet, either maroon-coloured or blue, closed at the

Albanian skull-cap: refers to a cap worn by the Illyrians, people in the northwest part of ancient Greece

chest with a double row of hanging buttons of gold or silver, which begin at the shoulders, and approach

Island Male Costume

each other towards the waist, forms the principal feature in their attire; it is generally bordered with gold lace, and fastened with a sash of coloured silk. The lower part of their dress, which is called *thoraki*, is deserving of particular description. It resembles a wide sack, made generally of blue cotton, with holes at the corners, through which the legs are thrust, the superfluous cloth hanging in folds between the legs; these trousers are supported by the silk sash already mentioned : this garment is sometimes exchanged for the short white Albanian petticoat, unconfined at the knee, and resembling the Highland kilt, which is a much more graceful dress than the thoraki.

The legs are covered with white cotton stockings, and shoes are worn on the feet, with very large buckles. Another and more elegant covering for the feet is a sandal made of undressed leather ; it fits the foot tightly, and is strapped across the instep and up the lower part of the leg : this sandal, however, is only worn by the lowest ranks, chiefly the goat-herds. These last also have a thick cloak, made of the hair of goats, or the wool of sheep, with the addition of a hood to protect the head.

The women in these islands wear their beautiful long hair plaited in many tresses, and it often grows

Highland: Scots dress

with such luxuriance, that it frequently reaches to the ground; a handkerchief, folded corner-wise, generally covers the head. The gown is made like the vest worn by the men; it is of purple or maroon velvet, richly embroidered with gold, and with a very long waist. A beautiful girdle is worn under the vest, which always floats open; the girdle is fastened with an immense gold or silver ornament at each side, formed in the shape of a shield. The petticoats worn with this robe are of rich blue or pink silk, beautifully embroidered and spangled. In these islands stays are unknown. The most graceful form of the vest is its fitting quite close to the waist; the female peasants also wear high heels to their shoes, ornamented with silver buckles.

Embroidery appears, from all the ancient authors, to have attained the greatest perfection in these islands. It was first invented by the Phrygians, and we frequently find it mentioned both in the " Iliad" and the " Odyssey." Not only were the dresses of the ladies beautifully worked by their own delicate fingers, but they also appear to have embroidered pictures or stories. Thus, the lovely Helen, we are told, was occupied in this manner:

> " Meantime to beauteous Helen, from the skies,
> The various goddess of the rainbow flies;
> (Like fair Laodicé in form and face,
> The loveliest nymph of Priam's royal race);
> Her in the palace at her loom she found;
> The golden web her own sad story crown'd,
> The Trojan wars she weaved (herself the prize),
> And the dire triumphs of her fatal eyes."— HOMER.

Phrygians: now a region of central Turkey, Phrygia was an independent kingdom in the
    8th–6th centuries B.C.
Helen: Helen of Troy

The warriors, also, of " olden time," wore girdles or belts covered with the richest embroidery :

> " Stiff with the rich embroider'd work around,
> My vary'd belt repelled the flying wound."—HOMER.

Woman of Scio

The women of Scio, who have always been celebrated for their beauty, have a very picturesque dress, which is thus described by Dr. R. Chandler: "They wear short petticoats, reaching only to the knees, with white silk or cotton hose; their head-dress, which is peculiar to the island, is a kind of turban of linen, so fine and white that it seemed like snow. Their slippers are chiefly yellow, with a knot of red fringe at the heel; some wore them fastened with a thong. Their garments were of silk of various colours, and their whole appearance so fantastic and lively, as to afford us much entertainment."

In Cyprus the female dress is very becoming. The head-dress is modelled upon the kind of *calathus* which is often seen represented upon Phœnician idols and Egyptian statues : it is worn by all classes. Their hair, which they dye with henna till it becomes of a fine brown colour, hangs down behind in a great many glossy braids or plaits. Round the face ringlets are arranged in a very graceful manner, and among the " hyacinthine waves " of these shining curls are placed the flowers of the jessamine, which are strung

Scio: Chios, island off the coast of Turkey near Izmir
Dr. R. Chandler: Richard Chandler, "Travels in Asia Minor and Greece", 1817
Cyprus: island to the south of Turkey
calathus: an ancient vase-shaped basket

together upon slips cut from the leaves of the palm-tree. This coiffure, which is as simple as it is elegant and beautiful, is much admired by all strangers who visit the island.

In their dresses they are fond of displaying the brightest and most gaudy colours. The upper robe is generally of a rich crimson, scarlet, or green silk, profusely embroidered in gold; their yellow or scarlet trousers are fastened round the ankles, and they wear yellow boots, or slippers. Their love of ornament is very great, and they adorn the head and neck with gold coins, chains, and various other trinkets. Around the waist also they wear a large and massive belt or zone, clasped in front by large and heavy brass plates: the waist of the robe is made as long as possible. But though very handsome, the women of this island are naturally rather corpulent; and as stays are there unknown, they of course have no means, even if they wished it, of diminishing their size.

In Casos the women wear a boddice without sleeves, opening a little towards the top; a robe of the whitest and finest cotton, edged with a purple border four fingers wide, and elegantly embroidered, descends to their feet, and the waist is loosely girded by a sash, which floats gracefully around them.

The dress of the men consists of a short jacket and waistcoat, without a collar, very full breeches, with a red sash round the waist, a small red cap fitting close to the crown of the head, and shoes resembling our slippers; the legs and throat are generally bare. They wear moustaches, but never beards; and though they do not shave the fore part of the head, like the Albanians, yet the hair is

Casos: Kasos, island in the Dodecanese

made to lie back, and falls down the neck to a great length.

The women of Cephalonia wear their hair wreathed in broad plaits over a small thin turban, which is fastened in a knot on one side of the head. The gown, which discloses the neck and shoulders, is closed at the breast, and confined at the waist by a shawl; it flows loosely from the girdle, and is open in front. Under it is worn a pair of loose white trousers. The *bpákz*, mentioned in a fragment of Sappho as being worn at Mitylene, are supposed to be fac-similes of these trousers; they are drawn tight above the ankle, and leave to view the bare feet, on which are worn a pair of low light slippers that just cover the toes and heels.

Woman of Ios

The dress of the women of the isle of Ios is simple and graceful. A light under-dress gives the outlines of their elegant forms, without incommoding their movements. Their petticoats are short, and ornamented round the bottom and round the front of the bosom; they also wear loose jackets, and a kind of turban, one end of which hangs down upon the left shoulder.

It is the custom in some of the islands for a bride, on the day of her marriage, to wear a veil of red silk. This practice has been

Cephalonia: largest of the Ionian islands
Sappho: Greek poetess, fl. 600 B.C., lived on the island of Lesbos
Mitylene: Mytilene, chief city of the island of Lesbos
Ios: island, near Naxos in the Cyclades

transmitted from the ancient Grecians, with whom the *flamen*, or red veil, was in general use on this occasion.

The women of Argentiera have the singular fancy to admire clumsy legs, and those to whom Nature has denied this perfection make up for it by wearing several pair of very thick stockings; they also have velvet boots, either embroidered or ornamented with silver buttons. Their petticoat, which is very short, to shew their legs, is white, with a red embroidered border; the rest of their dress consists of an enormous mass of linen, which hangs about them without much shape.

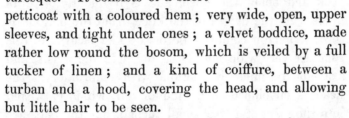

Gala-Dress in Argentiera

Their gala-dress is very picturesque. It consists of a short petticoat with a coloured hem; very wide, open, upper sleeves, and tight under ones; a velvet boddice, made rather low round the bosom, which is veiled by a full tucker of linen; and a kind of coiffure, between a turban and a hood, covering the head, and allowing but little hair to be seen.

The most curious part of the costume is a very short ornamented apron, which is sewn into the boddice, about half-way between the neck and the waist, and quite conceals the symmetry and grace of the latter.

The costume on a *jour de fête*, or any great occa-

Argentiera: we have been unable to place this town; the costume resembles that of the region of Anogeia, on Crete, except that long bloomers take the place of the layers of stockings mentioned

sion, in the isle of Naxos, is very curious. The head is covered with a turban of fine white muslin, edged with embroidery; a white linen vest is clasped round the throat; over it is an open boddice with a very broad ornamented girdle: the sleeves of this boddice are tight to the wrist, and the petticoat reaches below the knee. But the extraordinary part of this dress is a short upper robe, immensely full, and curiously arranged in close plaits and folds, in such a manner that, from the hips, it suddenly spreads out into two enormous wings or fans, giving the wearer a most grotesque appearance. A short cloak, richly embroidered, and having holes through which the arms are passed, the short apron above-mentioned, and shoes with very thick soles and large bows, complete the attire, which is ornamented with coloured borders and embroidery in every part.

In Tinos the dress is very simple. It consists of a garment not unlike a chemise, which reaches to the neck and below the knee, and is frequently of white linen. At the height of the knee, from the bottom, is sewn a narrow-coloured border. The sleeves of this robe are very wide and loose down to the wrists, and are edged round the bottom with embroidery; the head is enveloped in a kind of veil, which is twisted into the form of a very small turban, but the ends are brought round the face, crossed on the neck, and then allowed to float down the back; the stockings are neat, and the shoes have high heels. Altogether it is a simple and elegant costume.

In Patmos the robe is confined at the waist by a girdle, from whence falls the narrow embroidered

Naxos: largest of the Cyclades islands
Tinos: Tenos, island in the Cyclades known for its silk
Patmos: one of the Dodecanese islands off the Turkish coast

apron; the sleeves are nearly tight down to the wrists, and an open jacket is worn that reaches as low as the hips. The head is ornamented with a simple but elegant turban of very fine white linen. In some of the islands, and even in some parts of the continent, unmarried women braid their hair and ornament it with natural flowers; others adorn their heads with the most tasteful and elegant-shaped turbans, formed of light-coloured muslins.

NIO

Island Maiden

THE TOILETTE IN ALBANIA.

Male Costume

CHAPTER XXXVIII.

HO has not read of

" The wild Albanian kirtled to
his knee,
With shawl-girt head, and
ornamented gun,
And gold embroider'd gar-
ments fair to see ? "

These brave and hardy people wear a graceful
and a fanciful costume. The better classes have an
outer mantle, made of coarse woollen stuff, bordered
and embroidered with scarlet threads; this mantle,
being long, falls loosely from the shoulders down the
back, and reaches as low as the knees. Two vests
are always worn, and the higher orders even have

Albania: Illyria and Epirus, northwestern area of ancient Greece

three : the outer one is open, and the inner one laced down the middle, and richly figured. In their broad sash or belt are suspended one or two pistols, the handles of which are very long, and often curiously wrought and ornamented in silver. The shirt, made of coarse cotton, hangs from beneath the belt like a kilt, and the drawers are of the same material. Their legs are clothed in variously-coloured stockings, or high socks and sandals; they have also metal greaves or coverings for the knees and ankles.

Male Costume

The head - dress consists generally of a small red skull-cap, to which is added a shawl, wound round in the form of a turban. The most remarkable part of an Albanian's dress, however, is the capote, or cloak, worn indiscriminately by all ranks, the lowest as well as the highest. It is generally made of white or grey wool, but black horsehair is also used occasionally. This garment has wide open sleeves, and a square flap or cape behind, that serves sometimes as a hood. This cloak, which is generally thrown over one shoulder, gives a theatrical appearance, which is much increased by the stately manner in which an Albanian always walks.

Unlike the Turks, who are said to leave only one lock of their hair in its original state of nature, that Mahomet may draw them up to heaven by it, this people wear their hair long, in the ancient Spartan fashion.

Mahomet: Mohammed
Spartan: Sparta was a major city of the Peleponesus (Greece)

" An Arnaout girl, in costly garb, walks with graceful pride."

This verse of an Arnaout, or Albanian song, shews that a love of display is not erroneously attributed to the females of this nation.

The difference between the habiliments of the higher and lower orders consists only in the splendour of the material, the form of the garments being always the same. A napkin is fastened tight over the forehead, falling to the shoulders behind, and on each side in front, as far as the chin. Quantities of silver or gold coins hang about the forehead and under the chin, and are braided into the hair, which hangs in long tresses down to the calves of the legs. The shift is embroidered very richly in front, and entirely covers the arms. The sash or girdle is of blue stuff. An embroidered jacket is worn over the shift; it reaches to the elbows, and is trimmed with fringe: another rich jacket is also worn, which is rather shorter than that beneath it, and has no sleeves. They wear yellow boots and slippers.

The Albanian soldiers are generally splendidly attired; the ornaments on their knees and ankles being of silver filigree, and the sandals studded with silver stars. The officers frequently wear jackets of the richest velvet, embossed with gold and silver, till they are as stiff as a coat of mail.

Mr. Morrit, describing one of the chieftains of the country of Maina, says: " He wore a close vest, with open sleeves, of white and gold embroidery, and a short black velvet mantle, edged with sables; the sash which held his pistols and his poignard, was a shawl of red and gold. His light-blue trousers were

Mr. Morrit: John Bacon Sawrey Morrit wrote "The Letters of John B. S. Morrit of Roka-
    by, descriptive of journeys in Europe and Asia Minor in the years 1794-1796"
Maina: Mani, a rugged, isolated area of the Peleponese, not actually part of Albania

gathered at the knee, and below them were close
gaiters of blue cloth, with gold embroidery, and silver-
gilt bosses to protect the ankles. When he left the
house he flung on his shoulders a rich cloth mantle,
with loose sleeves, which was blue without and red
within, embroidered with gold in front and down the
sleeves in the most sumptuous manner. His turban
was green and gold."

THE TOILETTE IN INDIA.

CHAPTER XXXIX.

THE sweet, harmonious tinkling of golden anklets now invites us to repose under the shade of the sacred banyan, while the soft balmy breeze wafts towards us the elegant blossoms of the oleander, the myrtle, the jasmine, and " love's own creeper,"* in the land where

"Flowrets and fruits blush over every stream :"

Hindu Female

* The cálamatá (called by Linnæus *Ipomœa*) is the most beautiful of its order, both in the colour and form of its leaves and flowers ; its elegant blossoms are " celestial rosy red, Love's proper hue," and have justly procured it the name of cálamatá, or love's creeper."—SIR W. JONES.

Ipomæa: family of fleshy-rooted vines; the cálamatá referred to here is probably Ipomæa Horsfalliæ, or Horsfall's Morning Glory, which is native to India and produces masses of $2\frac{1}{2}$-inch magenta-crimson flowers

where we may

> "Gather the rich anana, India's pride
> Of vegetable life; beyond whate'er
> The poets imaged of the golden age."

Where the blue water-lilies bathe their azure blossoms in the crystal waves of the "Lake of Pearl," near whose sunny banks the bird of a "thousand songs" serenades his lovely rose, and where the stately elephant reposes under the shade of the high palmeto and the spreading tamarind. Such is the far-famed country of Hindostan—the land beneath whose bosom lie concealed the most precious jewels, and the beds of whose rivers teem with gold—while the fields, groves, and gardens are filled with the richest spices, and adorned with the loveliest flowers.

The ordinary dress of the inhabitants of this favoured clime is described by Lord as follows: " In India a people present themselves to our eyes clothed in linen garments, somewhat low descending; of a gesture and garb we may say maidenly, and well-nigh effeminate."

Forbes, in the " Oriental Memoirs," tells us that in most of the Hindoo tribes the men shave the head and beard, but leave the moustaches on the upper lip, and a small lock of hair on the head. The better sort wear turbans of fine muslin, of different colours, and a *jama*, or long gown, of white calico, which is

Male Costume

anana: pineapple
Lord: P. B. Lord was Assistant Surgeon of the Bombay Army; he wrote memoirs detailing
    his travels, and was killed in battle in 1841
Forbes: James Forbes, 1749–1819; his "Oriental Memoirs, a 17-Year Residence in India"
    was published 1813

tied round the waist with a fringed or embroidered sash.   The shoes are of red leather, or English broad-cloth, sometimes ornamented, and always turned up with a long point at the toe.   Their ears are bored, and adorned with large gold rings, passing through two pearls or rubies, and on the arms they wear bracelets of gold and silver.

The princes and nobles are adorned with pearl necklaces and gold chains, sustaining clusters of costly gems ; their turbans are enriched with diamonds, rubies, and emeralds, and their bracelets composed of gold and precious stones.

The dress of the inferior castes usually consists of a turban, a short cotton vest, and drawers, but some wear only a turban and a cloth round the waist ; although the poorest among them usually contrive to purchase a silver bangle, or bracelet, for the arm.

Female of the Lower Caste.

The costume of the Hindoo women is peculiarly becoming.   It consists of a long piece of silk or cotton

Hindoo: Hindu

tied round the waist, and hanging in a graceful manner to the feet; it is afterwards brought over the body in negligent folds: under this they cover the bosom with a short waistcoat of satin, but wear no linen. Their long black hair is adorned with jewels and wreaths of flowers; their ears are bored in many places, and loaded with pearls; a variety of gold chains, strings of pearl, and precious stones, fall from the neck over the bosom, and the arms are covered with bracelets from the wrist to the elbow. They also have gold and silver chains round the ankles, and abundance of rings on their fingers and toes; among the former is often a small mirror. They perfume their hair with oil of cloves, cinnamon, sandal, mogrees, and sweet-scented flowers, and those who can afford it use the oil or ottar of roses; they also make use of henna and antimony, like most other Eastern nations, to heighten their beauty.

The costume of the Mahomedans in India is much like that of the Hindoos, especially the turban, the long white gown, sash, and shoes; but, in addition, they wear full trousers, usually of satin, with gold and silver flowers, and a *catarra*, or short dagger, in their girdle. The Mahomedan women adorn themselves with a variety of jewels, worn over a close gown of muslin, with long sleeves and a short waist; silk or satin drawers reach to the ankles, and a transparent veil covers the head.

When the Hindoos and Mahomedans are baptized into the Christian faith, the women lay aside their Eastern dress, and put on a jacket and petticoat; and the men wear as much of the European apparel as they can, with the exception of a coat and stockings,

Mahomedans: Moslems

which are only worn on festivals and days of ceremony.

The Brahmins seldom wear a turban in the temples, and the upper part of their body is usually naked; but they never appear without the zennar, or sacred string, passing over them from the left shoulder, and a piece of white cotton tied round the waist, falling in graceful folds below the knees.

The costume of a Mahratta chieftain, described by Forbes, is gorgeous in the extreme. "He wore," says that writer, "a muslin vest, and drawers of crimson and gold kincob; his turban and sash were of purple muslin, the former adorned with sprigs of diamonds and rubies, and a very valuable emerald; from his neck depended two rows of beautiful pearls, sustaining a cluster of diamonds; his ear-rings, according to the Hindoo fashion, were four large pearls, and as many perforated, transparent rubies, on gold rings two or three inches in diameter; he wore a rich bracelet on the right arm; the handle of his catarra, or short dagger, was studded with jewels, the hilt of his broad sword plain gold."

Mahratta Chieftain

The Armenian merchants residing in India adopt the Turkish dress, only instead of a turban the men wear a high cap of black velvet, and the women conceal the mouth with a muslin handkerchief.

The manners and customs of the Indians in the time of Alexander, as described by Arrian, were much the same as those of the modern Hindoos. He mentions

Brahmins: highest caste in Indian system, the Hindu priesthood is reserved to them
Mahratta: Marathi-speaking people of west-central India
Forbes: see note p. 413
kincob: Indian embroidered fabric, usually metallic
Armenian merchants: see chapter 36
Alexander: Alexander the Great, King of Macedonia, 356–322 B.C., was in India in 326
Arrian: Greek historian, fl. 2nd century B.C., wrote about Alexander's travels in
    India

their garments of cotton of an extraordinary whiteness, the custom of men wearing ear-rings, parti-coloured shoes, and veils covering the heads and great part of the shoulders; the custom of daubing their faces with colours, and the principal people having umbrellas held over them. Strabo also mentions most of these particulars, and Herodotus speaks of their manufacturing fine cotton wool for clothing.

Strabo: Greek historian and geographer, circa 63 B.C.–24 A.D.
Herodotus: Greek historian, 5th century B.C., wrote about the Graeco-Persian War

THE TOILETTE IN THE MOGUL EMPIRE.

CHAPTER XL.

" * * * * In ample mode
A military robe of purple flowed
O'er all his frame ; illustrious on his breast
The double clasping of the king confest:
In the rich woof a hound, Mosaic drawn,
Bore on full stretch and seized a dappled fawn.
Fine as a filmy web beneath it shone
A vest, that dazzled like a cloudless sun ;
A sabre, when the warrior pressed to part,
He gave, enamelled with Vulcanian art;
A mantle purple tinged, and radiant vest,
Affection grateful to an honoured guest."—*Odyssey.*

Ancient Male Costume

Ancient Female Costume

HE dress of the princes and nobles in Homer's time resembled the jama, girdle, and kincob drawers, flowered with gold and silver, now worn by the Moguls, as we find by the above description of Ulysses in his royal attire ; and it is worthy of notice that the custom of making presents of garments, as mentioned in the last two lines, has continued ever since, and is still prevalent among Eastern nations. In the description of

Odyssey: Greek epic poem by Homer
jama: long gown of white calico (muslin)
kincob: see note p. 416
Moguls: Moslem Turks and Afghanis who conquered northern India in the 12th century

the reception of the ambassadors sent by the Uzbek Tartars to Aureng-Zêbe, we read that he commanded there should be given to each of the ambassadors a *seraph*, or vesture from head to foot—namely, a vest of brocade, a turban, and a sash of silk in embroidery.

The dress of Hyder Ali, the most formidable enemy the English ever met with in the East, like that of most of the natives of India, consisted of a robe of white muslin, with a turban of the same. The vest, which is fashioned much like the gown of a European lady, is fastened at the body and sleeves by strings; the rest of the robe hangs loosely in folds, so that the grandees of India, when they walk, have a page to support their train.

Hyder Ali, though so brave a warrior, was greatly devoted to the duties of the toilette, and generally bestowed two or three hours every morning on the adornment of his person, much of which time was taken up by his barbers. In the army this great nabob wore a military habit, invented by himself for his generals. It was a uniform composed of a vest of white satin with gold flowers, faced with yellow, and attached by cords or strings of a similar colour; drawers of the same materials and boots of yellow velvet, a scarf of white silk round the waist, and a turban of red or yellow. Hyder Ali, though so fond of dress, never wore jewels on his turban or clothes, neither did he adorn himself with ear-rings, necklaces, or bracelets. In this particular he followed the ancient fashions, as well as in his slippers, which were very large and had very long points turning backwards.

The *petits-maîtres* of his and other Indian courts adopted the mode of wearing little caps, which scarcely

Uzbek Tartars: Uzbekistan is on the Afghanistan border in southern Russia
Aureng-Zêbe: 1618-1707, Emperor, son of Shah Jahan
Hyder Ali: (Haiden-Ali) 1722-1782, ruler of Mysore
petits-maîtres: dandies

covered the tops of their heads, and slippers so small as hardly to admit their toes. Forbes, in his "Oriental Memoirs," says that the slippers, girdle, and other parts of a Mogul dress of both sexes, are embroidered with gold, silver, and coloured silks, upon velvet, satin, or scarlet cloth. The *jama* is often richly embroidered. This is the name of the muslin robe worn by the Hindoos and Mahomedans, which falls in full folds from the waist to the feet. The upper part is made to fit close to the body, and, crossing over the bust, is made to tie by the Hindoos on the left side, and by the Mahomedans on the right.

Forbes gives the following description of the dress of a Mogul lady :—" Her drawers of green satin, flowered with gold, were seen under a chemise of transparent gauze, reaching to her slippers, which were richly embroidered. A vest of pale blue satin, edged with gold, sat close to her shape, which an upper robe of striped silver muslin, full and flowing, displayed to great advantage. A netted veil of crimson silk, flowered with silver, fell carelessly over her long braided hair, which was combed smooth and divided from the forehead, where a cluster of jewels was fastened by strings of seed pearl. Her ear-rings were large and handsome—the ring worn in her nose, according to our idea of ornament, less becoming. A necklace, in intermingled rows of pearl and gold, covered her bosom, and several strings of large pearls were suspended from an embroidered girdle set with diamonds ; bracelets of gold and coral reached from her wrist to her elbow, golden chains encircled her ankles, and all her toes and fingers were adorned with valuable rings."

Forbes: see note p. 413

The silk net veil of a crimson or purple colour, embroidered in silver, which the Mogul ladies wear, either to cover the face or to throw back over the shoulders as an ornament, is similar to that mentioned in the "Odyssey" as being presented by Helen to Telemachus : —

> "The beauteous queen, advancing, then displayed
> A shining veil, and thus endearing said:
> ' Accept, dear youth, this monument of love,
> Long since in better days by Helen wove ;
> Safe in thy mother's care the vesture lay,
> To deck thy bride and grace thy nuptial day.'"

The court of Hyder Ali was the most brilliant of his time in India. His company of comedians was very celebrated, both on account of their riches and the beauty as well as the harmonious voices of the Bayadères or dancing girls. The dimpled cheeks of these lovely creatures are tinged a yellow colour, which, though a strange adornment in the eyes of a European, is much admired by the Orientals. Their black hair hangs in flowing tresses to the ground. Their dress is always made of fine gauze, very richly embroidered with gold, and they are covered with jewels. The head, neck, ears, breast, arms, fingers, legs, and toes, have each their own peculiar ornament, and even the nose is adorned with a diamond. Small bells are frequently used as ornaments by these fair maidens.

> "A zone of sweet bells
> Round the waist of some fair Indian dancer is ringing."

The Sikhs, the most rising people of modern

Helen: Helen of Troy
Telemachus: son of Odysseus
Hyder Ali: see note p. 419
Sikhs: religious sect, founded in the Punjab in the 15th century

India, next come under our observation. Runjeet Singh, their celebrated chief, like Hyder Ali, had a great taste for the adornments of fashion, and was imitated in his love of fine clothes by his whole court, which was in this respect unequalled in all the East.

The Sikhs wear a small flat turban, which becomes them well, and a short tunic, which only descends as far as the knee, leaving the rest of the leg exposed. Costly brocades and shawls lined with fur are employed by the great for these tunics. The Sikhs wear their hair long; the ladies of the tribe knot it at the crown, and throw over the head a robe, which also envelopes the body and gives them a singular appearance. They pull the hair so tight to form this knot that the skin of the forehead is drawn with it, and the eyebrows are considerably removed from the visual organs.

The glowing descriptions in the "Arabian Nights" are not more gorgeous than the realities often met with in India. Sir Alexander Burnes, in a letter addressed to General John Ramsay, thus describes the interview of the "Lion of the Punjab," Maharaja Runjeet Singh, with the Governor-General of India, which he justly says rivalled the "Field of the Cloth of Gold" in splendour and magnificence.

"Early in the morning of the 26th, Kurruck Singh crossed the Sutlege, to conduct the Governor-General to his father's camp. His lordship departed under a royal salute, accompanied by his personal staff, all the public functionaries, and the principal European gentlemen present. Runjeet Sing advanced to the water's

Runjeet Singh: Ranjit Singh, 1780–1839, founded a Sikh kingdom in the Punjab
Sir Alexander Burnes: Sir Alexander Barnes, travelled in India 1805–1841, see note
    p. 444
"Lion of the Punjab": this meeting was with Charles Metcalfe, 1785–1846, then the
    British Agent, later Governor-General, who drew up the Treaty of Amritsar in 1809
"Field of the Cloth of Gold": meeting of Henry VIII of England and Francis I of
    France in 1820; see appendix C
Sutlege: Sutlej River; it formed the border of the Punjab

edge, about a mile from the camp, where his lordship left his own elephant and proceeded in the same houda with the Maharaja. The spectacle which now presented itself was truly grand. There were seventy elephants advancing with Sikh chiefs and European gentlemen in full uniform. The Maharaja's troops were drawn up at some distance from the road. The procession was preceded by a band of music, and the 16th Lancers and body-guard closed it. It would be impossible to give a description of the magnificence exhibited at the Sikh encampment on this occasion. Two regiments of infantry were drawn up at right angles to each other; at the apex of the triangle was a spacious and lofty triumphal arch, covered with red cloth and gilded ornaments, lined with yellow silk. Another arch, more splendid than the first, was erected a short distance in advance, and proceeding through both of these we reached the court-yard. His highness's suite of tents occupied a rising ground overlooking the Sutlege, and inside the screen that entirely surrounded them the troops of the household were drawn up in order, forming a perfect wall of soldiers. There was a silence among this mass of men that made the scene most imposing. On alighting from the elephants Runjeet conducted the Governor-General to a pavilion where the court was held, and seated his lordship between himself and his son. The chiefs occupied the space immediately behind his highness, and the European gentlemen sat on two rows of chairs that formed a street for the approach of the different personages of rank who were to be introduced. The whole court was shaded by a lofty arcade of yellow

houda: howdah, the passenger box carried by elephants on their backs
16th Lancers: British Army unit
Sutlege: Sutlej River

silk.   On the floor were spread out the richest carpets and shawls of Cashmere, and behind the Maharaja stood a spacious tent glittering with every ornament; it was composed partly of crimson velvet, yellow French satin, and Cashmere shawls.   It realised every notion of Eastern grandeur.   But the Maharaja himself was a greater object of attraction than this magnificence. He was robed in green satin; on his right arm he wore that splendid diamond the 'Koh-i-noor,' and his wrist and neck were encircled by superb pearls. *   *   *   *   About three hundred chiefs were introduced.   Some appeared in chain armour; and one individual, Soojet Singh, a raja, and high in favour, wore a casque surmounted by a white plume, splendidly adorned with pearls and diamonds; he was the handsomest man at court, and on this day the admiration of both Europeans and natives.   On a golden footstool in front of the Maharaja sat a youth, the nephew of this person, and the only individual in the Punjab who is allowed the honour of a seat. He wore the largest necklace of pearls which I have ever seen, and the intelligent physiognomy of the little fellow seemed to speak favourably for Runjeet's choice."

A scene which took place at the Maharaja's court at Lahore is also worthy of description.   "The hall of audience is built entirely of marble, and is the work of the Mogul emperors; part of the roof was gorgeously decorated by a pavilion of silken cloth, studded with jewels.   The Maharaja himself wore a necklace, armlets, and bracelets of emeralds, some of which were very large; the nobles likewise dis-

'Koh-i-noor': a fanciful statement; the Koh-i-noor, or "Mountain of Light", diamond was taken from India to Persia in 1738, along with the Peacock Throne, by Nadir Shah.   Acquired by Ahmad Shah, Nadir's general and the founder of the Durrani dynasty in Afghanistan, it was surrendered by Ahmad's descendant Shah Suja to Ranjit Singh in 1814 when Suja was a refugee in the Punjab.   As the meeting described occurred in 1809, Ranjit Singh could not have been wearing the stone.   The diamond passed to the British Crown in 1849 when Ranjit Singh died, was worn by Queen Victoria, and is now in the crown of Queen Elizabeth the Queen Mother.
casque: helmet or head armor
Lahore: was the Sikh capital in the 19th century, now part of Pakistan

played upon their persons vast quantities of jewels, and all the court was habited in yellow, the favourite colour of the nation."

The neighbours of the Sikhs, the Scindians, from religious motives, wear garments of dark colour, and form their turbans of tight and round folds of cloth.

The weaving and embroidery of India are justly celebrated, and have been so for many ages. The stuffs of Mooltan and Bhawalpoor are now interwoven with gold, and frequently of a purple colour; and we read that Aureng-Zêbe had a tent lined with Masulipatam chintzes, figured with flowers, so natural in appearance, and of such vivid colours, that the tent resembled a real parterre.

The muslin drawers worn by the women in India are frequently most richly and beautifully embroidered with needlework, and some of them are of so fine a texture as only to allow of once putting on. Satins and silks are also embroidered in the hand, in great quantities. One of the garments worn by Aureng-Zêbe is described as having been a vest of white delicately-flowered satin, adorned with a silk and gold embroidery of the finest texture and the brightest colours.

In this country men as well as women devote much time to embroidery; and it is not unusual to see several of the former seated cross-legged on a mat employed in a manner that in Europe would be considered effeminate, and quite below the dignity of the nobler sex. But in India the *needle* does not belong exclusively to woman; her prerogative is there

Scindians: Sindhis, from Sind (now part of Pakistan)
Mooltan: Multan, city in Punjab which was a trading center for silks from Bokhara and also known for its indigo dyes
Bhawalpoor: Bahawalpur, Moslem state between the Sutlej and Indus Rivers, known for its silks
Aureng-Zêbe: 1618-1707, Emperor, son of Shah Jahan
Masulipatam: now known as Bandar, city on the Bay of Bengal, a center of the cotton trade

invaded; and the most delicate patterns of tinted flowers, or muslins fine as the spider's web, are ornamented in gold and silver threads by these industrious workmen.

Peasant Costumes

THE

TOILETTE IN THE BIRMAN EMPIRE.

CHAPTER XLI.

Male Costume

THERE is no country in which a more minute attention is paid to the ornamental parts of dress than in this division of the East. The *tsaloc*, or chain, is the badge of the order of nobility, of which there are different degrees, distinguished by the number of strings or rows of precious stones which compose this ornament. These strings are fastened by bosses where they unite. Three strings of open chain-work mark the lowest rank ; three of twisted wire is the next, then of six, of nine, and of twelve. No subject is allowed more than twelve ; the king alone wears twenty-four.

With the Birmans many articles of daily use, as well as of ornament, indicate the rank of the possessor. The shape of the betel-box, which is carried by an attendant after the people of distinction; the ear-rings, cap of ceremony, horse furniture, and even the metal drinking-cup,—all indicate the different degrees of society; and woe be to him who assumes the insignia of a rank to which he has no legitimate right!

The common dress of a man of distinction consists of a tight coat with long sleeves made of muslin, or of very fine nankeen, and a silk wrapper fastened at the waist. The court-dress of the nobility is very becoming: it is formed of a long robe, either of flowered satin or velvet, reaching to the ankles, with an open collar and loose sleeves. Over this there is a scarf, or flowing mantle, that hangs from the shoulders; and on their heads they wear high caps made of velvet, or silk embroidered with flowers, according to the rank of the wearer. Ear-rings are an indispensable part of the attire. Some of them are made of gold tubes about three inches in length, expanding into a ball at the lower end; others consist of heavy masses of gold, the weight of which often drags the ear down to the extent of two or three inches.

Colonel Symes, in his account of an " Embassy to the Kingdom of Ava," thus describes the appearance of the Birman king :—" His crown was a high conical cap, richly studded with precious stones; his fingers were covered with rings; and in his dress he bore the appearance of a man cased in golden armour, whilst a gold wing on each shoulder did not add much lightness to his figure. He advanced but slowly, and appeared not to possess a free use of his limbs. I was informed,

Birmans: Burmese
betel-box: highly decorated box for carrying betel nut, lime powder and betel pepper
  leaves; betel nut is a fruit of the areca palm, betel pepper is a plant totally
  unrelated; chewing the combination provides a mild narcotic which is quite bitter
  and eventually ruins the teeth because of the action of the lime powder on the
  enamel
Nankeen: a tough, highly durable fabric from Nankin, China
Colonel Symes: Michael Symes' "Embassy to the Kingdom of Ava in 1795" was published
  1826
Ava: capital city of the Burmese kings to 1723 and then from 1823 to 1837

however, that this appearance of weakness did not proceed from any bodily infirmity, but from the weight of the regal habiliments."

White is the royal colour, and the state umbrellas are always of a snowy hue, richly bespangled with gold. None of the Eastern courts display more splendour and magnificence than the Birman. A European is quite dazzled by the brilliancy of the officers of state, with their glittering garments, rich palanquins, and large gilded fans, as well as by the dancing girls, who are thus described by Moore:—

> " Around the white necks of the nymphs who danc'd
> Hung carcanets of orient gems, that glanc'd
> More brilliant than the sea-glass glittering o'er
> The hills of crystal on the Caspian shore ;
> While from their long, dark tresses, in a fall
> Of curls descending, bells as musical
> As those that, on the golden shafted trees
> Of Eden, shake in the Eternal Breeze,
> Rung round their steps, at every bound more sweet,
> As 't were the extatic language of the feet ! "

The Birman women have their distinguishing ornaments as well as the men : their hair is tied in a bunch at the top of the head, and bound round with a fillet, the embroidery and jewels of which mark their respective ranks. Their dress consists of a short chemise, and a loose jacket with tight sleeves. Round their waist they roll a long piece of silk, or cloth, which reaches to the feet, and sometimes trails on the ground.

When women of distinction go abroad, they put on a scarf, or shawl, made of silk, which they throw around them with much grace and elegance. Women in full dress stain the palms of their hands and their

Moore: Thomas Moore, 1779-1852; Irish poet who contracted with Longmans, the publishers, for a "metrical romance" on an Eastern theme and received what was at that time the highest advance in publishing history. "Lalla Rookh" appeared in 1817, and "The Loves of the Angels" in 1823 -- he had got no farther east in his researches than Paris. Eventually, he went to Italy, where he received Byron's memoirs to hold in trust; he destroyed them. His reference to the 'Caspian shore' obviously has as much to do with Burma as Paris does, although the Burmese Empire was quite large; any supposedly factual references from Moore must be taken with a large pinch of salt

nails of a red colour, and rub their faces with powder of sandal-wood, or of a bark called *sunneka*. Both men and women tinge the edges of their eyelids and their teeth with black, which in the latter case gives them a disagreeable appearance. The lower class of females often wear only a single gar-ment, in the form of a sheet, which, wrapped round the body and tucked in under the arms, descends to the ankle.

Female of the Lower Class

Men of the working classes also wear a very limited quantity of cloth-ing; a mantle or vest is, however, highly prized in the cold season.

Their neighbours, the inhabitants of Siam, wear very little clothing, which may, perhaps, be accounted for by the excessive heat of the climate. People of rank tie a piece of calico round the waist, and allow it to hang down to the knees. The lower classes wear a garment that resembles breeches. All have a muslin shirt without a collar, and open in front, with large loose sleeves, and no wristbands. When the weather is cold they throw a piece of painted linen over their shoulders, like a mantle, and twist it round their arms.

The women's dress is much the same. They wrap a cloth round the waist, and let the ends hang to the ground; they also cover the neck and shoulders, but never wear any ornament on the head. They cover their fingers with rings, and wear numerous bracelets and immense ear-rings. All classes have very pointed shoes, but no stockings.

Siam: Thailand

The king is distinguished by a vest of rich brocaded satin, with tight sleeves to the wrist; and it is unlawful to wear this dress unless it is presented by the sovereign as a mark of favour to a subject.

The court wear red dresses, and the king a cap shaped like a sugar-loaf, surrounded by a circle of precious stones, and fastened under the chin. Officers of rank have coronets of gold or silver. In travelling, hats are used, but in general no covering is worn on the head: the hair is very thick, and both sexes cut it quite short to the ears; the women make it stand up straight from the head. Beards are never worn in Siam.

THE TOILETTE IN PERSIA.

CHAPTER XLII.

" The moon hath risen clear and calm,
    And o'er the Green Sea palely shines,
Revealing Bahrein's groves of palm,
    And lighting Kishma's amber vines.
    Fresh smell the shores of Araby,
        While breezes from the Indian Sea,
Blow round Selama's sainted cape,
    And curl the shining flood beneath,
Whose waves are rich with many a grape,
    And cocoa-nut and flowery wreath,
        Which pious seamen, as they pass'd,
        Had tow'rd that holy headland cast."

Female Equestrian

HE Persian women are strictly confined to the seraglio, and pass the whole day at their toilette, which, with these beautiful prisoners, is almost the only amusement. The Persian ladies take great pains to heighten their beauty, and call to their aid washes

"The moon hath risen": poem probably by Moore, see note p. 429
Bahrein: island in the Persian Gulf off the coast of Saudi Arabia
Kishma: Kishm Island, called Zazirah-ut-Tul, or "long island", in the Persian Gulf
Araby: archaic form of 'Arabia'

and paints, not only of a red, white, and black colour, but also of a yellow hue. Ornamental patching, once so much the fashion in Europe, is still employed by them, and few female faces are to be seen without one or more *khals*, as they call these artificial moles, which are so often mentioned with admiration by the poets of their country. In the earliest accounts that we possess of Persia, we find this fashion mentioned, as well as that of padding the petticoats to improve the shape of the figure, of concealing the ruthless attacks of time by the use of false hair, and of adorning the head with feathered ornaments.

In an Eastern manuscript, adorned with drawings of the heroes and heroines of the tales, are represented several Persian female figures, whose dresses bear in many respects a strong resemblance to the fashions of Europe. Some of them are drawn without any ornament on the head, the hair falling in ringlets over the neck and shoulders; others have round their heads a kind of diadem set with precious stones, from which rise one or more tufts of feathers, the quills being set in sockets of gold or gems. Some of the figures are adorned with the nose-jewel, that singular ornament to which the Asiatic ladies were formerly so partial, and the antiquity of which is indisputably proved, by its being mentioned among the Jewish trinkets in the Old Testament. They have also ear-rings attached to the upper as well as the lower part of the ear, and necklaces consisting of many rows of jewels of different kinds.

The dress of most of these heroines consists of a robe, the upper part of which fits tight to the shape, while the petticoat, being long and wide, falls in graceful folds; a girdle of great width covered with embroidery and precious stones; trousers; and a head-dress like that now generally worn, consisting of a low-crowned cap, terminating in a point, round which are wreathed several folds of silk or fine linen: to this is fastened, with a gold bodkin, a large veil, which shrouds the whole figure.

In Mr. Morier's "Travels in Persia," the costume of the Persian queen is thus described:— "Her dress was rendered so cumbersome by the quantity of jewels embroidered upon it, that she could scarcely move under its weight. Her trousers in particular were so engrafted with pearls, that they looked more like a piece of mosaic than wearing apparel. Padded with cotton inside, stiffened by cloth of gold without, they were so fashioned as to exclude the possibility of discovering the shape of the leg, and kept it cased up, as it were, in the shape of a column."

Persian Princess

He also mentions that the queen's daughter, who was celebrated throughout the country for her beauty, was greatly disfigured in the eyes of a European by the immense quantity of red and white paint with which her face was daubed, and that her eyebrows, which were arched, were connected over the nose by a great stripe of black paint, and her eyelids and lashes strongly tinged with antimony.

The ordinary dress of a Persian female consists,

Mr. Morier: James Morier, 1780-1849; "A Journey through Persia, Armenia and Asia Minor in the years 1808-9 in which is included some account of his Majesty's Mission under Sir Harford Jones, Bart., to the court of the King of Persia" published 1812
Persian queen: the Shah at that time was Fath Ali, 1794-1834; he had hundreds of wives and numbered 46 daughters among his offspring

when in-doors, of a large black silk handkerchief round the head, a gown which descends to the knees, a pair of loose trousers, and green light-heeled slippers.

The interview of the English Ambassadress with the Queen of Persia is mentioned in these words by an Eastern traveller:—"The ambassadress was introduced into a large open room, at one corner of which was seated the queen, dressed out in truly Persian splendour. Large gilded knots appeared on her head-dress, which was of great size, and the other parts of her attire, like that of Zobeide, the Caliph's favourite in the "Arabian Nights," were so loaded with jewels, that she could scarcely walk. In a corner of the room stood some of the king's children, so stiffened out with brocade, velvet, furs, and jewellery, that they almost looked like fixtures. Great numbers of women were ranged in rows without the room, all ornamented with jewellery."

The bestowing of dresses is a mark of honour constantly practised in Persia, and is one of the most ancient customs of Eastern nations; it is mentioned both in sacred and profane history. We learn how great was the distinction of giving a coat that had been worn, by what is recorded of Jonathan's love for David. "And Jonathan stripped himself of the robe that was upon him, and gave it to David; and his garments, even to his sword, and to his bow, and to his girdle." (1 Samuel, xviii. 4.) And in Esther also (ch. vi. 7, 8), we read, "And Haman answered the king, For the man whom the king delighteth to honour, let the royal apparel be brought which the king useth to wear."

The maidens of Yezd, a town situated near the Ghebers' "holy mountain," wear a head-dress composed of a light gold chain-work set with small pearls,

English Ambassadress: Lady Sarah Jones, wife of Sir Harford Jones, Bart., who was Ambassador 1809–1811
Haman: anti-Semitic advisor to the King of Persia, who was Esther's husband (Esther was Jewish)
Yezd: textile and caravan center in central Iran

with a thin gold plate hanging from the side, about the size of a crown-piece, on which is inscribed an Arabian prayer, thus described by Moore :—

> " A light golden chain-work round her hair,
> Such as the maids of Yezd and Shiraz wear,
> From which, on either side, gracefully hung
> A golden amulet, in the Arab tongue
> Engraven o'er, with some immortal line
> From holy writ, or bard scarce less divine."

The females of Khorassan wear ear-rings of very large dimensions, with great quantities of turquoises suspended from them, for these stones are of but little value

> " In that delightful province of the sun,
> The first of Persian lands he shines upon,
> Where all the loveliest children of his beam,
> Flowrets and fruits, blush over every stream ;
> And, fairest of all streams, the Murga roves
> Among Miron's bright palaces and groves."

Male Costume

We must not take leave of the fair sex of Persia without mentioning the Squadanus, or Bebees, the female descendants of Mahomet, who go about veiled, or rather with a long white robe thrown over the whole body, having netted orifices before the eyes and mouth.

The men in Persia pay as much attention to their beards as the women do to their hair; they perfume them highly, and frequently dye them of different colours.

The ancient kings of Persia wore their hair very long.   During

Moore: see note p. 429
Khorassan: Khurasan, carpet-weaving area in northeastern Iran
Murga: Murgab River, forms the border between Turkestan and Afghanistan
Miron: unknown

the war between the Romans and Persians, a comet appeared, which was looked upon by the former as a bad omen. The Emperor Vespasian, however, laughed at it, and said, if it portended ill to any one, it must be to the King of Persia, because, like him, it wore long hair. The Persians now generally shave their heads. Men of rank wear very magnificent turbans. They are very particular about keeping the head warm, and never take off its covering, even in the presence of royalty. Among the common orders, a cap of black lamb-skin is generally worn.

The rest of the costume of all classes consists of a straight under-garment, open at the chest and throat, as is also the upper vest, which is fastened round the waist by a girdle; over this is worn a short loose kind of pelisse. The legs are clothed in socks and slippers, generally of a green colour. The pelisse is cut out nnder the arms, so that the sleeves can either be drawn in or thrown behind the back. The material of these vests consists, with the poorer orders, of coarse cloth, but with the richer they are formed of the most expensive furs, and of muslins, and silks richly embroidered with gold and silver.

The sash, with the higher ranks, is made of the finest cashmere shawls. In it is always carried a dagger, ornamented with jewels of every variety; diamonds, rubies, pearls, and amethysts are there seen glittering in all their brilliancy and splendour, dazzling the eyes of the beholders.

In a work, called " Sketches of Persia," there is the following description of the king:—" His beard attracted much of our attention; it was full, black, and glossy, and flowed to his middle. His dress

Vespasian: Roman Emperor, 69–79 A.D.
King of Persia: actually the King of Parthia, Phrates III
"Sketches": "Sketches of Persia, from the Journals of a Traveller" by Sir John Malcolm, published 1828

baffled all description. The ground of his robes was white; but he was so covered with jewels of an extra-ordinary size, and their splendour, from his being seated where the rays of the sun played upon them, was so dazzling, that it was impossible to distinguish the minute parts which combined to give such amazing brilliancy to his whole figure."

The Jitra

The *jitra*, an upright ornament of jewellery, the distinguishing mark of Persian royalty, is worn on the front of the crown. Another ornament, which also indicates sovereignty, called *bazubend*, is fastened on the arm above the elbow; it is always composed of precious stones of the greatest value, and is never worn but by the king and his sons.

In the book of Samuel we read, that the Amalekite who brought David word of the death of Saul said unto him, "And I took the crown that was upon his head, and the bracelet that was on his arm, and have brought them hither unto my lord;" whence it may be inferred that a bracelet and a crown were in those days marks of royalty.

The shoes worn in Persia have iron heels, which render them no mean instrument of punishment: in that country they are always considered as vile, and never allowed to enter sacred or respected places; while to be smitten with one is to be subjected to the greatest ignominy and disgrace.

The author of the " Kuzzilbash" thus describes the Persian costume :—" These people wear first a very short shirt, without a collar ; it has long loose

"Kuzzilbash": an unknown work

sleeves. Next come a pair of very wide, large trousers, down to the ankle, and drawn round the waist with a string. Over this a vest, fitting tight to the shape as far as the waist, with wide-flowing shirts down to the ankle. This is cut in the breast to shew the shirt, which is generally made of gauze or some light, pretty material. Over this they wear another dress, made just in the same manner as the former, only larger in every way. They have short shawl-stockings, and shoes with high heels, and so short, the heel comes to the middle of the foot. They universally wear on their heads a black fur conical-shaped cap; the young beaux have one long curl on each side of the face, just behind the ear, and all who can, wear a beard."

We must not quit Persia without mentioning the Gheber belt, which distinguishes this sect from the members of every other religion, thus spoken of by the poet Moore:—

> " —— as wild he flung
> His mantle back, and shewed beneath
> The Gheber belt that round him clung."

The Ghebers lay so much stress upon their *cushee*, or girdle, that they dare not be one instant without it: it is generally formed of leather, or of woollen cloth.

The peasants in the province of Mazenderan tie folds of cloth round their legs, and fix them with a low shoe and lacing cords. The men wear dark clothes, and the women generally dress in blue or red, the two colours which are the most easy to dye. Many of the people wear caps of felt instead of lamb-skin.

In Khorassan the slim, long-faced Kuzzilbash is

Ghebers: Zoroastrians, also known as Parsees after the Moslem conquest of Persia
cushee: kusti, the Gheber belt, a cord, part of the sacred initiation garment; it
    is a thin woollen cord of 72 threads, representing the 72 Has or chapters of
    the Izashne, a sacred book
Mazenderan: province in northern Iran along the Caspian Sea, also called Tabaristan
Kuzzilbash: possibly the Kusana or Kushan, an Indo-Scythian people in this area and
    central Asia

often met, with his fur cap on his head and his ringlets curling up behind.

Strabo describes the garments worn by the ancient Persians as the same as those employed by the Medes. A tiara, or kind of cap, the point of which bent over in front; a shift, composed of a material which was white in the inside, and covered with flowers on the outside; a tunic, with lined sleeves, reaching to the knees; a cloak, sometimes of a brilliant scarlet or purple, and sometimes figured, and of various colours; and socks, are the principal garments mentioned by him, as well as by Xenophon and other ancient authors, as having formed the Persian costume in the early ages.

Strabo: Greek historian and geographer, circa 62 B.C.–24 A.D.
Medes: Indo-European people who lived in western Iran and merged with the Persians
Xenophon: Greek historian, circa 434–355 B.C., who wrote on the Persian Wars

THE TOILETTE

IN

BOKHARA, CIRCASSIA, AND CASHMERE.

CHAPTER XLIII.

Female on Horseback

 WHEN Lalla Rookh rose in the morning, and her ladies came round her to assist in the adjustment of the bridal ornaments, they thought they had never seen her look half so beautiful. What she had lost of the bloom and radiance of her charms was more than made up by that intellectual expression, that soul in the eyes, which is worth all the rest of loveliness. When they had tinged her fingers with the henna leaf, and placed upon her brow a small coronet of jewels of the shape worn by the ancient queens of Bucharia, they flung over her head the rose-coloured bridal veil, and she proceeded to the barge that was to convey her across the lake."

"Lalla Rookh": see note p. 429
Bucharia: Bokhara, Bokara, part of Uzbek Russia since 1868

So says, or rather sings—for his prose is scarcely less musical than his verse—the poet Moore.

This favoured land, once the seat of a more powerful empire than that of Rome or Greece,—the cherished residence of the far-famed Zengis Khan, who enriched " proud Bokhara's groves" with the spoils of the Eastern world, is now peopled by numerous wandering tribes. There may be met

> " —— chiefs of the Uzbek race,
> Waving their heron crests with martial grace ;
> Turkomans, countless as their flocks, led forth
> From the aromatic pastures of the north ;
> Wild warriors of the turquoise hills, and those
> Who dwell beyond the everlasting snows
> Of Hindoo Kosh, in stormy freedom bred,
> Their fort the rock, their camp the torrent's bed."

The dress of these various tribes differs considerably. Ponderous turbans formed of innumerable folds of white muslin are to be seen, as well as the talpak, or Tartar conical fur-cap. In that paradise of the East, " holy Bokhara," the general costume of the men consists of a large white turban, a flowing sash, and three or four pelisses, the upper one, which is called *chogha*, being generally of a dark colour. On great occasions, this latter garment is replaced by a mottled vest of silk, called *uzrus*, made of the brightest colours.

The higher classes clothe themselves in brocade : the different gradations of rank may be ascertained by the texture of this outer garment. Stockings are never worn ; but an inhabitant of Bokhara, whether mounted or on foot, is never seen without his boots, which have heels an inch and a half in height, ta-

Moore: see note p. 429
Zengis Khan: Genghis Khan, circa 1167-1227, conquered Bokhara in 1220
Uzbek: Turkic people, originally of the Golden Horde (Mongols)
Turkomans: Turkic tribal people, mostly living in modern Russia
Hindoo Kosh: the Hindu Kush, a mountainous part of Afghanistan, bordering Pakistan
    and China

pering to a point, which renders walking in them very difficult to those who are not accustomed to it. Some men of rank wear a shoe over the boot, which is taken off on entering a room.

The ladies sometimes appear abroad on horseback, riding like men, or on foot, but always veiled, not only with a muslin screen, through which at times a transient glimpse of a pretty face may be caught, but often with an impenetrable veil of black hair-cloth. They wear the same pelisses as the men, only that the sleeves, instead of being used as such, are tucked together and tied behind. They also wear, even in the house, huge Hessian boots made of velvet, and highly ornamented. They braid their hair, and let it hang in tresses down their shoulders; on the head they wear a large white turban, but a veil covers the face. The exhibition of beauty, in which so much of a woman's time is spent in more favoured countries, is here unknown. A bride wears a rose-coloured veil on her marriage-day.

Deep blue is the distinctive mark of mourning in this country.

> " In that deep blue, melancholy dress
> Bokhara's maidens wear in mindfulness
> Of friends or kindred, dead or far away."

Strict adherence to the established dress is nowhere more thought of than in Bokhara. The costume described is nowhere enjoined by the Koran, nor was it assumed for two centuries after the Prophet, when the prejudice of some of the caliphs discovered that the " Faithful" ought to be distinguished from those who were not Mahomedans. Stockings are the chief

riding like men: i.e., astride
Hessian boots: high boots with tassels at the top front

emblem of distinction between the infidel and the true believer.

Sir A. Burnes thus describes the " Great King :" —" He was plainly dressed in a silken robe, or *udrus*, with a white turban. He sometimes wears an aigrette of feathers ornamented with diamonds. His suite did not exceed a hundred people ; most of them were dressed in robes of Russian brocade, and wore gold ornamented swords—I should call them knives—the mark of distinction in this country."

The Turkomans are a warlike and handsome race. They wear the talpak, a square or conical black skull-cap of sheep-skin, which is about a foot in height, and much more becoming for a warrior than a turban. They are very partial to bright colours, and generally choose light red, green, or yellow for their flowing *chumpkans*, or pelisses. Long brown boots are universally worn.

To the ladies of this tribe belonged the beautiful and delicate Roxana, the bewitching queen of Alexander, that Peri of the East whose beauty, like the perfume of the rose, is remembered with pleasure long after the casket which enshrined it is mouldered in the dust. They wear a head-dress consisting of a lofty white turban, shaped like a military shako, but still higher, over which they throw a red or white scarf that falls in folds down to the waist. As these ladies are generally rather on a large scale, this head-dress becomes them.

They attach a variety of ornaments to their hair, which hangs in tresses over their shoulders. Unlike most other Eastern women, they do not consider a veil a necessary appendage to their dress. The rest of

Sir A. Burnes: Sir Alexander Barnes, his "Travels into Bukhara being an account of a Journey from India to Cabool, Tartary and Persia 1831-33" was published 1834
Great King: Nasr Allah (Nasrullah) reigned 1827-1860 and was described as "ferocious"
Turkomans: see note p. 442
Roxana: married Alexander the Great in 327, at the time he conquered Bokhara
Peri of the East: 'Peri' is a fallen angel in Persian mythology, and a fairy or elf in English; this must refer to her legendary "fairy-like" beauty, rather than to any supposed fall from grace

their costume consists of a long gown of a bright colour that reaches to the ankle and conceals both it and the waist, those standard points of beauty with most nations.

And now we must say a few words of

> " The maids, whom kings are proud to cull
> From fair Circassia's vales,"—

they whose charms the historian from the earliest times has immortalised, and the poet sung. The costume of these houris is simple, and not remarkable for beauty. It consists in a long loose gown of divers colours, tied about the waist with a sash. The hair is worn in tresses, which hang on each side of the face, surmounted by a black coif, over which is placed a white cloth, which passes under the chin, where it is tied in a bow.

The apparel of the men of Circassia, like that of the women, is composed of one or more gowns, made of silk or cotton. They are sometimes ornamented, and among the higher ranks are frequently of stuff, woven with flowers of gold and silver in beautiful and delicate patterns. Their head-dress consists of a high conical cap, and they wear a cloak of coarse cloth or sheep-skin.

In Thibet, the country of the Grand Lama, which mighty personage resides in a sumptuous pagoda on the mountain of Patoli, near Lassa, and is supposed by his worshippers to be immortal, the people wear coarse woollen stuffs of their own manufacture, which they line with the

Head-Dress in Thibet

Circassia: area on the eastern Black Sea and in the Caucasus, ceded to Russia in 1829
Thibet: Tibet, high mountainous country between India and China, overrun by China in 1950
Patoli: Potala Palace, former residence of the Dalai Lama
Lassa: Lhasa, the capital of Tibet before its conquest by the Chinese, still an administrative center

skins of any animal they can procure. The better classes, however, are attired in European cloths, or in rich China silks, which they line and trim with American furs of the finest and most expensive kinds; thus rendering their attire at once warm, costly, and magnificent.

Linen is a luxury unknown among these people, who, however, have made some advance in civilization. The ambassador of the Deb Rajah, who rules a country tributary to Thibet, is represented to have been dressed, on his arrival at Bengal with a letter to the governor, Mr. Hastings, exactly like a Chinese grandee in his summer costume, or, at least, like the pictures we have of that people in their own paintings. His hat was of a conical shape, his tunic of splendid flowered brocade, and his feet were encased in thin boots.

Cashmere, that "paradise of nations," has long been celebrated for its manufacture of shawls, which gives occupation to the entire population of the country, even down to the children, and thus promotes the wealth of the nation. There are two sorts of shawls manufactured; one is made of the wool of the country, the other of the hair (called tonz) found on the breast of a species of goat which inhabits the Great Thibet. The tonz shawls are much more esteemed than those made with the native wool. The tonz, which is softer and finer even than the hair of the beaver, is of a dark grey colour; it is bleached by means of a preparation made of rice-flour. The yarn made from it, after being dyed, is woven and then washed. The border, which usually displays a variety of figures and colours, is attached to the

Deb Rajah: former title of the ruler of Bhutan, a country the size of Switzerland
    high in the mountains, bounded by Tibet and India, near Nepal and Sikkim
Bengal: province of eastern India; its chief city is Calcutta
Mr. Hastings: Warren Hastings, who became Governor-General of India in 1774
Cashmere: Kashmir, province in the northwest of India, in the mountains
tonz: the undercoat of wool from the neck and belly
Great Thibet: the Tibetan plateau

shawl after fabrication, but in so nice a manner that the junction is not discernible. The value of these shawls is often greatly enhanced by the introduction of embroidery.

The unrivalled excellence of the manufactures of Cashmere is attributed to certain properties in the water of that country, for though great pains have been taken to manufacture similar shawls at Patna, Agra, and Lahore, they never have the delicate texture and softness of those of Cashmere. Sir A. Burnes, in the description of his journey through the Vale of Cashmere, says : " Our approach to the Mahommedan countries became evident daily, and shewed itself in nothing more than the costume of the women, many of whom we now met veiled. One girl whom we saw on the road had a canopy of red cloth erected over her on horseback, which had a ludicrous appearance. It seemed to be a framework of wood ; but as the cloth concealed every thing as well as the countenance of the fair lady, I did not discover the contrivance. The costume of the unveiled portion of the sex had likewise undergone a change. They wore wide blue trousers, tied tightly at the ankle, and which taper down and have a graceful appearance. A narrow web of cloth, sixty yards long, is sometimes used in a single pair, for one fold falls upon the other."

Over the hair, which is worn in a single braid, they place a cap generally of a crimson colour, to the back of which is attached a triangular curtain of the same stuff, which falls upon the shoulders and conceals much of the hair ; round the lower edge of the cap is folded a shawl or piece of cotton or

Patna: capital of Bihar State, northeastern India on the Ganges River
Agra: city in northern India on the Jumna River, site of the Taj Mahal
Lahore: now in Pakistan, was the capital of the Sikh Kingdom
Sir A. Burnes: Sir Alexander Barnes, travelled in India 1805-1841, see note p. 444
Vale of Cashmere: high valley containing the city of Srinagar and its lake, a famous
    resort for Europeans during the hot Indian summer

woollen cloth, which gives it much the appearance of a turban.

The dress of the men consists of a large turban, a great woollen vest with wide sleeves, a girdle composed of many folds of cloth, a shirt, and drawers.

Cashmerian Costume

THE TOILETTE IN AFFGHANISTAN.

CHAPTER XLIV.

Dress of an Affghan

IN Elphinstone's "Caubul" we find a description of the dress of many of the inhabitants of Persia, Tartary, and India ; among the rest, of the Affghans. "The dress of the men," says the author, "varies ; but that now worn in the west appears to me to be the original dress of the whole nation. It consists of a pair of loose trousers of dark-coloured cotton ; a large shirt, like a wagoner's frock, but with wider sleeves, and only reaching a little below the knee ; a low cap (shaped like a Hulan's cap), the sides of which are of black silk

G G

Elphinstone: Mountstuart Elphinstone, 1779–1859, was English Envoy to Suja Shah in
    1808
"Caubul": Kabul, capital of Afghanistan
Hulan: Uhlan, a lancer in the Prussian and Austro-Hungarian cavalries

or satin, and the top of gold brocade, or of some
bright-coloured cloth ; and a pair
of half-boots of brown leather, laced
or buttoned up to the calf : over
this, for a great part of the year, is
thrown a large cloak of well-tanned
sheep-skin, with the wool inside, or
of soft and pliant grey felt.   This
garment is worn loose over the
shoulders, with the sleeves hanging down, and reaches to the
ankles.

Winter Attire

"The women wear a shirt like
that of the men, but much longer ;
it is made of finer materials, and
generally coloured or embroidered
with flowers in silk ; in the west it is often entirely
of silk.   They wear coloured trou-
sers, tighter than those of the
men, and have a small cap of
bright-coloured silk, embroidered
with gold thread, which scarcely
comes down to the forehead or the
ears ; and a large sheet, either
plain or printed, which they throw
over their heads, and with which
they hide their faces when a stranger approaches.   In the west the
women often tie a black handkerchief round their heads over their
caps.   They divide the hair over their faces and plait
it into two locks, which fasten at the back of their
heads.

Dress of an Affghan Female

" Their ornaments are strings of Venetian sequins, worn round their heads, and chains of gold and silver, which are hooked up over the forehead, pass round the head and end in two large balls, which hang down near the ears. Ear-pendants and rings on the fingers are also worn, as are pendants in the middle cartilage of the nose, which was formerly the custom in Persia, and still is in India and Arabia. Such is the dress of the married women ; the unmarried are distinguished by wearing white trousers, and by having their hair loose."

Another tribe of the Affghauns are thus described : " The ordinary dress of the men is a cotton tunic, made to fit the body down to the waist, and then loose and full down to below the knees ; it is either dark blue, or dyed grey with the bark of the pomegranate - tree. They also wear a large loose white turban, a pair of cotton trousers, and a pair of sandals ; but their dress is not complete without a *loongee* (a handkerchief of blue silk and cotton mixed), which hangs over the shoulder and reaches below the middle, both before and behind. It is sometimes used for a cloak and sometimes for a girdle. They have always a better suit of clothes for Fridays and great occasions. The tunic is then made longer and fuller below, and is puckered up about the waist in numerous plaits. The

Affghan of another Tribe

rest of the holyday clothes are of silk, except the turban.

" The women wear a gown, close over the breast and very wide below. They wear many gold and silver ornaments, like those used in India. Neither sex wear the long shirt that is so common among the other Affghauns. The women of the Eusofzyes are carefully concealed, and never leave their houses with-out putting on the cloak called a *boorka*, which covers them from head to foot.

" The Turcomanlees wear the Affghaun *camess* (a shirt), and a little cap of wrought silk.

" The Khyberees wear, in winter at least, dark blue turbans and long dark blue tunics, sitting close to the body and reaching to the middle of the leg. They wear neat sandals of straw or the leaf of the dwarf-palm.

" In winter the tribes of the Peshawur generally wear dark blue coats of quilted cotton, which are thrown aside as the summer advances, when a large Affghaun shirt, and a white and blue turban, form the dress of the greater part of the people. A *loongee*, either twist-ed round the waist or worn over the shoulder, is always part of their attire."

Warrior of the Peshawur

" The people of the tribe of Damoun wear long hair and beards. Instead of the long wide shirt and cap of the Affghauns, they wear a close dress of white cotton, tied across the

Eusofzyes: very proud tribal people of the North West Frontier, near Swat
Turcomanlees: Turkomen, Turkic people of Iran, Russia and Afghanistan
Khyberee: Afridi tribes around the Khyber Pass
Peshawur: Peshawar, city in northwest Pakistan near the Khyber Pass
loongee: the lunghi; see p. 451, second paragraph
Damoun: none of our sources included information on this tribe; it is possibly a
    typesetter's error, as the Dooraunees, p. 454, seem to wear the same type of
    clothing

breast, and reaching a little below the knee; even in winter they wear turbans, but they are extremely large and loose, while those of the Indians are rolled close round their head in a regular shape, that has little grace or elegance. At that season they also wear brown and grey woollen great-coats and posteens."

" The dress of the Seeaposh Caufirs is composed of four goat-skins; two of them form a vest, and two a sort of petticoat. The skins have long hair on the outside, the upper ones do not cover the arms; the whole is fastened on with a leathern belt. They go bareheaded unless they have killed a Mussulman, and shave their heads, except for a long tuft on the crown and perhaps two curls over the ears. They also pluck out the hair from the upper lip, cheeks, and neck, but wear beards four or five inches long. Those in good circumstances, and those near the Affghauns, wear a shirt beneath their vest; and in summer the shirt forms the whole of their dress, as it always does with the women. The great do not wear goat-skins, but cotton cloth or black hair-cloth; some also wear the sort of white blanket woven in the neighbourhood of Kaushkaur. The blankets are put on like Highland plaids, come down to near the knee, and are fastened with a belt; they also wear cotton trousers, which, as well as their shirts, are worked all over with flowers in red and black worsteds : the trousers are slit at the bottom, so as to make a sort of fringe. They also wear worsted stockings, or perhaps worsted fillets, rolled round their legs, and the warriors wear half-boots of white goat-skin.

posteen: postin, an Indian garment of leather with the fleece left intact
Seeaposh Caufirs: Siah Posh Kafirs, a tribal people of northeastern Afghanistan who were not converted to the Moslem faith until 1896; Kafirstan is now Noristan
Kaushkaur: Kashgar, also called eastern Turkestan, both a city and a state; the city is a major trading center and great crossroad for travellers
Highland: as in Scotland

" The dress of the women differs little from that of the men, but they have their hair plaited and fastened on the top of their head, and over it a small cap, round which is a little turban : they have also silver ornaments and many cowry shells.

" The Dooraunees wear a cotton shirt, over which is a tunic sitting close to the body, with skirts reaching half-way down the leg, which come quite round, and cross each other in front. This is called the *ulkhaulik*. It is generally made of chintz, and that of Masulipatam, which comes from India by the circuitous channel of Persia, is most admired. Over this is a tunic called the *kubba*, shaped very like the other, and either made of a very coarse brown woollen cloth, or of a very strong cloth made of cotton, and called *cudduk*. This upper garment is sometimes of a bright colour, but generally dark, and bottle-green is the commonest colour. It is tied across the breast, but the strings are concealed, and a row of covered silk buttons runs down one side of the front, with a row of silk loops on the other, though at much too great a distance to button. The sleeves are closed with a long row of buttons and loops, which run up the inside of the arm. They wear wide coloured trousers of silk or cotton, short stockings in winter, and Persian shoes, which are round and broad at the toes and narrow towards the heels ; they are shod with iron like German boots, and the inner part, on which the heel rests, has a piece of wood to fit it, covered with a thin plate of ivory, in which some figures are inlaid in black. The shoes are made of brown leather, well tanned.

Dooraunees: Durranis, Afghanis of the Durrani dynasty of Ahmad Shah, see note p. 424
    on the Koh-i-noor
Masulipatam: now Bandar, city on the Bay of Bengal in Madras State, see note p. 425

" The head-dress is a cap, about six inches high, made of quilted silk or chintz; a *loongee*, or coarse shawl, is always worn round the waist as a girdle, and the old men often twist another *loongee* round their caps, like a turban.

Male Head-Dress

" Many people of the lower order wear the *ulkhaulik*, or under-tunic, only, without the *kubba*, and all wear a cloak over the rest of their dress. In summer it is made of some light cloth, and in winter of sheep-skin or felt.

" The dress of the Uzbek Tartars is a shirt and trousers of cotton, a coat or tunic called *chuppaun*, of silken or woollen cloth, tied on with a girdle; and over it a gown of woollen cloth, posteen, or felt. Some wear in winter a little cap of broad cloth, lined with fur, sitting close to the head, and others a pointed silken cap,

Head-Dress of the Uzbek Tartars

called a *calpauk*, alone; but the national head-dress is a large white turban worn over the calpauk. All wear boots at all hours; the poor have the same description as that used in Caubul, but those in easy circumstances have a kind called *mukusee*, for constant use, and only put on the others in winter or on journeys. The *mukusee* is of thin and light sea-green leather, without heels or soles, so that the wearer is obliged to put on shoes when he goes out. All wear

kubba: see p. 454, second paragraph
Uzbek Tartars: originally Mongols of the Golden Horde, settled in Uzbek (now Russia)
Caubul: Kabul, the capital

bandages round their legs instead of stockings; even the women wear boots. The rest of their dress is like that of the men, but longer. They tie a silk handkerchief round their heads, throw a sheet of silk or cotton over all, wear golden and silver ornaments, and plait their hair into a long queue, which hangs down from the middle of the head like those of the Chinese."

A plume of white heron's feathers in the turban is the distinctive badge of a chief among the Uzbek Tartars.

The dress of the Parthians, or ancient Affghans, is often met with on the Arch of Severus. It consisted of a tunic reaching to the knee, with long sleeves, a belt round the waist, and over the tunic a cloak or chlamyde, fastened on the shoulder by a brooch or buckle. Shoes without any shape, almost like a bag, were generally worn, with wide buskins resembling gaiters, and a Phrygian cap.

The Medians, we learn from Plutarch, painted their faces, and wore false beards, as well as false hair. In this fashion they were imitated by Surena, a king of Parthia, who, unlike the generality of his countrymen, whose hair and beards were long, flowing, and untrimmed, wore his curled with the greatest precision. From the representations of several of the succeeding kings of Parthia, which are met with on ancient medals, we find much attention must have been bestowed on the hair and beard; and in many instances they appear to be so abundant, that it is impossible but Art must have assisted Nature to render them so flowing and luxuriant.

Parthians: from Parthia, area southeast of the Caspian Sea, Asian tribal people who conquered Persia and Afghanistan
Arch of Severus: in the old forum of Rome; Septimius Severus, Roman Emperor 192–311, defeated the Parthians
Phrygian cap: liberty cap, see upper illus. p. 387
Medians: Medes, people of western Persia who merged with the Persians
Plutarch: Greek biographer, circa 46–120 A.D.
Surena: Surenas, died circa 53 B.C.

THE TOILETTE IN CHINA.

CHAPTER XLV.

Chinese Military Mandarin

THE inhabitants of the Celestial Empire seem to agree with Beauty, in considering that Fashion mars, instead of improving, the charms of her votaries, for, ever since the days of the wise and renowned Confucius, they have steadily resisted all her blandishments, closed their ears to her flatteries, and followed, in every respect, the ordinances of their great lawgiver with regard to dress.

By this decree the poorer classes are obliged to wear their clothes of a dark blue, red, or black colour. The emperor and princes of the blood are alone allowed the privilege of having yellow dresses, and many of the most delicate colours are reserved exclu-

Confucius: Chinese sage and philosopher, circa 551–479 B.C.

sively for the ladies. Pure white is the emblem of mourning, among all classes.

So strictly is every thing relating to the toilette managed among this grave people, that even when the seasons change they are not allowed to clothe themselves in thick or thin coverings, according to their fancy, but must wait with patience to change the winter for the summer, or the summer for the winter garb, till the viceroy of the province has performed this important ceremony, when the whole outward appearance of the people alters as if by magic; and a stranger to their laws, who, the evening before, had seen the streets of Pekin crowded with people, all enveloped to their chins in the warmest furs, would imagine every body struck by a magician's wand, when, on going forth the following day, he finds the same people all, by one accord, habited in their summer attire.

Mandarin of Pekin

Female of the Higher Class *

The dress of the men is suitable to the grave de-

Pekin: Peking (Bei-jing), capital of China
* Both visually and in terms of the description given, this should be "Male of the Higher Class".

portment that they so universally affect. It consists of a long robe, which reaches nearly to the ground, and is fastened on the shoulders with gold or silver buttons. The sleeves, which are wide at the top, grow narrower towards the wrist, and end in the shape of a horse-shoe, covering all the hands except the ends of the fingers. This robe is fastened round the waist with a broad silk sash, to which are suspended a purse, and two small sticks, called chopsticks, which are used as forks.

In the summer they wear trousers made of linen, silk, or satin; but during the winter, particularly in the colder parts of the country, they are made of furs of different kinds. In the summer also they have their necks uncovered, but in the winter they are shielded from the cold by collars of quilted satin or furs. The higher classes frequently wear a sur-tout of silk, satin, or velvet; this garment is very short, has large sleeves, and is lined with the most costly furs. The men formerly wore their hair as long as they could induce it to grow, and plaited in tails hanging down their backs; but now they only allow two or three tufts on the crown of the head.

They either wear hats, in shape and size resembling large umbrellas, or else small conical caps, made of beautifully wrought cane-work, and frequently painted in flowers or birds. They also have another cap, which, though richer in material, is not so graceful as the former; it is of the same shape, but made of black velvet, with blue silk in the middle, and a red tassel surmounting the top.

The upper dress of the Chinese ladies resembles

that of the lords of the Celestial Empire; but it is more decorated with rich and beautiful embroidery. The trousers are tied round the ankle, so as to give a full view of their small feet, encased in highly ornamented shoes. They appear anxious to conceal, rather than to display, the elegance of their figure, though a small waist is much admired. Their sleeves being very long, protect their hands, and render gloves unnecessary.

Costume of Married Ladies

The married ladies tie the hair on the top of the head; and, to make the tuft as large as possible, add a quantity of false hair, and stick it full of long gold or silver pins, or bodkins, the ends of which are frequently highly ornamented with jewels; while the young women wear their jet black ringlets clustering on each side of the face. Artificial flowers are also often used to ornament the head. But the favourite coiffure, the object of a Chinese lady's greatest admiration, is an artificial bird, formed of gold or silver, intended to represent the Fong-whang, a fabulous bird, of which the

Costume of Unmarried Ladies

ancients relate many marvellous tales. It is worn in such a manner that the wings stretch over the front of the head; the spreading tail makes a kind of plume on the top, and the body is placed over the forehead, while the neck and beak hang down. The former being fastened to the body with an invisible hinge, it vibrates with the least motion.

In a Chinese novel, called by the euphonius title of " Hung-how-Mung," is the following description of a Chinese *élégante:*—" On her head, her knot of hair was adorned with gold and silver, and eight precious stones pendent. It was fastened with a pin of pearls dropping from five little eagles. An ornament of virgin gold, enlivened with insects, embraced her neck. Around her waist was an upper dress of deep red-coloured silk, on which was embroidered an hundred golden butterflies fluttering among flowers. Over this a narrow garment made of the skins of stone-blue *mice,* and silk of five different colours. Below all was a petticoat of foreign *crêpe,* of a green colour, sprinkled with flowers."

The distinctive mark of different ranks among the mandarins consists in the colour and value of the button worn in the cap, in the jewels that adorn the girdle, and in the quality of the embroidery that ornaments the robe.

The Chinese wear their nails of an immense length; and neither men or women are often seen without a painted fan in their hands, many of them most beautifully figured.

The extraordinary admiration of this people for small feet subjects them to much pain and incon-

"Hung-how-Mung": "Dream of the Red Chamber", Ts'ao Chan, translator; a famous novel of classical China, its actual name is "Hung-lo Meng"

venience. As soon as a female child in the higher ranks is born, the toes are bent under the foot, and tightly bandaged day and night, till the growth of the foot ceases. This barbarous custom is attributed by some old writers to Takya, the wife of one of the first Chinese emperors. She is represented as having been very beautiful, but haughty and imperious. She persuaded her husband to allow her to make what laws she pleased, and having very deformed feet, she bound them with fillets, and, ordered all the ladies of the country to imitate her example; thus attempting to make a deformity pass for a beauty.

Chinese Boot

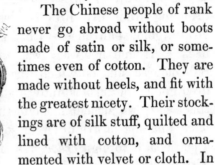

The Chinese people of rank never go abroad without boots made of satin or silk, or sometimes even of cotton. They are made without heels, and fit with the greatest nicety. Their stockings are of silk stuff, quilted and lined with cotton, and ornamented with velvet or cloth. In summer they have light slippers, and the common people black cotton shoes. Besides wearing quantities of false hair, the Chinese women also employ paint to heighten the charms of their complexion.

In the "Journal of the Embassy to China," by Henry Ellis, we read that the dress of ceremony of the mandarins consists of blue gauze or crape, with some flowered satin beneath; and that it is plain and not unbecoming. An embroidered badge, marking their rank, whether civil or military, is fixed upon their robe, either before or behind. The peacock's feather,

"Journal of the Embassy to China": published 1818

or more properly tail of peacock's feather, answering to our orders of knighthood, is worn behind. Two of these are equivalent to the garter.

In the journal of Dr. Thunberg we find the following account of the dress of the Japanese:—" The fashion of their clothes has remained the same from the highest antiquity. They consist of one or more loose gowns, tied about the middle with a sash; the women wear them much longer than the men, and dragging on the ground. In summer they are very thin; but in winter, quilted with silk or cotton wadding. People of rank have them made of silk; the lower class of cotton stuffs. Women generally wear a greater number of them than the men, and have them more ornamented, often with gold or silver flowers woven into the stuff. These gowns are generally left open at the breast; their sleeves are very wide, but partly sewed up in front, so as to make a kind of pocket, into which they can easily put their hands. Men of consequence are distinguished from those of inferior rank by a short jacket of thin black stuff, which is worn over their gowns, and trousers open on the sides, but sewed together near the bottom part, into which the skirts of the robe are thrust. Some use drawers, but all have their legs naked. They wear sandals of straw, fastened to the feet by a bow passing over the instep, and a string which passes between the great toe and that next to it, fixing it to the bow. In winter they have socks of linen, and in rainy or dirty weather, wooden shoes.

" In their sash they fasten the sabre, fan, and tobacco-pipe. They never cover their heads but on a journey, when they use a conical cap made of straw;

Dr. Thunberg: Carl Peter Thunberg, 1743–1828, a Swedish botanist, wrote "Travels in Europe, Africa and Asia performed between the years 1770–79" which was published in 1794
N.B.: Japan was still closed to the West at this time; Admiral Perry forced the gates in 1853

at other times they defend themselves from the sun or rain by fans or umbrellas. Their hair is universally black; and such a sameness of fashion reigns throughout this whole empire, that the head-dress is the same from the emperor to the peasant. The mode of the men's head-dress is singular; the middle part of their heads, from the forehead very far back, is close shaven; the hair remaining round the temples and nape of the neck is turned up and tied upon the top of the head into a kind of brush, about as long as a finger; this brush is again lapped round with white thread, and bent a little backwards. The women preserve all their hair, and, drawing it together on the top of the head, roll it round a loop, and, fastening it down with pins, to which ornaments are affixed, draw out the sides till they appear like little wings; behind this a comb is stuck in. Physicians and priests are the only exceptions to the general fashion; they shave their heads entirely, and are by that means distinguished from the rest of the people."

THE

TOILETTE IN PALESTINE AND SYRIA.

CHAPTER XLVI.

Dancing Girl

N Dr. Clarke's "Manners and Customs of the Ancient Israelites," he says, that "the shape of their dress cannot be exactly known. There is every reason to suppose that it was similar to that of the ancient Egyptians, which consisted of a *tunic*, a *pallium* or cloak, and a girdle." All ancient nations seem to have had the same costume, formed of long garments, without much shape or ornament; and as these were all much alike, they descended from father to son for many generations. The colours most valued among the ancients appear to have been purple, red, and violet, but white was the most used by the Israelites. Young people wore variegated clothes, like the

Dr. Clarke: Edward Daniel Clarke, 1769–1822, also wrote "Travels in various Countries of Europe, Asia and Africa 1790–1800"

coat of Joseph (Gen. xxxvii. 23).   "And it came to pass, when Joseph was come unto his brethren, that they stript Joseph of his coat, his coat of many colours, that was on him."

Their garments, however, were richly ornamented with fringes, borders of colour or embroidery, and jewels; and they were ordered to put borders on their robes, to remind them continually of the law of God. On their heads they wore a sort of tiara, like that of the Persians, for, among this people, to be bare-headed was a sign of mourning.   Their hair was long, for shaving the head marked sorrow and affliction.

In the Scriptures, in various parts, we find descriptions of the manner in which the Jewish women attired themselves.   We read in Ezekiel of the fine stuffs of different colours, a silken girdle, purple shoes, bracelets, a necklace, ear-rings, and a crown or mitre; and in Isaiah, iii. 18, &c. we have a long account of their costume in all its varieties, when the prophet reproaches the daughters of Sion for their vanity and corruption; and truly, at that time, the love of dress and ornament must have been very prevalent, as we find by the numerous accessories to their toilette enumerated by the prophet.

In an old book on Palestine, written by Fuller, in 1650, we have a full account of the Jewish dress, taken from the Bible, and describing all the forms and peculiarities of their costume with the greatest precision.   "At first," he says, "the habits of this persecuted people were made of raw hides, such as sheepskins and goat-skins; secondly, leather, as the girdle of Elijah; thirdly, hair cloth; fourthly, coarse hemp, for mourners; fifthly, fine linen, very fashionable in

Sion: Mt. Zion, in Jerusalem; 'daughters of Zion' meaning Jewish women
Dr. Fuller: Thomas Fuller D.D., 1608-1661; his "A Pisgah-Sight of Palestine and
    the confines thereof ..." was published 1650

those parts, silk, cloth, scarlet, wrought gold, woollen, and jewels. As for the shape and making of the Jewish garments, they were no affecters of various fashions, but kept to the same form for many ages. Indeed, their clothes, being for the most part loose vestments, not exactly fitting to their bodies, but only cast over, wrapped about, or girded unto them, the less curiosity was required in their making. And because we meet not with the trade of a tailor mentioned all through the Scriptures, it seems anciently no distinct occupation among the Jews, being probable the men or their wives made their own clothes. Thus the state and gallantry of the Jews consisted not in changeable fashions, but in their various changes, orient colours, costly matter, and curious embroideries."

"Next to their skins," the same author observes, " the Jews wore linen, over that a coat which came down to their very feet, accounted modest, grave, yea, honourable among them."

These coats, it appears, were fastened with girdles about the waist, and had collars at the neck; they also had a fringe of blue round the skirts. Over this coat, when they went abroad, they wore a mantle or cloak.

Different vocations and degrees of people among the Jews were, however, differently apparelled; and when the luxuries of the East Indies, such as silk, came among them, they were not backward in using them for the adorning of their persons. It is said that they wore hats, though the shape of this covering for the head is never mentioned. Their legs were generally bare, and on their feet they wore sandals, and in winter, shoes, frequently made of the badger's skin.

They wore chains, bracelets, and signet-rings, but no other ornaments.

The dress of the Jewish women was splendid with gold and embroidery. The Queen of Judea was arrayed in a garment of wrought gold. "Thus," observes Fuller, " such gallantry was fashionable amongst the Jews, long before any thereof was used in the western parts, or Rome itself; indeed, a mantle of cloth of gold we find mentioned by Pliny as a great novelty, though such a one had been worn by the Jewish queens a thousand years before."

Their trousers and tunics were made of fine linen, and rich silks embroidered in gold and jewels; they wore also a veil, which fell over the whole person down to the feet. The anklets of gold or silver, often alluded to in Scripture, were very heavy, and made a ringing sound as the wearer walked. The pride and pleasure that the Jewish ladies took in making a tinkling with these ornaments, is severely reproved by the prophet Isaiah. It is supposed that the caul alluded to by the prophet was intended to describe the peculiar manner of dressing the hair. It was at that time divided into tresses plaited with silk threads, gold ornaments, and golden coins.

Besides the anklets, the Jewish women wore ear-rings, nose - jewels, chains of silver and gold, and bracelets. The ear-rings probably contained a verse from the Scriptures, to serve as an amulet or charm, in which most Orientals place much faith, as they believe these amulets have power to avert evils and obtain blessings. They also wore from the waist boxes or bottles containing rich perfume; these they fastened to a chain and hung to their girdles. The

Queen of Judea: Judea was the southern Jewish kingdom; the garment of wrought gold
    must have been ceremonial garb
Fuller: Dr. Fuller, see note p. 466
Pliny: Pliny the Younger, 62–112 A.D.

Jewish women are still very fond of jewels and ornaments of every kind, and, wherever they dwell, are usually as much celebrated for the costliness and splendour of their dress as for their great beauty.

Since the dispersion of the Jews over almost every nation of the globe, they have, as might be imagined, very much adopted the costume of the countries in which they reside. The only peculiarity to which they still strictly adhere in some countries, is in wearing their beards as long and flowing as in the time of the patriarchs. The Jews, however, do not wear their beards exactly of the form followed by the Christians and Mussulmans; for to distinguish themselves from the rest of mankind, they allow two tufts of hair to hang over the ears. The Jews of Arabia dare not wear a turban, but are obliged to be contented with a small bonnet, and they are only allowed to dress in blue habits, generally made of cloth; they are also forbidden to use the *jambea*. Indeed, in most countries, some mark of contempt and contumely have ever been assigned to this wandering race, to distinguish them from the people among whom they reside. A brimless hat marks the Jew in Turkey; at Algiers their heads are wrapped in a black silk cloth; at Tunis they have a black turban; at Tripoli a silk parti-coloured turban; and in old times in England they were obliged to wear a yellow cap of a high square form. The Jewish women at Tripoli bind a riband round their brows, and suspend from it pieces of money; sometimes the whole fortune of the husband is thus worn on the wife's forehead.

We must give the description of a court-dress, which is exactly according to the Jewish fashion, and

Mussulmans: Moslems
jambea: dagger or knife carried by Moslem men in their sashes

is borrowed from the " Tale of Zillah," which, though a novel, abounds in interesting and faithful records of the manners, costumes, fashions, and many other details of the Holy City.

"She accordingly wore the parti-coloured robe, which she had herself embroidered with flowers and gold thread, and of which the sleeves were of the richest gauze, decorated with ribbons and facings, curiously sewed together. These were blue, which, being a celestial colour, was in high favour, and much used for cuffs and trimmings; though it was not deemed decorous to have the whole apparel of this hue, since none more was used about the curtains and veils of the tabernacle. Her under-garment, of fine linen, reaching to the ankles, and bordered also with blue, had been decorated by her own skilful needle with clouded colours, which bore the name of feather-work. Across her bosom was a pectoral of byssus, a sort of silk of a golden yellow, formed from the tuft that grows on a large shellfish of the mussel species, found on the coasts of the Mediterranean, for the great men of the earth had not then begun to rob the silkworm of its covering. Her sandals were of badger-skin leather, secured with golden clasps. Her head-dress was of simple and, according to modern notions, of not very becoming form; for her black and luxuriant locks, being drawn behind the head, were divided into several tresses, their beauty consisting in their length and thickness, and the extremity of each being adorned with pearls and jewels, or ornaments of silver and gold, of which latter metal she also wore narrow plain circlets around her wrists and ankles."

"Tale of Zillah": "Zillah, a Tale of the Holy City" by Horatio Smith, 1828

In a work published in 1819, called "Letters from Palestine," we read: "The female costume of Palestine is not particularly graceful. The outward robe consists of a loose gown, the skirts of which appear as if hanging from the shoulder-blades; the arms, wrists, and ankles are bound with broad metal rings, and the waist is encircled by a belt, profusely studded with some shining substance, intended, probably, to resemble precious stones. The crown of the head is covered with a compact sort of network, interwrought with plates of gold and silver, so arranged as to conceal a part only of the hair, which flows in profuse ringlets over the neck and shoulders; yet even this natural ornament is much injured by a custom very prevalent, of interweaving the extremities with silk ribbons, that descend in twisted folds to the feet. The supplemental tresses would inevitably trail on the ground were it not for the high clogs, or rather stilts, on which women of condition are always raised when they appear in public; many of these are of an extravagant altitude, and, if the decorations of the head were of correspondent dimensions, a lady's face would seem as if fixed in the centre of her figure. The impression made on a stranger by such an equipage is certainly very ludicrous. There is, indeed, a whimsical fantasy here, almost universal in its application, which seems utterly irreconcilable with all ideas of female delicacy. Not only are the cheeks plastered with vermilion, the teeth discoloured, and the eyebrows dyed, but the lips and chin are tinged with a dark indelible composition, as if the fair proprietors were ambitious of the ornament of a beard."

The *haick* forms the principal garment of the

"Letters from Palestine": "Letters from Palestine, written during a residence there 1836–8" by J. D. Paxton; the publication date should have been set as 1839

modern inhabitants of Palestine.   It is of different
sizes and degrees of fineness, usually six yards long,
and five or six yards broad, serving frequently for a
garment by day and a bed and covering by night.
It is very troublesome to manage, often falling upon
the ground ; so that the person who wears it is every
moment obliged to tuck it up, and fold it anew about
the body.

Female of Palestine

Jewish females in the East do not wear stockings,
and generally use slippers of a red colour, embroidered
in gold.   They are very much addicted to the use of
ornaments.   From the lower part of the ears they suspend large gold ear-rings, and three small ones, set
with pearls, on the upper part.   They load their
necks with beads, and their fingers with rings ; their
wrists and ankles also are adorned with bracelets and
anklets of solid silver, and long gold chains hang from
their girdles.

"The dress of the Arabs in Syria," says Dr. Clarke, "is simple and uniform.   It consists of a blue shirt, descending below the knees, the legs and feet being exposed, or the latter sometimes covered with the ancient *cothurnus* or buskins."

Near Jerusalem the ancient sandal is frequently met with, exactly as it is seen on Grecian statues.

"A cloak," continues Dr. Clarke, "is worn, of very coarse and heavy camel's-hair cloth, almost universally decorated with broad black and white stripes, passing vertically down the back.   This is of one square piece, with holes for the arms."   In this we probably behold the form and material of our Saviour's garment, for which the soldiers cast lots, being without seam, woven from the top throughout.   It was the most ancient dress of the inhabitants of this country.

The women of Syria do not veil their faces so closely as those of Palestine.   They wear robes with very long sleeves, hanging quite to the ground; this garment is frequently striped in gaudy colours.

Woman of Syria

Druze Costume

Dr. Clarke: see note p. 465

The Druses, who inhabit part of Syria, wear a coarse woollen cloak, with white stripes, thrown over a waistcoat and breeches of the same stuff, tied round the waist by a sash. They cover the head with a turban, which is flat at the top, and swells out at the sides.

The women wear a coarse blue jacket and petticoat, but no stockings. Their hair is plaited, and hangs down in tails behind. They wear a singular shaped head-dress, called a *tantoor*. Page, in his "Travels," speaks of it as a silver cone, and says it is evidently the same as Judith's mitre. Dr. Hogg thus describes one: "In length it was, perhaps, something

A Druze Female

more than a foot, but in shape had little resemblance to a horn, being a mere hollow tube, increasing in size from the diameter of an inch and an half at one extremity to three inches at the other, where it terminated like the mouth of a trumpet." This strange ornament, placed on a cushion, is securely fixed to the upper part of the forehead by two silk cords, which, after surrounding the head, hang behind nearly to the ground, terminating in large tassels. The material of which it is made is silver, rudely embossed with flowers, stars, and other devices, and the tassels are often capped with silver. The tantoor of an unmarried female is generally made of stiff paper, or some similar material. On being married it is the custom for the bridegroom

Druses: Moslem Arabs of a minority sect who live apart from their neighbors in Syria as well as Israel and Lebanon

Page, "Travels": Pierre Marie François de Pages wrote "Travels Round the World in the Years 1767-1771"; his travels included a sojourn in Palestine

Dr. Hogg: Edward Hogg's "Visit to Alexandria, Damascus and Jerusalem during the successful campaign of Ibrahim Pasha" was published 1835

to present his bride with one of silver, or silver tinsel. A veil is thrown over the smaller extremity of this head-dress, which descends nearly to the feet, and is drawn over the face when the wearer quits the seclusion of her home.

Tyre, once the "Queen of Nations," was formerly celebrated for the renowned purple dye, which is often mentioned by ancient writers, particularly by Homer and Virgil, who generally arrayed their heroes in vests and tunics of Tyrian purple, sometimes plain, at others ornamented. We read in the "Æneid" of

"The vests embroidered of the Tyrian dye;"

and, in another part,—

"Then two fair vests, of wondrous work and cost,
Of purple woven, and with gold emboss'd,
For ornament the Trojan hero brought,
Which with her hand Sidonian Dido wrought."

This queen, so celebrated in olden time for being the supposed foundatress of the renowned city of Carthage, appears to have possessed the talents of her countrywomen in the use of the needle; for Virgil often alludes to her skill; and probably the scarf she presented to Æneas was the work of her own fair fingers. Her dress is thus described :—

"The queen at length appears: on either hand
The brawny guards in martial order stand.
A flower'd cymarr, with golden fringe, she wore;
And at her back a golden quiver bore:
Her flowing hair a golden caul restrains;
A golden clasp the Tyrian robe sustains."

Tyre: city-state of the Phoenicians, now in Lebanon; its leaders founded ancient
    Carthage; Tyre was famous for textiles and its purple dye
Homer: Greek poet of unknown dates who wrote the "Iliad" and the "Odyssey"
Virgil: Roman poet, 70-19 B.C., wrote the "Æneid"
Tyrian purple: purple dye made at Tyre from secretions of the marine gastropods of the
    genus Murex; so famous that the Phoenicians are named for it (phoinix=purple in Greek)
"Æneid": narrative poem by Virgil on the voyages of Æneas after the fall of Troy
Sidonian Dido: Sidon was another city-state of Phoenicia, but Dido was actually the
    daughter of the King of Tyre and became Queen of Carthage (modern Tunis)
Æneas: hero of the Æneid

THE TOILETTE IN ARABIA.

CHAPTER XLVII.

Ordinary Arab Costume

E learn from various writers, both sacred and profane, that the ancient inhabitants of this sweet-scented land were the most commercial and civilized of the world; and "Araby the blessed" is honourably mentioned by Ptolemy, Strabo, and even Eratosthenes.

" Beautiful are the maids that glide
　　On summer eves through Yemen's* dales,
And bright the glancing looks they hide
　　Beneath their litter's roseate veils ;
And brides as delicate, as fair,
As the white jasmine flowers they wear,
Hath Yemen in her blissful clime,
　　Who, lull'd in cool kiosk or bower,
Before their mirrors count the time,
　　And grow still lovelier every hour."—MOORE.

　　* Arabia Felix.

Ptolemy: circa 367-283 B.C., General of Alexandria and King of Egypt
Strabo: Greek historian and geographer, circa 63 B.C.-24 A.D.
Eratosthenes: Greek astronomer and geographer, 3rd century B.C., and head of the
　　Library at Alexandria
Yemen – Arabia Felix: 'happy Arabia', the southwestern corner of Arabia, now North
　　Yemen

The costume of the Arabs, like that of most Eastern nations, consists of long robes, large trousers, an embroidered leathern girdle, and generally some weapon of defence, either a sword, knife, or dagger. There is, however, a great variety in their dresses. Notwithstanding the heat of the climate, the men wear a most preposterous head-dress, frequently fifteen linen, cloth, or cotton caps, one over the other, the upper one being gorgeously embroidered in gold, and a sentence from the Koran worked upon it. Not satisfied with this curious coiffure, they add to it by wrapping round the outer cap a large piece of muslin, ornamented at the ends with silk and golden fringes, which stream loosely upon their shoulders.

Of so much importance is the coiffure with this people, that, though when at home they perhaps allow their heads to feel the luxury of coolness and lightness, by laying aside twelve or thirteen of the caps, still, when on any visit of importance or ceremony, they dare not appear without the proper number. Writers on Arabian manners even assert, that those who wish to pass for men of learning shew their pretensions to that distinction by the size and weight of their coiffure.

It has been suggested that these extraordinary wrappings may be necessary to secure the wearer from the intense heat of the sun. This opinion is the more probable, as in ancient Egyptian monuments the same head-dresses are frequently seen.

The common dress of the Arabs is very simple. It generally consists of a large white, or white and blue, shirt; and over this they sometimes wear a garment like a great-coat without sleeves: in the province of Lachsa, in particular, this robe is worn by both men and women. The lower orders merely gird a piece of linen about their loins, and throw another piece over the shoulders; but never wear less than two or three caps, and have neither shoes nor stockings. In the mountains, where the climate is colder, they have sheep-skin garments.

Persons of the middle class have sandals instead of shoes; they are single soles, or thin pieces of wood, fastened to the feet with leathern thongs. Richer people wear slippers, and the women always use the latter covering for the feet. In several parts of Arabia the men do not wear drawers; but these last, with the addition of a shirt, always form the female dress. At Hedsjas, as in Egypt, they veil their faces with a piece of linen, leaving only the eyes uncovered. In Yemen the veil is much larger, and covers the face, so that even the eyes are not discernible. At Sana and Mokha the women wear a transparent gauze veil, embroidered in gold. They are very fond of rings on their fingers, arms, wrists, and ears; they stain their nails red, and their hands and feet of a brownish yellow, with the juice of a plant called *el henne*; they also paint all round the eyelids, and even the eyelashes themselves, with *kochhel*, which renders them quite black. Men even sometimes imitate this fashion, but it is considered effeminate.

The women of Yemen make black punctures on the face, which they consider improves their beauty. Fashion shews its influence in this country most particularly in the manner of wearing the hair and beard. In the states of Sana all men, whatever their rank, shave their heads; in other parts of Yemen it is the

Lachsa: name unknown; could be Hasa, a province on the east coast between Kuwait and Qatar
Hedsjas: Hejas/Hedjas, region in northwestern Saudi Arabia; Mecca is the chief city
Yemen: see note p. 476
Sana: ancient city, capital of North Yemen
Mokha: Mocha, seaport on the south coast
el henne: henna
kochhel: kohl, powdered antimony, used by most Middle Eastern peoples to darken the eyes and protect them from bright sunlight

universal custom to knot the hair up behind, and wrap it in a handkerchief. Caps and turbans are not in use here. In the mountain districts the hair is left long and loose, and is bound with small cords.

There is one universal fashion respecting beards —they are never touched, but are allowed to grow to their full length; the moustaches only are sometimes shortened. In Arabia the men's beards are always quite black; sometimes, when whitened by age, they dye them red, but it is a fashion not much admired or followed.

Dress of a Bedouin Arab

We learn from Niebuhr that, in Arabia, the Bedouins, or wandering Arabs, wear only a white robe, bound round the waist with a leathern girdle, which is very broad, and made with one large, and several small clasps. In both winter and summer they have a large goat-skin cloak, striped in black and white. On their heads they have only a red cap, surrounded with a piece of cloth of the same colour, or mixed with white.

The princes also wear the same dress; their cloak only is different, being almost always black. Their drawers are of linen, and reach to the lower part of the leg. They wear slippers when at home, and half-boots for riding. The labourers wear sandals.

The dress of Arabs of distinction in Yemen consists of a pair of wide cotton drawers, with a shirt over them. The cutlass is suspended to a broad girdle,

Niebuhr: Corrsten Niebuhr, German traveller, 1733–1815; his "Travels through Arabia and other Countries in the East" was published 1792
Bedouins: nomadic tribes of the Middle East, desert dwellers

and they have a vest with tight sleeves, surmounted by another that is large and flowing. They have no

An Arab of Distinction

stockings, only slippers or half-boots. In Niebuhr's "Travels" the dress of the Iman of Sana is thus described: " His gown was of a bright green colour, and had large sleeves; on each side of his breast was a rich filleting of gold lace, and on his head he wore a great gold turban."

All Arabians of rank have one curious addition to their dress. It is a piece of fine linen upon the shoulder, which, probably, was formerly intended to keep off the heat of the sun, but is now used only as an ornament.

Carreri states, that the Arabian women wear black

Niebuhr: see note p. 479
Iman of Sana: an Imam is a religious leader, who often is also a Caliph or ruling
  prince
Carreri: John Francis Gemelli Careri's "A Voyage Around the World" was published 1732

masks, with elegant little clasps; and Niebuhr mentions their shewing but one eye in conversation. In Moore, also, we find these lines:

> " And veil'd by such a mask as shades
> The features of young Arab maids,
> A mask that leaves but one eye free
> To do its best in witchery."

In many parts of Arabia the women wear little looking-glasses on their thumbs. All the women of the East are particularly fond of being able to gaze upon their own fair countenances, and seldom go without a looking-glass.

The Arabian princesses wear golden rings on their fingers, to which little bells are suspended, as well as in the flowing tresses of their hair, that their superior rank may be known, and they may receive the homage due to them. The following lines of L. E. L. might serve for the description of an Arabian princess:

> " Her silken hair, that, glossy black,
> But only to be found
> There, or upon the raven's back,
> Falls sweeping to the ground.
> 'Tis parted in two shining braids
> With silver and with gold,
> And one large pearl by contrast aids
> The darkness of each fold.
> Close to her throat the silvery vest
> By shining clasps is bound;
> Scarce may her graceful shape be guess'd,
> 'Mid drapery floating round.
> Upon the ankle and the wrist
> There is a band of gold,
> No step by Grecian fountain kiss'd
> Was of diviner mould.

Moore: Thomas Moore, see note p. 429
L.E.L.: Letitia Elizabeth Landon, 1802–1838, was a poetess and novelist

In the bright girdle round her waist,
  Where the red rubies shine,
The kandjar's glittering hilt is placed,
  To mark her royal line."

And with these graphic verses will we terminate our account of the Toilette in Arabia; and, at the same time, close our " Book of Costume," in the hope that it may be found useful and interesting to the many readers who require general information on the subject.

THE END.

kandjar: a type of dagger

APPENDIX A

p. 142: "Nœud de rubans..." Knot of ribbons which women wear as part of their hairstyle, and which takes its name from Lady de Fontange.

p. 149: "L'usage des mouches..." The use of patches is not unknown to French women, but it is necessary to be young and pretty. In England, young, old, beautiful, ugly — all use patches up to their last years; I have several times counted fifteen or more patches on the dark and raddled visage of a woman of 70. Thus the English improve upon our styles.

p. 201: "On donne le los..." We generally give Queen Isabelle of Bavaria, wife of King Charles VI, the credit for introducing to France the pomp and the gorgeous materials necessary for women to dress in elaborate and brilliant fashions.

p. 205: "La mutation et..." Change and variety in dress has always been natural for the French, more than any other nation, from which they received more fame for inconstancy than benefit. For in this year 1461 the women of Lyon, who formerly wore long trains to their gowns, changed and displayed at their hems large, broad flaps, some of baby squirrel, or of marten fur, or of other similar materials, each according to her class, and all trying to surpass one another; and on their heads bearing pointed pads or cushions like steeples, most of them half or three-quarters of an ell tall [24"-36", using the Lyon ell of 47.75" as a guide]; and were called by some "big butterflies", because they had two wide wings, on either side, like butterfly wings, and this tall headdress was covered with a large veil, falling to the ground, which most carried on their arm [the hennin and veil]. There were others who wore a headdress which was composed in part of wool cloth, or of mixed silk, which had two horns, like two towers, and this headdress was short and flowing like a German hat, or crêpe-y like a calf tripe; and they wore gowns having very narrow sleeves from the shoulder to the hand, at which point they widened and were cut in waves. The women of the middle class wore hoods of wool cloth, made in several wide widths, or folded bands twisted around the head, and two wings at the sides, like a donkey's ears. There were others, of the upper class, who wore hoods of black velvet, an arm's-length tall, which we now find extremely ugly and strange. One can hardly describe the different fashions of women's clothes simply in words, and it is really necessary to see a picture. We can see many such styles in the tapestries at Lyon, and in church windows of that period. Besides all this, the young women, from the time they are betrothed until a full year after their marriage, wore a head ornament which the Lyonnais call a "Floccard", which they leave off after the first year, returning to the wearing of hoods as described above.

p. 231: "Imaginez vous..." Imagine a head combed peasant style over a two-inch pad; one cuts the hair at either side, layer by layer, from which are made great curls, round and casual, which barely fall more than an inch below the ear; it makes a very young and pretty style, like two large bouquets of hair, on each side. One must not cut the hair too short; but as it is necessary that these curls, which take up a great length [of hair], wave naturally, several women have been quite taken in, and their example makes others tremble. Ribbons are put on in the usual way, and a large curl between the pad and the coiffure; sometimes it is allowed to fall to the bosom.

p. 232: "Ces coëffures..." These hairstyles are awfully amusing: some make me want to box their [owners'] ears.

p. 232: "Je la trouvai..." I found her quite unkempt; no wig; a little cap of old Venice lace, a black scarf, a faded gray dress and an old petticoat.

p. 232: "Votre belle-sœur..." Your sister-in-law has a mouse which does quite well in her dark hair; amusing affectation!

p. 232: "Vous avez donc peur..." So you've been afraid of these poor little dark birds; I wondered about that, and laughed to myself: you think they have a sad look: but at least they aren't sulky at all; they don't have shrewish voices; and when you see what they know how to do, you'll find that — rather than being thought ugly — they make their hairstyle, at least, a thing of beauty.

p. 233: "Je voudrois que vous eussiez vu..." I wish you could have seen the excess which the presence of Termes and Flamarens has brought to the hairstyles and dress of two or three young ladies of this place: really, from six in the morning, everything is in a flurry, headdress, little curls all round the face, powdered, crimped; cap à la Bascule, rouge, patches, a long curl dangling in back, fan, bodice long and tight; I could faint from laughing.

p. 234: "Avez-vous oüi parler..." Have you heard tell of the 'transparents'? These are entire dresses of the loveliest gold or blue brocades one could see, and over this gowns of sheer black stuff, or of lovely English lace, or of velvety chenille on tissue, like the winter laces, which you have seen: this makes a 'transparent', which is a black gown and a gown all of gold or silver or a color, as you like; and there is the fashion.

p. 235: "M. de Langlée..." M. de Langlée has given Mme de Montespan a dress of gold on gold, embroidered in gold, interlined in gold, and over this a gold frisé embossed with gold mixed with a special gold, which makes the most divine fabric ever imagined: it was fairies who did this work in secret; not a living soul knew anything about it. Someone wanted to give it as mysteriously as it was made: Mme de Montespan's tailor brought her the dress she had ordered; he had cut it to a ridiculous size: there are wails and grumbling as you can imagine; the tailor says, shaking, 'Madame, as time is so short, see if this other dress which has appeared might not suit you, for lack of any other.' The dress is revealed; ah, it's so beautiful! ah, what fabric! did it fall from the sky? there is nothing else like it on earth: they try the dress on; it fits like a glove. The King arrives: the tailor says, 'Madame, it is made for you: one understands this is a gallant gesture; but who can have done it?' 'It is Langlée,' says the King; 'Assuredly, it is Langlée,' says Mme de Montespan; 'no one but he could have dreamed of such magnificence; it's Langlée, it's Langlée.' Everyone is saying, 'It is Langlée;' the echoes agree and say, 'It is Langlée,' and I, my daughter, I say to you, in order to be in style, 'It is Langlée.'

p. 236: "Madame de Coësquen..." Mme de Coësquen has had made a petticoat of black velvet with masses of gold and silver embroidery, and a dress of tissue in flame, gold, and silver: this outfit cost a vast amount, and when she is so resplendant, she looks like an actress.

p. 237: "Les manches du chevalier..." The knight's sleeves make a lovely scene at table; although they carry everything along with them, I don't think they carry me along, too; whatever weakness I may have for fashion, I have a great dislike for such dirtiness.

p. 238: "J'ai vu des manches..." I saw some sleeves like the knight's. Hmph, they are so beautiful in the soup, and on the salad!

p. 240: "Je vous dirai une nouvelle..." I shall tell you the greatest, most important news you could possibly hear, which is that M. le Prince had his beard done yesterday; he was shaved, it is no illusion, nor one of those rumors one hears, it is absolutely true: all his court were witnesses, and Mme de Langeron, taking her opportunity while he sat with his paws crossed like the Lion, dressed him in a doublet with diamonds in the buttonholes; a valet, also taxing his patience, curled his hair, powdered him, and reduced him finally to being the handsomest man at court, and a head which outshone all the wigs; there was the prodigy of the wedding: the Prince's outfit was beyond valuation, it was embroidered with enormous diamonds which followed the design of black cut velvet on a straw-colored ground, they say that the straw color was not a success and that Mme de Langeron, who is the inspiration of all the finery at Condé's house, was quite ill about it; anyway, this is the kind of thing which provides no consolation. The Duke, the Duchess, and Lady de Bourbon had three outfits decorated with jewels, a different one for each of the three days; but I forgot the best part, that the Prince's sword was decorated with diamonds —

> The famous sword
> Whose worth is assured without a victory.

The lining of the Prince's cloak was of black satin, quilted with diamonds like speckling.

p. 242: "Jamais les Français..." The French had never been more creative than at this period; never before had voluptuousness of all types so multiplied to surround a woman with their exquisite elegance. The staff of a perfectly correct woman's household never had fewer than two ladies' maids and nearly always there was a valet, also. A bathroom was essential, for an elegant woman did not pass two days without bathing; and then the perfumes in abundance, the lawns, the finest linens, the most costly laces, for each season, were on the dressing table, in the 'sultans' — amber-scented baskets covered in Spanish leather — which held the basic necessities for the toilette of a wealthy woman.

p. 247: "Ancien officier de cavalerie..." A former cavalry officer, he had retained, in spite of the times, reform, and revolution, the heavy, cuffed horseman's boots, the military bag wig, short on the top and at the sides, with a tightly tied pigtail; short breeches, the coat with big metal buttons, and the tight, close-fitting waistcoat. Below this waistcoat hung two immense watch chains, with such a collection of charms that, when I did not hear the noise he and his horse usually made, I was always forewarned as soon as he began walking up the stairs.

p. 248: "La noblesse..." The nobility were to be dressed in the following way: black coat, with waistcoat and facings in gold, silk cloak, lace jabot, and hat with curled plume in the style of Henri IV. The clergy were to appear in cassock, large cloak, square cap; bishops were distinguished by the purple robe and the linen surplice. As for the commons, their outfit was the most modest. They were condemned to a black wool suit, a plain black silk cloak, a linen cravat, and a flat hat with neither braid nor buttons. [Note: The sumptuary laws of Napoléon I were promulgated on the advice of the designer and painter Jean-Baptiste Isabey, whose portrait was painted by Gérard in 1795, wearing the "Titus" hairstyle, carmagnole jacket, hunting waistcoat or jerkin, and pantaloons, but soft leather shoes rather than sabots.]

p. 249: "Madame Leclerc..." Mme Leclerc's hair that day was arranged with strips of an expensive fur, I don't know its name, but a short fur on a very supple skin and sprinkled with small tiger-like marks. Above these bands of fur were arranged bunches of grapes in gold, but not so that the hair was as high as today's styles. A dress of India muslin, excessively delicate, with a border at the hem, four or five inches deep, of gold spangles embroidered in a design representing a garland of vine branches. A tunic of the purest Greek cut was draped on her pretty form and also had at the hem an embroidered border like the one on the dress. The tunic was held at the shoulders by extremely costly cameos. The sleeves, very short and lightly pleated, had a small cuff and were also held by cameos. The belt, set high, as we see it on statues, was made of burnished gold and the buckle was a superb stone engraved in Grecian style.

p. 250: "An nombre des folies..." Among the extravagances of this period, wigs played an important part. Nothing can be compared to the absurdity of this fashion. A brunette had to have a blonde wig; a blonde, a brown one. Finally, a wig became a necessary part of the trousseau. I have seen some that cost as much as 8,000 to 10,000 frances (but in credit notes, which amounted to 150 or 200 francs in silver).

p. 250: "Les vêtemens..." Clothes suffered from the effects of political change. Good taste consisted of dressing like a soldier, which is to say wearing pantaloons and a jerkin. Those who observed fashion's dictates wore wooden shoes; rather than a cane, they carried a gnarled stick. Their hair was worn short and close to the head, and they wore a red [Phrygian] cap with a cockade; I have seen millionaires in this get-up. On November 22, in the Paris City Council, a rather lively discussion arose on the question of whether members of the local constituencies should be allowed only to wear the red cap, or if they should be given the freedom of deciding their headdress individually; it was decided that each could coif himself in his own way. The night before, this council had taken steps to proscribe dark wigs in the Jacobite style. Women, in their clothes, wore nothing out of the ordinary beyond the tricolor cockade on their caps, or on their hats, the shape of which was a truncated cone. Their hair fell loose on their shoulders and, cut short in front, covered half their foreheads.

p. 251: "Les Muscadins portaient..." The dandies wore grey frock coats with black collars and green ties; and their hair, rather than being arranged à la Titus like most young people's, was braided, powdered, and held by a comb in such a way that, at each side of the face, a long lock fell, which was called, in the style of the time, "dogs' ears".

p. 252: "D'une immense corbeille..." From an enormous basket or, rather, a trunk of pink Naples silk embroidered with black chenille, bearing my monogram and strongly scented with Spanish leather, a great quantity of little packets tied with narrow pink and blue ribbons appeared. There were chemises with crystal-pleated sleeves, embroidered, even embroidered as Mlle l'Olive does such work; handkerchiefs, petticoats, morning gowns, wrappers of India muslin, night gowns, night caps, morning caps in all colors, in all shapes, and all embroidered, with Val lace trim, or Malines, or English point. At this time, the excellent custom of not giving basketry had not yet begun; it was in a basket that one found the cashmere shawls, the English point lace veils, the dress trimmings in needle lace, or Brussels point, or in blonde lace for summer. There were also entire dresses of white blonde lace, and of black lace; lengths of India muslin, lengths of Turk-ish velvet that the General had brought back from Egypt, ball gowns suitable for a married woman; my presentation gown*; dresses of India muslin embroid-ered with silver sequins and artificial flowers from Mme Roux's shop; ribbons in all widths and colors, handbags, fans, gloves, scent from Fargeon and from Riban, sachets of Spanish leather and of herbs from Montpellier; in fact, no-thing had been forgotten. —— In the morning, 9 o'clock had hardly struck be-fore we began the semi-formal toilette I would wear to go to the Mayor's office. I had a dress of India muslin embroidered in feather stitch and openwork, as was then the fashion. This dress had a train, a high neck, and long sleeves; the border in front was covered with embroidery, as were the waist, the bodice, and the sleeve ends, which we called "amadis" at that time. ["Amadis" was the term applied to a series of sleeve styles which changed over time although "amadis" was used for them all.] The neck ruffle was of magnificent needle lace. On my head, I had a cap of Brussels lace, designed by Mlle Despaux; at the crown of the bonnet, a little circlet of orange blossom was attached, and from that point, a long veil of English lace fell to my feet, so wide I could have wrapped myself up in it. This ensemble, which was the one worn by all brides, and which dif-fered only in being more or less elaborate from one young bride to another, had, in my opinion, much more charm and elegance than those we see nowadays.

—— *Note: What was odd about this dress was that, since one never again wore a dress made especially for an appearance at Court, a custom which came in only under the Empire, Mme Germon felt herself obliged, hearing my mother say the words "presentation gown", to make a dress completely different from the others. This dress had a train, which was nothing unusual then, as they were always worn that way for evening. But it was the same style as the gowns worn on the stage. It was open, and showed [beneath] a petticoat in crêpe with silver sequins; the dress itself was of a rich Lyon fabric imitative of the Orien-tal silver brocades.

p. 254: "Ce costume était..." This costume was at that time very nearly what it is these days; the chérusque*, which fell out of favor very soon after, was very becoming for all that; the dress and petticoat were as we always wear them, with this difference, that in the beginning the embroidered hem of the dress could not be more than four inches wide; only the princesses had the right to wear dresses embroidered all over. Such were the original orders of the Emperor. It was, he had said to my husband, up to us to set the example of moderation and not, by excessive display, crush the wife of an officer with no fortune, or of a respect-able scholar.
    *Chérusque: [Medici] standing ruff with deep points of tulle outlined in gold or silver to match the overdress. [The coronation portrait of Napoleon I and Joseph-ine, painted by David in 1804, shows Josephine wearing a chérusque.]

p. 255: "La toilette de l'impératice..." The Empress's ensemble was admirable for its good taste and daintiness; she wore a dress of India muslin, one of those muslins one could almost say were made of air but which, in spite of its deli-cacy, had been embroidered in feather stitch with a sprinkling of little stars whose centers were filled with a spot of drawn work. The dress had a high neck and was cut like a frock coat; all around was a border of magnificent English lace, eight inches wide and heavily gathered; the neckline and front of the dress had similar amounts [of gathered lace]; at intervals there were knots of blue satin ribbon, so fresh, so pure a shade of turquoise blue, you have never seen anything so charming; the underskirt was of satin in the same blue as the ribbons; on her head, the Empress wore a cap whose lappets were of English point in the same design as that on her dress, but on a smaller scale, and gracefully arranged and set off by little clusters of the blue ribbon with no flowers in the arrangement at all.

p. 255: "La jupe et le manteau..." The petticoat and dress were alike; both of tulle embroidered with gold sequins, but with infinite delicacy. The pattern was of squares within squares, set on their points and interlocking, which formed, not a fabric of gold, but a beautifully composed network. A small fringe bordered the cape and the dress. Then around the bodice, the sleeves, the belt, all were embroidered in emeralds surrounded by diamonds. The tiara, the comb, the earrings ... all in emeralds.
  [cf. David's "Coronation of Napoleon", noted above, where Josephine wears both a tiara and a jewelled comb on the crown of her head.]

p. 299: "Je mis par-dessus..." I put on, over this monstrous mountain which surrounded me completely, a beautiful dress of white watered silk embroidered with gold sequins and caught up at the sides by large gold tassels, absolutely as if I were wearing a set of curtains. I put on my head a toque with six large white feathers held by a diamond clip, the base of the toque embroidered with clusters of diamonds; I also had them at the throat and on my ears; and, thus decked out, I left for Queluz Palace.

p. 300: "Elle avait ses cheveux..." She had her white hair pulled to the top of her head with a ribbon, as we still see it sometimes in pictures.
  [In this and the next quotation, the hair is arranged in what we now call a ponytail, drawn close to the head and falling from a rather high-placed tie or twisted into a bun around the tie.]

p. 300: "Il y a encore..." There are still many Portuguese women of high rank who wear their hair this way at home. Whenever they go out, they do their hair in the French style; but, for example in the interior of the country, I have seen some who never wear any other hairstyle.

p. 300: "C'était la plus étrange..." It was the strangest masquerade one could imagine as clothing for a Christian. It was a petticoat of heavy taffeta, quite thick, in deep blue, with a broad border of gold embroidery at the hem, and then along with it a tail, a gown, I don't know what, a piece of fabric of a startling red which hung behind them like a train. The oldest, just like our little chambermaid, wore a tiny toque, a sort of cap, quite close to the head (they were widows, I think) and on this cap was a big flower of the same blue as the petticoat.

APPENDIX B

Excerpts from The Art of Needle-Work, from the Earliest Ages, The Right Honourable The Countess of Wilton, ed. 1841 3rd edition, Henry Colburn, London; appended here for further information and not annotated.

"Needlework in Costume"

Manifold indeed were the varieties in mode and material before that beau ideal of all that is graceful and becoming — the "black breeches" — were invented. For though in many parts of the globe costume is uniform, and the vest and the turban of a thousand years ago are of much the same make as now, this is not the case in the more polished parts of Europe, where that "turncoat whirligig maniac, yclept Fashion," is the pole-star and beacon of the multitude of men, from him who has the "last new cut from Stultz," to him who is magnificent and happy in the "reg'lar bang-up-go" from the eastern parts of the metropolis.

It would seem that England is peculiarly celebrated for her devotion at Fashion's shrine; for we are told that "an Englishman, endevoring sometime to write of our attire, made sundrie platformes for his purpose, supposing by some of them to find out one stedfast ground whereon to build the summe of his discourse. But in the end (like an orator long without exercise) when he saw what a difficult peece of work he had taken in hand, he gave over his travell, and onely drue the picture of a naked man, unto whome he gave a paire of sheares in the one hand, and a piece of cloth in the other, to the end he should shape his apparell after such fashion as himselfe liked, sith he could find no kind of garment that could please him anie while together, and this he called an Englishman. Certes this writer shewed himself herein not to be altogether void of iudjement, sith the phantasticall follie of our nation, even from the courtier to the carter, is such, that no forme of apparell liketh vs longer than the first garment is in the wearing, if it continue so long and be not laid aside, to receive some other trinket newlie devised.

"And as long as these fashions are diverse, so likewise it is a world to see the costlinesse and the curiositie; the excesse and the vanitie; the pompe and the brauerie; the change and the varietie; and, finallie, the ficklenesse and the follie that is in all degrees; insomuch that nothing is more constant in England than inconstancie of attire.

"In women, also, it is most to be lamented, that they doo now far exceed the lightnesse of our men (who nevertheless are transformed from the cap even to the verie shoo) and such staring attire as in time past was supposed meet for none but light housewives onlie, is now become a habit for chast and sober matrons.

"Thus it is now come to passe, that women are become men, and men transformed into monsters."

This ever-revolving wheel is still turning; and so all-important now is THE MODE that one half of the world is fully occupied in providing for the personal embellishment of the other half and themselves; and could we contemplate the possibility of a return to the primitive simplicity of our ancient "sires," we must look in the same picture on one half of the world as useless — as a drug on the face of creation. Why, what a desert would it be were all dyers, fullers, cleaners, spinners, weavers, printers, mercers and milliners, haberdashers and modistes, silk-men and manufacturers, cotton-lords and fustian-men, tailors and habit makers, mantuamakers and corset professors, exploded? We pass over pin and needle makers, comb and brush manufacturers, jewellers, &c. The ladies would have nothing to live for; (for on grave authority it has been said, that "woman is an animal that delights in the toilette;") the gentlemen nothing to solace them.

"The toilette" is the very zest of life with both; and if ladies are more successful in the results of their devoirs to it, it is because "nous sommes faites pour
embellir le monde [we are made to embellish the world]," and not because gentlemen
practice its duties with less zeal, devotion, or assiduity — as many a valet can testify when contemplating his modish patron's daily heap of "failures." Indeed to put
out of view the more obvious, weighty, and important cares attached to the due selection and arrangement of coats, waistcoats, and indispensables, the science of "Cravat-
iana" alone is one which makes heavy claims on the time, talents, and energies of the
thorough-going gentleman of fashion. He should be thoroughly versed in all its varieties — The Royal George: The Plain Bow: The Military: The Ball Room: The Corsican:
The Hibernian Tie: The Eastern Tie: The Hunting Tie: The Yankee Tie: (the "alone original" one) — The Osbaldiston Tie: The Mail Coach Tie: The Indian Tie, &c. &c. &c.

Though of these and their numberless offshoots, the Yankee Tie lays most claim to
originality, the Ball Room one is considered the most exquisite, and requires the
greatest practice. It is thus described by a "talented" professor: —

"The cloth, of virgin white, well starched and folded to the proper depth, should
be made to sit easy and graceful on the neck, neither too tight nor loose; but with a
gentle pressure, curving inwards from the further extension of the chin, down the
throat to the centre dent in the middle of the neck. This should be the point for a
slight dent, extending from under each ear, between which, more immediately under the
chin, there should be another slight horizontal dent just above the former one. It
has no tie; the ends, crossing each other in broad folds in front, are secured to the
braces, or behind the back, by means of a piece of white tape. A brilliant broach or
pin is generally made use of to secure more effectually the crossing, as well as to
give an additional effect to the neckcloth."

What a world of wit and invention — what a fund of fancy and taste — what a mine
of zeal and ability would be lost to the world, "if those troublesome disguises which
we wear" were reduced to their old simplicity of form and material! Industry and tal-
ent would be at discount, for want of materials whereon to display themselves; and
money would be such a drug, that politicians would declaim on the miseries of being
without a national debt. Commerce, in many of its most important branches, would be
exploded; the "manufacturing districts" would be annihiliated; the "agricultural interest" would, consequently and necessarily, be at a "very low ebb;" and the "New
World," the magnificent and imperial empress (that is to be) of the whole earth,
might sink again to the embraces of those minute and wonderful artificers from whom,
I suppose, she at first proceeded — the coral insects; for who would want cotton! No,
no. Selfish preferences, individual wishes, must merge in the general good of the human race; and however "their own painted skins" might suffice our "sires,' clothing,
"sumptuous," as well as "for use," must decorate ourselves.

To whom, then, are the fullers, the dyers, the cleaners — to whom are the spinners
and weavers, and printers and mercers, and milliners and haberdashers, and modistes,
and silk-men and manufacturers, cotton lords and fustian men, mantua-makers and corset
professors, indepted for that nameless grace, that exquisite finish and appropriate-
ness, which gives to all their productions their charm and their utility? — To the
NEEDLEWOMAN, assuredly. For though the raw materials have been grown at Sea Island
and shipped at New York, — have been consigned to the Liverpool broker and sold to
the Manchester merchant, and turned over to the manufacturer, and spun and woven, and
bleached and printed, and placed in the custody of the warehouseman, or on the shelf
of the shopkeeper — of what good would it be that we had a fifty-yard length of calico to shade our oppressed limbs on a "dog-day," if we had not the means also to render
that material agreeably available? Yet not content with merely rendering it available,
this beneficent fairy, the needlewoman, casts, "as if by the spell of enchantment,
that ineffable grace over beauty which the choice and arrangement of dress is calculated

to bestow." For the love of becoming ornament — we quote no less an authority than the historian of the 'State of Europe in the Middle Ages,' — "is not, perhaps, to be regarded in the light of vanity; it is rather an instinct which woman has received from Nature to give effect to those charms which are her defence." And if it be necessary to woman with her charms, is it not tenfold necessary to those who — Heaven help them! — have few charms whereof to boast? For, as Harrison says, "It is now come to passe that men are transformed into monsters."

"Better be out of the world than out of the fashion," is a proverb which, from the universal assent which has in all ages been given to it, has now the force of an axiom. It was this self evident proposition which emboldened the beau of the fourteenth century, in spite of the prohibitions of popes and senators, — in spite of the more touching personal inconvenience, and even risk and danger, attendant thereupon — to persist in wearing shoes of so preposterous a length, that the toes were obliged to be fastened with chains to the girdle ere the happy votary of fashion could walk across his own parlour! Happy was the favourite of Crœsus, who could display chain upon chain of massy gold wreathed and intertwined from the waistband to the shoe, until he seemed almost weighed down by the burthen of his own wealth. Wrought silver did excellently well for those who could not produce gold; and for those who possessed not either precious metal, and who yet felt they "might as well be out of the world as out of the fashion," latteen chains, silken cords, aye, and cords of even less costly description, were pressed into service to tie up the crackowes, or piked shoes. For in that day, as in this, "the squire endeavours to outshine the knight, the knight the baron, the baron the early, the earl the king, in dress." To complete the outrageous absurdity of these shoes, the upper parts of them were cut in imitation of a church-window, to which fashion Chaucer refers when describing the dress of Absalom, the Parish Clerk. He —

"Had Paul 'is windowes corven on his shose."

Despite the decrees of councils, the bulls of the Pope, and the declamations of the Clergy, this ridiculous fashion was in vogue near three centuries.

And the party-coloured hose, which were worn about the same time, were a fitting accompaniment for the crackowes. We feel some difficulty in realising the idea that gentlemen, only some half century ago, really dressed in the gay and showy habiliments which are now indicative only of a footman; but it is more difficult to believe, what was nevertheless the fact, that the most absurd costume in which the "fool" by profession can now be decked on the stage, can hardly compete in absurdity with the outré costume of a beau or a belle of the fourteenth century. The shoes we have referred to: the garments, male or female, were divided in the middle down the whole length of the person, and one half of the body was clothed in one colour, the other half in the most opposite one that could be selected. The men's garments fitted close to the shape; and while one leg and thigh rejoiced in flaming yellow or sky-blue, the other blushed in deep crimson. John of Gaunt is portrayed in a habit, one half white, the other a dark blue; and Mr. Strutt has an engraving of a group assembled on a memorable occasion, where one of the figures has a boot on one leg and a shoe on the other. The Dauphiness of Auvergne, wife to Louis the Good, Duke of Bourbon, born 1360, is painted in a garb of which one half all the way down is blue, powdered with gold fleurs-de-lys, and the other half to the waist is gold, with a blue fish or dolphin (a cognizance, doubtless) on it and from the waist to the feet is crimson, with white "fishy" ornaments; one sleeve is blue and gold, the other crimson and gold.

In addition to these absurd garments, the women dressed their heads so high that they were obliged to wear a sort of curved horn on each side, in order to support the enormous superstructure of feathers and furbelows. And these are what are meant by the "horned head-dresses" so often referred to in old authors. It is said that, when Isabel of Bavaria kept her court at Vincennes, A.D. 1416, it was necessary to make all the doors of the palace both higher and wider, to admit the head-dresses of the queen and her ladies, which were all of this horned kind.

This high bonnet had been worn, under various modifications, ever since the fashion was brought from the East in the time of the Crusades. Some were of a sugar-loaf form, three feet in height; and some cylindrical, but still very high. The French modistes of that day called this formidable head-gear bonnet à la Syrienne. But our author says, if female vanity be violently restrained in one point, it is sure to break out in another; and Romish anathemas having abolished curls from shading fair brows, so much the more attention was paid to head-gear, that the bonnets and caps increased every year most awfully in height and size, and were made in the form of crescents, pyramids, and horns of such tremendous dimensions, that the old chronicler Juvenal des Ursins makes this pathetic lamentation in his History of Charles VI.: —

"Et avoient les dames et damoyselles de chacun coste, deux grandes oreilles si larges, que quand elles vouloient passer par l'huis d'une chambre il fallait qu'elles se tournassent de coste et baisassent, ou elles n'eussent pu passer;" that is, "on every side old ladies and young ladies were seen with such high and monstrous ears (or horns), that when they wanted to enter a room they were obliged perforce to stoop and crouch sideways, or they could not pass." At last a regular attack was made on the high head-gear of the fifteenth century by a popular monk, in his sermons at Notre Dame, in which he so pathetically lamented the sinfulness and enormities of such a fashion, that the ladies, to show their contrition, made auto da fés of their Syrian bonnets in the public squares and market-places; and as the Church fulminated against them all over Europe, the example of Paris was universally followed.

Many attempts had previously been made by zealous preachers to effect this alteration. In the previous century a Carmelite in the province of Bretagne preached against this fashion, without the power to annihilate it: all that the ladies did was to change the particular shape of the huge coiffures after every sermon. "No sooner," says the chronicler, "had he departed from one district, than the dames and damoyselles, who, like frightened snails, had drawin in their horns, shot them out again longer than ever; for nowhere were the hennins (so called, abbreviated from gehinnin, incommodious) larger, more pompous or proud, than in the cities through which the Carmelite had passed.

"All the world was totally reversed and disordered by these fashions, and above all things by the strange accoutrements on the heads of the ladies. It was a portentous time, for some carried huge towers on their foreheads an ell high; others still higher caps, with sharp points, like staples [steeples], from the top of which streamed long crapes, fringed with gold, like banners." Alas, alas! ladies, dames, and demoiselles were of importance in those days! When do we hear, in the present times, of Church and State interfering to regulate the patterns of their bonnets?"*

It is no wonder that fashions so very extreme and absurd should call forth animadversion from various quarters. Thus wrote Petrarch in 1366: —

"Who can see with patience the monstrous, fantastical inventions which the people of our times have invented to deform, rather than adorn, their persons? Who can behold without indignation their long pointed shoes; their caps with feathers; their hair twisted and hanging down like tails; the foreheads of young men, as well as women, formed into a kind of furrows with ivory-headed pins; their bellies so cruelly squeezed with cords, that they suffer as much pain from vanity as the martyrs suffered for religion? Our ancestors would not have believed, and I know not if posterity will believe, that it was possible for the wit of this vain generation of ours

*Lady's Magazine

to invent so many base, barbarous, horrid, ridiculous fashions (besides those already mentioned) to disfigure and disgrace itself, as we have the mortification to see every day."

And thus Chaucer, a few years later: —

"Alass! may not a man see as in our daies the sinnefull costlew array of clothing', and namely in too much superfluite, or else in too disordinate scantinesse: as to the first, not only the cost of embraudering, the disguysed indenting, or barring, ounding, playting, wynding, or bending, and semblable waste of clothe in vanitie." The common people also "were besotted in excesse of apparell, in wide surcoats reaching to their loines, some in a garment reaching to their heels, close before and strowting out on the sides, so that on the back they make men seem women, and this they called by a ridiculous name, gowne," &c. &c.

Before this time the legislature had interfered, though with little success: they passed laws at Westminster, which were said to be made "to prevent that destruction and poverty with which the whole kingdom was threatened, by the outrageous, excessive expenses of many persons in their apparel, above their ranks and fortunes."

Sumptuary edicts, however, are of little avail, if not supported in "influential quarters." King Richard II. affected the utmost splendour of attire, and he had one coat alone which was valued at 30,000 marks: it was richly embroidered and inwrought with gold and precious stones. It is not in human nature, at least in human nature of the "more honourable" gender, to be outdone, even by a king. Gorgeous and glittering was the raiment adopted by the satellites of the court, and, heedless of "that destruction and poverty with which the whole kingdom was threatened," they revelled in magnificence.

It was in a subsequent reign, that of Mary, that a proclamation was issued that no man should "weare his shoes above six inches square at the toes." We have before seen that the attention of the grave and learned members of the Senate, the "Conscript Fathers" of England, was devoted to the due regulation of this interesting part of apparel, when the shoe-toes were worn so long that they were obliged to be tied up to the waist ere the happy and privileged wearer could set his foot on the ground. Now, however, "a change came o'er the spirit of the day," and it became the duty of those who exercised a paternal surveillance over the welfare of the community at large to legislate regarding the breadth of the shoe-toes, that they should not be above "six inches square."

"Great," was anciently the cry — "Great is Diana of the Ephesians;" but how immeasurably greater and mightier has been, through that and all succeeding ages, the supreme potentate who with a mesh of flimsy gauze or fragile silk has constrained nations as by a shackle of iron, that shadowy, unsubstantial, ever-fleeting yet everexacting deity — FASHION! At her shrine worship all the nations of the earth. The savage who bores his nose or tattooes his tawny skin is impelled by the same power which robes the courtly Eastern in flowing garments; and the dark-hued beauty who smears herself with blubber is influenced by the selfsame motive which causes the fair-haired daughter of England to tint her delicate cheek with the mimic rose.

And it is not merely in the shape and form of garments that this deity exercises her tyrannic sway, transforming "men into monsters," and women likewise — if it were possible: her vagaries are infinite and unaccountable; yet, how unaccountable soever, have ever numberless and willing votaries. It was once the fashion for people who either were or fancied themselves to be in love to prove the sincerity of their passion by the fortitude with which they could bear those extremes of heat and cold from which unsophisticated nature would shrink. These "penitents of love," for so the fraternity — and a pretty numerous one it was — was called, would clothe themselves in the dog-days in the thickest mantles lined throughout with the warmest fur: when the winds howled, the hail beat, and snow invested the earth with a freezing mantle, they wore the thinnest and most fragile garments. It was forbidden to wear fur on a day of the most piercing cold, or to appear with a hood, cloak, gloves, or muff. They supposed or pretended that the deity whom they thus propitiated was LOVE: we aver that the autocrat under whose irreversible decrees they thus succumbed — was FASHION.

And, after all, who is this all-powerful genius? What is her appearance? Whence does she arise? Did she alight from the skies, while rejoicing stars sang Pæans at her birth? Was she born of the Sunbeams while a glittering Rainbow cast a halo of glory around her? or did she spring from Ocean while Nereids revelled around, and Mermaids strung their Harps with their own golden locks, soft melodies the while floting along the glistering wave, and echoing from the Tritons' booming shells beneath? No. Alas, no! She is subtle as the air; she is evanescent as a sunbeam, and unsubstantial as the ocean's froth; but she is none of these. She is — but we will lay aside our own definition in order that the reader may have the advantage of that of one of the greatest and wisest of statesmen.

""Quelqu'un qui voudrait un peu étudier d'où part en première source ce qu'on appelle LES MODES verrait, à notre honte, qu'un petit nombre de gens, de la plus méprisable espèce qui soit dans une ville, laquelle renferme tout indifféremment dans son sein; pour qui, si nous les connaissions, nous n'aurions que le mépris qu'on a pour les gens sans meurs, ou la pitié qu'on a pour les fous, disposent pourtant de nos bourses, et nous tiennent assujettis à tous leurs caprices."

[Anyone who would like to discover the main origin of what is called The Mode would see, to our shame, it is a small number of people, of the most despicable sort to be found in a city, which holds them to its bosom all the same; these, for whom, if we knew them, we would feel only the contempt that one has for people completely without morals, or the pity one feels for the mad, still control our purses, and keep us kneeling before their whims.]

APPENDIX C

Excerpts on "The Field of the Cloth of Gold", from *The Art of Needle-Work*

Who shall record, or even refer to the hopes, and feelings, and wishes, and thoughts, and reflections of the thousands congregated thither; each one with feelings as intense, with hopes as individually important as those which influenced the royal King of France, or the majestic monarch of England! The loftiest of Christendom's knights, the loveliest of Christendom's daughters were assembled here; and the courteous Bayard, the noble Tremouille, the lofty Bourbon, felt inspired more gallantly, if possible, than was even their wont, when contending in all love and amity with the proudest of England's champions, in presence of the fairest of her blue-eyed maidens, — the noblest of her courtly dames.

Nor were the lofty and noble alone there congregated. After the magnificent structure for the king and court, after every thing in the shape of a tenement in, out, or about the little town of Guisnes, and the neighbouring hamlets, were occupied, two thousand eight hundred tents were set up on the side of the English alone. No noble or baron would be absent; but likewise knights, and squires, and yeomen flocked to the scene: citizens and city wives disported their richest silks and their heaviest chains; jews went for gain, pedlars for knavery, tradespeople for their craft, rogues for mischief. Then there were "vagaboundes, plowmen, laborers, wagoners, and beggers, that for drunkennes lay in routes and heaps, so great resorte thether came, that both knightes and ladies that wer come to see the noblenes, were faine to lye in haye and strawe, and hold theim thereof highly pleased."

The accommodations provided for the king and privileged members of his court on this occasion were more than magnificent; a vast and splendid edifice that seemed to be endued with the magnificence, and to rise almost with the celerity of that prepared by the slaves of the lamp, where the richest tapestry and silk embroidery — the costliest produce of the most accomplished artisans, were almost unnoticed amid the gold and jewellery by which they were surrounded — where all that art could produce, or riches devise had been lavished — all this has been often described. And the tent itself, the nucleus of the show, the point where the "brother" kings were to confer, was hung round with cloth of gold: the posts, the cones, the cords, the tents, were all of the same precious metal, which glittered here in such excessive profusion as to give that title to the meeting which has superseded all others — "The Field of the Cloth of Gold."

This gaudy pageant was the prelude to an era of great interest, for while dwelling on the "galanty shew" we cannot forget that now reigned Solyman the magnificent, and that this was the age of Leo the Tenth; that Charles the Fifth was now beginning his influential course; that a Sir Thomas More graced England; and that in Germany there was "one Martin Luther," who "belonged to an order of strolling friars." Under Leo's munificent encouragement, Rafaello produced those magnificent creations which have been the inspiration of subsequent ages; and at home, under Wolsey's enlightened patronage, colleges were founded, learning was encouraged, and the College of Physicians first instituted in 1518, found in him one of its warmest advocates and firmest supporters.

A modern writer gives the following amusing picture of part of the bustle attendant on the event we are considering. "The palace (of Westminster) and all its precincts became the elysium of tailors, embroiderers, and sempstresses. There might you see many a shady form gliding about from apartment to apartment, with smiling looks and extended shears, or armed with ell-wands more potent than Mercury's rod, driving many a poor soul to perdition, and transforming his goodly acres into velvet suits, with tags of cloth of gold. So continual were the demands upon every kind of artisan, that the impossibility of executing them threw several into despair. One tailor who is reported to have undertaken to furnish fifty embroidered suits in three days, on beholding the mountain of gold and velvet that cumbered his shop-board, saw, like Brutus, the impossibility of victory, and, with Roman fortitude, fell on his own shears. Three armourers are said to have been completely melted with the heat of their furnaces; and an unfortunate goldsmith swallowed molten silver to escape the persecutions of the day.

"The road from London to Canterbury was covered during one whole week with carts and waggons, mules, horses, and soldiers; and so great was the confusion, that marshals were at length stationed to keep the whole in order, which of course increased the said confusion a hundred fold. So many were the ships passing between Dover and Calais, that the historians affirm they jostled each other on the road like a herd of great black porkers.

"The King went from station to station like a shepherd, driving all the better classes of the country before him, and leaving not a single straggler behind."

Though we do not implicitly credit every point of this humorous statement, we think a small portion of description from the old chronicler Hall (we will really inflict only a small portion on our readers) will justify a good deal of it; but more especially it will enlighten us as to some of the elaborate conceits of the day, in which, it seems, the needle was as fully occupied as the pen.

Indeed, what would the "Field of the Cloth of Gold" have been without the skill of the needlewoman? Would it have been at all?

"The Frenche kyng sette hymself on a courser barded, covered with purple sattin, broched with golde, and embraudered with corbyns fethers round and buckeled; the fether was black and hached with gold. Corbyn is a rauen, and the firste silable of corbyn is Cor, whiche is a hart, a penne in English, is a fether in Frenche, and signifieth pain, and so it stode; this fether was endles, the buckels wherwith the fethers wer fastened, betokeneth sothfastnes, thus was the devise, harte fastened in pain endless, or pain in harte fastened endles.

"Wednesdaie the 13 daie of June, the twoo hardie kynges armed at all peces, entered into the feld right nobly appareled, the Frenche kyng and all his parteners of chalenge were arraied in purple sattin, broched with golde and purple velvet, embrodered with litle rolles of white sattin wherein was written quando, all bardes and garments wer set full of the same, and all the residue where was no rolles, were poudered and set with the letter ell as thus, L, whiche in Frenche is she, which was interpreted to be quando elle, when she, and ensuyng the devise of the first daie it signifieth together, harte fastened in pain endles, when she.

"The Frenche kyng likewise armed at al pointes mounted on a courser royal, all his apparel as wel bardes as garmentes were purple velvet, entred the one with the other, embrodred ful of little bookes of white satten, and in the bokes were written a me; aboute the borders of the bardes and the borders of the garmentes a chaine of blewe like iron, resemblyng the chayne of a well or prison chaine, whiche was enterpreted to be liber, a booke; within this boke was written as is sayed, a me, put these two together, and it maketh libera me; the chayne betokeneth prison or bondes, and so maketh together in Englishe, deliver me of bondes; put to ye reason, the fyrst day, second day, and third day of chaunge, for he chaunged but the second day, and it is hart fastened in paine endles, when she deliuereth me not of bondes; thus was thinterpretation made, but whether it were so in all thinges or not I may not say."

The following animated picture from an author already quoted, has been drawn of this spirit-stirring scene: —

"Upon a large open green, that extended on the outside of the walls, was to be seen a multitude of tents of all kinds and colours, with a multitude of busy human beings, employed in raising fresh pavilions on every open space, or in decorating those already spread with streamers, pennons, and banners of all the bright hues under the sun. Long lines of horses and mules, loaded with armour or baggage, and ornamented with gay ribbons to put them in harmony with the scene, were winding about all over the plain, some proceeding towards the town, some seeking the tents of their several lords, while mingled amongst them, appeared various bands of soldiers, on horseback and on foot, with the rays of the declining sun catching upon the heads of their bills and lances; and together with the white cassock and broad red cross, marking them out from all the other objects. Here and there, too, might be seen a party of knights and gentlemen cantering over the plain, and enjoying the bustle of the scene, or standing in separate groups, issuing their orders for the erection and garnishing of their tents; while couriers and poursuivants, and heralds, in all their gay dresses, mingled with mule drivers, lacqueys, and peasants, armourers, pages, and tent stretchers, made up the living part of the landscape.

"The sounding of the trumpets to horse, the shouts of the various leaders, the loud cries of the marshals and heralds, and the roaring of artillery from the castle, as the king put his foot in the stirrup, all combined to make one general outcry rarely equalled. Gradually the tumult subsided, gradually also the confused assemblage assumed a regular form. Flags, and pennons, and banderols, embroidered banners, and scutcheons; silver pillars, and crosses, and crooks, ranged themselves in long line; and the bright procession, an interminable stream of living gold, began to wind across the plain. First came about five hundred of the gayest and wealthiest gentlemen of England, below the rank of baron; squires, knights, and bannerets, rivalling each other in the richness of their apparel and the beauty of their horses; while the pennons of the knights fluttered above their heads, marking the place of the English chivalry. Next appeared the proud barons of the realm, each with his banner borne before him, and followed by a custrel with the shield of his arms. To these again succeeded the bishops, not in the simple robes of the Protestant clergy, but in the more gorgeous habits of the Church of Rome; while close upon their steps rode the higher nobility, surrounding the immediate person of the king, and offering the most splendid mass of gold and jewels that the summer sun ever shone upon.

"Slowly the procession moved forward to allow the line of those on foot to keep an equal pace. Nor did this band offer a less gay and pleasing sight than the cavalcade, for here might be seen the athletic forms of the sturdy English yeomanry, clothed in the various splendid liveries of their several lords, with the family cognisance embroidered on the bosom and arm, and the banners and banderols of their particular houses carried in the front of each company. Here also was to be seen the picked guard of the King of England, magnificently dressed for the occasion, with the royal banner carried in their centre by the deputy standard bearer, and the banner of their company by their own ancient. In the rear of all, marshalled by officers appointed for the purpose, came the band of those whose rank did not entitle them to take place in the cavalcade, but who had sufficient interest at court to be admitted to the meeting. Though of an inferior class, this company was not the least splendid in the field; for here were all the wealthy tradesmen of the court, habited in many a rich garment, furnished by the extravagance of those that rode before; and many a gold chain hung round their necks, that not long ago had lain in the purse of some prodigal customer."

But we cease, being fully of opinion with the old chronicler that "to tell the apparel of the ladies, their riche attyres, their sumptuous juelles, their diversities of beauties, and their goodly behaviour from day to day sithe the fyrst metyng, I assure you ten mennes wittes can scarce declare it."

And in a few days, a few short days, all was at an end; and the pomp and pageantry, the mirth and the revelry, was but as a dream — a most bitter, indeed, and painful dream to hundreds who had bartered away their substance for the sake of a transient glitter:

> "We seken fast after felicite
> But we go wrong ful often trewely,
> Thus may we sayen all."

Index of some costume terms used in The Book of Costume

N.B. Since such terms as girdle, petticoat, robe, tunic, doublet, shoes, vest, veil, etc., are used on almost every page, they are not listed here. The author's use of terms descriptive of articles of dress reflects the language of her times. Students of costume are urged to check alternative listings when seeking specific items.